CONFRONTING STATE, CAPITAL AND PATRIARCHY

Confronting State, Capital and Patriarchy

Women Organizing in the Process of Industrialization

Edited by

Amrita Chhachhi
Lecturer in Women's Studies
Institute of Social Studies
The Hague

and

Renée Pittin
Associate Professor
Women and Development Programme
Institute of Social Studies
The Hague

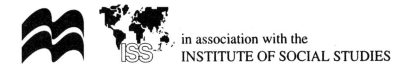

in association with the
INSTITUTE OF SOCIAL STUDIES

First published in Great Britain 1996 by
MACMILLAN PRESS LTD
Houndmills, Basingstoke, Hampshire RG21 6XS
and London
Companies and representatives
throughout the world

A catalogue record for this book is available
from the British Library.

ISBN 0–333–65443–9

First published in the United States of America 1996 by
ST. MARTIN'S PRESS, INC.,
Scholarly and Reference Division,
175 Fifth Avenue,
New York, N.Y. 10010

ISBN 0–312–12980–7

Library of Congress Cataloging-in-Publication Data applied for

10 9 8 7 6 5 4 3 2 1
05 04 03 02 01 00 99 98 97 96

Printed in Great Britain by
Ipswich Book Co Ltd, Ipswich, Suffolk

Contents

List of Tables

List of Figures

Preface

On 15–25 April 1991, a group of activists, researchers and policy-makers met at the Institute of Social Studies, The Hague, at a Workshop on 'Women Organising in the Process of Industrialisation'. The participants, from Argentina, Peru, Ghana, Zimbabwe, Nigeria, India, Pakistan, Philippines, Hong Kong, South Korea, Jamaica, United Kingdom and the Netherlands, spent two weeks in intensive sessions at the workshop, presenting and sharing their research and experiences. The present volume represents in part the fruits of that interaction.

In addition, the workshop, and this volume, are intended as a contribution toward the strengthening of an international action/research network in relation to women and industrialisation, a first step in the exchange of ideas and experiences to build a comparative framework which links analysis, planning and policy-making.

We would like to thank the Netherlands Ministry of Foreign Affairs for their support of this initiative, the Institute of Social Studies for logistic and administrative support, our colleagues in the Women and Development Programme, and Liesbeth van Nispen for her unfailing assistance throughout.

We should also like to acknowledge and thank each other, and recognise here both the extraordinary patience we have exhibited and the tremendous pleasure we have derived from working with each other in co-ordinating the workshop and editing this volume.

Amrita Chhachhi and Renée Pittin

Notes on the Contributors

Amrita Chhachhi is a Lecturer in Women's Studies at the Institute of Social Studies, The Hague. She has published numerous articles on and continues her research on women and industrialisation, and on the state, legal systems, identity politics and fundamentalism in South Asia. She is Co-ordinator of an ongoing action research project on Working Women and Organisational Strategies in India. She is also involved with feminist networks in South Asia.

Renée Pittin is an Associate Professor in the Women and Development Programme at the Institute of Social Studies, The Hague. She has written extensively about women and industrialisation, particularly in Nigeria and West Africa. She is engaged in an international research project on Women, Technology and Employment, and continues also her research on issues of changing ideology and economic access in relation to women.

Diane Elson is a Professor in the Department of Economics, University of Manchester. She has written widely on gender and development, and has acted as a consultant to the Commonwealth Secretariat, FAO and ILO. Her books include *Male Bias in the Development Process*, and *Women's Employment and Multinationals in Europe*, co-edited with Ruth Pearson.

Martha Roldan is a researcher with CONICET, the National Council of Research in Argentina, and is based in Buenos Aires at FLACSO, the Latin-American Faculty of Social Sciences. Martha has published many articles on trade unionism, on homeworking, and on industrial restructuring and technological change, particularly in relation to women. With Lourdes Beneria, Martha has co-authored *The Crossroads of Class and Gender: Industrial Housework, Subcontracting and Household Dynamics*.

Karamat Ali works with the Pakistan Institute of Labour Education and Research, Karachi, Pakistan. He is a trade unionist, actively involved in issues of workers' rights, women's rights, and child labour. He has initiated and is part of a number of networks linking trade unions and NGOs in South Asia.

Farhat Parveen works with the Pakistan Institute of Labour Education and Research, Karachi, Pakistan. She is engaged in research and action with women industrial workers.

Cecilia Olea Mauleón works with the Centro Flora Tristan, a feminist organisation which deals with a variety of women's issues in Peru. Cecilia is particularly involved as researcher and activist in the Women and Work Programme; the Programme provides for the promotion, training and support of women workers.

Jurgette A. Honculada is Director of the Labour Education and Research Network of the National Federation of Labour in the Philippines. She is also engaged in research and writes about, among other topics, the relation of gender to trade union activities and organisation.

Rohini Hensman has published numerous articles and books on industrial workers, trade unions and working women including, most recently, *To Do Something Beautiful*, a novel about women workers in Bombay. She has been part of the Union Research Group, Bombay, and has been involved in many other actions and investigations, including the Bhopal disaster, and assisting Tamil refugees in Sri Lanka.

Leith L. Dunn is a Jamaican activist and researcher. She carried out a pioneering study of free trade zones in Jamaica, which was followed up by the creation of a women's action committee to improve women workers' situation. Leith has written also on issues of worker participation and leadership, and upon export-oriented industrialisation in the Caribbean as a development strategy, and its impact on women. Her work as a project officer has provided an opportunity to link policy, research and action.

Loh Cheng-Kooi has worked for several years with the Committee for Asian Women, based in Hong Kong. The Committee for Asian Women assists in consciousness-raising, organising, and networking among women workers in Asia, and creating extended links of solidarity. Cheng has been programme officer for CAW, is on the editorial team of the *Asian Women Workers Newsletter*, and co-edited for CAW, with Cheung Choi Wan, the book, *Many Paths, One Goal: Organising Women Workers in Asia*.

Linda Shaw lectures in the Department of Sociology at the University of Manchester. She is a founder member of Women Working Worldwide, an organisation which concerns itself with the employment and working conditions of working women internationally, and which seeks to support women through networking, information exchange and education. Linda has written, campaigned and organised extensively on behalf of Women Working Worldwide.

Rudo B. Gaidzanwa is a Lecturer in Sociology at the University of Zimbabwe. Rudo has been engaged in research particularly on unwaged workers, and on wives of minors. She is also doing research on violence, and has written about and been involved in a series of actions concerning women in Zimbabwe. She is the author of *Images of Women in Zimbabwe*.

Mairo V. Bello has undertaken research on rural issues, on health and on the economy in relation to Nigerian women. She is a member of Women in Nigeria, an organisation which recognises that women are oppressed in relation to both gender and class, and which seeks to improve women's situation through research, education, policy and action. Mairo has held the offices of State Coordinator and National Treasurer in the organisation.

Young-ock Kim works as a researcher at the Korean Women's Development Institute. Her primary interest is women workers' problems, and she has done considerable research particularly on women homeworkers. She has written also on the position of women workers in manufacturing industries in South Korea. Young has recently completed a master's degree in Economics.

Nandita Gandhi has carried out research and written on a number of issues and actions, including the anti-price rise movement in Bombay and the situation of homeworkers. She is involved with a number of activist organisations, and is a member of the Forum against Oppression of Women. With Nandita Shah, she has recently published *Issues at Stake*, a book about the women's movement in India. She is presently engaged in the research project on Working Women and Organisational Strategies in India.

Introduction
Amrita Chhachhi and Renée Pittin

The contributors to this volume are part of emerging networks of research-ers/activists working on a variety of women's and labour issues interna-tionally. The linkages between North and South, and the global nature of industrialisation and organising inform the volume in general, and are demonstrated also in individual chapters. The different levels and forms of industrialisation and of organising, and specific linkages through shared networks are reflected in quantitative differences in regional and country representation. Asia, Africa and Latin America are particularly represented.

The contributors share a political commitment towards the struggles of women workers, and are located in both South and North. Many of the authors are both researchers and activists; some of the authors present analyses based on own research, while others were engaged in the actions they describe. A conscious attempt has been made to present analyses of struggles by women engaged in those struggles. The different entry points of the authors to the subject reflect differences in the nature and content of the articles themselves. Also, within a number of the articles, space has been made to present the voices of women workers as directly as possible.

The chapters in this volume focus on the myriad methods, strategies and forms of organisation elaborated by working women to confront the state, capital and patriarchy in the context of industrialisation. The structures of the state, capital and patriarchy are neither monolithic nor homogeneous, exhibiting wide variations in the nature of state regimes, patterns of capital accumulation and forms of patriarchal control in the countries covered in this volume. As these structures incorporate and constitute women's labour in specific ways, in particular socio-cultural and political contexts, they enter into conflict with each other and at other moments exhibit a coin-cidence of interests. The chapters reveal the wide variations in the forms and effects of the incorporation of women's labour into the process of industrialisation, and the strategies whereby women respond to the changing socio-economic situation. In spite of the variations, there also appears to be a convergence today at a macro level as more and more countries come under the sway of IMF/World Bank propagated stabilisation and structural adjustment policies. Numerous studies have documented the devastating effect of SAP in developing countries, in particular on women and chil-dren, and have raised fundamental questions concerning human survival and the future of malnourished generations in a manifestly unsustainable economic and political environment (Cornia *et al.*, 1989; Commonwealth Secretariat, 1989; Elson, 1989).

The issues raised are located within the broad problematic of the generalised economic crisis in the world economy and the restructuring of national economies. Although only one article (Bello) focuses specifically only on structural adjustment policies, almost all the countries included, i.e. Peru, Argentina, Pakistan, Philippines, Nigeria, and Jamaica, are engaged in structural adjustment programmes to overcome a crippling balance of payments crisis. India has joined this group, as an IMF package of structural reforms was initiated in 1992. Malaysia and South Korea, without being subject to these conditionalities, are in fact held up as the model for the policies contained in SAP, particularly its export-oriented industrialisation strategy. It is within this broad context that the changing situation of urban working women and their strategies for survival, struggle and organisation are examined.

The focus on strategies for organising feeds into two interrelated themes. The first theme underpinning the volume is that the present crisis is not only economic/political, but also 'discursive' (see Roldan, this volume). In the last decade, dominant models of development discourse and existing paradigms in the social sciences as well as certain orthodoxies in feminist theory have been challenged. Articles in the first section of this volume question conventional economic formulations, sociological analysis of technological changes and the labour process, and the focus on class and/or gender in contemporary feminist analysis. Feminist analysis has highlighted the significance of the household in the process of reproduction and maintenance of human resources, the economic value of unpaid women's labour within and outside the household, and the necessity to redefine 'the economy' to include the domestic sphere (Beechey, 1988; Elson, 1989). The use of sex-blind categories and the assumption that the 'average worker' is permanent, full-time and male continues to dominate in most mainstream analysis of industrialisation, even as empirical evidence increasingly challenges such an assumption. Discussions on flexible specialisation and the changes initiated in the labour force due to new technology continue to use the male worker as the norm (see Elson, this volume). Feminist analysis has made a significant contribution to the redefinition of work and conceptualisation of the economy, but its application to women workers in the process of industrialisation has remained caught within the dualistic formulations of class and gender. In addition, feminist categories often remain blind to race and ethnicity. A further challenge has been posed by the post-modernist deconstruction of key categories of feminist analysis such as 'woman' and 'patriarchy'. The chapters by Amrita Chhachhi and Renée Pittin, and by Martha Roldan respond to some of these issues, using new theoretical categories, while at the same time locating them within a materialist framework.

The second theme is concerned with the link between the particular experience of women workers and the generalised crisis of restructuring in the world economy. Given that the crisis today affects both men and women in such debilitating ways, does it make sense to focus only on working women? This question is increasingly being raised in discussions regarding the ghettoisation of women's studies in academia. In this volume we focus on working women not only because they are a very vulnerable section of society (country studies of SAP and the article on Zimbabwe show, however, that the effects of SAP are not uniform and that some women have benefited from the new economic policies), but because investigation of organisational efforts reveals possibilities for transformation which have a general validity, i.e. not only for women workers, but also for male workers, as well as in relation to broader perspectives for social change and solutions to the present crisis. A common concern informing the volume as a whole is therefore with identifying practical strategies which are transformative not only of gender relations but also of economic, political and other social relations and structures.

TRENDS IN INDUSTRIALISATION: FLEXIBILITY AND FEMINISATION REVISITED

The emergence of a new female labour force in the process of industrialisation in developing countries as well as in the advanced capitalist countries of Europe and North America in the last two decades has been the subject of research and policy formulations since the 1970s. In developing countries, it is estimated that women form around 18 per cent (Banerjee, 1985) to 26.5 per cent (Joekes, 1987) of the industrial labour force. This increase in women's employment is not only a reversal of earlier trends, for example in India, where women's employment in traditional sectors such as mines and textiles had declined, but also demonstrates an increase in several countries where total industrial employment is stagnant. A similar trend has been noted for advanced capitalist countries where over half of all adult women in most OECD countries are in the paid labour force, with their participation rate increasing at the same time as the male participation rate has been falling (Jenson, Hagen and Reddy, 1988). The increasing trend towards subcontracting production from the factory to small workshops right down to the household has also incorporated women's labour on a large scale. Trends towards a decentralisation of production with increasing centralisation of marketing and managerial control have been noted internationally (Mitter, 1986).

Analysts of this trend have put forward the thesis of 'flexibility' as the main characteristic feature of this phase of industrialisation, accompanied by processes of 'global feminisation' of the labour force in developing and advanced capitalist countries. In the 1980s there has been a major shift away from even the rhetoric of a development model committed to the achievement of a redistributive welfare state (Standing, 1989). The new global strategy has focused on structural adjustment and stabilisation where market mechanisms and cost competitiveness are given overwhelming emphasis. Development discourse became narrowed down to the magic of the market, open economies, trade liberalisation and the propagation of export oriented industrialisation as the only viable development strategy. Mechanisms of explicit and implicit deregulation were initiated whereby labour rights, protective legislation, other forms of social security, and the role of the public sector were seen as rigidities to be suspended or eliminated.

Deregulation and 'flexibilisation' stimulated by new technology have led therefore to a global trend wherein:

> the types of work, labor relations, income, and insecurity associated with 'women's work' have been spreading, resulting not only in a notable increase in female labour force participation but a fall in men's employment, as well as a transformation – or feminization – of many jobs traditionally held by men.
>
> (Standing, 1989: 1077)

Diane Elson (this volume) begins with an assessment of this thesis. She distinguishes three referents of flexibility: the organisational structure of firms, the operation of the labour market, and the pattern of production. The argument for flexibility rests on reducing fixed labour costs to increase profit margins. As part of the shift to flexible specialisation, there is a global trend to replace full-time workers with labour rights with temporary, casual and contract workers, most of whom are women. However, flexibilisation is not always associated with feminisation and that flexibility is not inevitably detrimental to workers, especially women. She argues that it is important to see the present form of flexibility, for example, in relation to subcontracting and alteration of job boundaries as only one strategy of capital accumulation. The content and context of labour flexibility is significant in determining present trends. An examination of the electronics and textile industries in various countries does not reveal an overall tendency towards feminisation in the 1980s. It appears therefore that flexibilisation does not necessarily lead to direct substitution of women for men in jobs traditionally held by men. The sexual division of labour structures the form flexibility takes.

Although an examination of international data on labour force participation does show a tendency for women's labour participation rates to rise and men's labour participation rates to decrease, it is possible that given earlier problems in measurement of FLP rates, this trend could be a result of increasing visibility rather than of growth due to monetisation and improvement in data collection methods. Secondly, the increase in the female share of manufacturing employment is more a reflection of an increasing share of manufacturing output from sectors of industry in which women are concentrated. Even in these sectors, recent studies have pointed out that as a result of technical change, women's share in employment is declining over time, for example in the electronics industry in Ireland, United States and Mexico.

While it is clear that the issues of flexibility and feminisation of the labour force have to be seen in relation to long-term strategies of capital accumulation, in particular the role of technological change, it is also necessary to highlight the fact that flexibility is also resorted to as a form of labour control. It is necessary to examine these trends in relation to specific contexts. In relation to Argentina for instance, Martha Roldan demonstrates that given the economic crisis, the partial adoption of Japanese-style Just-In-Time (JIT) technologies by a light engineering firm is limited by demand factors as well as the existing sexual division of labour. When a new product demanded changes in the women's section, which would have resulted in women entering male work areas, skill redefinitions categorised all the women as simple operators. In spite of the economic rationality of JIT and goal of maximum flexibility, the interests of management and male workers combined to keep women in their old enclave.

In Nigeria, even typically 'women's jobs' are being taken over by men. Technical change, especially automation, was still leading towards a masculinisation of the labour force. The Indian case studies revealed that women's employment has declined in the traditional industries, particularly textiles, as well as in the modern sectors such as pharmaceuticals, where companies stopped recruiting women from the 1960s onwards; in the 1990s, all recruitment in the permanent categories was stopped. Rohini Hensman (this volume) points out, however, that the decline in women's employment in the organised sector is offset by the increasing trend towards decentralisation of production which has led to a net increase in female employment in the unorganised sector. Rather than substitution, this seems to be a case of *transfer* of jobs from the organised to the unorganised or informal sector.[1] A comparison of electronics and electrical equipment factories in Nigeria and India by Amrita Chhachhi and Renée Pittin points out that the substitution of men by women workers and the replacement of women by men workers in these cases was due to labour control and the operation of gender ideology rather than being solely a result of technological changes.

Other components of the structural adjustment strategy in many developing countries affect women's employment in specific ways. In Sub-Saharan Africa, where industrialisation has been treated for more than two decades as a, if not the, key to long-term development (as demonstrated in the Lagos Plan of Action and myriad national policy documents), the 1980s and 1990s have seen a shift in practice to deindustrialisation, with massive retrenchments in industry, the demise of many large and medium-scale industrial enterprises, and a reorientation to 'resource-based development'. Both industrialisation and deindustrialisation have hit women harder than men in most countries in Sub-Saharan Africa, with women suffering proportionately greater losses through retrenchment and through systematic removal from permanent positions in industries over the past decade. At present, large-scale employment of women tends to be associated with foreign-owned or supported industries, and with foreign rather than local prioritisations. As structural adjustment programmes, with their massive devaluations and price increases, make moonlighting or a series of income-earning activities in addition to waged labour a necessity, the numbers working in the informal sector increase, including not only former factory workers but also those still employed. Unlike in other parts of the world, informal sector activities for women in Sub-Saharan Africa do not normally include sub-contracting labour or providing products to established industry; women may well use tools such as sewing machines and expertise gained from previous formal sector work, but generally for self-directed economic activities.

In Ghana, since the Economic Recovery Programme/SAP was initiated, there has been a change in the distribution of employment between sectors of the economy. The increase in employment in mining, timber logging, transport and communications has not benefited women since these are traditionally male preserves. In the public sector which employed a large number of women, retrenchment and a freeze on new recruitment have hit women directly. In those manufacturing industries where women still have jobs such as food processing, companies have resorted to restructuring the workforce through retrenchment, increasing work intensity and designating workers as casual labour (Mensah-Kutin, 1991). The lay-offs due to SAP in Nigeria affected a million workers, one third of whom were women (Bello, this volume). In both Ghana and Nigeria, structural adjustment programmes have led to a growth in the informal sector with women handling multiple jobs, a tendency identified in Peru also (Bello; Scott, 1986). Yet while women increase in numbers in the informal sector, the control over urban space and the repression of women therein by representatives of the community and the state, is also increasing (Pittin, 1991). Mairo Bello demonstrates that although there has been an increase in women's work in agriculture, women's labour remains unpaid at the same time as they are displaced by men in the new rice mills set up to develop agro-industries.

Studies on Latin America have also documented the increase in irregular, home-based or other informal sector work, with considerable labour being expended now in industrial work carried out as sub-contracted homeworking by women who had formerly been permanently employed for the same labour, as in the maquiladoras. In this respect the structural linkages between irregular, temporary, and other forms of informal work with work in the formal sector is stronger in Latin America than in Africa. The employment of particular categories of women (in relation to age, marital status, origin and skill levels) is specific to industrial sectors and labour processes, and neither country- nor certainly continent-wide generalisations can be made with regard to the character of the female industrial labour force. However, it is apparent that while both men and women have lost jobs in formal industry, women are not as easily rehired as men (Aguiar, 1988). The gendering of work in new labour processes is differently perceived by analysts with, for example, Martha Roldan (1993 and this volume) pointing out a reluctance in industry to invest in women in JIT processes, and other studies suggesting more significant employment of women (Humphrey, 1993).

Present trends in industrialisation in both developing and developed countries do not show a unidirectional tendency towards 'feminisation' or 'masculinisation'. In addition, flexibility should not be judged according to the male norm of a regular, full-time skilled job, since these have not been jobs that women have had. It is useful to distinguish different referents of 'feminisation', since these have often been conflated in recent studies. Feminisation of the labour force could refer to one or all of the following:

1. Increase in the female participation rate relative to men;
2. The substitution of men by women who take over jobs traditionally handled by men;

3. The increase in women's involvement in 'invisible' work, i.e. family labour and homeworking; and
4. The changing character of industrial work on the basis of new technology and managerial strategies whereby work is decentralised, low-paid, irregular, with part-time or temporary labour contracts, i.e. increasingly like 'women's work' (but which is *not* necessarily done by women).

Analysing data from Turkey, N. Cagatay and G. Berik (1990) point out that there has not been a feminisation of employment in large-scale manufacturing, although they do document an increase in homeworking.[2] Clearly, an analysis of trends depends on which aspect(s) we refer to in identifying 'feminisation'. If we combine all four points above, so as to include the total range of production sites which draw on women's labour, then it is possible, given recent studies, that there is an overall tendency towards feminisation of the labour force. Articles in this collection point not only to the transfer of jobs to the unorganised sector, which includes small-scale family units (see Hensman), but also to the phenomenal increase in homeworking.

The increase in unorganised or informal sector activities is often taken as an indication that workers losing jobs in the formal sector move into the informal sector. Hirata and Humphrey question the argument that manufacturing workers in São Paulo, Brazil, move into the informal sector or non-industrial occupations after job loss in the formal sector. They point out that entry into this sector is differentiated by gender, skill and marital status. Adult male skilled workers tended to remain in open unemployment and returned to factory work, while the pressure to move into the informal sector was greater for unskilled men and single parents. In São Paulo, women, particularly older women and single mothers, were forced into domestic service, cleaning, etc., after losing their jobs in factories. A significant point highlighted by the research was the fact that adult skilled male workers had a strong sense of identity as industrial workers/breadwinners and were able to hold on to this work identity even in a situation of crisis (Hirata and Humphrey, 1991). In discussions on feminisation of the labour force, it is important to be cognisant of their suggestion that labour markets are not very fluid in periods of crisis, and intersectoral mobility may apply more to the very poor rather than to workers in the formal sector. In addition, as Scott points out in relation to Latin America, the *selectivity* of the processes whereby women are incorporated, excluded or marginalised has to be assessed through specific studies and micro level analysis (Scott, 1986: 673).

An important dimension in discussion of feminisation (or defeminisation) is the relationship of capital to the state. Lack of feminisation could be due to gender typing of industries in the context of labour repression, which reduces the labour cost advantage of women workers in relation to men (Cagatay and Berik, 1990: 129). Present trends in fact highlight the crucial role of the state in industrialisation. One of the myths of contemporary development discourse concerns the idealisation of the free market as eminently superior to state intervention as a motor for industrialisation. It is difficult to sustain the argument that there is any economy today which is operating without some form of state intervention. Analysis of the 'East Asian miracle' has revealed that the superior industrial performance of the NICs is not due to the superiority of export-oriented industrialisation strategies over import substitution, or of the market against the state, but rather due to the ability of the state to make selective interventions to facilitate capitalist development (Jenkins, 1991; Amsden, 1990). The NICs have been characterised by a high degree of repression and state control over trade unions.

To support their industrialisation policies, many Latin American countries also revised their labour laws and curtailed union intervention and autonomous authority (see e.g. Acero, 1991, for Brazil and Argentina; the work of Humphrey for Brazil), while reducing the expense and extent of general social welfare provisions (Aguiar, 1988; Ramirez, 1988, for Colombia). Although infrastructure, resources and technologies differ, nevertheless countries in Sub-Saharan Africa[3] present a rather different picture in relation to industrial policies and workers' response to these. Tight state authority, whether in terms of linkage with or control over unions, has been profoundly changed with the retreat of the state and/or with efforts at democratisation. Thus, e.g. in Tanzania, loss of strong state control and the reduced role of state-linked trade union organisation has created a space for organising in and around informal networks and community-related organisations (Tripp, 1994). Lesotho built an export-oriented textile and clothing industry using its comparative advantage of absence of sanctions and cheap (female) labour within the enveloping South Africa. This strategy will be greatly affected by the democratisation of South Africa, while efforts by the Lesotho authorities to disregard labour legislation, ignore labour unrest and monopolise wealth, have been explicitly repudiated through strikes and disturbances which have in fact frightened away many actual and potential foreign investors the government sought to woo (Baylies and Wright, 1993).

State intervention in relation to industrialisation extends as well to measures which constitute a specifically gendered and ethnic labour force.

Explicit state ideology on women is often contradictory, particularly in relation to their entry into the labour market. Studies have pointed out the contradictions betwen the policies on women and development and the simultaneous articulation of state ideologies in Pakistan and Iran to restrict women in the 'private' sphere. Hamza Alavi argues for instance that state fundamentalist discourse to restrict the mobility of women through *chador* and *chardiwari* concurs with the increasing trend towards home-based production and the incorporation of women's labour in this form of capitalist production (Alavi, 1988). Alavi sees state ideology as a simple reflection of economic interests. Apart from the limitations of a mechanistic reflection theory of ideology and a narrow definition of the economic as referring only to production, such a formulation cannot explain the violence that often accompanies the process of asserting patriarchal control, nor can it account for the adaptation by women workers of 'purdah ideology' as they continue to work outside the home (see Parveen and Ali, this volume). Haleh Afshar, on the other hand, sees states as more autonomous and argues that most states exhibit a strong ideological fear of women who are not confined to the domestic sphere. This results, as in Iran and Pakistan, in repressive measures against women who have entered the labour market and the articulation of a state ideology to restrict their mobility and control their sexuality (Afshar, 1987). The danger in such a formulation lies in attributing an essentialist intentionality to the state.[4]

MULTIPLE IDENTITIES

A significant contribution of the present volume is its move away from focusing primarily on class and gender to the more fruitful concept of multiple identities, located in the context of the family, community, workplace and the state. A number of aspects of identity, including ethnicity, class, caste, marital status and level of education, are relevant as areas of cohesion and/or cleavage among women workers: gender does not create an automatic basis for affinity, although gender can be operationalised within particular contexts and is a possible basis for solidarity. Identities are constantly shifting, historically and contextually. They are selectively mobilised in response to economic, political and social pressures. It should be noted that the acknowledgement of 'difference' along axes of class, caste, race, etc. and the forefronting of multiple identities does not necessitate or imply the abandonment of the notion of patriarchy. Articles in this volume share a similar conceptual focus on patriarchy and capitalism as systemic social constructs, varying historically and contextually; individual authors differ in the emphasis they place on each.

Using comparative data from factory-based research in India and Nigeria respectively, Chhachhi and Pittin focus on the relationship between identity, consciousness and organisation among women workers. Analysis of data permitted re-examination of some common theoretical assumptions regarding women workers (such as, e.g. that women's focus on marriage and family precludes or minimises the possibility of industrial action): these assumptions were shown to be classist and Eurocentric.

The interaction of identity, consciousness and process, the interplay of multiple identities and multiple strategies, and the effects of this in relation to possible organisational forms and alliances, are interrelated areas which must be brought to bear in analysis and strategic planning (see also Parveen and Ali, this volume). There is a clear continuum between the many areas and arenas of women's lives, areas (such as waged labour and domestic labour; obligations as wife, mother and income earner) which are often segregated or compartmentalised in patriarchal ideology. In their chapter, Chhachhi and Pittin put forward a proposal for developing the use of coalescing strategies. Through the use of coalescing strategies, the continuum is recognised and efforts can be made not only to respond to these linked responsibilities, but also to compensate them through economic valuation and action.

Non-organisation by women at the workplace may operate as a critique of existing patriarchal organisational structures, composition, ideology, interests and strategies. Women workers' demands, the forms in which those demands are couched, and the strategies through which resolution and satisfaction are sought may differ from those of male co-workers. These findings have implications for the forms and structures wherein women workers may seek redress of grievances, and for the kinds of linkages with other support groups and organisations which may be created.

The dialectical relations, particularly between gender and class as these are represented in unionised and non-unionised contexts, is the focus of a comparison of women workers in two factories in Nigeria (Abdullah-Olukoshi, 1991). Both groups of women workers suffer gender-specific discrimination linked to the conflicting obligations of motherhood and waged labour, while each group is also subject to other forms of gender-based discrimination. Whereas workers in the non-unionised factory united to fight primarily for union representation and gender-linked concerns were relegated to secondary status in terms of immediate strategy, in the unionised context, women workers had the 'luxury' of seeking redress in relation to gender discrimination. However, the complexity of claims, representations, divisions and alliances among the workforce in both cases reflects also identities other than gender and class, including education, ethnicity and marital status.

Rudo Gaidzanwa (this volume) demonstrates how in Zimbabwe, an ideology of domesticity has informed and influenced the education and actions of several generations of women, although differently represented and operationalised in relation to race, class and historical context. At present, with limited waged labour and reduced value of income, some working-class women have parlayed the domestic craftwork of crocheting into international trade. Through barter across borders and mutual support within a network of women traders, women have created new sources of wealth, justified through reference to maternal obligations and provision for the family. Using sale of domestic goods to secure stronger currencies and to purchase luxury items for resale, these women challenge state policies and establish themselves as international entrepreneurs, in the process expanding their own horizons and knowledge. Women are concurrently confronting the state, supporting the state and using the state. They have forced action against body searches and harassment and precipitated debates concerning the ostensible and actual effects of government policy and its differential application in relation to class and gender. They have supported the state by reducing group pressures for economic reform (and the individual entrepreneurial nature of the women's socio-economic response has limited concerted action); and they have used the state through manipulation of policy and procedure.

TRADITIONAL TRADE UNIONS, NEW UNIONS, ALTERNATIVE ORGANISATIONS AND WOMEN

In general, there is a low rate of unionisation of industrial workers as a whole and women workers in particular. Jurgette Honculada (this volume) points out that in the Philippines, only 10 per cent of all industrial workers are organised into unions and of these only 25 per cent are women. In Pakistan, the analysis by Farhat Parveen and Karamat Ali (this volume) reveals that less than 5 per cent of the total industrial and commercial labour force is organised in registered unions. These limited unions are all male-dominated, with leadership positions being held by men. The neglect of women's issues is also a reflection of the continued orientation of the unions towards male workers. The reasons for the low participation of women range from the double burden of women's work and hence lack of time to attend union meetings, cultural restrictions on women's mobility, and the fact that women are working in sectors which are anyway difficult to organise. An ever-present concern in organising is the possibility of sexual violence being used as a woman-specific form of repression and control. And unions are often not seen as organisations which could take up issues which affect women most directly. This assessment has led to questioning whether unions are the most effective form of organisation for women workers.

To identify the reasons for the low rate of unionisation, a distinction between general issues and women's issues proves useful. General issues include the growth of the unorganised sector fostered by government policies and employer strategies towards decentralisation and casualisation of labour: these make unionisation difficult. Some issues which specifically affect women include maternity benefits, crèches, ban on night work, unequal wages and unpaid domestic work. Traditional trade unions have tended to ignore these issues, focusing on the male formal sector worker. Traditional trade unions have serious limitations given their patriarchal orientation, internal hierarchical structures, methods of functioning and the neglect of non-factory life and unwaged labour which exclude women as well as an increasing cross-section of casual labour. However, articles in this volume do not reject trade unions *in toto*, but rather suggest strategies for transforming existing union structures as well as establishing linkages with other organisations.

Organising Homeworkers

Unions have played a limited and often negative role in relation to homeworkers. With their focus on formal employment, trade unions have tended to treat homeworkers as competitors and as a threat to their members, and have sought to place the blame for this situation variously on employers, governments and on the homeworkers themselves, whose very vulnerability has made them particularly subject to exploitation. With the introduction and expansion of telework, some unions and union federations sought in the early and mid-1980s to ban the process altogether. This position has now become more moderate, with clear recognition of the dangers associated with telework as a form of homeworking, but also of the possibilities of additional employment generation (di Martino and Worth, 1990).

Homeworking, a form of labour with a centuries-old history, is presently on the increase, with increasing casualisation and flexibilisation of labour and the consequent continuing removal of labour from factory premises, and from the payrolls and responsibility of large industrial and manufacturing concerns into subcontractual and informalised arrangements. The very understanding of homework is subject to debate on a number of grounds. A definition of homework, suggested for an ILO meeting on the topic, is as follows:

> the production of a good or the provision of a service for an employer or contractor under an arrangement whereby the work is carried out at a place of the worker's own choosing, often the worker's own home, where there normally is no direct supervision by the employer or contractor.
>
> (ILO, 1990: 3)

This definition raises questions, among others, concerning the place of work (*not* necessarily of the worker's choosing), the issue of supervision (now common in telework, where spatial distance is irrelevant), the lack of recognition of differential dependency upon the employer, and of use of the labour of others (spouses, children, etc.) (ILO, 1990: 75–7). What is indisputable, however, is the predominance of women in homeworking[5] and the extensiveness of homeworking. Honculada notes that in the Philippines, there are seven to nine million documented women homeworkers.[6] Also indisputable are the profound impact of increasing homeworking on women, the economic and social constraints from within which women undertake homework, the differential situation of women and men, and the effects of nationality, ethnicity and class in relation to homeworking.

Discussion of homeworking in this volume brings out the specificities and conditions of homeworking, noting, for example, the problems of low wages, long hours, isolation, health hazards, insecurity of employment, and lack of employee status and associated benefits. But the possibility of earning reasonable wages with homeworking is also brought out, as is the fact that homeworkers do not necessarily want work on-site (see e.g. Young-ock Kim, this volume). However, the focus is particularly on issues of policy and strategy, and consideration of the possibilities of organising homeworkers.

In advanced capitalist countries in particular, homeworkers have been less likely to admit to homeworking for legal and social reasons, and thus to organise, than have women elsewhere. Indeed, the very residential and social structures in advanced capitalist countries, as well as the fear of state intervention, has increased isolation and hindered action among homeworkers and limited exposure of exploitation. In general, however, given that homeworking is often undertaken because of lack of viable alternatives, the threat of loss of income as well as the individualised nature of the work have frequently made organising untenable.

Suggested strategies for action in relation to homeworking include, for South Korea, its termination, and the incorporation of homeworkers into formal external waged labour (Young-ock Kim). Such a strategy would assist women to get away from the home, end the isolation of homework, provide a source of social relationships and establish a basis for organising, and create pressure for state-assisted support for children and the elderly. However, this is an optimal solution which demands intensive, sustained and coherent action between state and capital, for which the political will is certainly not yet evident. Alternatively, extant intermediate work arrangements can be utilised. For example, neighbourhood workshops established by South Korean manufacturers to supervise off-site workers, provide a context wherein women workers do meet each other and can work together towards improving their work conditions.

The profound consequences of present industrial restructuring provide now a basis and a space for radical rethinking and revision in the unions, as work moves increasingly into smaller, non-factory-based units, and the membership of traditional unions dwindles. Also, with Structural Adjustment programmes, as the real value of wages plummets with revaluation of currencies, not only has interest in securing waged work reduced, but also the waged workers are often compelled themselves by economic circumstance to seek additional income. They either move out of formal waged labour or become, concurrently, workers in the formal and informal sectors, at times home-based (Sanyal, 1991). Thus, the union member and the threatening competition may merge in one and the same person.

At present, unions tend to recognise that many workers are dependent on homework, and are more likely to support legislation to protect homeworkers, and better implementation of legislation. Some unions have begun to seek the integration of homeworkers into trade unions or stronger links between homeworkers and parent companies. However, these initiatives are still tentative, with many still at the level of suggestions for consideration.

Legislation is vital, but has a limited value if not actively implemented. Young-ock Kim notes that the Japanese Homeworkers Protection Law, instituted more than twenty years ago when the number of Japanese homeworkers reached two million, is honoured more in the breach than in compliance. While the Commission of the European Community suggests that over-rigid controls will drive homeworking underground, it notes also that there is no evidence that specific legislative instruments on homeworking have had the effect of controlling or regulating homeworking.[7]

The main thrust in homeworking strategy is for the removal of homeworkers' social and political isolation via the establishment of a series of

linkages between homeworkers and: each other; trade unions; other support organisations; employers. This has been the position, for example, of
Steunpunt Thuiswerk, a Dutch organisation created specifically to support
homeworkers. Too often the ties of homeworkers to each other, employers,
and possible support groups are tenuous or virtually non-existent, with
knowledge of the employer, for example, limited to the intermediary who
collects and pays for the finished product. Researchers can be instrumental
in uncovering these ties and establishing the chain of production around
which action can be taken. Suggestions for action[8] in relation to production include, among others, a proposal from a representative of IRENE,
the International Restructuring Education Network Europe, to 'cut the
chain', to work towards reducing the numbers of contractors and profit-
taking in order to increase the wages of homeworkers. Alternatively, action
could be directed along the lines of enforcing accountability for sub-
contracting excesses at the top of the chain, with the primary company.

Alternative Organisational Structures

Some of the most effective organisational strategies have taken a multi-
pronged approach and have sought to operationalise action along the line
of production, through the community, via the state, and tying into international structures. Perhaps the most successful effort thus far, and certainly
the best documented, has been that of the Self Employed Women's Association (SEWA) in Ahmedabad, India. Open to any women workers –
self-employed or casual wage earners – not represented by other trade
unions, SEWA has established a union, cooperatives, a bank, a trust, and
welfare facilities for its workers. Research is a conscientising, mobilising
and organising activity, and is a basis for initiating and extending actions
for and by the SEWA workers.

While SEWA representatives state that the SEWA experience is not
directly replicable, and indeed SEWA has had difficulty even in extending
its activities to other parts of India, yet the sheer originality and extensiveness of the SEWA effort has had tremendous impact. SEWA has reached
and organised unorganised women workers, created linkages with existing
unions and established new negotiating bases, exposed the non-availability
of credit sources and the limitations of extant facilities, established new
financial possibilities, utilised legal structures to support women workers,
created new work possibilities and situations, and conscientised both women
and men workers and the surrounding populace regarding the joint needs
and strength of the (previously) unorganised workers. The success of SEWA
has inspired other groups internationally in their efforts to organise.

Honculada examines the basis for the establishment in the Philippines in 1991 of one such organisation: the National Association of Home-based Workers (PATAMABA). Encouraged and facilitated by the rising global interest in homeworking, with access to learning of shared experiences and inspired in part by SEWA, PATAMABA reflects and reasserts the importance of a broad-based support network with assistance and advice from its rural-based parent organisation, which is itself experienced in organising, budgeting and income-generating, as well as in the building of cooperatives and in alliance-building with government and the universities, in order to establish a well-researched framework for viable new legislative, organisational and economic efforts.

The contradictions inherent in the creation of ventures and organisations designed for economic success yet intended to be more broadly responsive to their members' needs are elaborated in the analysis by Nandita Gandhi (this volume) within the context of India. The value of cooperatives as organisational conscientising yet economically effective structures is explored, as are the conflicting pressures placed on other organisations supporting women workers. Thus, for example, the workers' cooperative, Lijjat Papad Udyog, in its impressive rise to economic success alienated its workers/shareholders who responded by striking for better wages. In its efforts to assist its members, SEWA has engaged in commercial ventures which oblige it to enter into close economic relations with the very groups and individuals who had been responsible for the exploitation of the SEWA members. Also examined in Gandhi's work are the conflicts created by differing prioritisation and separation of gender and class issues. In some cases, the forefronting of economic issues has been paralleled by the marginalisation of gender concerns. Even within women workers' organisations, the reified nature of women's and workers' interests is not always acted upon, although there is increasing recognition of the inextricable linkages of these issues.

The chapters by Cheng-Kooi, Gandhi, and Honculada present the experiences of new unions which have emerged in Korea, India, and the Philippines respectively, and which have attempted to organise contract workers and workers in the informal sector. Through the formation of women's wings and caucuses, women workers are able to raise their issues. The emergence of women's unions and women workers' associations and women's centres is another trend (see also Parveen and Ali). A significant feature of these new organisations is the bridging of the gap between factory and community, and an attempt to raise 'personal' issues such as domestic violence, alcoholism, and housing along with wages and working conditions. Gandhi points out for instance that in raising and dealing with these 'personal and domestic' issues, these organisations have moved beyond the activities and brief of SEWA, often given as the definitive model for organising in the informal sector. In Pakistan, the Working Women's Centre has been instrumental in forming a women's union for garment workers and is also handling cases of divorce and sexual harassment. The experience of the Korean Women Workers Association is interesting and relevant. The KWWA represented a new phase in working-class organisation with single women workers becoming militant labour activists, establishing support structures for day care, laundry, etc. as well as building links between women wage workers and working-class housewives.

A multiple strategy approach to organising, linking the worker, the community, local structures and international support groups and organisations has provided an effective response for women working in the highly constrained and controlled free trade zones (FTZs). Emphasis and analysis of free trade zone industry has shifted over the past few years from a focus on issues of exploitation to issues of resistance and organisation.

Methods for organising in FTZs have largely excluded traditional trade unions; in many countries, traditional unions are forbidden by law to organise in FTZs. Leith Dunn (this volume) describes how FTZ women workers are organising in Jamaica and the Dominican Republic. In both countries, all relevant legislation exists to support trade union involvement which is, however, 'discouraged' in Jamaica, and had been, in the Dominican Republic, 'ignored', a situation which changed only in 1990 after three years of workers' unrest, and pressure from the ILO and the US AFL-CIO (American Federation of Labor and Congress of Industrial Organizations).

Dunn demonstrates that an array of support groups may be available to women workers outside the factory, such as food and housing cooperatives, medical centres, legal aid centres and local media. These may, and indeed usually are, linked with various organisations or institutions such as women's groups, religious sects or political parties. This linkage may strengthen the alliances which women establish as a collectivity – or may reduce the value and possibilities of ties, if workers perceive that recourse to the support group is only possible through affiliation to the parent organisation. The outside support groups have themselves been suggested as a base wherein women can develop organisationally and personally. The social solidarity and cohesiveness of local organisations[9] may then lead to the creation of the participatory structures needed to come to consensus on local issues, and thence to coherent political strategies.

More than anywhere else in the world, organising strategies among women workers in Latin America are spread throughout the community;

workers gather strength from the actions of their neighbours and compatriots in their own bargaining efforts. Initially in reponse to the authoritarian regimes within which they operated, some Latin American women workers developed decentralised alternative structures for action, which worked sometimes parallel to, sometimes in conjunction with, and sometimes in opposition to concurrent populist movements and feminist trends (see e.g. Souza Lobo, 1985, for Brazil; Villamil, 1992, for Uruguay). At the same time, grassroots actions have provided additional impetus for change in formal workspaces (Gogna, 1988), with popular movements and organis-ing efforts outside the formal workplace also creating the base for im-proved working conditions for all women through, for example, better child-care arrangements for neighbourhood children (Acero, 1991. See also Nash, 1990). The actions, needs and obligations of women as income earners, as mothers and wives, and as citizens, is nowhere so clearly in-tertwined as in Latin America, where the popular, feminist and labour movements have drawn from and continue to inform each other, and as the pressures of the multiple responsibilities of women require and effect response.

Experience has shown then that although support organisations are seen as important allies for women workers, nevertheless organisation is still crucial on the factory floor. Whereas women have resisted, struck, dem-onstrated and walked out in response to industrial grievances in spite of the lack of a formal workers' organisation or union, to gain fully from collective action an organisational structure is needed.

The advantages of in-house unions as possible structures with transitional potential, points of resistance where women could organise around their own issues and develop negotiating skills, and where they could be em-powered more effectively than traditional unions generally permit have been put forward by K. Rosa (1991). Although the disadvantages of in-house unions are pointed out in Rosa's work (e.g. the dangers of isolation, cooptation and/or control by management), she argues that these dangers might be diminished through active alliances with outside support groups. In discussing in-house unions, one must recognise and respond to the presence of state and organised labour control. In countries where the state permits only in-house unions (e.g. Malaysia and Pakistan), the move for democratisation tends to be in relation to broader union structures. On the other hand, in countries such as India, where the legal structure is such that only industry-level textile unions are allowed as for instance in the cotton textile industry, a move for additional autonomy and greater control for workers may be instead in relation to local level or company unions (Chhachhi and Kurian, 1982).

Autonomy: A Process and a Strategy

The experiences of women workers with traditional industrial unions and other organisations and associations highlight the significance of autonomy for women workers. Autonomy can best be seen as a *process* and a *strategy* rather than as a fixed, rigid position implying separatism. The need for *space* for women workers in autonomous organisations where they can articulate their own specific needs as well as develop skills of negotiation and leadership needs continuous emphasis. Equally, it is necessary to maintain a relationship with the general trade union, although such a relationship will remain one of constant struggle, bargaining and negotiation. Alternative organisations such as working women's centres and women workers' associations may function as mediating structures linking women workers with trade unions on one hand and the women's movement on the other (see Hensman; Parveen and Ali). The recognition of women workers' multiple identities also implies the necessity of dual or even multiple memberships in different organisations which could express women's various interests.

Indeed, organising strategies which incorporate the establishment of multiple alliances at local and international levels, while being intrinsically subject to fractures or divisions, nevertheless provide a broader base for action and a variety of forms and lines of support. Thus, alliances can be created within the factory, in the community, with traditional trade unions and trade union federations, as well as with, among others, women's bureaux, other women and the media.[10]

NETWORKING, LINKAGES AND ALLIANCES

Linkages and alliances at the local, national and international level become essential, given the connection between global processes of economic restructuring and changing gender relations in the process of industrialisation. Examples of regional and international strategising and action, linking workers of parent and dependent companies with tremendous effect, are documented by the Committee for Asian Women, an organisation which combines watchdog, liaising and support roles in relation to Asian women workers.

An example of international networking that went further than support and solidarity actions is presented by the work of Women Working Worldwide, described by Linda Shaw (this volume). The network aims to support the struggle of women workers through information exchange, international networking and public education. The significant feature of international networking is the attempt to link together women as workers and women as consumers, thus highlighting the interdependence of North and South. Campaigns and educational work are also carried out in the North, on aid and trade policies and on the role of multinational and local firms. Channels of communication and linkages are established not only between women workers in the South and women consumers in the North, but also between academics and activists, and trade unions and black/ethnic minority communities. In the present context there is need to strengthen such initiatives, with at the same time a cautionary note concerning the power of multinationals and international organisations to undermine such efforts. The lack of funding for such initiatives in the North and the relationship of non-governmental organisations with the labour movement are major barriers to the expansion of such initiatives.

Regional and international linkages give space to move from the stifling stranglehold of the local context and may provide some of the most powerful allies for local women workers. However the need for such linkages rests on more than emotions of solidarity, since given the global pattern of industrial restructuring and the interdependence between North and South, strategies and policies have to be formulated which relate to industrial processes of both North and South in order to have any significant effect. These should be multi-faceted, utilising interlocking industrial, economic and political structures and processes. Thus, a policy for improving wages and working conditions for women in the South has to recognise, query and incorporate regulations concerning multinational investments and development aid from the North.

TRAINING AND RESEARCH

The training of women workers is an integral part of several organisational strategies discussed in this volume (see e.g. Mauleón; Dunn; Honculada; Parveen and Ali; Elson). But, more significant than the inclusion of training *per se*, is the character of that training. Overwhelmingly, the training which is being planned or given is *not* in new work techniques or technology or work skills, but rather training in self-expression, decision-making, consensus-building, conflict resolution and organisational development. Women workers are being trained to be more effective advocates and negotiators, within the workplace, outside it and, as necessary, beyond it. The temporary and uncertain nature of any given job, and indeed the uncertainty surrounding even the continued presence of a particular factory or industry in a given place, in the context of industrialisation today, have contributed to a new focus in training. The emphasis has now shifted to teaching women to fight for their rights and interests not only within the workplace, but also within the community and the broader political arena.

The nature of the organisations offering training (e.g. women's groups, church groups etc.) in part explains this broader focus, but even within unions themselves, and in union-based women's groups, the emphasis is increasingly on social empowerment,[11] in and against the operative structures in which women live and work. Several chapters (Elson; Chhachhi and Pittin; Dunn; Mauleón) point out the integral and indivisible nature of the multiple forms of work in which women engage, and the artificiality of the distinctions which serve to compartmentalise women's lives. In the forms of training intended for women, this compartmentalisation is exposed and its effects and implications challenged. Honculada correctly states that our vision of the future must not include 'a patriarchal culture that force[s] [women] to choose between work and family, union and husband'.

Women are being trained to *communicate* – with each other, with other unions and other groups and organisations, locally, nationally and internationally. In this context, training also includes, in some cases, instruction in research methodology, dissemination of findings, and the development of data bases for campaigns and actions. The relatively high level of education of women in some industries underscores the possibility of immediate application of these efforts to ensure that women workers's voices are heard. Research and documentation should be undertaken by the workers themselves, expressed in writing or alternative media; such research should be supported and encouraged.

This research can be augmented by parallel or joint research by activists/researchers who are not necessarily employed in the specific workplace. Optimally, there should be an interactive relationship between workers, researchers, activists and policy-makers (none of these categories are mutually exclusive), whereby policy is informed by detailed data from researchers linked to persons actively engaged in organising. Training, research, theory and policy should be integrally linked to improve the conditions of women workers.

The political interests and background of the researcher should be revealed to the research subject: this avoids false 'objectivity', and recognises that activist research may be interventionist research, with the research itself possibly changing the content of the research setting. Difference and distance between researcher and subject are commonly evident in e.g.

class, caste, ethnicity and nationality. Difference *per se* does not preclude good research; but false representation, or an approach which is less than straightforward, may. And while researchers and research subjects of course have at least somewhat differing agendas, this does not justify the use of politically damaging or exploitative research methodology or information dissemination.

Honesty extends also to the recognition and acknowledgement of research assistance and to the return of documentation and analysis to the people whose work and experiences it represents; this is still all too infrequent. Groups should also make clear demands of researchers in terms of documentation, retrieval of information, and material assistance, so that there is an exchange of benefits and a mutually understood framework within which this interaction occurs. Indeed, in this context a *code of ethics* should be established to guide research and researchers, to avoid the exploitation of research subjects and to work towards ensuring that research findings and documentation are restored to the research group themselves.

CONCLUSION

Chapters in this volume highlight through explicit statement as well as implicit frameworks the need to move away from the dualistic and additive conceptualisations which have hitherto informed analysis of women workers in the process of industrialisation. The interface between capital and patriarchy is revealed in very specific contexts, in which the culturally gendered construction of masculinity and femininity is drawn in relation to industrial work, the household and the community. Positioning within the labour market as well as within household and community is constantly subject to change, affected by material and discursive processes which fuel capitalist production as well as reconstituting patriarchal controls. Nowhere is this more clear than in the contemporary context of structural adjustment. The chapters show that industrial restructuring can lead to seeming feminisation of certain sectors of industry as well as to a defeminisation of other sectors as the locations and definitions of women's work and men's work in different countries shift and change. This is predicated on considerations such as pre-existing ideological constructions, the emergence of new ideologies of the value of women's work and the degree of male unemployment.

A historically specific analysis of the changing structures of gender relations in the labour market, workplace, household and community as they are asserted, reconstructed and newly constituted in relation to contemporary trends of industrialisation, does not necessitate the abandonment of the concept of patriarchy, as some post-modernist analysis might demand. Even as the particularity of the structures of patriarchy are highlighted in each chapter, the volume as a whole also reveals the similarities as well as the (differentiated) universality of the subordination of women.

The state features in this process of definition and redefinition through institution of legal regulations and deregulation, and direct and indirect coercion. Yet, as many of the chapters show, the state is not monolithic nor unitary, thereby providing spaces for intervention by the women's movement and the labour movement. Drawing on notions of justice and citizenship, women workers have organised to defend and extend their rights and improve their situation, even in the unorganised sector and free trade zones often seen as unorganisable. All the chapters share a standpoint which sees women workers as conscious agents, making interventions which range from survival strategies to the proposing of transformative policies. This moves well away from the 'victimology' which has too often coloured studies on women workers. In so far as women do organise and form a collectivity, however brief, to assert a (or often more than one) identity, the volume reasserts the value of the conceptual category 'women', whose multiple identities are a source of both fragmentation and coalescence.

Organising independently and in coalition with others, and confounding ideological assumptions concerning their position, condition or place, women workers have acted in diverse circumstances and for differing purposes to confront the state, capital and patriarchy. The interactive effect of agency and the processes of mobilising and organising are evident in the confrontation by women, in the shifting of power relations this implies and generates, and in the changed consciousness and response which may be created through the action undertaken.

Within these contexts, confrontation may be direct and overt, or it may be more indirect and carried out at various levels. The chapters document campaigns and militant actions resorted to by women, as for instance the strikes for better working conditions and struggle for unionisation by free trade zone workers in Jamaica and the Dominican Republic in the 1980s, as well as by women garment workers in Karachi, Pakistan and the campaign for paternity leave by the KMK in the Philippines. In their attempts to gain access to foreign exchange and trade recognition, women traders in Zimbabwe have confronted the joint pressures of state, capital and patriarchy; their efforts to manoeuvre within and/or to circumvent the system(s), demonstrate not only the difficulties of the situation, but also the ingenuity of the women, and the series of strategies brought to bear.

There are examples of the formation of coalitions which act as pressure groups on the state, such as the Coalition for Construction Workers in India. At another level, the detailed analysis of the internal functioning and organisational structures in which women are involved reveals intangible, slow yet steady changes in consciousness, self-confidence and self-determination. This is evident, for instance, in the Livelihood Revolving Fund for Women in the Philippines, and in the case study of the Tamilnadu Construction Workers Union in India. Women workers have not only built alliances with trade unions and other organisations but have also formed international alliances, linking the local to the global and confronting the interdependence of the world economy in this phase of restructuring, as documented in the chapters by Linda Shaw and Cheng-Kooi.

Similar initiatives have been noted in other countries, as for example the actions of the Madres de la Plaza de Mayo in Argentina.[12] Strategies followed by women in many Latin American countries in the context of economic crisis have also asserted the principles of collectivity, raised the moral issue of the right to survival and have confronted the state (J. Nash, 1990). Describing survival strategies in Bolivia, Peru, Uruguay, Mexico and Chile, Nash suggests that the extended kin group, the neighbourhood and community, having become the prime sites for collective action among women, have provided a base, a forum, in some cases already operationalised, for additional political action. Indeed, the incapacity of the state to create the conditions to satisfy basic needs has rendered action by women and other impoverished compatriots imperative. Women could not afford *not* to join or initiate community protests or programmes, actions which in other contexts or countries would have been deemed too demanding of their already too limited time.

All the chapters, while pointing out that traditional forms are male dominated and the various ways in which patriarchy has operated in the labour movement, assert the necessity for joint actions, alliances and/or conscientisation of men workers. The focus on the particular experience of women workers in the context of industrial restructuring in this volume has shown that the issues which affect women, and around which they have organised, form a critical base for transforming gender relations as well as the structures of capitalist production and the state. For example, the existence of the hierarchical, non-participatory structure of trade unions mentioned in many of the chapters implies the exclusion not only of women workers, but also of rank and file workers in general. Raising the issue of women's participation and restructuring of traditional unions would contain within it a step towards the general democratisation of institutions of the state and civil society.

Similarly, in the process of organising around very specific issues, women workers have raised or sometimes even created structures and values which have relevance for society as a whole. Cecilia Olea Mauleón (this volume) discusses the ways in which communal kitchens emerged in Peru to deal with the immediate problem of food shortages, but in addition led to changes in the traditional sexual division of labour and access to the public sphere, as well as to increased confidence to propose social policies linking, for example, urban consumption to agricultural development.

The chapters show that a focus on issues of basic survival and the necessity to develop different strategies and policies to keep jobs for women, to get jobs for women and to improve terms and conditions of work, does not preclude changes in other areas of women's lives. In fact, these strategies will of necessity have to incorporate other dimensions of women's multiple identities to attain even these limited objectives.[13] So for instance a policy for women's employment must support strategies for changing gender ideology both inside as well as outside the factory. Notions of masculinity and femininity affect skill definitions, wages and working conditions, and the location of women within the production process as well as within sectors of industry. The integral link between household, factory and community affects women's work as well as their potential for organisation. Strategies and policies for increasing women's access to income generation have to incorporate policies recognising pressures of and ties with the household and the community as a whole.

The dual character of present trends in global restructuring, particularly for organising, provides a broad framework within which alternative strategies and policies in the present context could be located. An important point made by both Elson and Roldan is that there is a double character to the present trends in flexible specialisation, which allows also for the possibility of creating a basis for progressive social transformation.[14] Part-time work, for instance, could allow greater choice about hours and patterns of work if it included parity with full-time work in wages, benefits and rights. Other strategies include the possibility of adapting efficient technologies in women's cooperatives, extension of legal liabilities along the chain of sub-contracting, a code of conduct implemented by consumer organisations, redivision of budgets and allocations to local government bodies, supportive policies for women's work in the informal sector, and the inclusion of ILO Conventions in IMF conditionalities as ways to develop points of leverage towards social transformation. One recent and relevant approach is the Code of Conduct for Multinationals formulated by COSATU. This not only raises immediate labour issues such as conformance to ILO Conventions, workers' rights and employment creation, but also brings out the issues of apartheid and other forms of discrimination, and incorporates equality of opportunity, training and basic education, protection of the environment, and corporate social responsibility.[15]

The perspective that emerges moves away from a dichotomy of reform vs. revolution, to identifying strategies which are practical and viable in the short term and lay the basis for more fundamental structural changes in the long run. The advantages and limitations of linking alternative organisations with either the market or the state become questions of how much, which sectors (for instance, tapping local government resources for education and training rather than setting up a large income-generating project), in which way and with what amount of leverage and space for autonomy, rather than being a radical negative or blinkered positive response.

The contributions in this volume demonstrate the tremendous strength, initiative, resilience and resolve that working women have shown in their confrontation with the state, capital and patriarchy. In a context where the onslaught of structural adjustment programmes on working people has forced traditional workers' organisations into a defensive position, it is the actions of these women, and the theory and strategies derived therefrom, which can provide us with a basis for new directions, and for a coalescing of interests for the restructuring of state and civil society.

NOTES

1. The concepts of formal sector/informal sector and organised sector/unorganised sector have been the subject of massive political and theoretical debate since their introduction more than two decades ago. We use the terms as a shorthand method to reflect the integrating yet hierarchical linkages in industry and industrialisation, but with recognition of the limitations of these terms as either descriptive or analytical constructs.
2. See also Alison MacEwen Scott, 1986, concerning the limitations of the Female Marginalisation Thesis as a theoretical model to understand women's employment.
3. South Africa has been excluded from Sub-Saharan African reckoning and statistics by the United Nations and other agencies. However, South Africa has perhaps the most extensive and detailed history and contemporary analysis of both industry and industrialisation in relation to women of any African country (see e.g. the writings of Iris Berger, Belinda Bozzoli, Joanne Yawitch; and Debbie Budlender, 1991). Some of the South African unions have demonstrated historically the strong involvement of women. Contemporary union efforts include the provision of a basis for a more equitable sexual

division of labour through union-led shared parenting provisions (Daphne, 1992); and recognition of the need to assert and safeguard women's interests through the creation of union-based gender fora, women's spaces in the formal union structures (Horn, 1992).

4. See F. Anthias and N. Yuval-Davis, 1989, for relevant theoretical discussion on the state.

5. In Europe, present statistics demonstrate that women make up 90–95 per cent of homeworkers in Germany, Greece, Ireland, Italy and the Netherlands, 84 per cent in France, 75 per cent in Spain, and 70 per cent in the UK. Married women with children predominate. In Japan, according to 1988 figures, 93.5 per cent of homeworkers are women; in the Australian clothing industry 95 per cent of homeworkers are women, and in the Indian cigarette industry the figure is almost 90 per cent (ILO, 1990, p. 10).

6. Cagatay and Berik's analysis of Turkey also documents the increase in homeworking. According to the 1988 Urban Household Labor Force Survey, 30 per cent of women employed in manufacturing are homeworkers (Cagatay and Berik, 1990: 124). See also Young-ock Kim for data on homeworking in Korea.

7. For discussion of the legal classification, definition and regulation of homeworking in a number of countries, and the present possibilities for protection of homeworkers, see Vega Ruiz, 1992.

8. Put forward at the Workshop on 'Women Organising in the Process of Industrialisation', ISS, The Hague, April 1991.

9. The importance of local organisations, among others, at times superseding specifically 'workers' organisations, at times acting in conjunction with them, is becoming more clearly recognised and treated as an accessible workers' resource. See e.g. Sanyal (1991) concerning the 'axes of commonality' (e.g. proximity, ethnicity, gender) which may bind workers together in the informal sector.

10. The media comprise one of the most powerful tools and vehicles for organising and action, with input and efforts by women workers themselves providing an additional base of solidarity (or cleavage, depending on interests involved). For detailed discussion regarding the value and use of media among women workers, and as an exemplar of the medium itself, see *Many Paths, One Goal*, 1991, edited by the Committee for Asian Women.

11. 'Empowerment' is one of the most evocative and increasingly all too common terms in feminist writing today. A useful descriptor in its use is the distinction between 'power to . . .' and 'power over . . .'. Note, in the chapter by Gandhi in this volume, the example of how the former merged over time and with use into the latter.

12. The Madres de la Plaza de Mayo, for example, for years shamed the government of Argentina in their demonstrations, carried out in the busiest areas of the city, against the disappearance of their children, their husbands, their parents. Cloaking (and protecting) themselves in the garb of womanly authority, the women used the very imagery of maternal love and caring to defy and expose the state and to demand justice.

13. For a theoretical examination of the application of the distinction between practical and strategic interests, see Chhachhi and Pittin, this volume.

14. Ruth Pearson (1991) makes a similar point in relation to telecommunication

workers in Jamaica. She argues that although in terms of e.g. pay, conditions of work, opportunities for promotion and security of employment, the situation of women data-entry operators is similar to that of women workers in Free Trade Zones, there exist possibilities for data-entry operators to move into better jobs, created by the revolution in telecommunication technology. Rather than moving at the most into secretarial jobs, if these women were provided with managerial and information technology training courses, and their skills were redefined and enhanced, they could begin to provide professional services in the telecommunications field.

15. Code of Conduct for Multinational Companies Investing in South Africa, as discussed at COSATU's Economic Policy Conference in March, 1992.

REFERENCES

Abdullah, Hussaina. 1992. 'Trade Unions, The Democratic Process and the Challenge of Gender in Nigeria'. Paper presented at the Workshop on Women and Work: Historical Trends, Centre for Basic Research, Kampala, Uganda.

Abdullah-Olukoshi, Hussaina. 1991. 'The Dynamics of Gender and Class in Kano's Manufacturing Sector: Two Case Studies'. Paper presented to the International Workshop on Women Organising in the Process of Industrialisation, Institute of Social Studies, The Hague, The Netherlands.

Acero, Liliana. 1991. *Textile Workers in Brazil and Argentina: A Study of the Interrelationships between Work and Households*, United Nations University Press, Tokyo.

Afshar, Haleh. 1987. *Women, State and Ideology*, Macmillan, London.

Aguiar, Neuma. 1988. 'The Crisis in Latin America and its Impact on Women: A Summary of Research by Members of the DAWN Network in Latin America', in ISIS International & DAWN (eds), *Confronting the Crisis in Latin America: Women Organising for Change*, ISIS International, Santiago, Chile, pp. 11–22.

Alavi, Hamza. 1988. 'Pakistan: Women in a Changing Society', *Economic and Political Weekly*, June 25.

Amsden, Alice H. 1990. 'Third World Industrialisation: "Global Fordism" as a New Model?', *New Left Review*, No. 182, July/August.

Andrae, Gunilla. 1993. 'Gender and Unions: The Family Woman Worker in Garment and Tailoring Industry in Lagos'. Paper presented at a Colloquium on Transformation of Female Identities: Forms of Female Organisations in West Africa, held in Ngaoundéré, Cameroun, March 26–28.

Arriagada, Irma. 1988. 'Latin American Women and the Crisis', in ISIS International & DAWN (eds), *Confronting the Crisis in Latin America: Women Organising for Change*, ISIS International, Santiago, Chile, pp. 53–9.

Banerjee, Nirmala. 1985. 'Women and Industrialisation in Developing Countries', Occasional Paper No. 71, Centre for Studies in Social Sciences, Calcutta.

Bangura, Yusuf. 1991. 'Structural Adjustment and De-industrialisation in Nigeria: 1986–1988', *Africa Development*, Vol. XVI, No. 2, pp. 5–32.

Baylies, Carolyn and Caroline Wright. 1993. 'Female Labour in the Textile and Clothing Industry of Lesotho', *African Affairs*, No. 92, pp. 577–91.

Beechey, Veronica. 1988. 'Rethinking the Definition of Work: Gender and Work', in J. Jenson, E. Hagen and C. Reddy (eds), *Feminization of the Labour Force*, Polity Press, Oxford, pp. 45–62.

Budlender, D. 1991. *Women and the Economy*, C.A.S.E., Johannesburg.

Cagatay, Nilufer and Gunseli Berik. 1990. 'Transition to Export-led Growth in Turkey: Is There a Feminization of Employment?', *Review of Radical Political Economics*, Vol. 22, No. 1, pp. 115–34.

Chhachhi, Amrita and Paul Kurian. 1982. 'New Phase in Trade Unionism?', *Economic and Political Weekly*, Vol. XVII, No. 8, Feb. 20, pp. 267–72.

Committee for Asian Women. 1991. *Many Paths, One Goal: Organising Women Workers in Asia*. Committee for Asian Women (CAW), Hong Kong.

Commonwealth Secretariat. 1989. *Engendering Adjustment for the 1990s*. Report of a Commonwealth Expert Group, London.

Cornia, G. A., R. Jolly and F. Stewart. 1989. *Adjustment with a Human Face*, Clarendon Press, Oxford.

Daphne, Jeremy. 1992. 'The South African Commercial, Catering and Allied Workers' Union Policies on Parental Rights: Strategies for Change'. Unpublished MA Thesis, Institute of Social Studies, The Hague, The Netherlands.

Di Martino, Vittorio and Linda Wirth. 1990. 'Telework: A New Way of Working and Living', *International Labour Review*, Vol. 129, No. 5, pp. 529–54.

Elson, Diane. 1989. 'The Impact of Structural Adjustment on Women: Concepts and Issues', in Bade Onimode (ed.), *The IMF, the World Bank and the African Debt. Vol. 2: The Social and Political Impact*, The Institute for African Alternatives and Zed Books Ltd, London, pp. 56–74.

Gogna, Monica. 1988. 'Women in Labor Unions: Organization, Practices, and Demands', in ISIS International & DAWN (eds), *Confronting the Crisis in Latin America: Women Organising for Change*, ISIS International, Santiago, Chile, pp. 33–9.

Hirata, Helen and John Humphrey. 1991. 'Workers' Responses to Job Losses: Female and Male Industrial Workers in Brazil', *World Development*, Vol. 19, No. 6, pp. 671–82.

Horn, Patricia. 1992. 'Women and Work in South Africa: Transforming the World of Women's Work through Initiative and Struggle'. Paper presented at the Workshop on Women and Work: Historical Trends, Centre for Basic Research, Kampala, Uganda.

Humphrey, John. 1993. 'Introduction: Reorganising the Firm', *IDS Bulletin*, Vol. 24, No. 2, April, pp. 1–9.

ILO. 1990. *Social Protection of Homeworkers*. Documents of the Meeting of Experts on the Social Protection of Homeworkers, Geneva. MEHW/1990/7.

Jenkins, Rhys. 1991. 'The Political Economy of Industrialisation: A Comparison of Latin American and East Asian Newly Industrialising Countries', *Development and Change*, Vol. 22, No. 2, April, pp. 197–231.

Jenson, Jane, Elisabeth Hagen and Ceallaigh Reddy (eds). 1988. *Feminisation of the Labour Force*, Polity Press, Oxford.

Joekes, Susan. 1987. *Women in the World Economy – An INSTRAW Study*, Oxford University Press, New York, Oxford.

Mensah-Kutin, Rose. 1991. 'The Pattern of Women's Work in Ghanaian Industry: Issues and Strategies for Organising'. Paper presented to the International Workshop on Women Organising in the Process of Industrialisation, Institute of Social Studies, The Hague, The Netherlands.

Mitter, Swasti. 1986. *Common Fate, Common Bond: Women in the Global Economy*, Pluto Press, London.

Nash, June. 1990. 'Latin American Women in the World Capitalist Crisis', *Gender and Society*, Vol. 4, No. 3, September, pp. 338–53.

Pearson, Ruth. 1991. 'Gender and New Technology in the Caribbean: New Work for Women?' Paper presented to the International Workshop on Women Organising in the Process of Industrialisation, Institute of Social Studies, The Hague, The Netherlands.

Pittin, Renée. 1991. 'Women, Work and Ideology in Nigeria', *Review of African Political Economy*, Special Issue on Fundamentalism in Africa: Religion and Politics, No. 52, November, pp. 38–52.

Ramirez, Socorro. 1988. 'Women Confront the Economic Crisis and Demand Participation', in ISIS International & DAWN (eds), *Confronting the Crisis in Latin America: Women Organising for Change*, ISIS International, Santiago, Chile, pp. 25–31.

Riddell, Roger C. (ed.). 1990. *Manufacturing Africa, Performance & Prospects of Seven Countries in Sub-Saharan Africa*, James Currey and Heinemann Educational Books, Inc., London and Portsmouth, N.H.

Roldán, Martha. 1993. 'Industrial Restructuring, Deregulation and New JIT Labour Processes in Argentina: Towards a Gender-aware Perspective?', *IDS Bulletin*, Vol. 24, No. 2, April, pp. 42–52.

Rosa, Kumudhini. 'In House Unions – An Alternative Organisational Form for Women Workers in Export Processing Zones?' Paper presented to the International Workshop on Women Organising in the Process of Industrialisation, Institute of Social Studies, The Hague, The Netherlands.

Sanyal, Bishwapriya. 1991. 'Organising the Self-employed: The Politics of the Urban Informal Sector', *International Labour Review*, Vol. 130, No. 1, pp. 39–56.

Scott, Alison MacEwen. 1986. 'Women and Industrialisation: Examining the "Female Marginalisation Thesis",' *The Journal of Development Studies*, Vol. 22, No. 4, July, pp. 649–80.

Shettima, Kole Ahmed. 1989. 'Women's Movement and Visions – The Nigeria Labour Congress Women's Wing', *Africa Development*, Vol. XIV, No. 3, pp. 81–98.

Souza Lobo, Elizabeth. 1985. 'The Rising of Women Workers in São Paulo (Brazil)'. Paper presented at the Wenner-Gren Foundation for Anthropological Research International Symposium on Anthropological Perspectives on Women's Collective Action: An Assessment of the Decade, 1975–1985, Mijas, Spain.

Standing, Guy. 1989. 'Global Feminisation through Flexible Labor', *World Development*, Vol. 17, No. 7, pp. 1077–95.

Tripp, Aili Mari. 1994. 'Deindustrialisation and the Growth of Women's Economic Associations and Networks in Urban Tanzania', in S. Rowbotham and S. Mitter (eds), *Dignity and Daily Bread*, Routledge, London and New York, pp. 139–57.

Vega Ruiz, Luz. 1992. 'Home Work: Towards a New Regulatory Framework?', *International Labour Review*, Vol. 131, No. 2, pp. 197–215.

Villamil, Silvia Rodriguez. 1992. 'Women and Work in Uruguay: Historical Trends and Changing Gender Ideologies'. Paper presented at the Workshop on Women and Work: Historical Trends, Centre for Basic Research, Kampala, Uganda.

Part I – Reconceptualising Industrialisation and Organisation

The volume is divided into three parts which represent its major thematic, conceptual and theoretical foci. Part I presents new theoretical and conceptual approaches to the study of women organising in the process of industrialisation. The contributions to this section consider some key areas in industrialisation theory and feminist theory, and review and reanalyse them on the basis of detailed data from international, national and industry-specific research.

In the first chapter in this part, Diane Elson re-examines the concept of feminisation, particularly in relation to changing patterns of flexibilisation. The chapter challenges previous assumptions concerning questions of replacement of male by female workers, and points to issues of generalised job loss which are being ignored or masked by the (often misplaced) focus on feminisation in this process. Significant differences between industries, sectors, regions and countries are brought out in her findings, and the need for and value of specificity in analysis in relation to industrial process is brought clearly to the fore.

From the basis of several years' research in the Argentinian metallurgical industry, Martha Roldan raises disturbing questions concerning the development of feminist theory in relation to the profound socio-political changes taking place not only in industry, but also in relation to global economic restructuring more broadly. She notes that it is insufficient for women activists in industry, such as trade unionists, to focus on women *per se*. Rather, they must act on the basis of a gendered perception of the dynamics as well as the effects of economic and industrial processes. Such an approach would avoid the marginalisation and ghettoisation of women's issues and input, and would enable women to debate and discuss more effectively with their male colleagues, and create better strategies for women. Roldan uses her research on Just-In-Time technological innovation and employment and labour transfer to reflect also upon broader issues of deindustrialisation and economic restructuring.

In the third chapter in this section, Amrita Chhachhi and Renée Pittin introduce the concept of multiple identities, which permits a more nuanced and complex analysis and understanding of the theoretical and practical construction of industrial pattern and process, and of choice and action among industrial workers. Comparative empirical data from Indian and Nigerian industry provide the foundation for reconsideration of issues of identity and consciousness among factory workers, on the basis of the plethora of interests and understandings which they (and others) have of their priorities. Thus, considerations such as gender, class, ethnicity, caste, educational level and marital status come into play as workers respond to social, economic and other pressures. These identities inform their choices, their actions, and their alliances. Chhachhi and Pittin eschew the dichotomies within gender analysis *per se*, and of class and gender, and present a multivariate conceptual base for the analysis of the dynamics of the industrial process.

1 Appraising Recent Developments in the World Market for Nimble Fingers

Diane Elson

At the end of the 1970s, researchers' and policy-makers' attention was focused for the first time on how a new female workforce was being created in the course of industrialisation in many developing countries. The emphasis was on a new international division of labour: relocation of production from developed to developing countries, export-oriented world market factories, western-owned multinational corporations, and the massing together of hundreds of young women in export-oriented garment factories and electronics factories (Lim, 1978; Frobel, Heinrichs and Kreye, 1979; Elson and Pearson, 1981). Two dominant themes present in much of the literature were encapsulated in the title of an article published in *Signs*: 'Runaway Shops and Female Employment: The Search for Cheap Labor' (Safa, 1981).

In the early 1990s, concerns have broadened: not just women in export-oriented factories, but also women in factories supplying primarily local markets (Dennis, 1984; Pittin, 1984; Hensman, 1988); not just new electronics factories in developing, but also in developed countries (Goldstein, 1989; Pyle, 1990); not just factory work, but also outwork (home based production) (Beneria and Roldan, 1987; Ward (ed.), 1990). The emphasis in much of the literature has shifted from 'cheap' labour to 'flexible' labour (Mitter, 1986, 1991; Standing, 1989); and from relocation of production to deeper forms of economic restructuring,[1] involving changes not simply in individual production processes, but in the way production and consumption are articulated and whole economics are co-ordinated and reproduced (MacEwan and Tabb (eds), 1989; Beneria and Feldman (eds), forthcoming; Kaplinsky, 1985).

Debate continues about the benefits of industrialisation for women (Elson, 1988a; Lim, 1990; Ward (ed.), 1990; Stichter and Parpart (eds), 1990); and about its impact on women's consciousness (Rosa, 1989; Ward (ed), 1990). While activists welcome evidence of women workers organising to improve their situation, orthodox economists see this as one more 'distortion' impeding the efficient operation of the labour market.

This chapter will discuss some interpretations of recent developments and some implications of current trends. It is organised in three sections:

1. Capital Accumulation: the issue of 'flexibility' and 'feminisation';
2. State Regulation: the issue of 'distortions'; and
3. Social Organisation: the issue of moving beyond the factory.

CAPITAL ACCUMULATION: THE ISSUE OF 'FLEXIBILITY' AND 'FEMINISATION'

It is widely argued that the current phase of capital accumulation is marked by an emphasis on more 'flexibility' in both developing and developed countries. 'Flexibility' is used to refer to at least three different dimensions of the economic system: the organisational structure of firms, the operation of the labour market, and the pattern of production. The 'flexible firm' decentralises its organisation and uses measures such as dividing its workforce into a 'core' with secure jobs and a 'periphery' which can be dismissed and re-employed at will (Atkinson and Meager, 1986). It also sub-contracts much of its production to a network of other firms with which it has very close relations, sometimes referred to as 'systemofacture' (Kaplinsky, 1985). Labour market flexibility refers to changes in the regulations, contracts, customs and practices that govern the labour market so as to make it easier for management to hire and, more especially fire, workers; to casualise labour; and to raise and lower money wage rates in line with the profitability of the firm. (This is the major focus of Huws, Hurstfield and Holtmaat, 1989.) Flexibility in the pattern of production refers to an alteration of the technical division of labour so that it is less rigid. This is often discussed in terms of a new pattern of work organisation labelled 'flexible specialisation' which is defined as 'manufacture of a wide and changing array of customized products using flexible, general purpose machinery and skilled, adaptable workers' (Hirst and Zeitlin, 1990).

The outcome of these three types of flexibility can be seen as an increase in functional flexibility, numerical flexibility, and financial flexibility for the employer. Functional flexibility refers to flexibility across job boundaries, so that workers are called upon to undertake a different range of tasks and skills that cut across former demarcations. Numerical flexibility refers to flexibility in hours of work, both in total and in the shift pattern, and in numbers of workers. Financial flexibility refers to flexibility in the costs of employing labour, particularly through minimisation of the *fixed* costs of employing labour by minimising the employment of full-time permanent workers, enjoying job security and pension, sickness and holiday benefits. Functional flexibility is thus flexibility in terms of task; numerical flexibility is flexibility in terms of hours of labour time; financial flexibility is flexibility in terms of labour costs.

Flexibility has been associated with 'feminisation' of the labour force by a study of seven developed countries: Britain, Canada, France, Federal Republic of Germany, Italy, Sweden and the United States of America (Jenson, Hagen and Reddy (eds), 1988). This study argues that in the 1970s and 1980s firms have been searching for flexibility and that:

> Women have emerged as very desirable employees in these circumstances because their relationship to the labor market has traditionally displayed the characteristics of flexibility so much wanted in the current conjuncture. (p. 10)

The analysis of 'flexibilisation' and 'feminisation' has been extended to a global level by Standing, 1989, who argues that the dominant emphasis in accumulation today in *both* developed and developing countries is achievement of cost-competitiveness through reduction of labour-related rigidities (p. 1078). This has involved both labour market flexibility through an erosion of forms of labour market regulation which gave workers some rights to job and income security (to be discussed further in the next Section); and also functional flexibility: 'a more flexible approach to job structures, making it easier to alter job boundaries and the technical division of labour' (p. 1078). The aim of enterprises everywhere, argues Standing, has become the reduction of the proportion of labour costs that are fixed. As part of this:

> There is a global trend to reduced reliance on full-time wage and salary workers earning fixed wages and various fringe benefits. Companies and public sector enterprises in both developed and developing countries are increasingly resorting to casual or temporary workers, to part-timers, to sub-contracting and to contract workers. (p. 1079)

Standing also associates flexibility with 'feminisation', claiming that there is:

> 'feminization' of many jobs and activities traditionally dominated by men. (p. 1080)

and that:

> women are being substituted widely for men in various occupational categories, including manufacturing and production work. (p. 1086)

Many orthodox economists would interpret 'flexibilisation' as evidence of greater efficiency in the allocation of labour between different uses. But this optimistic view depends on the assumption that there is a strong intrinsic tendency of the market mechanism to produce full employment; that transitional costs of 'disequilibrium' situations can safely be ignored, and that workers can freely choose the type of work and conditions of employment they undertake. More radical economists point out that for workers, flexibility may instead mean insecurity and impoverishment, especially in conditions of rising unemployment.[2]

This is undoubtedly true, especially for women workers, and other contributions to this volume provide graphic examples. However, a note of caution needs to be sounded on two issues: flexibilisation is not *always* associated with feminisation; and flexibility is not *inevitably* detrimental to workers, especially women workers. It all depends whose needs flexibility is designed to serve.[3]

Let us first consider the issue of the 'feminisation' of the labour force. The data in the ILO *Yearbook of Labour Statistics* do indeed show that in the vast majority of countries women's share of total employment rose during the 1980s.[4] But this by itself does not indicate the 'feminisation' of many jobs and activities traditionally dominated by men as claimed in Standing (1989). It is quite compatible with the *disappearance* of many jobs of the type traditionally dominated by men, and the *expansion* of jobs of the type traditionally dominated by women. The study of feminisation of the labour force in seven developed economies to which we earlier referred found that although women's share of employment rose, the labour market remained highly segregated:

> women were confined to work ghettos which involved serving or caring, or which required patience and dexterity. The stereotypes, based on the deeply-rooted assumptions about proper gender roles and gender relations, shaped labour markets ...
>
> (Jenson, Hagen and Reddy (eds), 1988: 9)

The restructuring of labour contracts and the altering of job boundaries in the name of 'flexibility' is in fact much more likely to take place in a gender differentiated way than to be a force for overcoming the sexual division of labour. There are several case studies which show how this can happen in various types of manufacturing. For instance, Walsh (1987) discusses a case in the UK textile industry. Courtauld, the leading UK textile multinational, embarked in 1986 on a £120 million programme of new investment in yarn production aimed at greater flexibility in the range of colours and grades of yarn produced. The idea was to match production much more closely to the fluctuating pattern of demand and reduce the need to hold stocks i.e. to diminish the rigidities of physical capital. The new equipment required far fewer operators than the old; and it was decided to alter job boundaries, so that the machine operators also carried out some maintenance to reduce the time the equipment might stand idle awaiting a maintenance engineer. This required operators to be trained in a limited range of new technical skills – an example of 'flexibility' leading to the creation of 'better jobs', though at the expense of many workers who would have to be made redundant. The job losses fell disproportionately on women – the mill was expected in future to have a workforce 85 per cent male, on higher pay and working in cleaner conditions, though with regular night work. Both management *and* the trade union representatives in this case are reported by Walsh (1987) as seeing the displacement of women as inevitable because as the new jobs needed a wider range of technical skills and a willingness to adopt inconvenient shiftwork patterns, they were indubitably 'men's jobs'.

International comparative statistics on the female share of employment in the textile industry show no overall tendency towards 'feminisation' in the 1980s. In fact, in quite a number of countries, developing as well as developed, the statistics show a fall in the female share of employment.[5]

The electronics industry is generally regarded as a leading example of 'feminisation' – but even here there is evidence suggesting some tendency for women's share of employment to be falling over time in at least some countries. For instance, women's share of employment in foreign owned electronics plants in the Republic of Ireland fell from 62 per cent in 1973 to 51 per cent in 1983 (Jackson and Barry, 1989, p. 52).[6] In the USA, women's share of employment in semi-conductor production has been falling. Most women are employed as unskilled production workers, and the proportion of such workers to total employment has fallen from 72 per cent in 1965 to 55 per cent in 1977 and 44 per cent in 1980. From the mid-1960s to the mid-1970s, the decline was largely due to relocation of labour-intensive production activities to developing countries. But from the late 1970s onwards, it has been due to technical change in wafer fabrication, assembly and testing (Goldstein, 1989, p. 123). A study of Scotland's 'Silicon Glen' in the early 1980s suggests that the female share of employment in semi-conductor production there is set to decline considerably from a level of about 56 per cent, as automation of wafer fabrication reduces the requirement for assembly workers and increases the requirement for technicians and electronics engineers. In one firm even women's virtual monopoly of assembly jobs had ended: 53 per cent of such jobs were held by men and the jobs done by the men were defined differently to include a wider range of tasks, overlapping with those of technicians (Goldstein, 1989: 123–6). In this case 'flexibility' in the scope of jobs has led to jobs being done by men rather than by women.

This tendency is *not* confined to developed countries. Recent evidence on the border industries ('maquiladora') in Mexico indicates that between 1980 and 1985 the share of unskilled assembly workers ('operators') in employment fell from 84.0 per cent to 78.0 per cent in electronics assembly, and from 85.7 per cent to 79.5 per cent in electronic components. There was a corresponding rise in the share of technical, administrative and management staff. Since women are overwhelmingly confined to 'operator' jobs and account for the vast majority of operators, the result is a decline in women's share of employment (Pearson, 1991).

International comparative statistics on the female share of employment in the electrical machinery industry show no overall tendency towards 'feminisation' in the 1980s; and indeed show a falling female share in a number of countries.[7]

My conclusion is that 'flexibilisation' does *not* necessarily lead to direct substitution of women for men in types of work traditionally done by men; nor does it necessarily lead to a rising female share of paid employment in manufacturing industries. The gender division of labour, which tends to confine women to relatively subordinate and inferior positions in the organisation of monetised production, is not overridden by 'flexibility'. Rather it structures the form that 'flexibility' takes. This is as true in the so-called 'informal' sector as in the so-called 'formal' sector. MacEwen Scott (1991) shows how gender segments both the 'formal' and the 'informal' sector, so that the jobs done by women in both the 'formal' and 'informal' sector have the negative characteristics often associated by critics with the idea of 'flexible labour'; whereas the jobs done by men in the 'formal' *and* the 'informal' sector have the positive characteristics often associated with the idea of 'regular' labour. In a detailed analysis of Lima, Peru, she shows that, 'Although men also worked in the informal sector, indeed predominated there, they had access to occupations that facilitated skill acquisition, accumulation of savings and movement between formal and informal sectors.' (MacEwen Scott, 1991: 124.) Dennis (1991) comes to similar conclusions for Nigeria.

The second note of caution concerns the desirability of flexibility. There is a danger of judging the organisation of production and the operation of labour market according to standards which see full-time permanent life-long jobs (a 40–50 hour week, from 8 or 9 till 5), based on carefully demarcated craft skills, as the desirable 'norm' to which all workers do and should aspire. Anything that departs from this 'norm' may be regarded as not really a proper job; as merely secondary employment. (For a discussion of such attitudes, see Huws, Hurstfield and Holtmaat, 1989: 17.)

But this is a male 'norm' that most women have never enjoyed and many women do not want. The vast majority of women who have domestic responsibilities have an immediate interest in a more flexible job structure, in the sense of greater *choice* about hours and patterns of work and ways of getting skills recognised and used. As Huws, Hurstfield and Holtmaat (1989) point out:

> women have demanded, and in some cases won, such things as the right to work short hours to fit in with the standard schoolday; the right to take paid leave to deal with family illnesses; workplace creche provision; the ability to rearrange working hours to fit in with such contingencies as doctors' or dentists' visits or school holidays; and the right to extended maternity or compassionate leave. (p. 15)

Obviously, in the longer run, women have an interest in the redivision of domestic responsibilities so that men participate equally in housework, child-care, and looking after the sick and elderly; and an interest in more collective forms of responsibility for the care of those who need the care of others. But this too is likely to require more flexible ways of organising time spent in paid work, for men as well as for women. If men too had greater choice about hours and patterns of work, then this might have beneficial effects on the division of domestic responsibilities, with men able to take more role in the day-to-day care of family members (Hensman, 1988: 23). Existing male norms about the 'proper' way to organise working life need challenging, not reinforcing; but in ways that extend rather than diminish workers' rights to be treated as human beings, with lives outside paid employment, rather than simply inputs into production.

There is considerable debate about the use of the term 'flexibility' in relation to workers' needs. As pointed out by Huws, Hurstfield and Holtmaat (1989):

> some would suggest that the word has become so irretrievably linked to a notion of flexibility which is solely in the employer's interests that it should never be used in relation to the fulfilment of workers' needs. Others feel it is still useful, and could be re-appropriated to describe a re-organisation of work which is in the interests of workers, particularly women workers. They point out that the demand for flexible working hours was frequently raised by women's groups during the 60s and 70s . . . Such worker-determined flexibility would, however, take very different forms from that currently promoted by employers. It would,

for instance, presuppose long-term job security and a guaranteed income. (p. 13)

The key issue, I would argue, is not so much the disintegration of previous norms of 'regular' employment in 'proper jobs', which were always more applicable to men than to women; rather it is the erosion of workers' rights and ability to organise in defence of those rights. It is in relation to this that current forms of 'flexibility' need to be judged, rather than male norms of work.

STATE REGULATION: THE ISSUE OF 'DISTORTIONS'

There is no intrinsic reason why moves to more flexible work should lead to an erosion of workers' rights. In a democratic economy, part-time workers could have the same rights as full-time workers. Workers employed by sub-contractors could have the same rights as those employed by the firm to which their employer is sub-contracted. Temporary workers could have fringe benefits and income guarantees provided by the state rather than by employers. If enterprises take measures to reduce the proportion of labour costs that are fixed, there is no intrinsic reason why all the risk should be transferred to labour. The income security previously provided by long-term employment contracts could be provided by a social security system financed from general taxation. Absolute job security, in the sense of a right to a *particular* job for a very long period of time, is, it is true, not compatible with more flexible work patterns. But it is not clear that this right is necessary or desirable, provided that there are democratic mechanisms for re-allocating jobs.[8] A new set of rights relating to the allocation of jobs could replace old ones which were constructed on the basis of craft demarcations by mainly male workers.

However, as Standing correctly points out, the 1980s have seen in many countries an attack on workers' rights in the name of deregulation:

a whole set of labour and social rights became perceived increasingly as costs and rigidities. . . . fewer people are entitled to state benefits in industrialised countries. . . . In country after country, including many developing countries, governments have taken steps to make it easier for employers to dismiss workers or reduce the size of their labour force . . . . Governments have been urged to remove or weaken minimum wage legislation and institutional safeguards, on the ground that such wages reduce employment . . .

(Standing, 1989: 1078)

This erosion of rights cannot simply be read off from technological change, or attempts to match production more closely to consumption; it involves ideological and political processes as well as economic processes. A key ideological process has been the rise of neo-liberal thinking, deriving its arguments from the neo-classical and 'Austrian' schools of economics, embodied in the policies of the Reagan and Thatcher administrations, and in IMF stabilisation and World Bank structural adjustment programmes. These schools of economic thought depict the labour market as potentially an arena of freedom of choice, harmonisation of interests, and full employment, if only there were not 'outside intervention' through state regulation and collective organisations, such as trade unions. These 'interventions' are typically seen as distorting prices and creating secure employment for a privileged 'labour aristocracy', while denying it to a mass of others, including most women. Thus an economist at Yale University concludes a recent study of women's changing participation in the world labour force thus: 'It does not seem unreasonable that women are the main group that loses ground due to labour-market regulations and distortions in low income countries.' (Schultz, 1991: 481) It is important to engage with this thinking, since it appears so 'commonsensical' to many people, and has come to set the international agenda in the 1980s.

This approach pays little attention to the fact that all markets are social institutions and cannot exist without some degree of social regulation by both the state and collective organisations of various kinds to establish and defend rights (Hodgson, 1988). A labour market is particularly complex, because what is bought and sold in a labour market is people's time and effort, and whether that time and effort will be useful to the buyer is indeterminate at the time of purchase. Similarly, it is indeterminate how much effort (and often how much time) the seller will actually have to yield up, even when a standard working time is specified. Labour contracts are essentially incomplete, in the sense that it cannot be specified in advance exactly what work will have to be done – an idea that can be traced back to Marx's distinction between labour (the activity of work) and labour power (the capacity to work) (Hodgson, 1988: 164). To make such incomplete contracts 'operational' as a basis for production, rights additional to the mere right to buy and sell are required. The question is not *whether* there is labour market regulation, but *what kind* of regulation (Standing and Tokman (eds), 1991) – regulation that is individualistic and anti-collective or regulation that is co-operative and solidaristic; regulation that permits and even encourages the degradation of human capacities, physically and spiritually ('exploitation'); or regulation that is conducive to the self-sustaining development of human capacities; regulation that operates in the service of short-sighted money-making or regulation that operates in the service of long-run human needs.

The kind of workers' rights that are seen as 'distortions' in neo-classical economics can in fact help labour markets to operate better, both from the point of view of workers' welfare, and from the point of view of encouraging the improvements in real productivity that are required for self-sustaining development of the whole society (Standing and Tokman (eds), 1991: 22–38).

Thus health and safety regulations giving workers entitlements to safe working conditions can be seen not as distortions which prevent the most efficient use of resources, but rectifications which guard against preventable deterioration in human capabilities, and encourage improvements in the organisation of production.

In fact the right to healthy and safe working conditions is probably not regarded as a 'distortion' by most economists, but minimum wage legislation is a different matter. This is the textbook example of a 'distorting' regulation. But the standard critique of minimum wage legislation ignores the role that such legislation can play in *offsetting* a variety of market imperfections and rigidities.

Standard models of the labour market, in which markets are assumed capable of clearing to generate full employment, also assume that sellers of labour determine how much pay they require by comparing the benefits (assumed positive) they would derive from the leisure they could otherwise enjoy as compared to the benefits they derive from getting an income. This assumes that there is no *compulsion* to earn a basic income either because it is assumed that consumption is entirely discretionary and one could live on fresh air alone should one choose;[9] or because it is assumed that one has other adequate sources of income from the possession of other assets (e.g. land) or from access to income transfers from others on terms which do not generate costs such as loss of dignity. In the absence of these conditions, the bargaining power of sellers is generally weaker than that of buyers, because the fall-back position of the sellers is worse. That is, if the sellers do not sell their labour, they starve and leisure is useless; but if the buyers do not buy labour, they can live off income from their other assets until sellers become more amenable. In this situation, minimum wage legislation is not a matter of introducing a rigidity, but of offsetting a rigidity: the rigidity of irreducible basic human nutritional needs.[10]

It is often argued that minimum wage legislation is not the best way to try to provide people with a minimum income because many poor people do not participate in the wage economy. Ideally, the irreducibility of basic human needs should be dealt with by providing everyone with a basic minimum income through a 'welfare state'. But in most countries of the world such a system is not yet feasible (for social and political as well as economic reasons). In the absence of a basic income for everyone, minimum wages is a useful step forward.

Even when wage levels are generally well above the level required to cover basic nutritional needs, minimum wage legislation can play a positive role in providing information about wage 'norms' and helping sellers of labour decide what they can legitimately ask for. The standard model of the labour market assumes that the equilibrium wage level is somehow 'given' and buyers and sellers simply react to it, deciding how much to buy and to sell. But in most real labour markets employers make offers and employees either accept them or bargain for a better offer. When information is very fragmented employees have difficulty determining what kind of offer they should accept or reject. There is a particular problem for women who, as a result of their social subordination, often lack information about alternative offers, or underestimate their own worth, or find it difficult to separate their own interest from the interests of others, and thus do not have the well-defined preference functions which standard economic theory assumes all agents have (Sen, 1990). Here minimum wage legislation can play a declarative and legitimating function, enabling women to avoid under-selling their labour. Thus minimum wage legislation can help to offset existing social distortions[11] stemming from male bias (Elson (ed.), 1991). Minimum wage legislation can also have benefits for employers and customers by improving the *quality* of work done: workers who feel their services are properly valued may take more care in how they do their jobs (Bazen, 1991).

What about rights associated with domestic responsibilities, such as maternity benefits and child-care facilities? Again, obligations on employers to provide these can be seen as offsetting pre-existing social distortions – the distortions that arise because the costs of women's unpaid work in having and rearing children are not taken account of by markets. Women's unpaid reproductive work provides a positive externality from which enterprises benefit by having a continuous stream of new labour coming on to the market.

It may be objected that while these arguments engage with the ideological onslaught against state regulation and workers' rights, they do not deal with the problem that more rights may mean less jobs, if they impose costs for employers more than they confer benefits. For instance, Schultz (1990) argues that women are particularly likely to be excluded from the labour force by minimum wage legislation because women tend to be paid less than men (and hence are more likely to have their wages raised by minimum wage legislation than are men). In support of this he points to evidence 'that the overall labour force participation rates for women and, to a lesser degree, those for men decrease in periods when minimum wages increase as a proportion of GNP per adult' (p. 481).

One response to this is to accept that there is a trade-off between workers' rights and employment available. Standing, 1989, reports several studies suggesting that employers are deterred from recruiting women workers by maternity leave benefits or requirements for provision of child-care facilities (p. 1082) and concludes 'explicit and implicit deregulation may mean more employment of women, but on less favourable terms'. A somewhat similar point emerges from a study of manufacturing employment in India (Hensman, 1988). Measures can then be suggested to improve the terms of this trade-off for women, for instance by arguing for maternity and child benefits to be financed by general taxation and not be wholly borne by individual employers.

Here I argue that the trade-off between workers' rights and employment available is likely to depend on the overall state of accumulation. During a period of rapid growth and productivity improvements or when there are shortages of particular kinds of labour, the fact that workers have an extensive set of entitlements does not deter employment. During periods of slow growth and stagnating or declining productivity and when there are plenty of alternative suppliers of comparable labour, then workers' rights play a more deterrent effect. This interpretation would suggest a need to re-examine the evidence cited by Schultz (1990) to see if changes in labour-force participation rates and changes in the ratio between the minimum wage and GNP per adult are *both* correlated to changes in overall rate of growth. If my interpretation is correct, the costs of employing labour are the dependent variable; the rate of accumulation is the independent variable. From this point of view, austerity programmes which depress aggregate growth create an environment in which the costs associated with a decent standard of workers' rights become more onerous for individual enterprises and there is pressure to erode or circumvent them. To avoid this happening, policies of macro-economic and sectoral co-ordination, based on co-operative agreements such as industrial strategies and incomes policies, which maintain a steady rate of growth with full capacity utilisation, and ideally, full employment need to be devised and implemented. Foreign exchange and other constraints that prevent this happening need to be removed. The aim is to accommodate accumulation to a decent standard of workers' rights rather than accommodate workers' rights to the demands of capital accumulation.[12] Clearly, the standard must reflect social norms and levels of economic development in particular countries or groups of countries. There is no absolute quantitative standard that can be set for all countries. But qualitative standards could be the same everywhere (e.g. right to a minimum wage; to be represented by a trade union; to health and safety legislation; to compensation for dismissal; to conditions and remuneration for part-time work pro rata with full-time work; and for home based work comparable with factory or office based work; etc.). Obviously, until the way that patterns of accumulation are determined is changed to meet this aim, workers will have to contend with some degree of trade-off between rights and employment, and this trade-off will tend to be worse in poorer countries.

Of course, there is a difference between having rights on the statute book, and the actual enjoyment of these rights. Collective organisation is frequently necessary for individual workers to be able to exercise their rights. This is one way in which organisations like trade unions act to offset existing social distortions in the system. They also act to offset the disadvantages that workers have in bargaining with employers due to lack of information, necessity to meet basic consumption needs etc. Collective workers' organisations may also play another important role: that of a check upon the power of the state and a support for democracy. No matter how much 'liberalisation' there is, there is no way that the need for the state to play an active role in the development process can be eliminated (Killick, 1990). And so there is, as the World Bank has now come to realise, a need for countervailing centres of power in 'civil society'. One of the most important of these is autonomous trade unions, which have been bases for the struggle for democracy in many countries.

Even supposing the intellectual base for erosion of workers' rights can be undermined, there is still the problem that new forms of 'flexible production' may make maintenance and enforcement of rights extremely difficult. There is a need to develop new ideas about how workers' rights can be enforced in the new circumstances. One idea is to make large firms responsible for the rights enjoyed by workers in the small firms to which they sub-contract – so that large firms do not just exercise quality controls for the products produced by sub-contractors, but also quality controls for the working lives of their employees. Another is to mobilise consumer organisations to use the power of the purse in support of workers' rights – on an international as well as a national basis. Another is to decentralise responsibility for enforcement of labour market regulation to local government (in the way that environmental and health regulation is often decentralised). Another is for governments to make part of the resources they allocate for enforcement of labour market regulation available to autonomous campaigning groups (e.g. Homeworkers Campaigns, Low Pay Units) as grants, to enable them to monitor and publicise breaches of workers' rights. Another might be to argue for ILO Conventions to set performance criteria in international policy-related lending rather than World Bank and IMF conditionality.

SOCIAL ORGANISATION: THE ISSUE OF MOVING BEYOND THE FACTORY

Workers are never completely quiescent in response to the demands made on them by employers, not even women workers who are supposedly docile. Many studies have documented the day-to-day resistance to the logic of profit-making engaged in by women workers, even those not formally organised in any way (for example Hossfeld, 1990; Harris, 1989; Rosa, 1989). But that day-to-day resistance needs to be translated into some kind of collective organisation if workers are to gain more rights and greater control[13] over their own lives.

Large-scale factory employment, with 'normal' labour contracts based on secure and regular work and specific skills, suggests trade union organisation as the appropriate form of collective organisation; and the conditions of large-scale factory organisation facilitate trade union organisation. But as is well documented, traditional forms of such organisation, with their narrow focus on the workplace and their failure to take into account the demands that domestic activities make on workers' time, fail to meet many of the needs of women workers.

'Flexibility' weakens the organisational base of traditional trade unionism, but it may foster the development of new forms of trade unionism that reach out from the workplace into the community, and encompass a wider understanding of the needs of workers, taking into account their roles as parents, sons, daughters and citizens, as well as their role as workers.[14]

'Flexibility' also highlights the importance of other forms of collective organisation based on religious, community or civic concern. Such forms of organisation have grown up in many developing countries, especially where the attack on workers' rights has made trade union organisation difficult, and even impossible (see Rosa, forthcoming). They include Welfare Centres that offer help to workers with personal problems and provide recreational facilities for them; Legal Centres that educate workers about what rights they do have and help them to exercise these rights; Women's Centres that offer education, advice and recreation in ways that particularly address the issue of women's subordination; and campaigning and publicity organisations which help women workers give voice to their problems and take these problems to a wider public through meetings, newspapers and newsletters, pamphlets, and exhibitions.

A major challenge is integrating these diverse and innovative forms of organisation. If the process of capital accumulation can no longer be relied upon to mass together large numbers of workers in one workplace (and it always did this less for women than for men), then the process of social organisation must bring scattered workers together. We can learn from the decentralised forms of networking organisation being developed between firms (Kaplinsky, 1985). Parallel networks have to be developed between the variety of organisations, including new forms of trade unionism, which are being developed with and for women workers with the process of industrialisation. And given that the internationalisation of production has intensified, not lessened, with 'flexibility', these networks need to be international as well as national.

Such networks enable organisations to be mutually strengthening rather than competitive. They facilitate the interchange of information – about health and safety, management strategies, bargaining tactics, successful and unsuccessful campaigns. They mobilise support and solidarity for workers in particular disputes. They enable workers in different situations to appreciate what they have in common as well as how they differ. They have the potentiality of mobilising stronger groups of workers in support of weaker ones – for instance, workers in large factories organised in trade unions might be persuaded to take up the issue of the rights and conditions of workers working for sub-contractors. They also have the potentiality of mobilising larger groups of citizens in support of particular groups of workers – through consumer action, for instance.

It is generally much harder to get funding for networking between different organisations than to get funding to set up a Women's Centre; a Homeworkers Campaign Unit; Legal Advice Centre; a Women's Cooperative, etc. But my experience with one project involved in networking – the Women Working Worldwide 'Labour Behind the Label Project', focusing on women in the textile and garment industry internationally – indicates that resources put into networking can increase the productivity of a whole range of organisations concerned with women workers and their rights.

We tend usually to focus on the problems of women workers organising. We also need to take into account the implications of success. When workers do successfully organise and are able to mobilise to campaign for improvements in pay and working level, and even to the point of organised disruption of production (go-slows, strikes), they are nevertheless still confronted with the fact of the employers' control over the means of production. In the long run, a firm can be relocated elsewhere, where workers are not so well organised; or new technology can be introduced which displaces large numbers of workers. The case of the Bataan Export Processing Zone in the Philippines is instructive. This is a Zone which has experienced a wholly exceptional level of workers' organisation (mainly in trade unions), including at least one general strike of almost the whole Zone. But firms have been relocating elsewhere, and today the Zone employs only a fraction of the people it once did.

So how can this contradiction be handled? I have two suggestions. The first is that organisations of and for women workers should always be concerned with enhancing the skills and education of those workers, so that if workers lose their jobs, they have acquired something of permanence – more self-confidence, more organisational and advocacy skills, more knowledge of how their society works. This means that organisations need to be judged not only in terms of what they achieve for women in terms of pay and conditions, but the kind of opportunities for self-development that they give to women. These opportunities are likely to be larger if the organisation is interactive and democratic, rather than hierarchical and bureaucratic.

The second is that organisations of and for women workers cannot limit their horizon to what happens in paid work at each specific point of production. They need a wider horizon, that takes into account how getting a living is integrated with raising children and looking after the sick and the old; and how different kinds of production are integrated with one another and with consumption. In other words, with how the reproduction of the entire society is co-ordinated.

The drive to undermine workers' rights in the name of 'flexibility' is often justified as a way of improving that co-ordination, of making markets more 'perfect', of enabling a closer match between what is produced and what people want to buy. But it has contradictions of its own, which throw up new impediments to the co-ordination of the entire economy. In particular, it undermines the social fabric on which market co-ordination[15] rests by tending to increase insecurity and intensifying exploitation for a large number of people. If labour rights are weakened and the ability to organise collectively in defence of them is weakened, then it is not surprising if people turn to other, less progressive, ways of seeking security – including criminal gangs, inward-looking communalisms and nationalisms, and religious fundamentalism of all kinds – all of which have the capacity to violently disrupt even the most 'flexible' forms of accumulation.

Those who see a positive role for social organisations of and for women workers will have to be able to argue for this in the face of a dominant ideology in international financial institutions (especially the World Bank and IMF) which sees collective workers' organisations as distortions which hamper the efficient functioning of the labour market. One way to do this is by showing how a so-called 'free' labour market in fact may reduce efficiency by inhibiting workers from fully developing and using their potential.[16] The kind of 'flexibility' fostered by present forms of accumulation is a very limited and impoverished kind of 'flexibility' compared with the creative range of activity that most people are capable of. Collective social organisations, if they are appropriately structured, can make an enormous contribution to the development of human capabilities.[17] We can argue that women organising in the process of industrialisation to secure and defend a wider set of rights should not be seen as a force that reduces efficiency, but as a force that promotes a less one-sided development, more efficient at meeting human needs and more conducive to democracy than 'flexible' market forces.

NOTES

1. Restructuring is admittedly rather a vague term, meaning different things to different authors. Some use the term to refer merely to the emergence of a global assembly line (Ward (ed.), 1990: 1). Here it is used more specifically to refer to changes in the way that production and consumption are co-ordinated and reproduced.
2. For more discussion of these views see Standing and Tokman (eds), 1991.
3. Anna Pollert (1988), at the conclusion of her critical discussion of the literature on flexibility, makes the following point:
'In spite of unemployment and the appropriation of "flexibility" as a managerial and market concept, the organisation of work and employment continues to be socially negotiated (whether through formal industrial relations or informal means), and labour can, as in previous periods, recoup and transform managerial initiatives to its own ends. However, such outcomes depend . . . on the ground work of worker organisation and self-confidence. Whether the libertarian legitimation of casualisation and "flexible" working lives can thus become re-appropriated by labour as positive improvements in terms of working hours and arrangements, paid for by capital, not labour, is an open question' (p. 70).
4. The relevant statistics are contained in ILO, *Yearbook of Labour Statistics 1981*, Table 2A and ILO, *Yearbook of Labour Statistics 1989/90*, Table 2A.
5. The relevant source is ILO *Yearbook of Labour Statistics 1991*, Table 5B, from which it can be ascertained that the female share of employment in the

textile industry fell in the 1980s in Kenya, Mauritius, Hong Kong, India, Republic of Korea, Singapore, Austria, Belgium, Czechoslovakia, Finland, France, Norway, Sweden, Australia, Zimbabwe.

6. Pyle, 1990, attributes this to discriminatory policy practised by the Irish Development Authority which wanted foreign firms which provided jobs for men (pp. 107–10). But the main reason is likely to be changes in product mix and technology. Production of computers and peripherals tends to be considerably less female intensive than production of semi-conductors.

7. The relevant source is ILO *Yearbook of Labour Statistics 1991*, Table 5B, from which it can be ascertained that the female share of employment in the electrical machinery industry fell in the 1980s in Kenya, Australia, Federal Republic of Germany, Hong Kong, Republic of Korea, Singapore, Austria, Belgium and Czechoslovakia.

8. For a brief discussion of how such mechanisms might work, see Elson, 1988b.

9. Of course, it is not so baldly put. But 'modern resource allocation theory assumes for the most part that each person's consumption possibility set is convex, and that in particular each person can survive even if he or she were not to engage in any transactions with others in the social system in question.' (Dasgupta, 1991) – which amounts to much the same thing.

10. Or as Dasgupta, 1991, put it:

> There is a fixed cost, measured by what is called the resting metabolic rate in the bio-medical literature, which each person must cover before he or she can do anything else over the medium and long run.
>
> (Dasgupta, 1991: 23)

This introduces a non-convexity or rigidity into the resource allocation process.

11. The distinction between price distortions and social distortions is made in Standing and Tokman (eds), 1991: 22. A price distortion is defined in terms of the concept of Pareto optimality; a social distortion can be defined in terms of other criteria, such as greater equality or development of human capabilities.

12. For more discussion of these issues see Standing and Tokman (eds), 1991.

13. Standing, 1989, offers a useful typology of varieties of control that are relevant to women.

14. For discussion of some examples in Britain and The Netherlands, see Huws, Hurstfield and Holtmaat, 1989.

15. For more discussion of the way in which market co-ordination rests upon a set of social relations and moral norms, see Platteau, 1991.

16. For examples, see Standing and Tokman (eds), 1991: 32–8.

17. The development of human capabilities is at the heart of the development process, as is increasingly recognised by the IMF and World Bank, with their new emphasis on 'human resource development'.

REFERENCES

Atkinson, J. and N. Meager. 1986. *New Forms of Work Organisation: IMS Report 121*, Institute of Manpower Studies, Brighton.

Bazen, S. 1991. 'Recent Developments in the Economic Analysis of Minimum Wages: A Partial Survey', mimeo, University of Bordeaux I.

Beneria, L. and S. Feldman (eds). forthcoming. *Economic Crisis, Persistent Poverty and Gender Inequality*, Westview, Boulder.

Beneria, L. and M. Roldan. 1987. *The Crossroads of Class and Gender*, University of Chicago Press, Chicago.

Dasgupta, P. 1991. 'Nutrition, Non-Convexities and Redistributive Policies', *Economic Journal*, Vol. 101, No. 404.

Dennis, C. 1984. 'Capitalist Development and Women's Work: A Nigerian Case Study', *Review of African Political Economy*, No. 27/28.

Dennis, C. 1991. 'The Limits to Women's Independent Careers: Gender in the Formal and Informal Sectors in Nigeria', in D. Elson (ed.) op. cit.

Elson, D. 1988a. Review of Joekes, op. cit., and Mitter, op. cit., *Journal of Development Studies*, Vol. 25, No. 1.

Elson, D. 1988b. 'Market Socialism or Socialisation of the Market?', *New Left Review*, No. 172.

Elson, D. (ed.) 1991. *Male Bias in the Development Process*, Manchester University Press, Manchester.

Elson, D. 1991. 'Male Bias in Macro-economics: The Case of Structural Adjustment,' in D. Elson (ed.), 1991, op. cit.

Elson, D. and R. Pearson. 1981. '"Nimble Fingers Make Cheap Workers": An Analysis of Women's Employment in Third World Export Manufacturing', *Feminist Review*, No. 7.

Elson, D. and R. Pearson. 1989. *Women's Employment and Multinationals in Europe*, Macmillan, London.

Frobel, F., J. Heinriches and O. Kreye. 1979. *The New International Division of Labour*, Cambridge University Press, Cambridge.

Goldstein, N. 1989. 'Silicon Glen: Women and Semi-conductor Multinationals', in D. Elson and R. Pearson (eds) 1989, op. cit.

Harris, L. 1989. 'Women's Response to Multinationals in County Mayo', in D. Elson and R. Pearson (eds) 1989, op. cit.

Henderson, J. 1989. *The Globalisation of High Technology Production*, Routledge, London.

Hensman, R. 1988. 'The Gender Division of Labour in Manufacturing Industry: A Case Study in India', Institute of Development Studies, Discussion Paper No. 253, University of Sussex.

Hirst, P. and J. Zeitlin. 1990. 'Flexible Specialisation vs Post Fordism: Theory, Evidence and Policy Implications', Public Policy Centre Working Paper, Birkbeck College, University of London.

Hodgson, G. 1988. *Economics and Institutions*, Polity Press, Oxford.

Hossfeld, K. 1990. '"Their Logic Against Them": Contradictions in Sex, Race and Class in Silicon Valley', in K. Ward (ed.), op. cit.

Huws, U., J. Hurstfield and R. Holtmaat. 1989. *What Price Flexibility? The Casualisation of Women's Employment*, Low Pay Unit, London.

Jackson, P. and U. Barry. 1989. 'Women's Employment and Multinationals in the Republic of Ireland: The Creation of a New Female Labour Force', in D. Elson and R. Pearson (eds) 1989, op. cit.

Jenson, J., E. Hagen and C. Reddy (eds). 1988. *Feminisation of the Labour Force*, Polity Press, Oxford.

Joekes, S. (ed.) 1987. *Women in the World Economy*, Oxford University Press, New York.

Kaplinsky, R. 1985. 'Electronics-based Automation Technologies and the Onset of Systemofacture', *World Development*, Vol. 13, No. 2.

Killick, T. 1990. *A Reaction Too Far: Economic theory and the Role of the State in Developing Countries*, Overseas Development Institute, London.

Lim, L. 1978. 'Women Workers in Multinational Corporations: The Case of the Electronics Industry in Malaysia and Singapore', Michigan Occasional Papers No. 9, University of Michigan.

Lim, L. 1990. 'Women's Work in Export Factories: The Politics of a Cause', in I. Tinker (ed.) 1991, op. cit.

Mitter, S. 1986. *Common Fate, Common Bond: Women in the Global Economy*, Pluto Press, London.

Mitter, S. 1991. 'Computer-aided Manufacturing and Women's Employment: A Global Critique of Post-Fordison', in I. Eriksson, B. Kitchenham and K. Tijdens (eds), *Women, Work and Computerisation*, Elsevier, Netherlands.

Pearson, R. 1991. 'Male Bias and Women's Work in Mexico's Border Industries', in D. Elson (ed.) 1991, op. cit.

Pittin, R. 1984. 'Gender and Class in Nigeria', *Review of African Political Economy*, No. 31.

Platteau, J. P. 1991. 'The Free Market is Not Readily Transferable: Reflections on the Links Between Market, Social Relations and Moral Norms', Paper given at 25th Jubilee of Institute of Development Studies, University of Sussex.

Pollert, A. 1988. 'Dismantling Flexibility', *Capital and Class*, No. 34.

Pyle, J. 1990. 'Export-led Development and the Under-employment of Women: The impact of Discriminatory Development Policy in the Republic of Ireland', in K. Ward (ed.) 1990, op. cit.

Rosa, K. 1989. 'Women Worker's Strategies of Organising and Resistance in the Sri Lanka FTZ', IDS Discussion Paper No. 266, University of Sussex.

Rosa, K. forthcoming. 'Women Organising in FTZ: Malaysia, Philippines and Sri Lanka', WIDER, Helsinki.

Safa, H. 1981. 'Runaway Shops and Female Employment: The Search for Cheap Labor', *Signs*, Vol. 7, No. 2.

Schultz, T. P. 1990. 'Women's Changing Participation in the Labor Force: A World Perspective', *Economic Development and Cultural Change*.

Scott, A. M. 1991. 'Informal Sector or Female Sector?: Gender Bias in Urban Labour Market Models', in D. Elson (ed.) 1991, op. cit.

Sen, A. K. 1990. in I. Tinker (ed.), *Persistent Inequalities*, Oxford University Press, Oxford.

Standing, G. 1989. 'Global Feminisation Through Flexible Labor', *World Development*, Vol. 17, No. 7.

Standing, G. and V. Tokman (eds) 1991. *Towards Social Adjustment: Labour Market Issues in Structural Adjustment*, ILO, Geneva.

Stichter, S. and J. Parpart. 1990. *Women, Employment and the Family in the International Division of Labour*, Macmillan, London.

Tinker, I. (ed.) 1990. *Persistent Inequalities*, Oxford University Press, Oxford.

Walsh, J. 1987. 'Capital Restructuring and the British Textile Industry: A Case Study', Industrial Relations Unit, University of Warwick.

Ward, K. (ed.) 1990. *Women Workers and Global Restructuring*, ILR Press, Cornell University.

2 Women Organising in the Process of Deindustrialisation

Martha Roldan

LOCATING THE PROBLEMATIC IN THE CONTEXT OF FEMINIST THEORY AND RESEARCH

Women organising in the process of industrialisation or deindustrialisation in the 1990s face the challenges posed by a rapidly changing international economy. The sustained growth experienced in the developed central economies in the aftermath of World War II (the 'Golden Age' of the Fordist regime of accumulation (Lipietz, 1987; Marglin and Schor, 1990), was followed by successive crises in the late 1970s; the monetarist shock of the early 1980s, the restructuring of these same economies, and the consolidation of main blocks (the USA/Canada, the EEC, Japan, NICs) originating different modes of articulation with countries of the periphery or even with regions of this same periphery.

In the case of Latin America in particular, world (centre) restructuring shattered old patterns of insertion that had allowed relative growth before the 1980s. In contrast with other regions of the world (or some countries therein), the last decade has been aptly labelled by ECLA (Economic Commission for Latin America, 1990) the 'Lost Decade' of the Latin American and Caribbean economies, on the basis of the magnitude of the crisis and retrocession in social and economic development suffered by the majority of the countries of the region.[1] Three crucial features of this process should be stressed: firstly, and with country variation, the deindustrialisation of the area as a whole, within a context of a growing gap between the world's most advanced technological developments and their application in the region (ECLA, 1990: 38). Secondly, the internationalisation of the domestic economies, with the result that Latin America has become a net exporter of financial resources. It is estimated that during the last eight years this accumulated transference in which excessive indebtedness played a determinant role, came to more than 200 thousand million dollars (ECLA, 1990: 47). Thirdly, the costs of regressive 'structural adjustment' policies have been disproportionately borne by the working population (ECLA,

56

1990: 36). One may add, by the poor women of the area, according to other documents.[2]

In the context of Latin American countries looking for new ways of insertion into the international economy, again with considerable country variation, a heated debate is taking place on the ways or even possibilities of finding any path of sustained economic growth before the beginning of the new century. The problematic of women organising in the process of industrialisation assumes, therefore, a new character in relation to the crisis. As a corollary, feminist theory and research useful for this practice is also experiencing a crisis.

I will elabourate these points with particular reference to my experience in Argentina. For the last two years, in the context of an economy further plunging into recession, women and men trade unionists[3] in the metal-lurgical (engineering) industry, one of the most severely hit by the crisis and the same industrial branch where I have been carrying out protracted case study research, have been making new demands upon 'concerned researchers' in Buenos Aires. Favourite topics are world dynamics, centre-periphery relations, industrial branch prognosis, technological innovations, regional integration (problems with Brazil competing with Argentina for the same domestic markets), ideas on how to create successful small or micro enterprises for former members made redundant, among others. Women trade unionists who do not want to continue being relegated to the Women's Branch to discuss 'women's issues in reproduction' or 'the effects of the crisis or of technological change' on women's situation, have realised that they can no longer leave the discussion of those subjects that pertain to their industry's survival in men's hands. It is no longer a matter of an equal share in a growing industry, but of finding new ways of sub-mitting counter proposals to employers' strategies, of fighting each and every one of the points of new factory agreements, or skill reconversion, or conditions of work.

As a consequence, women trade unionists are now asking for feminist production of knowledge of a new type, concerned not only with the effects of processes on women, but also with the dynamics of those processes, and their gender dimension. This information is sought on two grounds: to be able to discuss with male colleagues at a similar level of expertise, and to plan for women's own strategies. The new challenge, which I have been told is not peculiar to Argentina, but also holds true for at least Uruguay and Brazil, finds most researchers in the social sciences somewhat unprepared to meet those demands.

Research pursued along the lines of the 'Women's Studies' paradigm, the dominant line of thinking in most countries of Latin America, with a focus on women's activities, attitudes, values, etc. provided the necessary first step in the eradication of male bias in development discourse. They were useful to women organising, yet it may also be argued that the concentration of feminist studies on 'making women visible' in a number of related topics and issues: women in industry, in the informal sectors, in rural change, as targets of the crisis, during the last decade, is largely responsible for today's growing irrelevance of this literature for the problematic of women organising in the context of crisis and restructuring. A second consequence of that restriction is the ghettoisation and marginalisation of these same contributions. Although with significant inter-country differences, feminist contributions in the field of development studies remain, unfortunately, outside mainstream academic and political practices.

It is time, therefore, to again become responsive to our constituencies' demands.[4] But in the Southern Cone of Latin America at least, and I believe in many other areas of the world as well, we have no gender-aware theory of centre–periphery relations, of socio-economic development, of industrial growth, of technological innovations. Under the guise of 'neutral' scholarship, androcentric interpretations of reality signify our frameworks, creating and recreating our social worlds. *Feminist scholarship in the social sciences can no longer ignore this site of struggle.* Theoretical discourses in development/restructuring studies should now be our target; the citadel of male power that must be challenged and overcome. We have a chance to succeed because the crisis is not only economic and political, but discursive as well. The theoretical interpretation of the nature of those intertwined links in the context of 'internationalised' domestic economies constitutes a contemporary contested domain.[5]

Having raised the issue of the relationship between feminist research and women organising in the process of deindustrialisation in Latin America, the purpose of this chapter is to present a preliminary exercise in the deconstruction of that general problematic as well of the socio-economic discourses that now signify development and restructuring processes in only class terms. To this effect the chapter draws on research on JIT technological innovations in the engineering industry that I carried out in the city of Buenos Aires. The chapter has four further sections. The next Section conveys a critique of main theories purporting to explain technological innovations in manufacturing. Section 3 introduces some principles of JIT productive systems. Section 4 presents the case study material, while Section 5 examines some of the implications of the factory analysis and relates them to the broader issues of development discourse.

TECHNOLOGICAL INNOVATIONS AT WORKPLACE LEVEL: ANDROCENTRIC THEORETICAL FRAMEWORKS AND FEMINIST CORRECTIONS

Androcentric Approaches in Sociology

How are we to explain the dynamics of technological change at factory level in small-scale manufacturing and the logic and consequences of their 'gendering'? Sociology offers a continuum of theoretical frameworks that range between two poles: 'Impact' perspectives and Labour Process approaches. Both positions offer contradictory representations of the nature of technological innovations within organisations, their rationality and consequence. Both poles share, however, rather similar deterministic and androcentric underpinning that privileges the external origin of innovating dynamics. Feminist interventions challenge these views while attempting to explain the 'gendering' of the productive sphere and its relation to the Sexual Division of Labour (SDL) at the level of the global society. I will briefly summarise some main tenets of these approaches.

'Impact' Approaches: Physical Technologies as Determinants of Work Organisation in Industry

Impact theories emphasise, firstly, the primacy of physical technologies, usually understood as EBATS (electronics-based automation technologies), as key determinants, or as the autonomous explanatory variable, of factory organisations; and secondly, the external impetus of technological innovations which are imposed on the diffusing organisation by commercial and technical imperatives of competitiveness. (See MacLoughlin and Clark, 1988; Wilkinson, 1983; Hill, 1981.) The firm that decides to innovate must then choose – with some degrees of freedom, or none according to Woodward's (1980) interpretation, which is the form of industrial work organisation which is most conducive to the rational utilisation of its new technologies.

A common denominator of Impact theories is their negation of the social conflict that underlies the capitalist organisation of production. As a result, the introduction of technologies is seen as an 'event' of industrial life that represents, for the enterprise, unions and workers, a matter of adjustment and adaptation that the firm must face through adequate policies, for example, by educating unions and its own workers about the economic reality that imposes this change (MacLoughlin and Clark, 1988). In this view, Wilkinson (1983) argues, technologies would be neutral inputs into individual productive systems. Eventual consequences such as the de-skilling of labour and a greater degree of management control over the workforce would only be incidental outcomes of the changes introduced. Finally, the view that science and technologies are neutral tends to be accompanied by the assumption that there is a linear progression towards systems of production which are more humane, implying the integration of workers by means of tasks which are intrinsically more gratifying, qualified and responsible, and the decline of differences between the manual and the intellectual labour force (Woodward, 1980).

This sociological perspective may be located within the line of thinking that Kaplinsky (1984) calls 'Technological Darwinism', that is, that variety of the social sciences which implicitly or explicitly maintains that technological progress is endowed with a logic of its own, following an autonomous trajectory which is neutral in its relationship with society.[6] Not surprisingly, Impact theories have been criticised for a number of reasons. In the first place, several authors (Mackenzie and Wajcman, 1985; Wilkinson, 1983; Rose, 1978; Silverman, 1970; among others) reject the thesis that physical technologies by themselves may produce 'impacts' on recipient organisations, and find the thesis basically wrong on theoretical and empirical grounds. Followers of the Strategic Option approach, to which I return below, argue that the notion of Impact leads to a technological determinism that ignores specific micro-political processes that accompany and signify the nature of the innovations introduced. In the case of JIT technologies, that approach is misleading because it is the JIT organisation of work *per se*, that is, social technologies (and not machines or equipment), that guarantees flexibility and competitiveness, with or without the incorporation of EBATS. Finally, Technological Darwinists' rejection of class conflict conveys the view of an absolute consensus between capital and labour, depoliticising the structural dimensions of technological innovations. Logically, if class cleavages are not incorporated into the analysis, gender conflicts are also invisible in the study of workplace reorganisation.

Labour Process Theory

This perspective, in contrast, emphasises the conflictive nature and the historical construction of work, science and technologies. Although this theory originates in Marx (Volume I of Capital), its contemporary renewal in the Anglo-Saxon context owes a great deal to Harry Braverman's 1974 *Labor and Monopoly Capital*. The book inspired more than a decade of theoretical thinking and research that accepts, re-elaborates or rejects some of its fundamental theses. I shall touch upon some elements of Braverman's study that bear directly upon the nature of technological innovations in the productive sphere.

Braverman follows Marx's classical analysis. The capitalist labour process, implying the unity between production and valorisation and thus basis of exploitation and accumulation, necessarily implies a structural conflict in the relation between capital and labour. The relations between the enterprise and its workers and processes of technological innovations must be seen in the light of this fact (MacLoughlin and Clark, 1988: 35). Explaining the historical de-skilling of craft-work and its role in the process of global accumulation, Braverman postulates that the primary function of management under industrial capitalism is the control òf the labour process. From this imperative emanated the necessary evolution towards de-skilling (Thompson, 1983: xiv). The trend towards de-skilling culminates in the 'degradation' of work in the twentieth century, that is, work which lacks intrinsic content, is routine, fragmented, mechanical and results in the formation of a homogeneous working class.

How is technological change at factory level understood from this perspective? Technological innovations (generally defined as the incorporation of physical technologies, nowadays EBATS) originate in management's strategy to control the labour process through de-skilling. There is no technological determinism in his approach because machines, *per se*, do not produce any 'impact' upon organisations. On the contrary, they attain their *raison d'être* only within the context of the labour process into which they are incorporated, and that the firm needs to control in order to guarantee the dynamics of accumulation. To sum up Braverman's interpretation: the dynamics of technological changes at workplace level emanate from inter-class conflict. Thus technological change is not a neutral or autonomous phenomenon, a simple rational response to commercial or technical pressures impinging upon the firm (as Impact theories would lead us to believe). Rather, it constitutes a political class weapon in the conflict between capital and labour.

Braverman's work inspired research into the nature of labour processes in capitalist societies and, in particular, on the topic of de-skilling and control in relation to EBATS incorporation in advanced industrial societies. However, the evolution of the debate itself meant the abandonment of its classical multidisciplinary emphasis and its replacement by a sociology of de-skilling and control (Cohen, 1987). The economic rationality of the firm became subsumed under its political logic.

Simultaneously, the development of the debate itself raised a number of important criticisms to Braverman's original formulations, such as his view of a single universal pattern of development of industrial capitalism. As critics point out, there are a variety of historical applications of Taylorism and Fordism, with different degrees of concomitant de-skilling. Besides, empirical research shows that although every capitalist labour process needs control systems to transform labour power into concrete labour, there are a number of ways of attaining this control with no need of absolute de-skilling as implied in an orthodox application of Taylorist methodologies. Other criticisms indicate the need to look at workers' reactions to the restriction of control (Edwards, 1979; Friedman, 1977; Burawoy, 1985) and to the diversity of mechanisms of control, including its subjective dimensions (Burawoy, 1985). It must also be emphasised that while these authors object to Braverman's treatment of the topic of control, they do not reject his conception of technological change. Other critics, such as Liff (1986, 1988) and Thompson (1983) touch upon the latter. For instance, Thompson (1983), in an excellent review of the debate, accepts that there is a main trend towards de-skilling and control, but argues that we need a more sophisticated analytical framework for the examination of technological change in organisations. This would include the consideration of labour markets, product markets, flexibility demands that may explain outwork, export of fragments of processes abroad, domestic and international political contexts, and the role of unions and workers' committees. What is important here is that Thompson, as Liff (1986), opens Braverman's scheme to include factors that touch upon the economic rationality of the enterprise, and the need to attain competitiveness, in itself a crucial element of today's restructuring. MacLoughlin and Clark (1988) and Walker (1989) stress the independent, (but not autonomous) role played by physical technologies in the construction of labour processes, and the influence they exert in the shaping of work features and workers' skills. This is an important correction to the tendency of Labour Process theory to ignore the material aspects of machines, equipments and tools in the design and implementation of technological change at plant level.

Strategic Choice Approaches

Any reformulation of Braverman's analytical framework may gain from another sociological perspective, which introduces a third path, or alternative between 'Impact' and Labour Process approaches: the Strategic Choice perspective (MacLoughlin and Clark, 1988; Wilkinson, 1983; Child, 1985, among others). This approach applies Social Action theory of industrial and organisational sociology (Rose, 1978; Silverman, 1970) to the specific study of technological change and labour processes. According to Mac-Loughlin and Clark:

> The key to this new approach is the assumption that the outcomes of technological change, rather than being determined by the logic of capitalist development, or external technical and commercial imperatives, are in fact socially chosen and negotiated within organisations by organisational actors. (1988: 40)

Thus there does not exist one uniform trend of transformation when EBATS are introduced; rather, changes observed will probably show great variations among firms, even when the technology and organisational circumstances are similar. This approach leads us to look at the intervention of managers, unions and workers as active participants in implementation.

However, one must not forget the insertion of these organisational actors in the wider structures of class and gender relations that very much constrain the possibility of implementing their goals, values and individual and group proposals in the technological domain. Besides, the Strategic Choice focus does not offer any alternative interpretation of why technological change takes place in an organisation, although its insights may be usefully incorporated as a correction of the more deterministic interpretations of Labour Process theory.

The Labour Process debate had reached a virtual point of saturation or impasse (Kelly, 1985) when world restructuring itself showed the need to revitalise it in the light of new developments. The deterministic restrictions and ethnocentrism of Western researchers had long ignored the technological innovations of Japanese JIT techniques and concomitant construction of workers' multi-skills. These are so important that authors such as Piore and Sabel (1984) and Hoffman and Kaplinsky (1988) locate them at the centre of another stage of capitalist accumulation on a world scale. It is necessary, therefore, to reformulate the analytical framework to be able to capture the dynamics and complexities of contemporary restructuring. But first, it is crucial to look at the contributions of feminist scholars and to the corrections they introduce in this debate.

The Challenge of Feminist Criticism to Labour Process Approaches

What are the features of feminist intervention in the theme of labour processes and technological changes at workplace level? The debate had evolved in terms of the capital–labour relationship, as if the gender of male and female participants did not matter or have influence on the specific, historical organisation of productive activities. Feminist literature based on empirical studies in central economies (Cockburn, 1983, 1985; Game and Pringle, 1984; Knights and Willmott (eds), 1986, among others) or peripheral societies (Elson and Pearson, 1981; Benería and Roldan, 1987; Lobo, 1988; de Souza, 1988, to name a few) shows, on the contrary, that as soon as we leave the most abstract level of analysis in order to explore concrete social phenomena, labour processes lose their apparent 'gender neutrality'. An SDL is embedded in each social and technical division of labour. Each technological innovation experiences a process of 'gendering' when defined as feminine or masculine. Men and women tend to participate in different labour processes or sub-processes, to be located in different spaces, shops or sections in a factory when they usually operate/set up different physical technologies that apparently require skills or knowledge also defined as male or female. As feminists have shown, horizontal divisions are not innocent, they do not indicate a 'natural' complementarity between women's and men's jobs or functions, but they are usually accompanied by a vertical SDL which is the main cause of the tremendous wage gap and other hierarchies found between them at work.[7]

Feminists have also shown how these work hierarchies are closely linked to pre-existing forms of gender subordination, in particular in the area of social reproduction. Because forms of SDL at the workplace are so important and tenacious, much feminist analysis, especially from a sociological viewpoint, has consisted in the exploration of that relationship, ascertaining through which 'gendering' mechanisms the technological innovation introduced has differently and hierarchically affected men and women in the workshops studied. This priority plausibly explains, in my view, why, in the area of sociology at least, the theoretical analysis of technological innovations themselves has been neglected by feminist scholars. We also still lack appropriate analytical frameworks for the study of the construction of innovations at the level of production. This may be explained as follows.

In very broad terms, and with differences in emphasis and 'texture' according to authors, feminist interventions implicitly or explicitly re-elaborate Braverman's thesis, which is then 'feminised' by introducing patriarchy and gender relations, that is male interests, into the analysis of capital–labour relations. (Huws, 1982; Barker and Downing, 1985; Cockburn, 1983, 1985; Game and Pringle, 1984; Knights and Willmott (eds), 1986, among others.) The main line of argument is that the technological change under analysis, usually EBATS incorporation, should not be seen only as a means through which the enterprise seeks to de-skill and control an undifferentiated working class in general, but also, and crucially, as a vehicle of male control over the female workforce in particular.

Men's interests exert their own influences in the struggle for control at the workplace, reflecting the inequalities and antagonisms of the SDL in the wider society.[8]

Within the labour process literature itself, or in a parallel line of analysis, there exist a gamut of positions which emphasise the role of different agents or mechanisms in the 'gendering' of productive transformations. For instance the enterprise, which takes advantage of pre-existing gender differences and the domestic SDL in the structuring of occupational segregation, through employment practices and the 'political' definition of workers' skills. (See in particular Beechey, 1987 and Cockburn, 1983.) Some authors stress the importance of symbolic practices, or a 'factory culture' (Lamphere, 1985; Willis, 1979), the role of sexist ideologies and the appeal to workers' gender identity as forms of company manipulation accompanying the introduction of innovations (Game and Pringle, 1984); the active intervention of trade unions through collective contracts or plant agreements to keep the best positions as enclaves for men (Rubery, 1980; Cockburn, 1983); while the emphasis of other studies lies in the very practices of working men themselves, and in their uses of cultural processes and ideologies to hold on to their jobs (Cockburn, 1983; Crompton and Jones, 1984). In these cases it is plausible that it is not only economic interests which are at stake but also psychological or cultural dimensions related to men's gender identity, threatened by the very diffusion of the innovation studied.

Cockburn, in a series of analyses (1983, 1985, 1987, 1990), explores in detail cultural and identity elements in the forging of the links between technologies and the SDL. In the first two, she suggests the use of the verb 'to gender' transitively, arguing that it is not only people but also machines and workplaces that are 'gendered'. This process continues along everyone's lifetime, and it is active and instrumental in the delimitation of occupational territories and boundaries. In the third contribution, on the basis of research among young women, she suggests that occupational choices represent a negotiation of gender identities. Technical competence has become an attribute of masculinity: this fact, and not only the firm's recruitment patterns, explain why young women, in search of an adequate positive femininity, prefer not to start a technical professional training or apprenticeship.

In 1990, Cockburn returned to this idea to postulate a link between masculinity and technical competence and femininity. Her concern is to explore the most appropriate way to analyse the link between technologies and the construction of gender differences on the bases of recent findings in the areas of cultural and language studies. Her main thesis is that women's subjectivities are intimately structured by technology. Therefore, and given that women need technical knowledge to attempt their reunion with technology and to ensure their autonomy, feminist struggle in the technological domain must focus not only on the acquisition of professional skills *per se*, but, crucially, on the very processes of 'gendering/ungendering' of socio-economic processes in their links with the cultural and psychological dimensions of women's lives.

This set of contributions challenges, corrects and enriches the analysis of the effects of technological innovations in the area of production and widens traditional spheres of feminist interest and research. The most important insight, in my view, is the recognition of factory life as a fundamental arena of construction and renegotiation of gender relations, a sphere where the interests expressed are not only those of capital but also those of the male dominant gender. But the importance of this literature goes beyond the correction of the androcentric underpinnings of the labour process debate, to open new lines of research, raise issues and in general enrich technology studies with the analysis of cultural and psychological dimensions (area of subjectivities). They therefore create tensions which have not yet been resolved in a number of theoretical domains, for example in the rethinking of social class construction and systems of stratification.

But it is important to stress that these pioneer sociological studies do not purport to analyse *process innovations per se* at a theoretical or an empirical level. Their conceptualisation of the labour process and of technological change must often be deduced from the treatment of their effects on women workers under study. Their starting point is an uncritical acceptance of Braverman, including his subsumption of the totality of enterprise logic in the dynamics of political de-skilling and control (in this connection, see Liff's comments, 1986 and 1988). It may be argued, therefore, that feminist sociological adherence to one interpretation of capitalist rationality as the only historical trend in international capitalist development deserves, as far as its implicit or explicit conceptualisation of process innovations is concerned, the same critiques that were expressed with regards to non-feminist contributions in this debate.

Several consequences follow from this restriction. To accept one type of technological change defined in terms of de-skilling/control as the normal one in capitalist labour process, its theoretical foundation and lack of an alternative feminist interpretation,[9] becomes a crucial obstacle for the understanding of new social technologies that indicate a trend towards workers' polyvalence (multi-functionality) although authors differ in their evaluation of the nature and levels of newly required skills.[10] JIT economic rationality requires functional polyvalence and reunification of tasks instead of fragmentation as under Taylorist or neo-Taylorist regimes that served as models for Braverman's conception, although the level of JIT-related skills actually deployed on the shop floor is highly controversial. To accept a priori women's de-skilling before every instance of technological change in the workplace by the joint logic of capitalism-cum-patriarchy, not only prevents feminist participation in the search for new answers to old problems (women's subordinated patterns of employment), but also may become particularly demobilising, as I found in my own research (pp. 72ff below).

Furthermore, because the type of technological change studied as 'normal' has a 'craft' tradition with its own meaning of skill (implying the unity of conception and execution), it is unable to capture other varieties of contributions of women's labour to technological innovations which cannot be encompassed within the framework of Braverman's scheme. This is very important in the context of Third World small-scale manufacturing where there are few instances of EBATS incorporation, but a high degree of use of women's unrecognised 'natural' skills in a professional setting. This is the famous 'nimble finger' argument and the use of gender traits for the same objective (see here the pioneer work by Elson and Pearson, 1981, and Beneria, 1987, among others). In these cases there is no de-skilling, but different forms and levels of exercise of knowledge and dexterity, involving a very important participation of women in the valorisation of capital. I suggest that instead of lamenting a taken-for-granted de-skilling of women in every instance of technological change, it might be more useful politically to establish how and by what means (scales for skill evaluation, for instance) trade unions may force the recognition of women's unrecognised contribution to the process of technological transformation.

One last caveat refers to the material dimensions of physical technologies. Mainstream feminist discussion (with the exception of Cockburn, 1983) appears to regard technologies as 'neutral', and devotes its preferential attention to the analysis of the labour process that acts as 'recipient' of tools and machines. This focus suggests that human-liberating interventions in the realm of technologies could be limited to process innovations or to the design of the final product. It does not explore, therefore, the extent to which machines, in particular non-automated machines, and the scientific knowledge that underlies them as socially-constructed artefacts, do or do not incorporate the relations of domination of the society that generates them. A second unintended consequence of this restriction is that ergonomics, an important site of workers' struggle, seems to remain outside the borders of feminist enquiry.

Feminist sociological analysis of labour processes cannot continue being limited to the effects of technological changes, or to its 'impact' on women's condition, or to the study of 'gendering' mechanisms if it wants to remain theoretically and politically relevant for the discussion of contemporary world restructuring. It is necessary to correct its unique vision à la Braverman and *give priority to the analysis of technological innovations at workplace level as complex socio-economic processes 'in construction'*, to examine the economic rationality of the model of change introduced, as well as its policy of control. Material and ideological dimensions are both crucial, and the agency of different actors – the enterprise, unions, women and men workers – their articulation and contradiction constitute a *sine qua non* component of any analysis of change.

SOME PRINCIPLES OF JIT/JER/TQC PRODUCTIVE SYSTEMS

In First World current debate and to lesser extent in countries of the periphery, a labour process approach has been integrated into theories of growth, crisis and possible 'solutions' to the crisis of the 1970s and 1980s.[11] 'Flexible' manufacturing techniques are now considered key elements of international competitiveness, and even a precondition for another stage of sustainable economic growth. Briefly elaborated below are some principles of this model.

The label 'JIT/JER/TQC'[12] manufacturing normally refers to a 'package' of highly interdependent practices and ideologies concerning the organisation of the industrial labour process, sub-contracting links between purchasing and supplying firms, skills of the labour force, industrial relations and control systems regulated by an appropriate 'external' socio-economic institutional environment; in this scheme, the role of the state is paramount. Three dimensions are typical of the Japanese techniques: *JIT* (instantaneous production), with *JER* (minimum waste), and *TQC* (ideally perfect quality).

JIT manufacturing refers to 'work [that] is only done when needed, in the necessary quantity and at the necessary time' (Sayer, 1986: 53). The second and perhaps most important feature is JER, the goal of eliminating all types of 'waste' (*muda* in Japanese), i.e. machinery, tools, inputs and labour that may be any time idle or non-contributing to the production of selling goods of the right quality. It aims to leave:

> every plant with just enough – and only just enough – human and material resources to keep production going . . . that is to say it strips away layer after layer of redundant manpower, materials and motions

until a plant is left with the barest minimum of resources needed to satisfy production requirements, in both quality and quantity. The system tolerates no waste, it virtually leaves no room for errors.

(Fucini and Fucini, 1990: 341)

Under the JIT system no reserve inventory of parts and supplies is allowed to cover for disruptions in delivery schedules. No back-up pool of workers is available to draw on when illness, injury or vacation remove employees from the JIT workforce. Instead, temporary employees are brought in and work is routinely based on overtime.

A crucial principle is *kaizen*, i.e. the permanent seeking of new ways to eliminate waste and further improve production, i.e. how to get the job well done with fewer resources, be they workers, time and/or material inputs. In other words, a JIT process is never static but is by definition dynamic and always being improved.

The *TQC* principle requires tight control over the production itself as upstream stations must deliver not only the right amount of components JIT, when needed, but also with no errors. Specific procedures to attain 'defect free production' are developed. These include elimination of separate departments devoted to quality control, autonomation (machines provided with mechanisms to stop production automatically when a defective part is discovered), rejection of any component with defects, Quality Circles, etc.

Skills and Workers' Polyvalence

The effective functioning of JIT/JER/TQC systems is based on sets of mutually reinforcing internal and external conditions. Internally JIT production requires a reduction in lot sizes and flows of material to be simple and straightforward. This is typically achieved by means of production lay-outs which require multi-tasking and/or multi-skilling of labour, including quality control and preventive maintenance. It is also worth emphasising that *kaizen* application leads to an extremely high degree of intensity of work that employees label 'Management by Stress' (Parker and Slaughter, 1988). JIT work practices would necessitate the re-emergence of the craft worker, a novel reincarnation of the unity of conception and execution of work attributed to traditional artisans. These workers would be dexterous, versatile, in charge of scale neutral and non-skilling micro-electronics technology. In addition they would be able and willing to participate in decision-making and to provide suggestions and experience to improve a non-alienating labour process.

A key external condition for JIT production is the establishement of tiers of sub-contracting firms. JIT production needs frequent delivery of small quantities of products of guaranteed quality. A further major external factor is the regulation and co-ordination of the state. This is seen clearly in Japan, where the state implements long-term economic and industrial policies.

The Economic Rationality of JIT/JER/TQC Systems

There are a number of advantages associated with JIT techniques. Briefly these include:

- more efficient use of working capital through reduction of levels of inventories and stocks, allowing capital to be released and used more productively elsewhere. JIT cuts down work-in-progress and the cost associated with space and storage, materials handling, etc. If one thinks about the high costs of financial capital needed to cover these expenses, savings may be important.
- reduction in lot size and elimination of buffers improves quality and productivity. Acccording to Sayer:

   The smaller the buffer, the more sensitive the system is to error, and hence the greater the visibility of the source of the error and the greater the incentive to remedy it and prevent it to happen again . . . . Conversely, the more quality is 'built in', the less the need for buffer and the greater the responsiveness of the system. (1986: 52)

- flexibility in meeting customers' demands, a crucial competitive advantage where market environment is unstable.
- even without team work, worker's polyvalence and multi-tasking provides a number of advantages. Coupled with a very intense work pace, it reduces the porosity of the working day, allowing for greater productivity. In the case of Toyota, Suzaki, quoted by Sayer (1986), refers to the experience of a worker who carried out 35 different productive processes in a cycle lasting 8 minutes and 26 seconds, with a tolerance of more or less two seconds and who walked six miles a day to fulfil his assignment! Of course, job rotation, as Sayer comments, allows a further advantage to the company revealing which are the machines that do not need to be constantly tended and liberating the worker to fulfil another job, allowing for further *kaizen*. Besides, as team members fill in for absent team-mates, there is a self-regulating attendance

system which relies on peer pressure to discourage tardiness and absenteeism (Fucini and Fucini, 1990: 137).

The Logic of Discipline and Control of JIT Systems

How are JIT social technologies reproduced and changed, in time and space? This is another topic of heated debate between those who advocate religious and cultural forces and those who prefer a material explanation based on secular practices, such as company-based welfare schemes, seniority-based payment systems and lifetime employment for 'core' workers, a dual labour market, the use of 'green labour' from rural areas who undergo a process of 'incubation' in economic and ideological terms among others.

Finally, in relation to unions it appears that if they are allowed to exist they ought to accept functional flexibility and rotation between jobs. This is very different from the rigid job demarcations characteristic of Just-in-Case (JIC) systems. In return the employer's guarantee of stability of employment and peaks in production are dealt with by compulsory overtime, temporary employment and certain types of sub-contracting. All of these factors make workers vulnerable to the exercise of informal, diffuse and paternalistic forms of control.

Centre and Peripheral Workers and the Uses of Gender

The JIT/JER/TQC model is based on a dual economy in which workers in central firms receive high wages and stable employment, while the same benefits are denied to workers in peripheral firms. This consolidates segmented labour markets. According to Godet (1987), it is estimated that less than 30 per cent of the Japanese labour force falls within the privileged category, enjoying high wages and stable employment. Besides, the commitment to *kaizen and muda* elimination makes JIT a work system that does not foster high levels of national employment, at least in 'core firms'. The security of male workers is based on the insecurity of the many workers in large firms with temporary contracts, and workers in smaller, sub-contracting firms.

Broadly speaking, the theorists of JIT systematically ignore the gender dimension of the Japanese system. It is important to stress that aspects such as lifetime employment and non-monetary benefits are only extended to the male workers in large companies. As Sayer comments, the objective is to obtain low absenteeism and 'responsible' workers, which is achieved by recruiting people who are not distracted by domestic obligations. In a patriarchal setting, this means a preference for men. Women are marginalised by central companies and are generally found in peripheral enterprises.

JIT SYSTEMS AND INDUSTRIAL RESTRUCTURING: SOME EVIDENCE FROM SMALL-SCALE MANUFACTURING IN ARGENTINA

I will now refer to some findings of research into gendered JIT restructuring within light engineering manufacturing (filter production) in Buenos Aires.[13]

My study took place in a medium (now small) size industry, and patterns investigated did not involve EBATS, but old, unsophisticated physical technologies common in any metallurgical workplace (lathes, welding machines, 'balancines', drillers, plus other specific machines, tools and equipment linked to filter manufacturing: 'bobinadoras', paper plaiters and many others). I examined the evolution of process innovations from the end of the 1950s to the 1990s, involving three different types of social technologies: 'shop organisation', 'line' organisation and contemporary JIT forms. The specific stage I am concerned with in this chapter is the transition from the JIC system (line production of filters for motor cars) to JIT techniques (small batch or custom-made filters for any type of industry).

By means of extended field work, days of concentration and 'desertion' of factory life, I followed the factory and its workers on the shop floor and at home between 1986 and 1990. I was able to explore some dimensions of the construction of technological innovations at the workplace level. I also wanted to examine the agency and responsibility of different actors in the shaping of social technologies (i.e. labour processes) and the uses of gender relations to this effect. That is, to understand management and workers' logic not in only class terms but also in gender terms, seeing them, simultaneously, as 'gendered' agents, i.e. men and women who may be recreating or questioning gender hierarchies in each technological innovation, thus affecting its very design or implementation.

Many questions and options in research methodology and techniques were involved in this search. To start with, I questioned pre-existing definitions of the whys and modalities of technological change at workplace level. Instead, I tried to establish the economic and political rationality of each model of social technology studied ('shop', 'line' under JIC; new JIT configuration). Is there a coincidence or potential conflict in that logic? How is the conflict resolved, if at all? Skill definition is crucial in this context. We are used to think along the lines of Babbage's principle (divide the craft to cheapen its parts). Is there a reversion of this trend in the industry studied? And if control was not achieved via de-skilling, what were the other mechanisms used in this crisis situation? What is the contribution of women's labour to capital valorisation? In jobs that mean access to machines, in 'only manual' tasks, with greater or less reflection upon practice? I was also interested in the making and deployment of gender ideologies (in the sense of definition of masculinity and femininity) in the implementation of technological change. Was there one gender ideology or several, who were the originators and how did these ideologies articulate with class practices? Was there always an alliance between management and male workers via skill and 'femininity' (gender trait) definition, or was it possible to detect contradictions, interstices that women can use to their own advantage?

These issues and questions required a reformulation of the analytical model and key concepts: industrial labour process, the distinction between different definitions of skills ('technical', 'political', 'personal') and systems of control.[14]

SOME FINDINGS OF THE ARGENTINE STUDY: THE APPLICABILITY OF THE MODEL IN SMALL BATCH MANUFACTURING IN A PERIPHERAL COUNTRY IN A CRISIS SITUATION

The experiences of Argfilsa show that the Japanese 'classical' model may be partially but 'successfully' emulated by a small firm, in small batch or custom-made production, with traditional physical technologies, in a crisis situation. This is probably a common but still unreported or undetected phenomenon: the literature abounds in examples of JIT techniques in mass production, typically in the automobile and electronics industries.[15] It seems logical to think that 'crisis' oriented industries like plastics and steel, and to a certain extent also automobile manufacturing, may apply different versions of JIT techniques, including EBATS incorporation and the use of increasing sub-contracting. This is reported to be the case for the automobile industry. The economic rationality that underlies the Japanese model still holds in a peripheral economy. However, it shows a number of 'distortions', with different consequences for both capital and labour. The sources of these distortions are mainly external: lack of a favourable institutional setting, and domestic demand which places limits that the firm by itself cannot overcome.

Argfilsa is a typical example of an industry which was founded and consolidated during the 'Golden Age' (1950s and 1960s) of import-substitution industrialisation in Latin America, and particularly in Argentina. Argfilsa had previously developed JIC forms of organisation, well suited to mass line production of filters for the automobile industry. During that period, it enjoyed the advantages associated with a heavily protected domestic market, in a period when, as some commentators have pointed out, industries did not need to be efficient to be profitable.[16] The State was a 'buffer' between management and unions, and rising wages were passed on to prices in decades of relative prosperity (by Latin American standards).

The firm experienced the transition from JIC to JIT logic switching from mass to small batch or custom-made production, but in a completely different context when, one by one, each of the old premises no longer held. There was an opening of the Argentine economy to the external world; (its 'internationalisation' operated to a large extent through the services of the external debt). The State withdrew from economic performance and to a great extent lost its regulatory role. Industrial protection became largely a policy of the past, and the domestic market collapsed. A wild, aggressive form of capitalist restructuring is taking place in Argentina under Menem's administration, far from the careful, long-range planning, industrial 'grooming' and financial set-up of the Japanese State.

Yet, in spite of these drawbacks, the firm has survived largely through JIT sound economic rationality. At the end of 1990, it even showed signs of slow revival. But it may be argued that this peripheral experience bears some resemblance to the type of 'JIT of crisis' (my term) that, in the view of Oliver and Wilkinson, 1988, seems to prevail in the UK. There is an emphasis on the cost-cutting elements of JIT and total quality principles, without the development work essential for long-term success (p. 171). Thus, on the whole, the future of Argfilsa is still very uncertain.

The decline and crisis of the Argentine economy in the 1980s impinges upon the firm and constrains it 'to screen' outside technological innovation. Its operational objectives are very short term, through trial and error of new social technologies. But there are no commercial or technological imperatives *per se*, as Impact and Labour Process theory would lead us to expect. In spite of the pressures, the firm still makes micro-strategic choices regarding a 'gendered' JIT version that management tries, negotiates and eventually imposes, helped by the indifference of the metallurgical union (Union Obrera Metalurgica (UOM)).

For the JIT/JER/TQC set of the equation, the model holds. Thus, we find instantaneous production, strict elimination of 'muda', 0 stock of inputs, TQC carried out by all workers, reduction in setting-up time of machines, beginning of new relations with supplying firms, but no great amount of sub-contracting (with idle capacity the firm does not see the advantages of homework production, as in the past). We have noted above the advantages associated with all these practices.

There is, however, a big difference in the organisation of work, with a very original version of group technology that management calls Temporary Technological Group (TTG) or, more familiarly, 'the amoeba'. It is so-called because this type of cellular manufacturing is so flexible that it may involve from two to all the persons present at the workplace for production of a given model of a 'family' of filters. It grows and diminishes according to need, depending on daily schedule decisions by management, articulation with production of other models, availability of inputs, and so forth. However, the very high efficiency and productivity associated with group technology in the Japanese model is not present in the Argentine example. The group is temporary, and it does not need to perform every day, given the low overall level of filter demand.

TTGs at the firm are shaped to attain maximum flexibility to accommodate very short notice rescheduling of any model requested with minimum multi-skilled personnel. This requires an 'open mentality, away from old demarcation' in the view of management, and certainly saves on wages and social costs. Consider the number of people that would be needed to manufacture a similar variety of products, at practically no notice, if workers were trained to perform only one function as under Fordist arrangements. A second difference is the lower intensity of work, in comparison with the Japanese model. There is no need to request a comparable speed, as it might lead to worker redundancies. Indeed, workers are not used to working at very high speed even on peak production days when full or partial 'amoebas' are formed. Thus, the TTGs are a reservoir for the future. If exports materialise, for instance, workers will be requested and expected to perform at maximum speed. As management explains, 'the "Amoebas" are efficient for our goal of flexibility, not of maximum productivity'.

JIT Systems, Skills, and Gender Relations

The core of the articulation between the model's rationality and pre-existing gender hierarchies is via the dynamics of skilling/de-skilling, a process that has different connotations according to the shop concerned. It should be noted that in the firm's 30 years of existence, management has always segregated women in the so-called 'Women's Section', while men were grouped in two other sections, called Mechanical and Metalwork Shops ('Talleres de Mecanizados' and 'Hojalateria').

The Women's Section

Women are multi-skilled in the sense of performing a great variety of functions and tasks (which include both machine operation and 'only manual' activities) which, according to our own scale of evaluation, involve skill levels two and one, and not the maximum three that involves the setting up/preparation of machines. In broad terms, the Babbage principle does not hold in relation to women's work. These multiple tasks have always been carried out within the limits of the women's own section, until 1990, when a new model of 'metal candle filters' with a partial change in the old SDL demanded women's 'invasion' into the male work areas. With one exception, all women are classified as 'simple operators' (unskilled labour), according to the categories of the collective agreement with the Metallurgical Union, and their multi-functionality is paid at level one.

To explain the non-recognition of women's skills and the uses of gender to further the economic rationality of the model, we need to make several distinctions. First, we must separate tasks that involve the operation of machines from 'only manual' ones. In the case of the former (in a limited way protected by the collective agreement), the above-mentioned level two of skills would mean at least a 'semi-qualified' ranking if the agreement were properly applied. To a certain extent it was, but only for a short period in the history of the firm, during the Peronist government (1973–76), when several shop stewards were elected in the plant.

What is important to stress here is that women were never trained to operate or set up the key 'skilled trades' machine tools (lathes, 'balancines', drillers). These are the tools specifically mentioned in the collective agreement and, for this reason, the 'qualifying technologies' in any Argentine metallurgical concern.[17] By being excluded from this knowledge women are, by the same token, 'politically' disqualified and deprived of the right to accede to the highest categories in the metallurgical ranking of trades. Besides, in the case of all the other machines that women operate, with only one exception, the company keeps the division between operation and setting up, the latter function safely remaining in men's hands. As the collective agreement demands both the operation and setting up of tools and equipment of any machine to 'climb the engineering ladder' to officers' status, this restriction remains a formidable obstacle to women's advancement.

As the collective agreement only protects 'trades' skills linked to machine tools, the performance of any manual task, even if it involves the performance of very high-calibre artisan's knowledge, expertise and dexterity of level three, is by definition 'politically' disqualified. This disqualification is reinforced by the 'nimble' finger argument pointed out by Elson and Pearson, and Beneria, among others. That is, real skills acquired by women informally in a domestic setting are not given professional recognition. The functions and tasks that require them are also disqualified, and women's objective contribution to capital valorisation is ignored. So we do not have the process of 'technical' de-skilling (in Braverman's sense), but a problem of 'political' disqualification, an altogether different matter.

As in previous stages of this factory's history, the 'gendering' of machines, space, 'families' of filters produced, and process innovation hides women's real contribution to the firm's accumulation. But it is not only capital which has benefited by this renewed exercise of women's subordination but also men of the working class as well. With the assistance of the collective agreement, and through their own shop-floor hostile practices against 'advancing' women, and the deployment of specific gender ideologies, men very much contribute to the final gendered outcome.

The Male Shops (Mecanizados and Hojalateria)

In these sections we find the core and the real periphery of the firm. There is a mini-nucleus of two core men who combine tasks and processes of skill levels three, two and one: they have the highest ranking in the factory. One is the supervisor, who also works at the shop floor and who epitomises the core worker of the Japanese model, with a long period of 'incubation' within the same concern. The expertise of both men is recognised by the collective agreements, and by the firm itself: the Babbage principle does not apply in their case. However, because the collective contracts are still worded to protect strict job demarcation (i.e. do not contemplate JIT multi-functionality), the multiplicity of tasks they perform is not paid for. But the use of gendering in male shops, on the other hand, still protects their public professional pride and self-esteem. They are paid at level three (although they also perform at levels two and one). Finally, it should be noted that although core men perform some work previously defined as women's jobs, at levels two and one, they are not placed in charge of the most specialised 'nimble finger' women's jobs, still the preserve of the latter. (Because of productivity considerations, according to management [private conversation].)

The real periphery is made up of men ranked as simple operators (unskilled), performing all level one tasks including some non-specialised tasks at the Women's Section. Again they are paid for one job, but not for their multi-functionality, if only at level one. In this sense, and in spite of the new JIT flexibility, intra-gender male hierarchies have not disappeared, as these peripheral men are also deprived of machine tool training, at least under present 'JIT of crisis' arrangements.

THE LIMITS OF JIT RATIONALITY WITH SDL BOTTLENECKS

During the course of the decade, the firm demanded both men and women to become multi-skilled. This applies mainly to men, as women, during most of the history of the firm, *were* multi-functional, in particular in 'only manual' jobs. But this multi-skilled workforce involves male invasion into the women's area (in non-'nimble finger' jobs), without an equivalent process in the opposite direction.

During 1990, the firm experimented with a new family of filters which required 'watchmaker abilities', and women's nimble fingers came to the rescue. Two women were trained to operate traditional male welding machines, and thus we witnessed the only movement of women into the old male enclave. However, the firm keeps the old separation between setting up and operation of machines and equipment that only 'skilled men' can carry through. This caused a number of bottlenecks (admitted to me by management in private, but not publicly). The 'skilled men' had to feed these machines, and of course there were delays with their rotation in different functions in the formation of TTG, and additional lead time which could have been averted if women had also been trained in setting up the welding machines. (In fact women wanted and attempted to do this, and were severely reprimanded by their supervisor.)

Other episodes came with sequences of high levels of 'objective skills' that women learned to perform, but that skilled men recovered. (Probably both an interest in overtime, and professional pride were involved here.) Another bottleneck came with the setting up of the main 'female' machine (bobinadora) and the TTG in another family of filters. Maximum production peaks could not be maintained if the skilled man in charge of this machine was sick or on leave, as there was no 'buffer' of qualified personnel to replace this man's expertise. (In this instance the supervisor helped, but then the production of another 'family' came to a halt.)

What then are the limits of JIT multi-functionality in connection with the SDL? One may ask why management keeps the contemporary SDL if it comes into conflict with economic rationality and the goal of maximum flexibility. TTGs keep a certain rigidity that could be eliminated if women were allowed and trained to set up the 'bobinadora', the welding machines and in general all the machines. According to management's comments in private, the firm experiences the tension of the situation: between an economic urge to reintegrate functions and tasks, and become even more flexible at peak time (saving on lead time) by further erosion of the SDL and the inertia of leaving things as they are and benefiting from the economic advantages previously described. This latter course of action also avoided additionally risking core men's co-operation.

Management readily admits that it might consider further changes in the SDL and allow more advanced machine training of women if it suited the firm's interests, according to levels of production, if the situation improves and exports materialise – *only* then, and not before. In the words of the Chief Plant Engineer:

> I only pass on knowledge if and when I want to. I am conservative now, I do not want further troubles with new training. I do not keep efficiency criteria, just survival, not maximum productivity.

Another reason why management prefers not to innovate in this sense is core men's hostile reaction (including verbal abuse) when women were allowed into their old enclave. In this fashion, the male mini-core keeps its predominance at shop-floor level and reproduces the fragmentation of the firm's working class. However, the enterprise, by imposing its own class interests is slowly eroding old gender hierarchies through the multi-flexibility of JIT techniques. In JIC times, the interests of the industry and of men coincided in more direct fashion, keeping a given SDL. There are possibilities, therefore, for the development of different scenarios, but we must bear in mind that women's flexibility is not paid for now. What would happen if they had to pay? What are the limits of the firm's 'ungendering'?

There is an obstacle here, in that women lack technical know-how in the setting up and operation of given machines. To acquire these skills, either management must train them in non-peak time, or the union or vocational schools must provide this experience (a possibility now being discussed by some women trade unionists). For the time being, the firm's interests and union indifference at *top national levels*, a collective agreement that does not contemplate multi-functionality and which has never recognised women's skills in 'only manual' tasks, all help to maintain limited erosion of the old SDL and restricted qualifying training. Let us see now how gender ideologies are constructed and deployed in this regard.

The Conflictive Reproduction of JIT Systems. Gender Ideologies as Control and Workers' Response

It has become commonplace to conflate gender ideologies with an apparently universal ideology of domesticity. My findings, on the contrary,

show a much more complex construction and deployment of gender signification at factory level. Thus I found different versions, shaped and
deployed by different actors, changing in time (a different 'mix' of component elements) and according to the context where discourses were
expressed (at the workplace: the 'public script'; or at home: 'private
scripts').[18]

Management before the Height of the Crisis (A Time of Multi-skills with No Change in the SDL)

Control systems were rarely expressed in an openly instrumental or coercive
fashion, but rather were accompanied by representations that sought to
legitimate those strategies not only before visiting third parties, but, primarily, before the firm's own workers. Two main public discourses were
used to justify JIT changes and unpaid multi-functionality. In class terms
the firm deployed 'the script of the crisis': as sacrifices were needed at a
time of economic decline, workers' co-operation and identification with
management's plight would be taken for granted. But the firm, in talks
with visitors and with workers, also appealed to males' assumed gender
identity expressed through stereotypical gender traits: physical strength to
operate heavy machinery; courage to deal with dangerous equipment or
tasks; capacity to put up with dirty sequences or spaces; and technological
competence, although the latter was not expressed in essentialist terms.
The link between technical skills and masculinity was not natural, but
historical, originating in men's access to technical training.

Women were referred to in the usual ideology linking complementary
traits that would find femininity associated with physical weakness, fear of
dangerous machines, unwillingness to do untidy or greasy jobs, and technological incompetence, also expressed in historical rather than essentialist terms. Apart from these negative connotations, management views also
exalted women's manual dexterity, concentration, endurance capacity and
assumed docility. These gender meanings justified the SDL and hierarch-
isation of sections and shops, and had the economic repercussions mentioned
above.

Also at the beginning of field work, male workers, in public and at
home, deployed a masculine ideology similar to that of management. Simultaneously, they expressed a different view on femininity. The latter was
not equated with physical weakness, cleanliness at worksite, and the rest
of the gender stereotypes that the firm assumed to be normal for working class men's taste. Thus male workers could conciliate neatness and

delicacy with a reasonable amount of physical strength. They wanted their women to be *polentonas* – robust, physically generously endowed. Skinny women were good as TV models, but not to their liking. They could also find female work mates attractive even if temporarily 'dusty' with cotton or 'dirty' with lubricants. Furthermore, they did not think that lack of technological knowledge was in itself an attribute of femininity. They also gave this trait a historical turn. They all thought domestic work was mainly women's domain, but they said they would see nothing wrong with helping with housework or children.

Women's gender representations agreed only partially with men's. There was some coincidence between masculinity and physical strength, but within limits, because 'one cannot deny that there are men who are not very tall or big, and they are not less manly because of that'. At the workplace, women did not express other public views on masculinity, keeping silent about men's assumed courage to work with machines, bravery, capacity to endure dirty jobs and other expressions of masculine gender traits. At home their private script did not express differences between men and women as far as facing the challenges of complex machines, provided women were well-trained, and the machines not extremely heavy (three exceptions were mentioned). Dirtiness was not found a particularly attractive trait for men or women (everybody should take a shower after work). The link between technical skills and masculinity was seen as historical: men are not inferior males because they do not know how to operate a machine, although it is handy to have a mate with some knowledge about electricity and home appliances.

Women's public script with regard to femininity at the beginning of field work approached that of men's and, if management allowed them to get away with it, they refused work that might make their hands or hair too dirty, or was dangerous or heavy. At home, however, they expressed different views. Women's private discourse rejected and laughed at male representations. They did not accept the ideologies that show them as weak, afraid, and lacking in strength and the degree of technological know-how needed for the factory's survival. That is, at shop-floor level, in a context where they lacked power to express what they thought, *they deployed the same gender stereotypes that downgraded them in comparison to men*. In instrumental terms, this was a convenient excuse to avoid carrying out functions and tasks that would not be translated into higher salaries or status. This play of representations, however, a 'hidden ideological rebellion' against management and working males, enters in an invisible contradiction with JIT flexibility, an additional bottleneck whose origin management could not easily detect.

The Contemporary Situation (Multi-skills with Some Changes in the Old SDL)

The factory is a microcosm that reflects and intensifies the conflicts and uncertainties found in the wider Argentine society. Labour–management relations are very fluid: that workers accept and are ready to give their best for the company's survival and growth. The 'discourse of the crisis' is enough to explain the consolidation of JIT forms, to the extent that gender meanings are not even brought up by management to justify class events.

For labour, the impossibility of carrying out group mobilisation against the violations of the collective agreement has displaced the struggle onto individual workers' own response, careerism and intra-class competition. The shop floor is thick with strife, rumours, and acute hostility towards the women who dared to invade their old enclave. On days when the production of the new model does not take place the conflict subsides, but tension is always there. But this response that fragments the working class is not expressed in 'neutral' class terms, but rather through gendered practices and signification. Core male workers do not represent JIT technological changes as instances of labour–capital relations, but rather in sectoral terms, in which male mini-groups or individuals, in changing alliances, struggle for the definition of their own multi-skills as indispensable for the factory's survival. As in the past, the symbolic reply is channelled through representations that construct, negotiate and recreate gender signification.

We have now three different public scripts that convey an appeal to alliances within the firm, and that originate from the core males and from the female periphery. (Men of the periphery, being the most dispensable of all, remain silent.) In the three discourses, men and women defend and recreate their multi-functional flexibility in gender terms, as an indispensable element in the company's survival.

This battle of significations is as active as daily work routines. At one extreme we have the lathe operator, the metallurgical officer who has arrived but feels threatened. He is the most active constructor of new gender meanings, and also the most hostile of men *vis-à-vis* 'uppity women'. He tries to safeguard metallurgical know-how, professional self-esteem and a highly qualified position in a very restricted labour market. Management's power of late shows him that his previously safe career may be shaken if women are trained. Moreover, he may no longer assume that his job is assured because he is a man. It is interesting to note that he has now extended his kit of masculine gender traits to include 'delicate manual dexterity and neatness' ('I am not afraid of being seen as a woman just because I can do a woman's job'). So in his own representation, he is so absolutely flexible that he is even superior to women in the latter's special jobs. (It must be noted here that the firm does not accept this version and that he is sent to perform only 'easy' women's jobs, not the ones demanding particular 'neatness and dexterity'.) Simultaneously, the metallurgical officer has modified the ideology of femininity. Now he represents technical know-how as an essential male gender trait: those 'dumb women will never learn to set up a really complex machine'.

In the middle of the spectrum, the other core man, the Supervisor who feels 'safe' because nobody can possibly substitute for him after so many years in the plant, has not openly changed gender representations. He shows reservations, however, concerning women's readiness to learn a trade, and tells management so. He has also actively tried to restrain women from the setting up of welding machines.

In the women's camp we find the only semi-skilled female operator caught between men and women alike. Men do not accept her, and women do not like her being the only one with recognised semi-qualified status among them. At the level of public scripts, their respective versions have not appreciably changed, although the vanguard operator tries to induce her female workmates, 'the expectant ones', into asking management for additional training as a prerequisite for future promotion.

The shop floor continues to be a site of signification, tension and struggle. Unfortunately it does not unite, but rather additionally fragments an already divided working class (JIT core/periphery divisions). Core men do not participate in the battle of signification over the consolidation of JIT forms at a more global level. This wider meaning could have been more egalitarian, stressing the negative relation between capital and labour in terms of unpaid multi-skills, deleterious for all workers, but particularly for women. Instead, they are breaking workers' class unity and increasing inter-class fragmentation. Their class representation at factory level demonstrates a discourse in which potential elements of class resistance are tarnished in their attempts to consolidate their superiority over women, offering themselves and their craft as the indispensable components in the company's future. Women, on the other hand, are not sure how to face the slowly eroding SDL, how far to accompany employers in their search for survival on unequal terms with their male co-workers. In this fashion, practices and ideologies sustained by the agency of the company, indifference of the union, and desperation and uncertainty of women and men are not conducive, at least in the short run, to 'ungendering' further this metallurgical concern.

A final word on differences in findings between my work and Cockburn's regarding the association between technological competence and femininity. These differences may be due to a number of factors, such as different class extraction (although it is possible that middle-class Argentine women may agree with English women's equation), rural versus urban origin. But Argentine women are used to very heavy physical work in a context in which femininity is not equated with bodily weakness. Rather, the opposite holds true. They are adult women, not adolescents, and they operate in an environment where a feminine woman is not assimilated to a skinny one. They are also women sure of their sexuality, with husbands or boyfriends who do not diminish them because they are strong factory workers. To exercise a degree of physical strength in their work, within some limits, does not diminish them personally or for men in general, whatever management's public views on the subject may be.

ISSUES FOR FURTHER REFLECTION ON JIT APPLICATION

How are we to evaluate JIT technologies from the point of view of workers' interests, in particular women workers' interests? The efficiency and growth of Japanese industry is an undeniable phenomenon. JIT systems, in Japan and wherever applied, are instrumental to this final effect. The question remains, however, as to the real degree of JIT's negative effects on workers' situation. The system has been called both one with 'high respect for humans' (as quoted by Oliver and Wilkinson, 1988) and 'cruelly inhuman' (Kamata, 1972). High work intensity and control over workers' lives are the most common complaints. The evidence in favour of the recreation of the 'flexible artisan' remains elusive and many trade unionists have labelled it a case of Hyper-Taylorism.[19]

I focus here on the implications of the diffusion of JIT social technologies, considering workers' – and first and foremost women workers' – needs and strategies. It is useful to distinguish between: 1) JIT practices as applied now or potentially by private enterprises, and the role of unions and shop stewards, if allowed at plant level, therein; and 2) the possibility of application of JIT practices by co-operatives or other forms of social production with workers' control (micro or small productive enterprises organised by women, for example).

With regard to 1) we note that available evidence originating from field work research, workers' and trade union sources coincide in negative evaluation of JIT models, in particular with regard to workers' skills developed and exercised at plant level, working conditions, and the invasion and control of men and women workers' private lives. However, this same evidence suggests also the possibility of a (small) degree of negotiation of some of JIT features according to the particular relationship of forces between capital and labour, as well as the nature of inter-gender relations. Divisions within the labour force and the union movement, state, group and trade union pressures possible in a context of crisis (or expansion) may help in the shaping of a different and perhaps more humane model.

The application of the model in the US (Fucini and Fucini, 1990) suggests that there are no intrinsic gender dimensions associated with it. Core firms do not need to exclude women like in Japan. It is a matter of workers' and their organisations' choice of response to negotiate at least some of the terms of its gendered application. Access of women to appropriate technical skills is a crucial condition to effect this. Of course, union action is also dependent on workers' own judgement of their particular workplace situation, 'how far to go on with a struggle' which in a time of crisis may certainly restrict that capacity.

With regard to 2), it should be possible to adapt JIT systems to women workers' co-operatives and other units of the social sector. Workers controlling their own labour process may check the intensity of the work pace (a big drawback in the original model), and also the timing of daily routine, to suit women's reproductive activities. JIT patterns require multi-skills: women may organise the work in the manner most gratifying to them – similarly with job rotation, and the possibilities of additional development of women's expertise. In addition these projects may be linked with other community organisations at neighbourhood and city levels, thereby enhancing women's consciousness raising and organising experiences. But any successful co-operative JIT launching requires the 'grooming' of the state and the financial community, and a favourable institutional environment. All these are presently substantial obstacles in the Argentinian and Latin American social landscape of industrial restructuring today.

One final reflection concerns the need of a debate on new production systems and their institutional frameworks. Such an inter-disciplinary debate would help to illuminate both the situation of national economies and also the many links these economies have at both intra-regional and inter-regional level. The final aim of feminist analysis must be to 'degender' transition paradigms and new production systems: Post-Fordism, JIT techniques, Flexible Specialisation etc. It is essential to do this because current interpretations of the crisis and solutions to it have an influence on policy. At present androcentric discourses on JIT and its relation to transition theories are not yet solidified. There is still time to prevent interpretations based on male experience being taken as representative for all men and women workers. However, achieving this goal involves political as well as theoretical work. Competing with androcentric models will not be easy. Rediscovering gendered history involves power relations and is part of the struggle for an equitable society.

APPENDIX I

WORKERS' EVALUATION OF JIT 'OF CRISIS' APPLICATION

In broad terms, there is consensus among Argfilsa workers, women and men alike, to reject JIT techniques in favour of a return to the past, even if by skills criteria the new arrangements of production are less boring or repetitive.

There are some positive elements in JIT: women and men find multi-functionality attractive; they are less *encajonados* (constrained by the task); they find there is more room for creativity. (After all, this *kaizen* of crisis is always impinging upon them to develop ideas on how to save on inputs, or otherwise increase efficiency of production, demanding a higher degree of experimentation.) Being required to 'accompany the factory' in manufacturing models which are more difficult, or never tried before, and to be 'consulted' by the Plant Engineer, makes the workers feel more useful and capable. There are here clear elements of professional pride.

As to the negative aspects: it is 100 per cent more stressful when TTGs are formed. The workers' worries (many tasks and different requirements – not the fixed routine of Japanese JIT) lead, reportedly, to stomach ulcers and nerves, although it is difficult to separate here the elements due to JIT itself and the general economic situation. The need to identify with the company also worries many workers:

> You know that they are not OK financially and that they rely on what they are extracting from you. You are worried because you know that what you are working at is the source of what you get at the end of the month, so you see the factory as if it were yours. Wrongly, of course: they are always the bosses.

The loss of the old anonymity also hurts workers. The lathe operator admits:

> Basically, before, you could make a mistake and remain anonymous. Now I also feel that the supervisor is 'sucking' our knowledge: 'Why do you do it this way?' We can't hide from the bosses and besides I know I can be creative, but I do not need to show it there. What we want is to have creativity paid or to have the chance to go elsewhere, but where nowadays?

The general opinion was one of rejection of JIT techniques, from different angles. Innovative, challenging aspects do not compensate for the risks, tensions and added responsibility without a fair economic compensation. It is not so much the physical stress, but rather the added emotional stress as well, because participation is expected (even without Quality Circles) and for further *kaizen*.

At home, core men admit that they need to be competitive to show how important they are. But in more quiet moments they regret the fight and abuse against women co-workers who, after all, are doing their best. As the vanguard woman comments:

> Yes, creativity is nice but when there is some material compensation. Both together are even nicer.

Nobody advances any prognosis about the future. The workers are worried about the present, the survival of the company, and job stability. They do not know how long the company will be able to survive with this type of JIT organisation; they keep their expectations. Most workers believe that they cannot go on like this, innovating every week or day, and they hope that the company might find it more profitable to stabilise in some type of mass production and return to JIC lines. Then they note that Argentine industry and its markets have changed and that, by all accounts, this evolution is irreversible, there is no return to the past.

All workers are pro-union, for instrumental reasons (in the past the best collective agreements and social services, hospitals, vacation sites and others, were those attained by the metallurgical union), but also on political grounds, for the union defence of workers' rights. Now the situation is different. Services have deteriorated, there are no new agreements, and wage increases are always below inflation rates. Workers of course would like the union to make national arrangements, via collective agreements, so as to have multi-functionality recognised and paid for. They would like shop-floor arrangements to have the contract applied according to the specific needs of the company concerned. But the main problem in a small enterprise is that there are no shop stewards as in the past, no buffer between workers and employers. So the workers do not want to *hacer olas*, stir up the shop; they want to avoid problems with management.

The high bureaucracy of the UOM is very close to the government, and has not yet admitted the existence of JIT practices among its flock. Dissident metallurgical unions are negotiating at plant level, defensively, but are showing what they call a 'creative response' that avoids strike action, and are thus following the lead of the metallurgical unions in São Paulo, Brazil.

NOTES

1. ECLA's 1990 thoughtful study, which cannot be suspected of 'excessive radicalism', provides very useful data on regional and country levels, and one of the most talked-about proposals for the transformation of Latin American productive activities with equity. It is, at the same time, one of the best examples of androcentric theory and research to be found in contemporary Latin America, and one of our main 'targets'.

2. See, for example, UNICEF, *Adjustment with a Human Face*, 1987, and UNDP, 1988, among others.

3.	I am referring to progressive, pluralistic and democratically elected middle echelons of the national union (UOM), not to its top leadership.

4.	There are several possible and perhaps simultaneous constituencies of our feminist research, apart from working women and their organisations, such as the academic community, national planning bodies, and international development agencies. While in times of economic growth their interests may coincide or at least not contradict each other, in times of economic crisis and deindustrialisation, in a context of anti-labour laws and severe adjustment policies (Argentina is a case in point), this is no longer necessarily the case.

5.	There are many interpretations of the Global Economy, Centre–Periphery relations, the new world emerging from restructuring in the 1990s, the central countries themselves, the high-technology revolution, etc. For example, compare some 'classics': Frobel *et al.*, 1989; and Aglietta, 1979; with Ominami, 1986; Lipietz, 1987 (Regulation School); Piore and Sabel, 1984; Castells, 1986; Marglin and Schor, 1990. For an interesting review discussion, see Lauridsen, 1988.

6.	See Kaplinsky, 1984, pp. 172–3 in particular for an account of Technological Darwinism and the consequences of its adoption for an understanding of Third World manufacturing.

7.	For case studies on these issues, see Walby, 1988.

8.	Perhaps the most illuminating case studies on this specific topic are Cockburn's long list of contributions. See References.

9.	I have not seen Liff's background papers and research reports. I suspect, hopefully, that she might be working on the type of theorisation we so much need in these times of 'uncertainty and restructuring'.

10.	The debate on JIT systems in the developed economies has not remained static. Some fissures have appeared in a formerly overall 'optimistic' view of 'transition' paradigms. See Tomany, 1990, as an example of this literature.

11.	Various theorisations of this 'transition' are on offer. For example, neo- or post-Fordism (Aglietta, 1979; Lipietz, 1987), post-Taylorism (Stankiewicz, 1991), Flexible Specialisation (Piore and Sabel, 1984), Lean Production (Womanck, Jones and Roos, 1990), Systemofacture (Hoffman and Kaplinsky, 1988), and the move from Just-in-Case to Just-in-Time (Sayer, 1986).

12.	I borrow the expression JER (Just Enough Resources) from Fucini and Fucini, 1990. In addition, it must be borne in mind that there are many 'visions' of JIT systems. For instance: Nakane, 1973; Morishima, 1982; Schonberger, 1982; Sethi, S. *et al.*, 1984; Cusumano, 1985; Dohse *et al.*, 1985; Sayer, 1986; Hoffman and Kaplinsky, 1988; Oliver and Wilkinson, 1988; Acroy *et al.*, 1988; Fucini and Fucini, 1990; Womack, Jones and Roos, 1990, among many others.

13.	Thanks are due to the Wenner-Gren Foundation Grant #5014, for the funding of this research.

14.	I explore these topics at length in Roldan, 1993b and c.

15.	Referring to the Argentine case, Novick, 1990, mentions examples of JIT practices in steel, automobile, plastics and shoe manufacturing, her own research (with no reference to the SDL) focusing on the last industry. See Roldan, 1993a for examples in steel, plastics, light engineering and electronics; Roldan, 1993b for the autopart industry; and Vispo and Kosacoff,

1990 for an IBM case study. From my conversations with colleagues, trade unionists and rank and file workers, I surmise that most industries in Argentina are implementing some variety of JIT reorganisation, although adapting different dimensions of the same basic model.

16. See Katz and Kosacoff, 1989 and Kosacoff and Aspiazu, 1989 on this issue.
17. The metallurgical collective agreement clauses to be applied in small enterprises have a very ambiguous wording. The result is that in the case of machines not actually mentioned in the contract, it would be extremely difficult to make a claim for the 'qualification' of any given machine. This, of course, is a matter of union's strength at the point of production. In small firms, with no shop stewards and with regard to machines used by women, I am afraid this is an instance of a lost case under present, and even pre-crisis, circumstances.
18. The use of 'script' terminology is taken from Scott, 1985.
19. For illustrations of these practices see Garrahon and Stewart, 1992; Fucini and Fucini, 1990; Parker and Slaughter, 1988 and Kamata, 1972.

REFERENCES

Ackroyd, S., G. Burrell, M. Hughes and A. Whitaker. 1988. 'The Japanisation of British Industry', *Industrial Relations Journal*, Vol. 19, No. 1, pp. 11–23.

Aglietta, Michel. 1979. *A Theory of Economic Regulation: The US Experience*, New Left Books, London.

Amsden, A.H. (ed.). 1980. *The Economics of Women and Work*, Penguin, Harmondsworth.

Barker, J. and H. Downing. 1985. 'Word Processing and the Transformation of Patriarchal Relations of Control in the Office', in D. Mackenzie and J. Wacjman (eds).

Beechey, Veronica. 1987. *Unequal Work*, Verso, London.

Beneria, Lourdes and Martha Roldan. 1987. *The Crossroads of Class and Gender: Industrial Homework, Subcontracting and Household Dynamics*, The University of Chicago Press, Chicago.

Braverman, Harry. 1974. *Labor and Monopoly Capital. The Degradation of Work in the Twentieth Century*, Monthly Review Press, New York.

Burawoy, Michael. 1985. *The Politics of Production*, Verso, London.

Catells, Manuel. 1986. 'High Technology, Economic Policies and World Development, *BRIE*, Working Paper No. 18, Berkeley.

Child, J. 1985. 'Managerial strategies, new technologies and the labour process', in D. Knights *et al.* (eds).

Clarke, J., C. Crichter and R. Johnson (eds). 1979. *Working Class Culture*, Hutchison.

Cockburn, Cynthia. 1983. *Brothers: Male Dominance and Technological Change*, Pluto Press, London.

Cockburn, Cynthia. 1985. *Machinery of Dominance: Women, Men and Technical Know-How*, Pluto Press, London.

Cockburn, Cynthia. 1987. *Two-Training: Sex Inequalities in the Youth Training Scheme*, Macmillan, London.

Cockburn, Cynthia. 1988. 'The gendering of jobs: workplace relations and the reproduction of sex segregation', in S. Walby (ed.).

Cockburn, Cynthia. 1990. 'Technical Competence, Gender Identity and Women's Autonomy'. Paper prepared for the World Congress of Sociology, Madrid.

Cohen, Sheila. 1987. 'A Labour Process to Nowhere', *New Left Review*, No. 165.

Crompton, Rosemary and Gareth Jones. 1984. *White-Collar Proletariat: Deskilling and Gender in Clerical Work*, Macmillan Press, London.

Cusumano, M. A. 1985. *The Japanese Automobile Industry*, Cambridge University Press, Cambridge, Mass.

Dohse, K., U. Jurgens, and T. Malsch. 1985. 'From Fordism to Toyotism? The social organisation of the labour process in the Japanese automobile industry', *Politics and Society*, 14.2.

ECLA/CEPAL. 1990. *Transformacion Productiva con Equidad*, Santiago de Chile.

Edwards, R. 1979. *Contested Terrain: The Transformation of Work in the Twentieth Century*, Heinemann, London.

Elson, Diane (ed.). 1992. *Male Bias in the Development Process*, Manchester University Press, Manchester.

Elson, Diane and Ruth Pearson. 1981. 'The Subordination of Women and the Internationalisation of Factory Production', in Kate Young, Carol Wolkowitz, and Roslyn McCullagh (eds).

Friedman, A. 1977. *Industry and Labour*, Macmillan, London.

Frobel, F., J. Heinrichs, and O. Kreye. 1980. *The New International Division of Labour*, Cambridge University Press, London.

Fucini, J. and S. Fucini. 1990. *Working for the Japanese*, The Free Press, New York.

Game, Ann and Rosemary Pringle. 1984. *Gender at Work*, Pluto, London.

Garrahan, P. and P. Stewart. 1992. *The Nissan Enigma, Flexibility at Work in a Local Economy*, Mansell Publishing, London.

Godet, M. 1987. 'Ten unfashionable and controversial findings on Japan', *Futures*, August.

Hill, S. 1981. *Competition and Control at Work*, Hutchison, London.

Hoffman C. and R. Kaplinsky. 1988. *Driving Force*, Longman, London.

Huws, Ursula. 1982. *Your Job in the Eighties: A Woman's Guide to New Technology*, Pluto Press, London.

IDS Bulletin. 1989. 'Restructuring Industrialisation', Vol. 20, No. 4, October.

Kamata, S. 1972. *Japan in the Passing Lane*, Pantheon, New York.

Kaplinsky, Raphael. 1984. *Automation, the Technology and Society*, Longman, London.

Katz, J. and B. Kosacoff. 1989. *El proceso de industrializacion en la Argentina: Evolucion, retroceso, y prospectiva*, Cedal-Cepal, Buenos Aires.

Kelly, J. 1985. 'Management's Redesign of Work: Labour Process, Labour Markets and Product Market', in D. Knights, H. Willmott and David Collinson (eds).

Knights, David and H. Willmott (eds). 1986. *Gender and the Labour Process*, Gower Publishing Co., Aldershot.

Knights, David, H. Willmott, and David Collinson (eds). 1985. *Job Redesign: Critical Perspectives on the Labour Process*, Gower Publishing Co., Aldershot.

Kosacoff, B. and D. Azupiazu. 1989. *La industria argentina. Desarrollo y cambios estructurales*, Entro Editor-Cepal, Buenos Aires.

Lamphere, Louise. 1985. 'Bringing the family to work: Women's Culture on the Shop Floor', *Feminist Studies* 11, No. 3, Fall.

Lauridssen, L. 1988. 'New Technology, New International Division of Labour and Gender'. Preliminary paper for CEDLA Workshop on Gender, Technology and Global Restructuring. Views from Europe with Relevance to Latin America. Amsterdam, November.

Liff, Sonia. 1986. 'Technical Change and Occupational Sex-Typing', in D. Knights and H. Willmott (eds).

Liff, Sonia. 1988. 'Review article on Machinery of Dominance', *Capital and Class*, No. 32, Summer.

Lipietz A. 1987. *Mirages and Miracles: the Crisis in Global Fordism*, Verso, London.

Littler, C. 1989. 'Deskilling and Changing Structures of Control', in S. Wood (ed.), 1989.

Lobo, Elizabeth. 1986. 'Division Sexual del Trabajo: el trabajo tambien tiene sexo' in GRECMU, *Mujer y Trabajo en America Latina*, Montevideo, Ediciones de la Banda Oriental, SRL.

Mackenzie, D. and J. Wajcman (eds). 1985. *The Social Shaping of Technology*, Open University Press, Milton Keynes. See their Introduction herein.

MacLoughlin, Ian and Jon Clark. 1988. *Technological Change at Work*, Open University Press, Stony Stratford.

Marglin, S. and J. B. Schor. 1990. *The Golden Age of Capitalism. Reinterpreting the Post War Experience*, Oxford University Press, New York.

Morishima, M. 1982. *Why has Japan 'Succeeded'? Western Technology and the Japanese Ethos*, Cambridge University Press, London.

Novick, M. 1990. 'Argentina, la profundizacion del cambio tecnologico y la nueva logica de accion sindical'. Paper presented to the XIV Entro Anual ANPOCS, Caxambu, MG, Brazil, October.

Oliver, N. and B. Wilkinson. 1988. *The Japanisation of British Industry*, Basil Blackwell, Oxford.

Ominami, C. 1986. *Le tiers monded ans la cris*, Edition La Decouverte, Paris.

Parker, M. and J. Slaughter. 1988. *Choosing Sides: Unions and the Team Concept*, South End Press, Boston.

Phillips, A. and B. Taylor. 1980. 'Sex and Skill': Notes Towards a Feminist Economics', *Feminist Review* 6.

Piore, Michael J. and C. F. Sabel. 1984. *The Second Industrial Divide*, Basic Books, New York.

Roldan, M. 1993a. 'Industrial Restructuring, Deregulation and New JIT Labour Processes in Argentina: Towards a Gender-Aware Perspective?, *IDS Bulletin*, Vol. 24, No. 2, April.

Roldan, M. 1993b. 'Reality in Search of Theory: Gendered JIT/JER/TQC Practices and Ideologies in Times of "Critical" Restructuring.' Paper presented at the Workshop on Intra-Firm and Inter-Firm Reorganisation in Third World Manufacturing, Institute of Development Studies, University of Sussex, April 14–16.

Roldan, M. 1993c. *Procesos de Trabajo, Restructuracion Industrial y Divisiones Generico-Sexuales en el Universo Fabril*, Buenos Aires, forthcoming.

Rose, M. 1978. *Industrial Behavior: Theoretical Development since Taylor*, London, Penguin.

Rubery, J. 1980. 'Structural Labour Markets, Worker Organisation and Low Pay', in A. Amsden (ed.), *The Economics of Women and Work*, Penguin, Harmondsworth.

Sayer, Andrew. 1986. 'New Developments in Manufacturing: The Last Just-in-time System', *Capital and Class*, 30, Winter.

Schonberger, R. 1982. *Japanese Manufacturing Techniques*, The Free Press, New York.

Scott, James. 1985. *Weapons of the Weak: Everyday Forms of Peasant Resistance*, Yale University Press, New Haven.

Sethi, S., N. Namiki and C. Swanson. 1984. *The False Promise of the Japanese Miracle*, Pitman, London.

Silverman, D. 1970. *The Theory of Organisations*, Heinemann, London.

Tomaney, J. 1990. 'The reality of workplace flexibility', *Capital and Class*, No. 40, Spring.

Thompson, Paul. 1983. *The Nature of Work. An Introduction to Debates on the Labour Process*, Macmillan Press, Hong Kong.

UNDP RI A-85-004. 1988. 'The Declaration and Agreements from the Regional Conference on Poverty in Latin America and the Caribbean', Cartagena de Indias, Colombia.

UNICEF. 1987. *Adjustment with a Human Face*, Oxford University Press, New York.

Vispo, A. and B. Kosacoff. 1990. 'Difusion de tecnologias de punta en la Argentina. Algunas reflexiones sobre la organizacion de la produccion industrial de IBM' *Documento de Trabajo*, No. 38, CEPAL, Buenos Aires.

Walby, S. (ed.). 1988. *Gender Segregation at Work*, Philadelpia, Milton Keynes.

Walker, Richard. 1989. 'Machinery, Labour and Location', in S. Wood (ed.).

Wilkinson, B. 1983. *The Shop Floor Politics of New Technology*, Heinemann, London.

Willis, Paul. 1987. 'Shop Floor Culture, Masculinity and the Wage Form', in J. Clarke *et al.* (eds).

Womack, J. P., D. Jones and D. Roos. 1990. *The Machine that Changed the World*, Rawson Macmillan, New York.

Wood, Stephen (ed.). 1989. *The Transformation of Work. Skill, Flexibility and the Labour Process*, Unwin Hyman, London.

Woodward, Joan. 1980. *Industrial Organisation: Theory and Practice*, 2nd. ed., Oxford University Press, Oxford.

Young, Kate, Carol Wolkowitz and Roslyn McCullagh (eds). 1981. *Of Marriage and the Market. Women's Subordination in International Perspective*. CSE Books, London.

3 Multiple Identities, Multiple Strategies[1]

Amrita Chhachhi and Renée Pittin

This chapter is based on reflections arising from research on women factory workers over a number of years.[2] The issues and questions in each phase of research changed as our own understanding grew, along with changes in the general political and economic environment. In spite of variations in research objectives, there were certain common themes concerning the ways in which women were perceived and their self-perception as workers, and as women, the possibilities and the limits to organising, the differences between the interests of women and men workers as well as the differences between women workers themselves. These issues are explored in this chapter. The chapter is divided into three sections. In the first section we discuss the theoretical implications of the relationship between identity, consciousness and strategies. In the next section we raise issues concerning strategies and organising/lack of organising on the basis of two case studies of women factory workers in electronics and electrical equipment factories in India and Nigeria.[3] The final section looks at existing struggles within the theoretical perspective elaborated earlier.

Considerable work has been done in recent years on women's employment, locating features ranging from restructuring at an international level to labour control on the factory floor and the use of gender divisions to place women workers in low-paid, unskilled, part-time and casual jobs (Elson and Pearson, 1981; Mitter, 1986; Redclift and Mingione, 1985). Theories of women's employment have moved from a critique of dual labour markets and orthodox Marxist categories to highlighting the linkage between production and reproduction, domestic labour and wage labour and the necessity to study gender construction within the labour process as well as within the sexual division of labour in the household (Beechey, 1986).

One theoretical area which remains 'underdeveloped' is the question of women workers' consciousness. The issue of consciousness is essential to any discussion on strategies for organising, and in this chapter we will explore certain areas which link identity, consciousness and strategy. The relationship between perception and action is extremely complicated. We examine two approaches – the Marxist and post-structuralist feminist analyses of the relationship between identity, consciousness and strategy – and then elaborate a tentative framework.

The dominant model in orthodox Marxist debates has been the model of dual consciousness initiated by K. Kautsky and Lenin, and systematised by G. Lukács. On the one hand is actual consciousness, i.e. what the worker normally thinks, and on the other hand is ascribed consciousness, i.e. the consciousness that the worker ought to have given his position within the production process. Identity in this formulation is singular, fixed and derived from positioning in the production process. This model not only constructed an ideal type model of class consciousness, but it also assumed a one-to-one correspondence between the objective class structure and consciousness. Further, this conception transferred the locus of radical consciousness from the working class to the intelligentsia. Since classes are seen as passive objects determined by economic functions, their conciousness is also seen as completely controlled by dominant ideologies. The concept of 'false consciousness' not only ignores the existence of 'everyday forms of resistance', but also reduces a worker's identity to that of class positionality.

An alternative to the above orthodox problematic was developed through rich historical studies of the 'moral economy' and resistance of working classes and slaves in the work of E. P. Thompson and E. Genovese, as well as more specific studies of the labour process and the politics around the points of production by M. Burawoy (Thompson, 1963; Genovese, 1974; Burawoy, 1985). These studies have highlighted that there is no 'objective' notice of class prior to its appearance in action, as for example in Thompson's well-known formulation of class as a 'happening' whereby classes are constituted in history. Rejecting the distinction between 'objective' and 'subjective' as arbitrary, Burawoy also emphasises the need to look at the formation of consciousness as an effect of the combination of economic, political and ideological realms. He also highlights the formation of a specific type of consciousness arising specifically from the structures of the workplace.[4] Instead of the notion of 'habituation' used by H. Braverman, which refers to an extreme form of objectification, eliminating the subjective moment, Burawoy uses 'adaptation' and examines, in the struggles over the labour process, the ways in which 'fragmented arenas of subjectivity expand into collective struggle, or, more narrowly, under what conditions . . . adaptation turn[s] into resistance' (Burawoy, 1985: 76).

The application of Gramsci's notion of 'commonsense', the discovery of counter hegemonic discourses developed by subaltern groups, and the acknowledgement of covert forms of resistance in recent historical and contemporary studies have opened the way towards developing a more 'grounded' theory of consciousness (Gramsci, 1985; Scott, 1985; also see the work of the Subaltern Studies group). For instance James Scott, in his sensitive study of peasant resistance through the creation of an oppositional culture, points out that:

> Class after all, does not exhaust the total explanatory space of social actions. . . . within the peasant village, . . . class may compete with kinship, neighbourhood, faction, and ritual links as foci of human identity and solidarity. Beyond the village level, it may also compete with ethnicity, language group, religion, and region as a focus of loyalty. Class may be applicable to some situations but not to others; it may be reinforced or crosscut by other ties; it may be far more important for the experience of some than of others. Those who are tempted to dismiss all principles of human action that contend with class identity as 'false consciousness' and to wait for Althusser's 'determination in the last instance' are likely to wait in vain. In the meantime, the messy reality of multiple identities will continue to be the experience out of which social relations are conducted.
>
> (Scott, 1985: 43)

Scott's work has moved from a critique of the Gramscian concept of hegemony and the notion of false consciousness, to emphasise the creative capacity of subordinate groups to reverse or negate dominant ideologies. A similar project is envisaged by the Subaltern Studies historians who recover the subject in the social history and resistance of subordinate groups in the colonial period. However, although both Scott and the Subaltern Studies group do look at men and women in struggles and point out areas of gender discrimination, their work does not incorporate the categories and relations of the sex/gender system into the analysis of the construction of wider political relationships.[5] It is to feminist theory that we have to turn for a re-conceptualisation of working women.

The first fracture in the notion of a monolithic working-class identity was in fact made by feminists when they highlighted the fact that the working class had two genders.[6] The specificity of women workers lay not only in that they had special issues, e.g. maternity benefits, equal pay, sexual harassment, but also that their position in the labour market was determined by their position within the household. The double burden of wage work and domestic labour, and the ideology of domesticity implied that women entered the labour market already determined as 'inferior bearers of gender'. Elson and Pearson succinctly identified three tendencies in the dialectic of capital and gender: 'a tendency to intensify the existing forms of gender subordination; a tendency to decompose existing forms of gender subordination; and a tendency to recompose new forms of gender subordination' (Elson and Pearson, 1981). Women workers therefore had to struggle as workers as well as women. The lack of participation by women in trade unions was located in certain structural features: male domination in unions, the internal structure of union organisation, the dead-end nature of women's jobs, the fact that women were employed in industries which are difficult to organise, the double burden which implied that women simply did not have the time for union activities. However, in many studies on women workers, the traditional Marxist model of consciousness still operates. The focus on gender has also led to the setting up of another model of 'feminist consciousness', and women who do not exhibit these characteristics are seen as victims of patriarchal ideology, backward and reactionary (for critique, see Beechey, 1986).

Another approach to women workers' (lack of) consciousness has argued that women's lack of participation in unions was due to gender socialisation and the reinforcement of women's roles as mothers and wives through the ideology of domesticity. An extreme formulation of this argument, and one that is often used in developing countries, is that women's consciousness is based on a 'fatalistic approach to life' (Purcell, 1981). Women workers were seen as more fatalistic than men in that they had little or no control over most aspects of their lives, a fact that was reinforced in the working environment as well. Further studies emphasised the 'familial orientation' of women workers (Pollert, 1981). These concerns of women are not seen as a sign of backwardness, but as a reflection of the fact that for women 'it is gender subordination which is primary, while capitalist exploitation is secondary and derivative' (Elson and Pearson, 1981: 89). N. Banerjee for instance points out that 'the ideology of the superior male worker' does not originate in the labour market, but rather arises from the position men occupy in other areas where their dominance is guaranteed by 'powerful social institutions of the family, religion and the state' (Banerjee, 1991: 307). However, such a formulation could result in focusing only on social institutions outside the labour market, depicting women workers as trapped within a vicious circle of 'traditional patriarchy'.

Recent socialist feminist theory on women's employment has stressed the importance of looking at all areas, i.e. the labour market, household, and labour process as well as the state and other institutions as sites for the construction and reconstruction of women's subordination. Cynthia Cockburn has argued for the significance of the 'socio-political and the physical dimensions as constituting the material basis for male domination'. A focus on these dimensions and on *processes* opens up examination of:

questions about male organisation and solidarity, the part played by institutions such as church, societies, unions and clubs for instance. And the physical opens up questions of bodily physique and its extension in technology, of buildings and clothes, space and movement.

(Cockburn, 1986: 96)

While these formulations have been useful, in the 1980s the notion of dual identities was challenged further as the significance of race, caste and ethnic differences in structuring the labour force as well as in being a locus of consciousness was highlighted. It is no longer possible to use the category 'woman' without specifying distinctions such as race, caste, ethnicity, and stage in the life cycle. In trying to accommodate these differences, there has been a tendency to stress the primacy of one identity over the other, or simply to add together gender, ethnicity and class as parallel identities based on parallel systems of domination: patriarchy, colonialism, racism and capitalism.

On the basis of research and discussions with women workers, we feel that there are serious limitations in the priority as well as the additive approaches. Further work in the area of consciousness would have to account for the pluralistic expressions of feminism and consciousness on the basis of multiple identities, rather than subsuming them under class or gender.

Feminist theorising on women's employment has to take on the challenge of multiple identities and the deconstruction of the category 'woman', articulated by black and Third World feminists, as well as the analyses presented by the corpus of theory referred to as post-structuralist feminism.[7] In pointing out the limitations of the concepts of 'double and triple jeopardy' (discrimination on the basis of race, sex and class) for assuming that the relationship between various discriminations are merely additive, Deborah King argues not for the simultaneity of several oppressions but for the multiplicative relationships among them, i.e. that these are imbricated into each other in interlocking and mutually determining ways (King, 1988). The capacity of black women to encompass mutually contradictory positions and sets of attitudes also points to multiple and creative ways whereby women have handled these multiple identities.

Post-structuralist feminism has addressed this issue by questioning unitary, universal categories and has attempted to develop a theory of subjectivity. De Lauretis highlights what she calls the 'third moment' in feminist theory as:

1) a reconceptualisation of the subject as shifting and multiply organised across variable axes of difference; 2) a rethinking of the relationship

between forms of oppression and modes of formal understanding – of doing theory; 3) an emerging redefinition of marginality as location, of identity as dis-identification; and 4) the hypothesis of self-displacement as the term of a movement that is concurrently social and subjective, internal and external, indeed political and personal.

(de Lauretis, 1990)

Although there are differences within post-structuralist feminist approaches, the notion of identity as the locus of multiple and variable positions which are historically grounded, the significance of the nexus 'language/subjectivity/consciousness' in the constitution of the subject, and the recognition that the subject is defined not only in relation to the polarities of masculinity and femininity, provide an important corrective to the limitations of theoretical formulations elaborated earlier. This approach also maintains a focus on *agency*, i.e. women and men are seen as active subjects rather than as passive victims, a perspective developed by social historians such as E. P. Thompson as well as A. Giddens.

There remain problems, however, in the formulations of some post-structuralist feminists such as Teresa de Lauretis, in the recourse to psychoanalytic approaches as explanations for the construction of gender identities. The fundamental assumptions of psychoanalytic discourse about the acquisition of gendered subjectivities and sexual difference lie in an almost inevitable model of psycho-sexual development. The difficulty of transforming such a realm, as well as the universalism implicit in such models, leaves such approaches open to well-established criticism.[8]

The post-structuralist feminist perspective, whatever its other shortcomings, does warn against a notion of essential women's consciouness as well as the privileging of a particular definition of consciousness as *the* feminist or non-feminist consciousness. The construction of ideal feminist/ truly feminist concerns and issues projected as universal, without articulation of the location from which such a formulation is made, continues in contemporary women's studies. For instance, a formulation which is widely used in women's studies as well as in policy formulation today is the distinction Maxine Molyneux introduced between practical gender interests and strategic gender interests.[9] This distinction is also based on a certain assumption of what feminist consciousness should be, i.e. that it should be oriented towards action on strategic gender issues. It has been pointed out that it is difficult to make such a distinction in relation to issues (Whitehead, 1990).

A struggle around wages or water taps shifts power relations, and the above-mentioned distinction leaves out the importance of the changes that occur in any context of mobilisation and struggle. Here, the concepts of agency and process are vital: the subject as actor, and the struggle itself, are key components in these changing relations.

The use of 'gender' to refer to what are specifically women's issues (though differentiated by class, etc.) is confusing, since gender refers to men as well. If it is implied that such issues are also in the interests of men (as Molyneux in fact does), then it is necessary to distinguish between short-term and long-term interests. In an immediate sense, many of these issues (most of the ones included in the practical as well as strategic interests categories in Molyneux's article) ensure men's interests and women's demands/organisation to change these will necessarily involve confrontation and conflict. The conflation of gender with women in this case completely negates the basis of women's subordination: a patriarchal system implies that men benefit from the denial of women's interests.

Caroline Moser substitutes 'needs' for 'interests', arguing that this separation is essential because:

> of its focus on the process whereby an interest, defined as a 'prioritized concern' is translated into a need, defined as the 'means by which concerns are satisfied'.
>
> (Moser, 1989: 1819, endnote)

A further distinction is developed by Kate Young (1988) between 'strategic gender interests' and 'practical gender needs'. She points out that the distinction made by Molyneux differentiates theoretically deducible interests from empirically verifiable wants or needs. She, however, finds it more useful to talk of practical needs and strategic gender interests.

The concept of 'interests' is a contested concept, yet in all these formulations the differing basis of the concept of interests and needs in distinct theoretical approaches is not examined. The notion of interests emerged historically and is located in the utilitarian view that society consists of rational, economic men seeking to maximise their satisfactions. Some feminists have rejected the use of interest theory on the grounds that:

> human beings are moved by more than interests. The reduction of all human emotions to interests and interests to the rational search for gain reduces the human community to an instrumental, arbitrary, and deeply unstable alliance, one which rests on the private desires of isolated individuals.
>
> (Irene Diamond and Nancy Hartsock, 'Beyond Interests in Politics . . .', *American Political Science Review* 75(3), 1981: 719, cited in Jónasdóttir, 1988: 45)

They argue for needs as an alternative to 'interests' and 'rights'. Others such as Anna Jónasdóttir feel that a clearer, historically-located notion of interests which emphasises its *form* rather than a particular *content*, could be useful for feminist analysis. The concept of interests has consisted of two aspects: the form aspect which is the 'demand to be among' (from the Latin base), which implies the demand for participation in and control over society's public affairs; and the content aspect which concerns the substantive values put into effect and distributed in relation to groups, needs, wishes and demands. In this sense then, the notion of 'interests' only emerges in a context where there is not acceptance of authority as immutable, divinely ordained or natural.

If the focus is on the formal aspect of interests, the content aspect is kept open. Interests then could be seen as extending the conditions of choice without presuming the content of the choices offered. Jónasdóttir points out that discussions of content are better expressed by needs and desires. However, she sees the use of 'needs' in political analysis as based on a view from above, i.e. it is the perspective of socially-engaged experts, of administrators, who design policies for weak groups who have their needs met without 'first having to overcome their weakness and fight for their own positions of influence' (Jónasdóttir, 1985: 48).[10]

Three crucial questions arise in discussing the application of the concept of 'interests' to women. Can one ascribe to women objective interests, irrespective of their subjective consciousness? Do all women have common interests, given class and other forms of differentiation? Do women and men have different interests? Jónasdóttir puts forward the proposition that given the pervasive mobilisation of women in history and society against their oppression, it is possible to ascribe to them objective interests. In spite of differences between women, there is agreement on a 'minimal common denominator' that all women share: an interest in not 'allowing themselves to be oppressed as women, or, in fighting patriarchy' (1988: 38). She argues that women and men do have different interests, due not to essentialist/biological differences, but to the sexual division of labour which allocates different and hierarchical positions to them.

We feel that such a notion of women's interests, which is both theoretically deduced as well as historically located, can be useful in examining women workers' actions and strategies for organising. The focus on the *form* aspect of 'interests' does not impose any specific content on what ought to be feminist interests, which is a problem in Molyneux's formulation of strategic gender interests. Women's interests would therefore imply extending the conditions for choices to be made about the sexual division of labour etc., without presuming what these choices have to be to qualify for inclusion into a 'feminist' agenda.

We outline a series of propositions which form a grid, or a shifting of lenses through which we examine and develop a further understanding of women's work and consciousness, and strategies for organising.

1. The contradictory and historically specific impact of patriarchy, colonialism and capitalism has resulted in a fragmentation and wide diversity of women's experiences. Both men and women workers possess multiple identities. Identities refer to subject positions which are made available and mobilised in specific historical contexts.[11]

2. Identities are selectively mobilised in response to economic, social, political and cultural processes. Identities therefore may be constantly shifting, not only historically, but also at a given point in time.

3. Identities involve the interplay of objective and subjective factors; class, gender, caste, race, ethnicity and age, for example, therefore have both a material and ideological existence.[12]

4. Consciousness cannot be read off from objective positions. The expressions of adaptation and resistance, overt and covert, are the result of complex processes (hidden and public scripts), which are constantly constructing the subjectivity of actors in multiple subject positions.

5. Women's interests are represented and reflected at all empirical and theoretical levels. Given the very nature of multiple identities, interests vary with the nature of the broader persona, or grouping, seeking change. Women's interests in this context represent the expansion of women's conditions of choice. The conditions of choice will change, as the process of asserting interests changes the subjects and the arena within which the protagonists contend.

6. The separation of private and public, of factory and home, of personal and political creates misleading dichotomies.

7. The double burden of women's work is not necessarily an impediment to organising; it can also be an impetus.

THE MESSY REALITY OF MULTIPLE IDENTITIES

In this section we present certain issues highlighted by electronic and electrical equipment factory workers in Nigeria and India. There are significant differences between the two countries – nature of the state, patterns of industrialisation, state ideology as well as gender ideology. However, without attempting to build a comparative framework, we felt that there were many similarities in the experiences and perceptions of life, work, as well as gender relations, of these women which provided a basis to raise more general questions about the relation between identity, consciousness and strategies for organising.

The Research Setting

The oil boom in the 1970s produced a number of initiatives on the part of the Nigerian government to encourage industrialisation in order to generate employment, strengthen the manufacturing infrastructure, and provide new investment opportunities. Multinational investments in Nigeria increased significantly at this time, as Nigeria offered the possibility of high profits, a possibility which was to be severely reduced with the oil glut. It was at this time of high hope and flowing oil that EMCON, the company under consideration here, was created.

EMCON, the Electricity Meter Company (Nigeria) Ltd, was established in northern Nigeria, in the city of Zaria in Kaduna State, to supply electric meters and circuit breakers for the expanding electrification programme of NEPA, the Nigerian Electric Power Authority. In 1976, a contract was signed between the Federal Government and the Swiss-based technical partners, Landis and Gyr, for the creation of EMCON, to be owned primarily by the Federal Government (60 per cent), and NEPA (20 per cent). In line with the increased manufacturing capability desired by the Federal Government, EMCON was intended to produce as well as assemble the electric meters and circuit breakers required.

Full production was begun only in 1982, at a time when the growing economic crisis in Nigeria was severely affecting most industrial production. By the end of 1983, many Nigerian companies had closed, or retrenched most of their workers. EMCON remained open, though few assembly-line workers were permitted to work throughout the year, or received their full wages. Periods of compulsory leave followed, and it is an indication of the parlous state of the Nigerian economy that few EMCON employees found work elsewhere. The company returned to full staffing at the end of 1984. This was maintained through mid-1985, the final date of the present study. EMCON later went through a dormant period of several years, re-starting full production in July, 1990.

Differing expectations and effects of capital and the state in Nigeria are reflected in the EMCON situation in terms of hiring practices and changing perceptions in relation to gender. EMCON began operations at a time when other Nigerian companies were systematically reducing their numbers of permanent women staff, replacing them with men. In Nigeria, few categories of work are seen as only 'women's work', and occupations previously available to women, such as secretarial work or nursing, become increasingly masculinised. The reduction of women's formal waged labour in Nigeria included considerations such as the constraints of protective legislation, the costs to capital of maternity and child-care benefits, and management perceptions of conflicts between domestic labour and waged labour responsibilities. EMCON, however, hired against this tide, employing so many women – more than a third of the 300-strong EMCON labour force – that it became the largest employer of women in Zaria.

In India the electronics industry has been state-supported with the government involved directly as a manufacturer, especially of high investment electronic items, and indirectly through support policies for private sector production. Since the 1970s the electronics industry in India has gone in for sub-contracting to small-scale industry, particularly in the area of consumer electronics. Domestic sub-contracting in the industry by large firms extends even to final assembly operations, with the company concentrating only on quality control, testing and marketing (Annavajhula, 1988). Corporate decisions favouring sub-contracting have been based on the over-investment and under-utilisation of earlier in-house capabilities which were highlighted in the slump in the mid-1970s, and to avoid worker militancy. For example, Philips, a multiplant multinational, has stepped up sub-contracting along with modernisation and automation programmes due to workers organising against productivity loads. Even a public sector unit like Keltron has sub-contracted production to women's co-operatives and welfare societies.[13] In 1982, colour transmission was introduced and an industrial and licensing policy for indigenous production of colour TV sets was formulated. Along with indigenous production of colour TV, however, international sub-contracting was also allowed to a certain extent. This took two forms – the provision of free trade zone facilities to local firms undertaking sub-contracting on behalf of foreign firms for re-export after processing, as well as sub-contracting by local firms, from Japanese companies in particular, for the domestic market.

Monica Electronics started the production of colour television sets in 1984 in collaboration with the Japanese company JVC. Initially the company imported kits and carried out screwdriver assembly, but now was using some indigenous components which were manufactured in other units. The company has had a phenomenal growth in sales turnover moving from $0.69 million in 1982–3 to $34.0 million in 1986–7. At an all-India level, 'Onida' (brand name) colour TVs ranked highest in sales and in ratings of reliability. The most important factor pointed out by management were the strong Quality Control Systems and regular training of technical personnel by the Japanese in the latest production techniques. Regular visits were also made by the Japanese and training workshops conducted by them on labour management relations.

Management strategies were akin to the post-Fordist shift to flexibility. Initially, the workforce was 80 per cent men, but by 1987, 70 per cent of the workforce were women. Confirming the general trend in Indian industry of a preference for male labour on the part of employers, the company first hired men (Banerjee, 1991: 310). Due to 'union trouble', they soon shifted to young unmarried women. However, when many got married and left at almost the same time, the company recruited married women. The personnel manager said that they found that a balance of married and unmarried women works out better. The advantages of a mixed workforce were also extended to recruitment of workers from Delhi and migrants from the southern state of Kerala. Out of a total workforce of 250 production workers, 179 were women, of whom 100 were from Allepy district in Kerala. Most of the women and men were between the ages of 20–29 and had finished secondary school. In the sample there were some women who were graduates, or were studying for their first degree through correspondence, while two men had done a short industrial technical course.

Shifting and Contradictory Discourses: The Construction of Masculinity and Femininity in the Workplace

The production process at Monica Electronics was divided into eight sections: Insertion, Auto-soldering, Touch-up, EHT fixing, Sub-assembly wire cutting, Pre-testing, Final testing, Servicing. In the Insertion section only women worked and in the Servicing section only men worked. Apart from the Auto-soldering section where again men did the soldering and women carried out visual checks, in the other sections both men and women worked on the same process. Management, women workers and men workers deployed contradictory and different discourses in relation to the sexual division of labour.

Women workers saw themselves as capable of doing any job on the production line, based also on the fact that they often substituted for men in situations of male absenteeism, during peak production periods, or for rush orders.

There is no difference between boys' and girls' work . . . although it is true that girls are more soft hearted (weak) however it is not true that girls work less. All are equal. How can there be a difference when we know that we can stand in for them? We can do their work equally well.

(Geeta, female)

Differences in individual capacity were stressed far more than gender differences in relation to the kind of work. However, differences in methods and attitudes towards work were seen as due to gender.

> Girls work better. They work consistently for one to one-and-a-half hours without moving on one job. Boys also work hard but they keep getting up, going for a cigarette . . . what can I say. That is why there are fewer boys now.

(Sarla, female)

Male discourses on work also acknowledged the similarity of tasks and, given the shared experience of working on the same jobs, there was acknowledgement that if women were trained they could handle most machines. However, a link was constantly re-established between heavy machines and masculine physical strength. Qualities of 'speed, dexterity and lightness', the hallmark of managerial constructions of essentially female qualities, were projected as essentially *masculine* attributes. *Feminine* qualities were located in fear, delicacy and sensitivity which impinged negatively on their capacity to work. Recognition of women workers' skill and competence at work was combined with a mixture of derogatory and paternalistic judgements on their naivety and vulnerability as women.

> Both girls and boys do the same work. Girls also do heavy work but there are differences. Men work on other machines – girls cannot work on them because it is too difficult. Girls would need to have speed, lightness, dexterity to do that. If girls are trained perhaps they could also work. They do work on similar machines but those are the Japanese type.

(Akhram, male)

> Girls get scared, they don't say anything. They are hardworking but so are men who have responsibilities. Those who do not have responsibilities tend to play the fool. Girls cannot do soldering because one needs to be quick with the machines and they can't bear the heat.

(Ram Naresh, male)

Managerial discourses, however, emphasised that these very same 'feminine qualities', i.e. dexterity, delicacy, 'the training by parents which made girls more responsible and diligent in their work', sincerity and docility, made women better workers than men. Women workers were seen as able to do the same jobs as men, and in fact better than men. Managerial ideals of a women-only workforce however had to be jettisoned due to the restrictions of protective legislation (ban on night work for women), given the frequency of overtime and rush production schedules.

> The fact that we have only girls as relief workers shows that the work in all sections can be done by anyone. We have learnt through past experience that girls are more sincere. They are easy to convince. They devote themselves to the work, since they are taught traditionally by parents to be more responsible – such training is useful for this kind of work.
>
> (Sushil Kumar, Personnel Manager, male)

The conflicting constructions of masculinity and femininity in these discourses have to be seen in the context of a three-way power struggle as management substituted women in place of men, and used this as a threat to discipline the men who were still employed. Tension between women and men workers was expressed in the shifting meanings of masculinity and femininity, where men tried to carve out and preserve an 'essentially' masculine 'heavy machine' area of work, while at the same time appropriating women's qualities for themselves.

Conflict between supervisors and production-line workers became simultaneously a gender struggle, since most of the supervisors (called group leaders) were women. Men found it difficult to accept women in supervisory positions.

> I want to leave this company because they do not give work according to capacity. I was shifted because I told the group leader I would slap her. I didn't abuse her or anything. She was hassling me about the target and I told her what's your problem – I'll do it in my own time. She started screaming at me so I told her I'll slap her – then they shifted me from that section.
>
> (Ram Naresh, male)

Managerial deployment of a discourse on the more productive capacities of women workers created a constant feeling among men that they could lose their jobs – one signifier of their masculinity. They identified negative feminine attributes in women workers which were presented as reasons for the incapacity of women to do certain jobs. In addition, men workers emphasised that the same feminine qualities were reasons for the lack of a joint alliance as workers against the management. Women workers were thereby represented by men as doubly incompetent – at their work as well as in unionisation and organising against management. In response to company policy and men workers' resentment, women began to flaunt their qualities of patience and diligence at work, reconstructing broader social models of femininity in the workplace.

In spite of the 'pro-women' slant in managerial discourses, skill distinctions and payment of bonuses created a hierarchy whereby men workers got a higher consolidated wage.[14] Although women did exactly the same kind of work as men, women were called production assistants, while men were called production technicians.[15] There was also a difference in the payment of bonus, with men getting 40 per cent and women getting 20 per cent of the turnover. No one – management, women or men workers – would give a reason for these differences. The arbitrariness of the gendered definition of the division of labour and differential remuneration reflected the continuing three-pronged power struggle between management, women and men workers.

The shifts in managerial discourses, in a context where an opposite process occurred i.e. women were substituted by men, and the changing discourses of women workers are evident in EMCON as well. In its hiring, EMCON acted on the basis of its world-wide production network and methods, seeking an amenable, inexpensive and replaceable labour force. Particular assembly-line tasks – the assembly of meters and circuit breakers, meter check and calibration – were to be primarily the work of dexterous women, with the well-known stereotypes indicated even in a local press release:

> the calibrating is being done by female employees. The meter demands the care of the feminine touch due to its sensitivity to accuracy and women are known for carefulness, the world over.
>
> (R. Anyamikegh, *New Nigerian*, 1 Sept. 1982)

The labour force was not, however, either inexpensive or replaceable. Women workers were not cheaper than male workers, where both were carrying out the same tasks, and had the same job description.[16] Neither women nor men were easily fired. Labour legislation provides a number of safeguards for workers, and the one area in which the (correctly) much maligned union *did* take some responsibility was in relation to the threat of unfair dismissal.

Over the course of the first few months, management found that the women workers were not the docile group they had expected, and that relations between intermediate staff and assembly-line workers were fraught. A number of the women workers felt that they were being discriminated against by their superiors and treated with discourtesy. They continued their work, but without enthusiasm or interest. At this point, management shifted discourses, abandoning their traditional stereotypes which favoured the recruitment of women. Now men were 'more obedient than women'; 'women workers in calibration were no more effective than men'; 'men weren't "proud" like women'; 'women weren't responsive to the problems of the company'(!). The company embarked upon a policy of hiring men rather than women: for some months, an unofficial ban was placed on the employment of additional women.

Women workers, however, continued to maintain the importance of women's special qualities – 'patience and carefulness' as essential and irreplaceable by men in the production process:

> It is only women that can do calibrating. The company knows the work of the women, and they won't employ men.

> Men are not patient enough to do calibration; they would overadjust the machines. This work must remain for women, who are more careful.

But section by section, men workers were brought into the formerly predominantly women-staffed sections.

Management discourses and strategies at both EMCON and Monica Electronics point to the arbitrary nature of the gender-linked stereotypes, and the ease with which employers shift emphasis on gendered requirements to maintain flexibility of hiring, as interests and production priorities, and labour relations change. Both women and men workers were also involved in changing and arbitrary definition of women's work and men's work.

Both case studies show that there is no unilinear trend towards masculinisation or feminisation of the workforce in these companies, and that shifts in discourses and recruitment practices are due more to labour control and disciplining the workforce rather than simply as a result of technological changes.[17] Whether the direction was towards substituting women for men or vice versa, managerial, women's and men's discourses constructed masculinity and femininity at the workplace as essentially different, though the content of these gender categories was fluid and shifting.

Agency and Illusion: Contradictory Consciousness

The treatment of factory work as temporary for women workers has been a feature in many studies of women workers in very different cultural settings. A. Pollert sees the temporary nature of factory work for women as reflecting 'shared female identity along a continuum of different stages in a woman's life cycle' (1981, p. 106). The socialisation of women into seeing marriage as their main aim in life is given as one of, when not the main, reasons that women lack a commitment to work, and therefore do not get involved with workplace organising. However, if we examine further the assumption of women's factory work as a temporary phenomenon, a number of questions arise, which must be addressed. For example:

1. Does the reality fit the assumption: Do women work only temporarily?
2. If no. 1 is true, *do* women leave work for marriage?
3. Is the notion of expecting to work temporarily specific to women workers?

In the Indian case study, almost every unmarried woman worker saw her job as temporary, as a means of 'passing time' until she married. In discussion with women garment workers in 1982, women focused on marriage as an exit from factory work, *even though many of these workers had been working for over six years.* Many of these women were earning money for their dowries, seeing a good dowry as a passport to marriage in a higher economic group. Coming from sections of a disintegrating middle class, they maintained the illusion of escape even though they knew that the rising cost of living meant that it was necessary to have two earners at least, even to maintain middle-class status. The story of Shanti brings out the operation of this illusion:

Shanti had been working in WINGS, a garment company which dismissed women when they married. She had been working for over seven years, 'passing time and earning for her dowry'. Her earnings, however, were being used not for dowry but rather for supporting the whole family, and she spoke with pride about the way in which she had paid for her brother's education and got her younger sister married. There was no way she could leave her job with so many family members dependent on her. Entering her thirties, Shanti had little chance of getting married, and even less chance of moving up the economic ladder to become a dependent housewife, for her 'dowry collection' had in fact disappeared in supporting her family. Yet she believed that the work she was doing was temporary.

In many cases this cycle has resulted in the emergence of the permanent single woman worker. In 1987, the women in the electronic factory also shared the same illusion, but there was a different attitude. They were also passing time, but were more conscious of reducing the burden at home and being 'useful'. But even older married women workers saw their work as temporary. They too dreamt of a time when it would not be economically necessary for them to work outside.

> Women should not have to work after marriage. There is so much work anyway and we can barely handle that. Cannot add more work. However if the economic situation is bad then of course women have to do it.
>
> (Geeta, female)

> Women work outside because they have to. If there was comfort at home then of course it is OK for women to go out and work. Men should also help – after all when both husband and wife are working outside, men should also help at home. That way housework would finish faster and that would benefit both.
>
> (Ramani, female)

In reality, factory work was not a temporary phase; marriage was not an inevitable part of a woman's life cycle; and even when marriage took place, it did not preclude the continuation of factory work. In computer terms, marriage and associated domesticity are 'the default setting', the norm, the ever-present point at which one arrives, or to which one returns, although other possibilities may (temporarily) intervene.

Monica Electronics women workers display contradictory consciousness, reflecting multiple identities, and multiple scenarios both actual and desired. Their own words reflect both acceptance of economic and social realities, the wish that that reality were different; and preferred alternatives. (In this context, one must note also, in the example of Ramani above, yet another permutation: that married women may *want* to work, even if they *need* not; and that, in that best of all possible worlds, the sexual division of labour should be more equitable.)

The women work and continue to work. They are agents, making choices which are in part compelled, supporting themselves and their kin (and taking pride in that support), yet keeping alive alternative not-yet-and-perhaps-never-to-be-realised realities. This may be seen as agency: taking on, though not fully accepting, the non-preferred alternative, the remaining, the only 'choice', taken from the stock of one available.

However, the Monica Electronics example, and the perception of women's factory work as temporary and ended with marriage, cannot be generalised for Indian women, much less more broadly. In India, amongst traditional working-class communities such as the Ahmedabad textile workers, who were also *dalits*, no workers said they were 'passing time'. Indeed, older women textile workers were only concerned that when they left work, their daughters should get jobs in the mills, since the mill management had stopped hiring women for factory work (Chhachhi, 1983).

EMCON women were very young when hired, most being recent secondary school graduates. In a 1982–3 survey of 95 EMCON women workers (more than 80 per cent of the female staff at that time), 57 women, three-fifths of the women surveyed, were 20 years of age or younger. More than four-fifths (76 women) were no more than 22 years old; the youngest were 17. Eighty of the women surveyed at that time were unmarried.

Most of the EMCON women had sought factory work en route to their next goal. But that goal is not marriage, but rather higher education. For some of the women, the reaching of that goal might be years away, if attainable at all. But women assembly-line workers saw themselves, ideally, as educated women with additional academic or vocational training in their future, and an excellent job as the endpoint. And indeed, EMCON assembly-line women are well-educated by Nigerian standards.[18]

Women worked to further their education, insofar as they could. Poor results could be overcome through application and good networking, and a prime reason for single women to take time off was for interviews, admissions tests, and repeat school certificate examinations. During the 1982–3 period, 20 EMCON women workers resigned; 13 of these women had gained admission for further education, and hopefully, ultimately a better occupation. Other women continue to apply for interviews, for tests, and for work outside the assembly-line. However, in present Nigerian economic realities, the latter is difficult to find, nor are school places easily available. Alternatively, some women worked towards opening a shop, or saving enough money to begin another venture.

For Nigerian women, marriage is not an alternative to earning an income.[19] Marriage does not end women's waged labour, and indeed, marriage and child-bearing virtually *require* women's earnings. Assisting kin, particularly junior siblings before marriage, Nigerian women partially or fully support their children, themselves and their kin, as possible, with marriage. Waged labour and domestic labour are not an either/or proposition, but rather are equally women's responsibilities. The colonial and neo-colonial ideology of housewifisation and domesticity has had relatively little purchase, fitting neither traditional nor contemporary marital and kin expectations and obligations, and manifestly impossible in the present period of economic crisis.

In Nigeria, where the optimum number of children favoured by women and men ranges between six and eight, additional economic support is not a luxury, but a necessity. By the middle of 1983, 13 of the 80 single women had married; nine were pregnant or had already delivered. Only one woman (who married the EMCON accountant) resigned her post on marriage. Marriage not only would not distract Nigerian women from waged labour; it could well concentrate their interests and organising efforts, if this would assist them in gaining additional economic benefit.

The idea of work as temporary varies along sections of the working class itself, as has been well demonstrated also in advanced capitalist countries, where many women cannot afford *not* to work. Women do continue to work, and we find further that the proposition that a woman's identity, given its social construction, necessarily orients her towards a narrow familial orientation, and away from workplace organising, cannot be sustained as a general theoretical argument. We take up this issue further below.

With regard to our third question, whether the expectation of temporary work is specific to women, we find that this is not the case. Men may also see their work in the factory as temporary, a means to another end.

In the interviews with male workers in Monica Electronics, one of them used the same term of 'passing time'; others hoped to earn enough money to return to Kerala either to own and ply an auto-rickshaw or set up an independent business, while others hoped to get further technical training and set up their own unit, manufacturing components or undertaking assembly work. At EMCON in Nigeria, men had more opportunities for advancement than women, and some men intended to stay with the company, working their way up the seniority ladder. But a number of men sought to improve their education and left EMCON when they gained admission for further studies, or planned to leave if they gained admission. Thus, some men too saw their work in the factory as temporary, a (paid) step in time, as they sought to make for themselves a better future.

Multiple Identities: Differences and Alliances

We have noted that identities are selectively mobilised, with different emphases and foci in different contexts. In this section, we address issues of identity important nationally in Nigeria and India; and consider whether these or other distinctions are relevant and to the forefront in the industrial context. We examine those identities which are actively brought into play in the factory, how this activation of particular identities may facilitate the creation of alliances, result in the dissolution of prior solidarity, or render such solidarity unlikely or impossible. In this context, gender is taken as one marker of identity (among others), selectively prioritised.

Women and men at EMCON act, are perceived, and see themselves on a variety of bases. Among the significant features which identify men and women in Nigeria are religion, ethnicity, gender, place of origin, education, marital status, and of course positioning in the labour process, the final three being particularly important in relation to women at EMCON.

Religion is a profoundly important issue in Nigeria today, with the division between Christians and Muslims having become a focus of riots, pogroms, and forms and sites of control over women not hitherto seen. On the other hand, it is less directly relevant at EMCON; almost none of the women, and few of the men, are Muslim. Christianity plays an important part in EMCON women workers' lives: bible classes, fellowship meetings, church organising and of course Sunday services are foci of women's non-working hours. None of these activities are carried out in the company, nor do the workers belong to the same sects.

The fact that the vast majority of the workers are Christian points up another feature of the EMCON community: most of the workers are labour migrants, representing several major areas of Nigeria. Among the women surveyed, more than a third were from the southern part of Kaduna State. Almost a quarter of the women were Igbo, from the east, while the third largest grouping were the Yoruba women from western Nigeria: few EMCON employees are indigenes of Zaria, or of the Muslim Hausa community which forms the vast majority of the local population. The widely diverging origin of EMCON women is mirrored in local residence: the workers are scattered through the city. Friendships, shared activities and alliances, certainly among women, tend to be contracted outside the company, rather than within it. Ethnicity and region did not form focal points for organising in the factory: the very multiplicity of areas and ethnic groups represented, and the split of workers into different parts of the production process, were not conducive to division, or organisation, along these lines.[20]

Marriage is a major dividing and uniting factor among EMCON women. Unmarried women are treated as girls, inexperienced and immature. Discussion of possible women's organisations often brought up the issue of the differences between married and single women. This was raised also in operationalised organising strategies: the union was ineffective in pursuing 'women's interests', but the issues involved – breast-feeding, maternity benefits, shiftwork[21] – affect directly married rather than single women. Gender did not create automatic affinity or shared action on these issues among women. Some married women saw the issues as 'personal'; others felt that married women must organise to fight for their rights. On the other hand, as women remained with the company, and the numbers of married women increased, this group would become larger and stronger, and could organise more effectively, possibly carrying the single women, who look to the married women as their seniors, with them.

We have noted that identities are available subject positions, selectively activated and mobilised. Yet that activation can be external also, as workers are forced into categorisations and identities which they reject. Thus, for example, images and stereotypes of the assembly-line worker ('rough', 'uncouth') were called up by women administrative staff (clerks, secretaries etc.) to distinguish and distance themselves from assembly-line workers. The distinction reflected hierarchy and privilege, objectively demonstrated in labour practice: different working hours and relations to management; more flexibility for administrative staff; different workplace dress. Assembly-line workers were even refused admittance to the administrative toilet facilities.

In the industrial setting, divisions were created which had hitherto not been experienced by the assembly-line women, in terms of inferior positioning reinforced by associated action. This was an issue which produced anger and bitterness among the assembly-line women. The EMCON assembly-line women workers were incensed at these derogatory images, particularly given their good education, generally better than that of the white-collar women who looked down on them. The distinction was particularly galling to the assembly-line women, for they aspired to become white-collar workers, yet knew both that EMCON labour policy precluded the move from assembly-line to administration, but that, nevertheless, their qualifications were as good as those of the administration workers. The two groups projected *the same identity*, that of the educated and socially-adept woman, in a bid to improve (or maintain) their situation and conditions. The assembly-line women and administrative staff did make periodic attempts to move beyond the unwelcome images and actions, generally through the mobilising of personal ties reflecting other identities (regional links, school networking, ethnicity etc.), extended to the broader group of workers.

The main division between the women at Monica Electronics was between the rural migrants from Kerala, and women from Delhi and other parts of North India. Keralite women complained that they were called 'madrasis' – a term used by many North Indians for anyone from Southern India which has a derogatory connotation. They found the North-Indian, and particularly Punjabi women, racist in their attitudes. They did not make friends with them, or meet them outside the factory.

However, there were close ties between the Keralite women themselves, since many of them were related or close friends and neighbours before they came to Delhi. The other women workers did not meet each other outside, living in scattered parts of the city. Some of the women came from relatively better off middle-class families (their fathers were middle-level civil servants) and were ashamed of working on the production line. Having a job at an Onida factory sounded glamorous, and that was all they said about their work to relatives and friends at home.

Regional and class differences came out more sharply in the discussions than differences based on religion or caste. Though there were a number of Christians and a few Muslims in the total workforce, the majority were Hindu.

In both studies, association created in the workplace was not carried outside, nor were other organisations or networks formed outside the workplace; support groups were not shared, and even issues such as maternity benefits were differently perceived and responded to. Vertical company lines of communication, sectional rivalries and gender conflicts exacerbated differences in the company context, and rendered horizontal linkages more difficult, although not impossible. Gender did not create an automatic basis for affinity, although such affinity could be built up over time.

Women's Interests/Men's Interests: Different Demands

Women workers at Monica Electronics had not organised actively around the issue of wages, although they had supported the initiative by men workers to demand a higher bonus. However, they *had* initiated and organised to demand transport and uniforms which had been granted by management. Both these demands related to specific problems they had experienced as women. Transport was essential to avoid the sexual harassment women faced in public transport buses, particularly late evenings when they worked overtime. A company bus which picked up and dropped off the women also allayed the fears of parents, particularly of unmarried women. Since overtime meant double pay, the demand also related to wages and wage differentials in an indirect way.

The demand for uniforms was explained by Sarla:

> Due to the fact that women in the factory come from different economic backgrounds and many cannot afford to wear a different dress during the week, we thought it would be nice to solve the hassle of what to wear everyday if we had uniforms. This also meant that now girls do not envy each other or pass nasty remarks and compare clothes.

Male workers interpreted these demands in a very different way:

> Girls do not know how to raise demands. They fall into the trap laid by management. They ask for general facilities while the real issue is wages.
>
> (Madhusudan M. R.)

This company tends to favour the women. Why? Because they keep quiet and accept everything. Onida has a big name, now the girls have a bus, uniforms so they are just happy with that. They don't ask for wages.

(Naresh)

They had been indifferent to the women's initiative, though some had supported them half-heartedly. Men wanted to form a militant union which would take up the issue of wages. They had raised the demand for bonus, which after a long period of negotiation, management granted, with a different rate for men and women – 20 per cent for women and 40 per cent for men.

EMCON women raised specific demands, although some of those demands (breast-feeding, maternity leave etc.) were not necessarily seen by the women themselves as relevant to all of them, or as demands to be taken up by all of them, given the distinction made by the women themselves between the married and unmarried women workers. Thus, these demands were not equally strongly pursued by women, and were certainly not followed through by the union.

Another demand made by the women reflected the strongly gender-linked differential treatment in the factory, and was relevant to many of the female production-line staff. These demands centred around issues of dignity, respect and shared humanity.[22] The women reported that men (some of the foremen, and others in authority) would shout at the women workers. They would clock women's toilet breaks, but not those of men, and in general they did not accord to women the same respect they gave to men. Women raised these issues with the union representatives. So strongly did the women feel these insults, and so strongly did they express them, that the former union president had been told, among other things, that the women 'felt they were being treated like animals'. These issues, however, were not taken up by the union.

Some issues affected and were relevant and of value to all workers. Thus, for example, union support and attention to issues of unfair dismissal benefited men and women, and were recognised as useful by all.

Other demands have been of interest only to men workers, but these demands have also been put forward as general demands. And where the EMCON men were particularly keen on a particular benefit, they applied themselves wholeheartedly. Thus, the union managed to obtain motorcycle loans, which they treated as a benefit available to *all* EMCON staff. However, given that Nigerian women do not generally drive motorcycles, this particular 'unisex' benefit was not relevant to them. The motorcycle loan was taken up by one hundred men – and two women.

Women's demands were different from men's demands in both case studies, reflected in the different forms and content of demands. Women's demands for improvement in general facilities linked together their identities as women and workers, in addition to being a disguised/indirect demand for an improvement of wages and working conditions. The derogation of women workers as women reinforced simultaneously the dominance of capital and patriarchy within the workplace.[23] Issues treated as general workers' interests tended to benefit men primarily (bonus and motorcycle loans). Women's interests were expressed in initiatives by women to raise specific demands and act together, though demands which were specific to a category of women (maternity benefit and breast-feeding) were not followed through. Monica Electronics women workers had gained tremendous self-confidence in relation to management and men workers through the process of independent mobilisation and action in pursuit of their interests.

Apathy, Indifference, Irrelevance or Covert Critique? Unions and other Organising Strategies

Monica Electronics has an organisation called the *sansad*, which handles grievances, and management called this a union. Members are partly appointed and partly elected. There was an attempt to form a union from outside, but this was scuttled by the management. The personnel manager, after giving a variety of inconsistent and contradictory reasons why women were being hired in preference to men, finally let on that the substitution of men workers by women two years earlier was due to the attempt to unionise.

The majority of women were against the formation of a union.

> If a union comes there will be fights, strikes, lock outs – too many problems. If a union is inside then it is OK and can help us but an outside union will lead to too many fights.
>
> (Ramani, female)

The *sansad* had responded to their demands for transport and uniforms. A crèche was not an issue because the married women had grown-up children, and there wasn't a wage differential in basic pay between men and women within each section.

The rejection of unions was not in itself a rejection of a worker's organisation. The distinction many women made between an inside union and an outside union was a reference to the fact that outside unions were affiliated to political parties, and inter-union rivalry had led to violence in many industrial sectors. A desire for an independent organisation which truly represented their interests was the underlying theme in discussions around unions.

Women also belonged to other organisations which expressed their regional/ethnic or religious identities. These organisations, like the Malayalee Association to which all the women from Kerala belonged, also functioned as support networks finding jobs, arranging housing etc. There was an enthusiastic response from all the women when a women's organisation was mentioned, and a number of them took the address of a local women's resource centre. Rather than apathy or indifference, women workers were not reluctant or hostile to the idea of organising. Their reactions to unions were far more a covert critique of unions as they were presently structured. Alternative organisations which reflected other identities were seen in a positive light.

Organising around women's issues was problematic at EMCON. Women did not necessarily ally with each other, given the different identities and interests evoked. The union was weak, suspect in relation to the administration, relatively unconcerned with women's issues, and active only in support of demands which were of interest to the male membership, which then might (e.g. dismissal, wages) or might not (e.g. motorcycle loans) be relevant to women workers.

Lack of promotion of women in some sectors was accompanied by (limited) promotions in others, and the waging of internecine battles (see Pittin, 1984), although it was the case that women generally were demonstrably being passed over for promotion and training. In this case (but not in others), the union insisted that 'promotion and training are not the union's business'. But union weakness meant that many issues, not only women's issues, were untouched. Women's dissatisfaction, associated with frustrated career opportunities and differential treatment, became more evident in individual reaction than in organised response, although there had been attempts to involve the union. Complaints had been brought to the union, but the union did not take up these complaints.

However, asked whether there were any kinds of organisations for women which they would like to see at EMCON, the women responded with a variety of suggestions, from what was virtually a women's caucus: 'We should talk about how the company is cheating us: we don't get enough time for maternity leave; we don't get our end-of-year bonus; and there are a lot of other things wrong too' to sports groups (a very popular idea), to groups which include married and single women, with the married women acting as advisers and mentors to the single women 'so that we can learn how to behave, and how to look after children'. The sting in the tail of this particular suggestion, echoed by others, is that complaints could also be aired in this group which could then act on them. Thus, the group would take on for women, among other responsibilities, the undone work of the ineffective union executive. The need to organise was reflected in women's expressed interests within the workplace, and demonstrated in their activities within the community.

On the basis of the studies in Nigeria and India, we discuss below the issues which arise in relation to our propositions.

MULTIPLE IDENTITIES, MULTIPLE SITES OF STRUGGLE

Women, with their multiple positionings in the family, the home, the workplace and the community, respond to the sometimes reinforcing, sometimes contradictory pressures arising from these contexts. These disparate positions are reflected in the nature, forms and categories of organising and struggle in which they engage, in the extensiveness and necessarily comprehensive nature of the terrain which they contest, and in the alliances which they create. The wide-ranging issues, foci, and organisations associated with the women's movement, for example, give a very partial picture of women's mobilising and organising, or of the extent of women's struggles, or of the breadth of the areas in which women act. Many of the struggles are carried out in the context of, or in alliance with, other groups with related interests and demands.

The very process of conscientising, mobilising, and organising inherent in struggle undermines the power and intended certainties of dominant discourse, and, as significantly, creates new perspectives for those engaged in confrontation. Thus, the mobilisation itself and the creation of coalitions, and the character of the organisations or categories involved, may act to modify or to transform the very sites, forms and direction of struggle, with structural, organisational, and individual effects.

While much organising is carried out independent of the state, the mobilising, organising and positioning undertaken is eminently 'political', in terms of the political dimension being represented in all social practice (Laclau, 1985: 29); and in terms of the agendas and priorities regarding recognised and contested relations of power symbolised and/or privately discussed in homes and in gatherings among disaffected others,[24] now gaining voice and impetus in fora of action and/or confrontation. Equally, it is political in terms of feminist theory linked to strategy, which recognises and forefronts the pervasiveness of hegemonic patriarchal ideology and practice, historically and specifically constructed. Within this ideology and practice, unequal gender-based power relations are the norm. Action which addresses these and associated structures and relations of inequality, and differential access to resources, reflects, where it does not directly confront, the structure and fabric of relations of power in society.

The varied nature of political cultures and pocesses, the development of a culture of civil society, and the nature of the relation between the state and civil society, necessarily affect the possibilities and forms of response to specific issues (Young, 1988). The contexts in which categories of women act, the bases on which they act, the issues which they address, the alliances and linkages which they create, and the contradictions and conflicts which arise, cannot be generalised. Differences among women may militate against, but do not preclude, general unity.[25] Alliances may be created on the basis of affinity (Haraway, 1991; Young, 1988). Affinity provides the scope for multiple and temporary alliances,[26] and for organising on numerous fronts.[27]

The possibilities of women organising are predicated on the availability and interaction of time, space and place. Time signifies not only time available to meet and organise, but also time *lacking*, the *constraints* of time, due to multiple obligations, which may prevent women from even beginning to organise or participate in struggle, or which may galvanise women into necessarily actively engaging in struggle, in a bid to reduce the pressures of those conflicting obligations. Place is intended here as primarily locational (the site of work, and/or struggle), while space has a broader meaning, indicating the psychological and strategic creation of, or perceived need for, room to manoeuvre, to negotiate, and to challenge existing structures and controls.

Confronting Capital and the State

The constraints imposed by the double burden of domestic labour and waged labour – or, in some countries, the 'triple shift' of domestic labour, waged labour, and party political activity – have had a profound impact on women organising. But with regard to this double burden, triple shift and multiple obligations of women, we have demonstrated above, and we would posit that *the very multiplicity of roles and plethora of pressures may provide both the impetus and the necessary networking and organisational structures or base for women to organise.*

The pressures of multiple forms of work may reinforce each other, with the contradictory nature of these obligations ultimately precipitating action and strengthening women's demands at the various work sites (Coulson,

Magas and Wainwright, 1982; Hunt, 1980). Conversely, workplace organising, in terms of process (conscientisation, negotiation, incorporation in struggle, re-examination and revision of demands etc.) and outcome, can lead to re-evaluation of other areas of labour and unequal power relations such as the home, and to unequivocal demands for change.[28]

The importance of the concatenation of women's multiple identities in women organising, in organising women, and in creating coalitions with other workers, and other categories of persons through alliances of affinity, has been demonstrated in numerous contexts. In South Africa, organising has been successfully carried out in relation to domestic service, the waged occupation most recalcitrant to the improvement of labour conditions. Here, through the growth and strength of community organisations, access to and support from the union organising body, sections of the women's movement, and the shared commitment and involvement of a large grouping of women united also by race and class, action was undertaken to organise and recognise the body of domestic workers.[29]

Conflicting demands upon women, and the ideology buttressing the sexual division of labour, have provided the basis for women's seeming incorporation in the reserve army of labour, moving in and out of waged employment as state and capital, working at times in conjunction, and at times in contradiction to each other, have decreed. However, this movement has been contested and resisted, with historical studies demonstrating that women's waged labour did change in form and locus, but that women retained, wherever possible, their stake and involvement in, and earnings from, waged labour. Thus, for example, Rosie the Riveter may have been forced out of heavy industry, but she moved into the office, the shop, the café.[30]

The very structures and institutions which define the public/private ideology, which has served to define and constrain women,[31] are changing, and being changed by women's actions. We have seen how women in developing countries have responded to pressures created by changed economic conditions, and have initiated or joined in actions at various levels to support themselves and their kin, with family and neighbourhood ties and relationships necessarily being modified in the process. Such changes may take very different forms depending on production relations, nature of the state etc. It has been suggested that US women are becoming less 'domestic' beings: fewer women remain in conjugal families, or marry at all; neighbourhoods are dispersed; and more women are engaged in waged labour (Kessler-Harris and Sacks, 1987). 'Family' concerns are then necessarily extended to a wider framework. Kessler-Harris and Sacks note:

> As women come to perceive 'family' issues as social and public ones,
> they move beyond the community to the national arena. . . . with a cor-
> responding shift in locus from community struggle to workplace and
> state-centered arenas. (1987: 81)

One sees a significant move to other levels and areas of struggle, and from
the privatised and localised arenas of the community and home, thus also
providing the context within which to broaden the struggle, and the issues,
as more persons are directly affected.[32]

Analysts differ with regard to the effects of state intervention in domestic
matters. Jónasdóttir (1988) suggests that in states with strong welfare provisions, changing state policy and increasing intervention in domestic
matters increase public consciousness concerning the possibility of transformation of oppressive living conditions and domestic relations. In this
case, she finds that it is the state-led revision which precipitates action
among women to make further gains. Others find that that very intervention
provokes confrontation with the state, as public/private boundaries shift.
From dependence on individual men, women seemed to have shifted towards dependence on the state. Given the cut-backs and dismantling of the
welfare state today, women are being forced to confront the state and
engage in party political actions. With the present massive changes in state
ideology and practice, and the move to free market economies in Eastern
Europe and elsewhere, women organise on new bases as they find long-
held and assumed rights affecting their bodies, their work, and all aspects
of their lives, swept away in waves of religious, ethnic, nationalist and
capitalist fervour.

Women have allied to question assumptions arising from the relations
between waged and domestic labour, and from the assumptions underlying
marital and domestic ideology, in order to assert alternative positions in
relation to the community and the state. For example, in a South Korean
case (Suh Myung Sun, 1985), issues regarding labour legislation, domestic
ideology, valuation of domestic labour, economic provisions for married
women, and the rights of the individual were raised and queried in the
context of an injury compensation case, fought to the highest level through
the support of a coalition of women's organisations. Perhaps the most
striking example of women's querying of and resistance to a hierarchical
and oppressive sexual division of labour was the national action taken in
Iceland, with the Women's Strike of 24 October 1975 (James, 1985;
Hardadottir, 1985).

The building of alliances in relation to women's mobilising around
issues of labour is and has been of the utmost importance, although this

is an area where the establishment of allies has long been problematic. Historically, there have often been uneasy, when not openly conflictual, relations between women and men within the formal labour force, and the history of First World trade unionism has not often exemplified worker solidarity in relation to gender. Coalitions which have been created have sometimes worked *around* formal union structures, rather than through them, and certainly even at present, women workers may find more immediate (and useful) support through women's organisations, the church, ethnic groups, civil rights groups etc., than through the labour structures, although this reflects also present limitations set on union powers, as in free trade zones.

Women sometimes tend to straddle opposing camps in labour relations, and indeed the growth of women workers' organisations, in-house unions as a preferred organising strategy, and 'active non-participation' in unions reflects these considerations. However, the creation of coalitions is an important and effective strategy for women workers; and of course certain benefits extend throughout the coalition. These may not relate directly to the workers or to the labour process, but rather to the changed consciousness brought from the shared perspectives of the coalition and the effects of struggle.

Coalescing Strategies

The actions elaborated above have led women workers into direct confrontation with capital, patriarchy and the state. All the examples discussed demonstrate the importance of *coalescing strategies*. By coalescing strategies, we mean the formulation of demands which overcome divisions such as factory and household,[33] wage work and domestic labour, private and public.

The practical demonstration of coalescing strategies has occurred in situations of economic, social and political crisis. However, even in 'normal' situations it should be possible to develop organisational strategies which go beyond defensive reactions, and address multiple identities and their multiple linkages. For instance, in relation to women workers in industry, the following demands could break through the constructed divisions of capitalist society, as well as the compartmentalisation of organisational action:

a demand to include domestic labour in minimum wage determination would link together strategically household and factory, as well as the interests of women and men workers;

a demand to redefine industry so that it would include the whole chain of sub-contracting in a particular industry, would therefore make it possible to extend labour legislation to a wide range of casual work, including home-based work and related work of rural women; and

a demand for compensation in relation to divorce, injury etc., incorporating proper recognition and valuation of domestic labour. This would link labour law with family law, ensure greater financial, social and possibly physical security for women, and be more effective than the notoriously elusive equal pay.

Such demands are practical and therefore could be the basis for discussions around these issues in unions, women's centres and other organisations. We need to move from criticism of the limitations of dichotomies in theory, towards confronting and challenging the divisions of practice, drawing on the praxis of struggle and resistance of working women as they have confronted state, capital and patriarchy.

NOTES

1. We should like to thank workshop participants and colleagues in the Social Movements Seminar for their comments on earlier drafts of this chapter. Special thanks to Wicky Meynen, Peter Waterman, Virginia Vargas and Nira Yuval-Davis.
2. During 1981–83, Chhachhi was involved in research with women textile workers in Ahmedabad and Bombay, exploring the reasons and experience of the massive retrenchment of women from the textile industry. In 1982–83, she worked with a research team interviewing women garment workers in the export garment industry in New Delhi. In 1987, she conducted a case study of an electronics factory manufacturing colour television sets in an industrial estate near Delhi.

    Pittin's research concerning women workers in an electrical equipment factory in Zaria, Nigeria, was carried out from 1982 to 1984, with an additional short period of research in May, 1985. The research was done by the author, with the voluntary assistance and advice of Ms. Patience Aliogo, who was Head of the Calibration Section, EMCON, and a fellow member of Women in Nigeria.
3. In Chhachhi's research on Monica Electronics, questionnaires covering basic data as well as issues concerning nature of work, changes in technology, relations and perceptions of management and men and women workers, etc. were distributed and returned by 100 workers. In-depth interviews on tape were conducted with 50 workers, of which 10 were men. The interviews took the form of discussions where the researcher herself was questioned,

particularly on her status as a single woman. Interviews were also conducted with the managing director and personnel manager, and a company profile from company documents and factory returns was compiled. The workers were interviewed within the factory. The emphasis was on recording the statements made by workers in their own language and style. Pittin's research methodology included in-depth interviews primarily but not exclusively with EMCON women workers. A series of open-ended questions focused on concerns and issues such as organisational structures and strategies, problems encountered in the workplace, and women's involvement with and attitudes towards the union. Other topics included the double burden, obligations and responsibilities, and women's aspirations and expectations. Most interviews were conducted in English, the only shared language of all EMCON workers. Additional discussion was held outside the workplace concerning matters of mutual concern, particularly in relation to interest in possibilities presented by Women in Nigeria to improve women's working conditions.

It is necessary to point out that what is offered here is an interpretation, based on the accounts provided by women workers supplemented by the researchers' observations and analysis of broader trends in industrialisation. This cannot be a complete account of experienced reality and consciousness since factors such as concealment, contradictory responses, responding to ideal types, etc. create limitations in research situations where the researcher still remains an outsider.

4.   See Martha Roldan, this volume, for an analysis of the gendered implications of technical and social relations at the point of production.

5.   This is a point made by Gayatri Spivak (1988) in her introduction to *Selected Subaltern Studies*.

6.   'The Working Class has Two Sexes', *Monthly Review*, No. 28, July–August 1976 initiated a critical review of H. Braverman's *Labour and Monopoly Capital: The Degradation of Work in the Twentieth Century*, New York, 1974.

7.   There is a wide range of theory within the post-structuralist feminist corpus. See, for example, Chris Weedon, 1987, and Linda Nicholson, 1990, for review and elucidation of some of the approaches.

8.   Another problem with many of these approaches is their exclusive focus on heterosexuality, and on lesbians as the definitive metaphor for self-displacement. Other categories of women (as, for example, women who remain single) may be perceived as equally or additionally marginalised, inasmuch as they lack the reinforcement and recognition even of the (jointly displaced) marginalised group.

9.   Molyneux's strategic interests include, for example, the abolition of the sexual division of labour, removal of institutionalised forms of discrimination, and the attainment of political equality. Practical gender interests include, e.g. domestic provision, child-care, and public welfare (1985).

10.   It should be noted that the division between interests and needs, strategic and practical, inductive and deductive etc. tends to (wrongly) hierarchise and prioritise particular ideologies, perceptions and actions. Thus, for example, 'practical interests', or 'needs', tend to relate to socio-economic areas; while 'strategic interests' relate to the ethereal, and seemingly superior, realm of politics. Needs *per se* often focus on women's vulnerability or survival.

11. 'Identity' is used in many different ways: to refer to sameness vs. difference, the search for an identity, the crisis of identity and/or the assumption of a political identity as in black feminist movements. We use identity to refer to subject positions rather than in the specific sense of a conscious political articulation of an identity.

12. This interplay is nicely expressed by Chris Weedon:

> How we live our lives as conscious thinking subjects, and how we give meaning to the material social relations under which we live and which structure our everyday lives, depends on the range and social power of existing discourses, our access to them and the political strength of the interests which they represent.
>
> (Weedon, 1987: 26)

13. The linking of women's co-operatives into the network of capital through sub-contracting is an example of the convergence of interests between the women in development strategy and capital's strategy to lower costs of production. In developing strategies, we need to question the relationship with the state and the market. Co-operatives may be established without sufficiently reflecting on the nature of the product (how socially useful it is), the kind of production process, the nature of the internal structure, and relations within the household. Over time, and in the context of capitalist relations, such co-operatives may become exploitative, or may collapse altogether.

14. Production-line workers, both men and women, received the same basic pay, most of them earning below Rs. 600 per month. Supervisors received much higher salaries which, combined with the fact that they were mainly women, fuelled further resentment amongst men workers.

15. The definition of skill on the basis of the sex of the job occupant rather than on the basis of any 'objective' assessment of job content has been pointed out in a number of studies. See e.g. Phillips and Taylor, 1986; also Martha Roldan in this volume.

16. This does not exclude the various ways in which women may be discriminated against through differential promotion, access to training, etc., points which are raised elsewhere in this paper. Nigerian law ostensibly requires equal pay for equal work for women and men, but there are numerous ways in which the work is rendered unequal. In other Nigerian factories, gender differentiation was maintained through the allocation of temporary and part-time work to women (di Domenico, 1983), and through differential categorisation and valuation of labour processes carried out by women (Dennis, 1984).

17. For further discussion on the issue of masculinisation or feminisation in industry, see Diane Elson, this volume.

18. Given the limited job and higher education opportunities in Nigeria, EMCON could and did recruit a relatively highly-educated female workforce: about 70 per cent of the women had completed secondary school. This paper qualification was offset by the women's generally poor performance in their final examinations, a prerequisite for further schooling. This combination was considered optimum in EMCON hiring policy: sufficient education to make training and paperwork reasonably easy; poor enough results to reduce the likelihood of women rushing to further their education, and suggesting

a lack of cleverness consonant with the monotony of assembly-line work. EMCON management was incorrect in its assumptions regarding women's lack of educational possibilities, as is demonstrated in the text.

19. Even secluded Muslim women in Nigeria earn income from house-based trade and petty commodity production, a fact which is not recognised in statistics or evident in dominant discourse.

20. In a study of Nigerian oil workers (all men), Adesina also notes that ethnicity cannot be assumed to be solidary or divisive in the industrial (or other) context, whatever its importance as a national political concern or mobilising point. He suggests from his research that a common working-class solidarity, with an 'African ethos' of sharing and support, can be instrumental in the 'deconstruction of ethnic loyalties' (1990: 143). The EMCON data, which demonstrated more fully controlled hierarchical labour relations, and divisions among the assembly-line workers, did not show that generalised solidarity or shared support.

21. These specific issues, and the relationship between domestic labour and waged labour, are the focus of Pittin, 1986.

22. James Scott (1990) notes that among the oppressed, slights to the dignity (of the individual or group) figure as often as material concerns in terms of areas of contention and unacceptable pressure.

23. The issues of dignity and self-respect have mobilised both men and women into resistance in many contexts elsewhere, including in the industrial setting.

24. Here, we refer to the dialogue and alternative discourse of the oppressed exemplified by Scott's 'hidden transcripts', 1985, 1990.

25. Jónasdóttir, 1988, suggests three levels of unity. In her formulation, *sisterhood* presupposes the greatest shared identity, with bonds of friendship and affection; and *solidarity* suggests supportive ties, with possible sacrifice and the sharing of burdens. *Alliances* reflect minimal linkages and represent the only level which could unite all women.

26. It should be noted that the linkages which women make, and the support which they receive, is often of a transnational or non-national nature (Walby, 1990; Frank and Fuentes, 1990), reflecting the broader (or less state-focused) nature of the issues raised; the less direct relationships which women have (or in some cases want) to the state *per se*; and the immediacy of certain issues, evoking individual response.

27. See, for example, Iris Berger, 1990, for the process and outcome of a series of actions by men and women workers in South Africa, linked through fora and groupings based on identity and affinity, wherein issues and discourse of gender, race, class and nationalism were mobilised to unite the workers in relation to and in confrontation with the state.

28. See e.g. articles by Lamphere, Ladd-Taylor, and Zavella in *Feminist Studies* 11, No. 3: 'Women's Work, Work Culture, and Consciousness', for exemplification of this latter process in the US.

29. Discussion with SADWU Executive Committee members Violet Motlasedi, Florence de Villiars and Myrtle Witpool, Institute of Social Studies, The Hague, November 1988. See also Gaitskell *et al.*, 1984.

30. Noted for the post-World War II USA by Kessler-Harris and Sacks, 1987.

31. An effect of this ideology is that women may not necessarily 'see' themselves, or develop a consciousness of themselves, as workers (Safa, 1990;

Mies, 1988), although this work may be a prime constituent of their daily life – often throughout their life – and of their survival.

32.   Not examined specifically in this chapter are the ways in which issues such as sexuality, consumption, representation and culture are also taken up by working women.

33.   The dynamics and effects of power relations within the household have been thus far only partially addressed in the context of coalescing strategies.

REFERENCES

Adesina, Jimi. 1990. 'The Construction of Social Communities in Work: The Case of a Nigerian Factory', *Capital and Class* No. 40, Spring, pp. 115–47.

Annavajhula, J. C. B. 1988. 'Subcontracting in Electronics: A Case Study of Keltron', *Economic and Political Weekly*, Aug. 27, pp. M103–17.

Banerjee, Nirmala. 1991. 'Conclusion', in Nirmala Banerjee (ed.), *Indian Women in a Changing Industrial Scenario*, Indo-Dutch Studies on Development Alternatives 5, Sage Publications, New Delhi, pp. 299–311.

Beechey, Veronica. 1986. 'Studies of Women's Employment', in Feminist Review (ed.), *Waged Work: A Reader*, Virago Press, London, pp. 130–59. First published in *Feminist Review* No. 15, 1983.

Berger, Iris. 1990. 'Gender, Race, and Political Empowerment: South African Canning Workers, 1940–1960', *Gender & Society*, Vol. 4, No. 3, Sept., pp. 398–420.

Burawoy, Michael. 1985. *The Politics of Production*, Verso, London.

Chhachhi, Amrita. 1983. 'The Case of India', in Wendy Chapkis and Cynthia Enloe (eds), *Of Common Cloth: Women in the Global Textile Industry*, Transnational Institute, Amsterdam, pp. 39–45.

Cockburn, Cynthia. 1986. 'The Material of Male Power', in Feminist Review (ed.), *Waged Work: A Reader*, Virago Press, London, pp. 93–113. First published in *Feminist Review* No. 9, 1981.

Coulson, Margaret, Branka Magas and Hilary Wainwright. 1982. '"The Housewife and her Labour under Capitalism" – a Critique', in Ellen Malos (ed.), *The Politics of Housework*, Allison & Busby, London, pp. 7–43.

de Lauretis, Teresa. 1990. 'Eccentric Subjects: Feminist Theory and Historical Consciousness', *Feminist Studies* 16, No. 1, Spring, pp. 115–50.

Dennis, Carolyne. 1984. 'Capitalist Development and Women's Work: A Nigerian Case Study', *Review of African Political Economy* No. 27/28, February, pp. 109–19.

di Domenico, C. 1983. 'Male and Female Factory Workers in Ibadan', in Christine Oppong (ed.), *Female and Male in West Africa*, George Allen and Unwin, pp. 256–65.

Elson, Diane and Ruth Pearson. 1981. 'The Subordination of Women and the Internationalisation of Factory Production', in K. Young, C. Wolkowitz and R. McCullagh (eds), *Of Marriage and the Market*, CSE Books, London, pp. 144–66.

Frank, Andre Gunder and Marta Fuentes. 1990. 'Civil Democracy: Social Movements in Recent World History', in Samir Amin, Giovanni Arrighi, A. G. Frank and Immanuel Wallerstein (eds), *Transforming the Revolution: Social Movements and the World-System*, Monthly Review Press, New York, pp. 139–80.

Gaitskell, Deborah, Judy Kimble, Moira Maconachie and Elaine Unterhalter. 1984. 'Class, Race and Gender: Domestic Workers in South Africa', *Review of African Political Economy* No. 27/28, pp. 86–108.

Genovese, Eugene. 1974. *Roll Jordan Roll*, New York.

Gramsci, Antonio. 1985. *Selections from Cultural Writings*, Lawrence and Wishart, London.

Haraway, Donna. 1991. *Simians, Cyborgs, and Women: The Reinvention of Nature*, Free Association Books, London.

Hardadottir, Wilborg. 1985. Woman and Development Seminar, Institute of Social Studies, The Hague.

Hunt, P. 1980. *Gender and Class Consciousness*, Macmillan Press, London.

James, Selma. 1985. 'The Global Kitchen', Housewives in Dialogue, London (mimeo).

Jónasdóttir, Anna G. 1988. 'On the Concept of Interest, Women's Interests, and the Limitations of Interest Theory', in Kathleen B. Jones and Anna G. Jónasdóttir, *The Political Interests of Gender: Developing Theory and Research with a Feminist Face*, Sage Publications, London, pp. 33–65.

Kandiyoti, Deniz. 1988. 'Bargaining with Patriarchy', *Gender and Society*, Vol. 2, No. 3, pp. 274–90.

Kessler-Harris, Alice and Karen B. Sacks. 1987. 'The Demise of Domesticity in America', in Lourdes Benería and Catharine R. Stimpson (eds), *Women, Households, and the Economy*, Rutgers University Press, pp. 65–84.

King, Deborah K. 1988. 'Multiple Jeopardy, Multiple Consciousness: The Context of a Black Feminist Ideology', *Signs*, Vol. 14, No. 11, pp. 42–72.

Laclau, Ernesto. 1985. 'New Social Movements and the Plurality of the Social', in David Slater (ed.), *New Social Movements and the State in Latin America*, CEDLA, Amsterdam.

Ladd-Taylor, Molly. 1985. 'Women Workers and the Yale Strike', *Feminist Studies* 11, No. 3, Fall, pp. 465–89.

Lamphere, Louise. 1985. 'Bringing the Family to Work: Women's Culture on the Shop Floor', *Feminist Studies* 11, No. 3, Fall, pp. 519–40.

Mies, Maria. 1988. 'Capitalist Development and Subsistence Production: Rural Women in India' in M. Mies, V. Bennholdt-Thomsen and C. von Werlhof, *Women: The Last Colony*, Zed Books, London, pp. 27–50.

Mitter, Swasti. 1986. *Common Fate, Common Bond: Women in the Global Economy*, Pluto Press, London.

Molyneux, Maxine. 1985. 'Mobilisation without Emancipation? Women's Interests, the State, and Revolution in Nicaragua', *Feminist Studies* 11, No. 2, Summer, pp. 227–53.

Moser, Caroline O. N. 1989. 'Gender Planning in the Third World: Meeting Practical and Strategic Gender Needs', *World Development*, Vol. 17, No. 11, November, pp. 1799–825.

Nash, June. 1990. 'Latin American Women in the World Capitalist Crisis', *Gender and Society*, Vol. 4, No. 3, September, pp. 338–53.

Nicholson, Linda J. 1990. *Feminism/Postmodernism*, Routledge, New York.

Phillips, Anne and Barbara Taylor. 1986. 'Sex and Skill', in Feminist Review (ed.), *Waged Work: A Reader*, Virago Press, London, pp. 54–66. First published in *Feminist Review* No. 6, 1980.

Pittin, Renée. 1984. 'Gender and Class in a Nigerian Industrial Setting', *Review of African Political Economy* No. 31, pp. 71–81.

Pittin, Renée. 1986. 'Carrying the Double Burden: A Case Study of Women Factory Workers in Nigeria'. Paper presented at the XI World Congress of Sociology, New Delhi, August.

Pollert, Anna. 1981. *Girls, Wives, Factory Lives*, Macmillan Press, London.

Purcell, Kate. 1981. 'Female Manual Workers, Fatalism and the Reinforcement of Inequalities'. Paper presented to the British Sociological Association Annual Conference, Aberystwyth (mimeo).

Redclift, Nanneke and Enzo Mingione. 1985. *Beyond Employment: Household, Gender and Subsistence*, Basil Blackwell, Oxford.

Safa, Helen I. 1990. 'Women's Social Movements in Latin America', *Gender and Society*, Vol. 4, No. 3, Sept., pp. 354–69.

Scott, James C. 1985. *Weapons of the Weak: Everyday Forms of Peasant Resistance*, Yale University Press, New Haven.

Scott, James C. 1990. *Domination and the Arts of Resistance: Hidden Transcripts*, Yale University Press, New Haven.

Spivak, Gayatri C. and Ranajit Guha (eds). 1988. *Selected Subaltern Studies*, Oxford University Press.

Suh Myung Sun. 1985. 'State and Women's Subordination: The Case of Korea since 1960'. MA Research Paper, Institute of Social Studies, The Hague.

Thompson, E. P. 1963. *The Making of the English Working Class*, Penguin Books, Harmondsworth.

Walby, Sylvia. 1990. 'Woman, Citizen, Nation'. Paper presented to the Conference of the European Network for Women's Studies, The Hague, November (mimeo).

Weedon, Chris. 1987. *Feminist Practice and Poststructuralist Theory*, Basil Blackwell, Oxford.

Whitehead, Anne. 1990. Women and Development Seminar, Institute of Social Studies, The Hague.

Young, Kate. 1988. 'Reflections on Meeting Women's Needs'. Introduction to Kate Young (ed.), *Women and Economic Development: Local, Regional and National Planning Strategies*, Berg/Unesco, Oxford, pp. 1–30.

Zavella, Patricia. 1985. ' "Abnormal Intimacy": The Varying Networks of Chicana Cannery Workers', *Feminist Studies* 11, No. 3, Fall, pp. 541–57.

Part II – Strengthening and Broadening the Base: Trade Unions and New Organisational Strategies

This part focuses particularly on the organising strategies, limitations and potential of trade unions, and of the many other organisations which are supplanting, superseding or providing bases of action in addition to unions. The contributions in this part make clear that, on balance, the traditional trade unions have not kept pace with industrial and economic restructuring and with changes in political processes. Changes suggested include improving extant trade unions; other contributions move beyond traditional trade unions to put forward or describe perceived or ongoing alternative organising structures and programmes. These include, among others, the creation of local, regional and global networks, the establishment of stronger North–South linkages, and ties between workers and consumers.

Introducing this part is the chapter by Farhat Parveen and Karamat Ali, who discuss the background, conditions of employment, and the organisational structures which are available to women industrial workers in several cities in Pakistan. Ali and Parveen describe an action research project to document the increased employment of women factory workers and their working conditions. The project purposively conscientises and raises the awareness of those workers, to enhance their capacity to organise and act to improve their situation as workers and as citizens. The creation of a Women Workers Centre is intended to provide a space for the workers, while linking with present unions and seeking to transform their policies and practices in relation to women. This is to be effected through maintaining equally strong links with women's organisations and the broader Women's Movement, to ensure a strong *locus standi* for the Centre in its struggles with the state, management, and the unions themselves.

The subsequent two chapters, by Cecilia Olea Mauleón and Jurgette Honculada, also outline strategies which are utilised in relation to existing trade unions, in Peru and the Philippines respectively. Mauleón contextualises the situation of the trade unions in Peru, which grew in strength as civil society joined together in the 1970s in opposition to the military regime, and as an improved economic base permitted positive response to union demands. Mauleón describes the union at that period as classist and sexist, and points out that increasing numbers of women had joined in the workforce, but were compartmentalised and differentially controlled. With the growth of the Women's Movement in the 1980s, women's groups began liaising and working with industrial employees. Through this liaison, they are working to map out the structure of industry, to identify problem areas of women workers, to elicit response from the trade union to women's demands, to train women leaders, and to provide alternative structures and strategies for action. Thus, again the Women's Movement and the trade unions are seen as twin bases from which to act, with the former providing a spur to action in relation to the latter.

Honculada, like most of the contributors to this volume, situates her discussion of industrial organisation within the context of national and international economic development. Her chapter, focusing particularly on homeworking, first examines the forms, strengths and limitations of available unions for women workers, with particular recognition of the male dominance which infuses the culture, society, and the unions themselves. As in Peru, the historic Women's Movement and the tradition of women activists have been instrumental in seeking to effect change in the union context. A new union has been established for homeworkers, and a small but expanding number of women are making gender an issue in and out of unions. At the same time, support structures are being created in the heart of the community, as well as in the workplace. Feminist methodology is being used to train women workers and female union staff.

Rohini Hensman is far less convinced than the preceding contributors of the efficacy of the trade unions in supporting women workers. Using the example of the pharmaceutical and food industries in Bombay, she demonstrates that women remain a cheap and disposable part of the labour force in spite of struggles by the trade union movement and the Women's Movement. She points out that the trade unions still maintain a hard core of male privilege, and are less than vehement in supporting demands which directly benefit women or suggest changes in the sexual division of labour in the workplace. The Women's Movement, on the other hand, does not necessarily take on the class-specific issues of women industrial workers. Hensman sees an autonomous working women's movement, linked within campaigns with the labour movement and the Women's Movement, as the optimal organisational structure at present for factory women.

Free trade zones are often established with the incentive to prospective employers, particularly transnational corporations, of non-unionised labour. In this chapter, Leith Dunn considers the strategies open to women in free trade zones in the Dominican Republic and Jamaica. In both cases, workers have managed to organise in spite of constraints against union activity. In the Dominican Republic, labour laws guarantee the right of workers to organise, although these laws were long ignored by companies located in the zone. In spite of arrests and loss of employment, union organisers have created personal contacts with workers in the factories, and have strengthened these ties in the community. The women do not seek only better wages and working conditions. They also seek better security at work and in the community and the home, and the elimination of harassment and gender-based labour structures at work. Networking with other unions, and media support, have strengthened the union created in the zone.

In Jamaica also, traditional trade unions were discouraged in the free trade zones; only one company, unionised prior to its entry into the zone, has union representation. Most organising has been carried out outside the workplace, through the church and community. Dunn details the successes of a neighbourhood group of women, mainly factory workers, which created a framework and network to improve skills, give support and organise in relation to the women's productive, reproductive and community obligations and roles. Assistance to improve working conditions has been sought from women's organisations and other NGOs, and government groups as well as trade unions. In addition, a housing co-operative has been established which not only provides shelter, but also creates new spaces for women workers and their families, and a basis for alternative and more participatory organising and solidarity.

The chapter by Loh Cheng-Kooi has a broader scope still, for it concerns in particular organising and networking between Asian industrial women workers. Focusing on women workers' groups and the issues they espouse, Cheng-Kooi notes that these groups take up women-specific issues such as increased security and gender-based job discrimination which traditional unions ignore, and attempt 'new ways of organising' which contrast with the more abrupt and hierarchical traditional male structures. The chapter concludes with a reminder of the need to sensitise both men and women workers, and of the role of the labour movement to support the struggles of women workers.

The final chapter of this part, by Linda Shaw, is a study of Women Working Worldwide, a British-based organisation with offices in London and Manchester. Working particularly in relation to the clothing, textiles and micro-electronics industries, all of which employ large numbers of women globally, Working Women Worldwide supports women workers through information exchange, international networking and public education. The organisation has created a data base to provde information and communication between activists and researchers in industry, and makes extensive use of the media to disseminate information. Through its efforts in relation to a Philippine industrial dispute, for example, Women Working Worldwide has provided support for Asian women workers' actions and created a base for stronger international solidarity. Another significant area of action is in the rallying of consumer purchasing power. The active support or disapproval of companies in relation to their labour practices can be effectively demonstrated through the purchase or boycott of their products. Often in conjunction with other national and international support groups, Working Women Worldwide works towards ensuring that consumers know when the products they might buy are the result of unfair or exploitative labour practices. Solidarity is thus extended from the worker to the consumer, with purchasing power providing an incentive for companies to treat their workers well.

4 Research in Action: Organising Women Factory Workers in Pakistan

Farhat Parveen and Karamat Ali

This chapter describes the experience of an action research project conducted in Pakistan. The project had the objectives of ascertaining the background, conditions of work and employment as well as the organisational situation of women factory workers in formal sector industries of the cities of Karachi, Lahore, Faisalabad and Multan: these constitute the largest urban industrial centres of Pakistan. We elaborate the process of conscientisation resulting from the research and the subsequent creation of a support centre – the Women Workers Centre – and its attempts at organisational work with women factory workers in the city of Karachi. Some general conclusions are drawn with reference to the role and effectiveness of various forms of organisation available to workers in general and women workers in particular, in their efforts to improve their working conditions and opportunities.

The project was initiated by the Pakistan Institute of Labour Education and Research (PILER) in June 1988, as a result of the realisation that while official statistics continued to indicate that only about 3.2 per cent of women were included in the labour force, common observation revealed that the number of women workers was conspicuously on the increase, especially since the early 1980s.[1] However, the most striking increase was observed in formal sector factories, particularly in sectors such as garments, electronics, and pharmaceuticals. Despite the visible increase in their numbers, however, women workers by and large remained unorganised. Even in factories with unions, women workers were not active participants in the unions. It was therefore felt that it was necessary to undertake comprehensive research to determine the extent of women's employment in the factories and to ascertain the reasons for the existing state of organisation, as well as to identify future organisational possibilities. The research was to be action-oriented so that the research process itself would contribute towards increasing awareness amongst women workers, and also lay the basis for their eventual organisation.

The research concentrated on production workers in those industrial sectors which were found to be employing most women, i.e. food and beverages, garments, pharmaceuticals, electronics, cosmetics, plastics, rubber, textiles, fisheries, carpets and brick-kilns. The survey covered 96 registered factories, which employed 11 500 workers, out of which 4345 (37.78 per cent) were women.[2] Altogether, 1200 workers, including 100 men, were interviewed. These workers were employed in registered factories.[3]

RESEARCH METHODOLOGY

It was decided first of all that the women workers must be interviewed only by women investigators. This meant that the research project had to incorporate a double process of consciousness-raising regarding feminist and labour issues, since the segregation and restrictions on mobility for women in Pakistan made it difficult for even educated young women to be aware of these issues.[4] A team of young women (six in Karachi and seven in the Punjab) were recruited in May 1988; all of them were graduates in social sciences. Most of them came from lower middle-class backgrounds, while some had a working-class background. In fact, two of the women had themselves been employed as production workers in the garment industry. Training workshops were organised where local and international feminist academics and activists interacted with the team to provide a conceptual framework as well as research skills based on feminist methodology. The women researchers were exposed to issues and similar projects related to women workers in South Asia to provide a broader regional perspective. Emphasis was placed on avoiding a top-down research approach, and the importance of empathising and identifying as women was highlighted in these training workshops.

In the beginning an attempt was made to undertake the interviews of workers at their respective workplaces. However, this strategy was dropped when it was realised that the workers could not respond freely under the gaze of management. Indeed, most of the management officials would not even allow the research team to enter their premises. It was then decided that the team would collect workers' addresses at the workplace and interview them at their homes either in the evenings or on holidays. This approach of course lengthened the duration of the survey considerably. However, it provided a unique opportunity for the survey team to acquaint themselves with the living conditions of workers and their families. In addition, a closer interaction developed with the workers which not only enriched the quality of information, but also laid the basis for future co-operation between the workers and the researchers. It also helped the researchers to develop a deep commitment to the problems of women workers and eventually led to the researchers' active involvement in the formation of the Women Workers Centre at Karachi. The women researchers identified about one hundred women workers who were either actively involved in trade union or community activities, or had the potential for such involvement. The team also left the contact address of PILER with every worker they interviewed, and informed them of the action objectives of the project. During the process of data analysis, group discussions with a selected number of the interviewed workers were held to assess their needs and the role that PILER could play in this regard.

INDUSTRIALISATION PATTERNS AND THE SOCIO-POLITICAL CONTEXT

At independence, Pakistan was a predominantly agrarian society with very few industries and limited infrastructure. In the 1950s, a phase of rapid industrialisation was ushered in, boosted by the Korean war. This phase was based on import substitution in textiles, sugar, cement and food. In the 1960s, there was a shift to export-oriented industrialisation, with emphasis on middle-range engineering and consumer goods. In both phases, industrialisation was heavily dependent on large doses of foreign capital, not in the form of direct investment but as loans channelled through various state institutions to local industrialists. Although the emphasis was on the private sector, a public sector was emerging alongside, mainly in steel, cement, chemicals, but also in consumer goods. In the 1970s, large-scale nationalisation resulted in rapid expansion of the public sector. In the 1980s, there was a return to deregulation and privatisation, and the initiation of a structural adjustment programme in 1988. The effects of these have been similar to other countries in the loss of job security, depressed wages, increase in sub-contracting and casualisation of the workforce. In spite of being subject to international trends in the economy, Pakistan society remains caught in feudal values, ruled mainly through military dictatorships. Democratic institutions and norms have not been allowed to take root. An extremely repressive state uses the religion of Islam to legitimise a highly iniquitous system.

This particular aspect has been further accentuated under the latest and the longest martial law regime of General Zia ul-Haq in the 1980s. The imposition of the so-called Islamisation programme began with the introduction of the Hudood Ordinances in 1979, and has continued even after the death of Zia ul-Haq with the imposition of the Shariat Bill in

1991.[5] These laws have brutalised the political and social culture of Pakistan. Women were the worst sufferers, in that these laws sought to reduce them to the status of second-class citizens, to further curtail their mobility and tighten the already restrictive socio-cultural controls exercised over them.

Structure of Women's Employment in the Manufacturing Sector

Contrary to official statistics, the number of working women in the urban economy is significant and growing in recent years. The share of female workers in the manufacturing sector as a percentage of females employed in all sectors increased from 5.45 per cent in 1973 to 15.27 per cent in 1981, according to a survey conducted by Sabeeha Hafeez. Her study points to significant variations in the female participation rate in different provinces. In Sind, there are 6.8 per cent women workers compared to 93.1 per cent men workers; in Punjab, 4 per cent compared to 96 per cent; and there is a very low percentage of women workers in the North West Frontier Province and Balochistan (Hafeez, 1983). Sector-wise, the study showed that in Sindh, textiles employed the largest number of women while in the Punjab, garments was the largest employer. In the national economy as a whole, an increase of women's employment in non-agricultural labour from 35 per cent in 1973 to 60 per cent in 1981 was noted. A large proportion of these women were employed in the informal sector.[6] In the 1980s, there appears to be a shift in the structure of women's employment in the manufacturing sector. Women are being employed in more diverse industries including electronics, ceramics, engineering goods, packaging, and industrial chemicals. From the survey conducted by PILER, it appears that a systematic policy to hire women emerged mainly in the 1980s. In the sample, 58 per cent of the firms had employed women in the eighties, 20 per cent in the seventies, 12 per cent in the sixties, less than 10 per cent in the fifties and only one earlier. In terms of sectors, there is also a shift, with garments becoming the main employer of women over-all, particularly in Sindh and Punjab.[7]

The profile that emerged from the study confirms the general pattern noted in other countries, in that the largest section of women were young (16–20 years old) and single (60 per cent unmarried women, 29 per cent married and the rest [11 per cent] either widowed, divorced or separated). In the fisheries, there was the largest number of widowed, divorced or separated women, while the brick-kilns hired married women due to the system of family labour. An interesting finding revealed the use of female child labour (5 per cent of the sample in the age group 10–15) mainly in the garment industries. The private sector employed the largest number of women, accounting for 68.6 per cent, while the government sector accounted for only 1.8 per cent of women workers. Most of the women are educated, with the largest share composed of secondary school graduates (27 per cent) followed by secondary school leavers. The more highly-educated women were concentrated in the pharmaceutical industry, while fisheries had the largest number of illiterate women. There was no link between education, skill or years of service, with women being designated skilled or unskilled usually on an arbitrary basis. Electronics is an exception, with the lowest share of unskilled female labour, and with a high level of education accompanied by a higher degree of women's labour designated as skilled.

Estimation of future trends in women's employment has to be located in the greater tendency towards the increasing decentralisation of industry in Pakistan in the 1990s. Decentralisation takes two forms: sub-contracting from the factory to the small-scale sector and to the household, as well as geographical dispersion. Due to ethnic conflict in Sindh, a shift to rural industrialisation, and the promotion of tax-free industrial zones in the hinterland of large cities, mainly in the Punjab, there has been a shift of industry out of the cities of Karachi and Hyderabad. As a result of past growth trends as well as government policies in terms of incentives, expansion is expected in consumer industries such as food manufacturing, textiles, garments, footwear, electronics and pharmaceuticals. All these already employ a large number of women. However, future employment of women, except in garments, will not be on a permanent or even temporary basis, but rather in home-based work linked through a series of sub-contracting arrangements with larger firms. In garments, the emphasis on quality control for export markets would still require hiring women in factories, though the implications of the adoption of new garment technology such as laser cutting and sewing have still to be assessed. Studies have indicated that home-based workers constitute close to 53 per cent of all employed women in the urban economy (World Bank, 1989). This number is expected to grow, with women working both as piece-rate workers and as so called 'micro-entrepreneurs', i.e. women involved as family labour in small enterprises or those who sub-contract work out further to other women.

ETHNIC AND GENDER SEGMENTATION

Ethnic divisions have become extremely important in determining political, economic as well as social issues in the country, particularly in the largest industrial city of Karachi. Karachi has a multi-ethnic population with 54 per cent Urdu-speaking, 6 per cent Sindhi-speaking, 14 per cent Punjabi-speaking, 9 per cent Pushtu-speaking, 4 per cent Baluchi-speaking, 1 per cent Hindko-speaking and 12 per cent who speak other languages. In the PILER survey, women workers in Karachi came predominantly from the Urdu-speaking community (85 per cent), the next major group being Punjabi-speaking (10 per cent) with fewer numbers who spoke Pushtu, Saraiki and Baluchi. It is significant that there were no Sindhi-speaking workers, although Karachi is located within Sindh province. Recruitment to factories was primarily (over 80 per cent in the sample) through kin and community networks, thus resulting in ethnic segmentation in industrial sectors. So for instance, fisheries is predominantly Baloch with some Punjabi workers, while all the other sectors are dominated by Urdu-speaking workers, with a few Punjabis found scattered in different industries. Neighbourhoods are also divided along ethnic lines, so that workers from different communities rarely interact socially with each other. A recent trend is the emergence of ethnic parties and groups, each creating its own trade union wing or a committee within each factory, thus institutionalising ethnic divisions and making collective action even more difficult.

Ethnic polarisation also extends to employers, and this has significant implications for organising and consciousness amongst workers. Employers often hold positions of power in the ethnic political groups, and use these positions to subvert the resistance of workers belonging to their own ethnic group. For example, most of the garment factories are owned by Urduspeaking and Punjabi owners, with professional managerial personnel as well as workers belonging to the same groups. It is significant that all the ethnic groups have been able to mobilise a large number of women in their communities to participate actively in demonstrations on ethnic issues. In the context of increasing ethnic conflict as well as the militancy of a Sindhi nationalist movement, alliances tend to relate to ethnic rather than class issues. Since 1985, ethnic riots have become a regular feature in the cities of Sindh, characterised by violence, arson and looting; this has led to the death of over 2000 people. The gulf between communities, and the constant polarisation and confrontation, have affected workers within their communities, workplaces and trade unions.

This ethnic segmentation runs alongside gender segmentation, whereby women are segregated into sections of the production process. Management differentiates between men's work and women's work on the assumption that jobs requiring heavy physical input and technical/mechanical skill are men's jobs and unsuitable for women. Wages are extremely low, with over 80 per cent of workers receiving monthly wages below Rs. 1000. In most industries, women get only two-thirds of men's wages. Wage differentials are highest in garments, food and rubber industries and lowest in pharmaceuticals, where women get 20 per cent less wages than men. Wages for women are highest in the pharmaceutical industry, although even here there are differences (almost 26 per cent) between unionised and non-unionised workers. Only 41.9 per cent of the women are permanent, with 29 per cent temporary and the rest casual workers. This is in spite of the fact that all the workers in the sample had worked for more than one year at their present jobs, and two-thirds had around five years of job experience. Almost all the workers are entitled to appointment letters, compulsory insurance, annual medical and festival leave, paid weekly leave, double-rate overtime, minimum standards of health and safety at workplace and other labour rights existing in the labour laws. But the majority of the workers have been deprived of all these facilities and benefits – almost 17 per cent of the workers in the sample are denied even the facility of a toilet. Most distressing is the lack of awareness that they are entitled to these rights. Clearly, existing wages and working conditions, as well as the contrast between unionised and non-unionised workers, revealed the need for organisation.

The ideology of *purdah* (veiling) is the dominant ideology, and is used by management and men workers, unionists and women workers themselves to justify the segregation and exclusion of women, but there exist considerable variations in the way purdah operates in practice. In the survey, a number of women workers used purdah to come to the factories so as to avoid censure from neighbours; they took off the veils once inside the factory. Others stated that purdah essentially meant 'modesty in the eyes' without necessarily requiring an external cover. In spite of the internalisation of *purdah* ideology, we found that it did not act in any way as a barrier to organising, once possibilities and opportunities for women to organise and improve their situation were presented to them.

UNIONISATION

The issue of organisation has to take account of the general state of unionisation in Pakistan. In 1990 there were 7080 registered trade unions, with 952 488 members. However, these official statistics do not give information on the numerous worker associations which have not been offically registered. In spite of this, though, the rate of unionisation is low:

less than 5 per cent of the total industrial and commercial labour force is organised in the registered unions, and less than 3 per cent of that labour force is organised in the Collective Bargaining Agent (CBA) unions. The CBA has the sole right to represent workers in negotiations with employers. The Industrial Relations Ordinance 1969 permits the formation of only plant-level unions by permanent workers. The procedures for the formation and registration of trade unions are unduly tedious. The law confers excessive authority upon the Registrar of Trade Unions and related Labour Department officials, who use that authority for personal gains. It is almost impossible for workers to exercise their right to organise without being victimised. The legal structure also allows the formation of multiple unions. An effect of this is a tendency towards factionalism, making it difficult for workers to press collectively for their needs on a more than local or very restricted basis. The pattern of trade union organisation is similar to the style of general political organisation in the country, where personalised leadership and individual power politics lead to continuous splits, and the participation of rank and file workers and structures of internal democracy are absent. The situation is complicated further by the anti-union attitude of the employers, who will go to any lengths to prevent the formation of representative unions by the workers.

These unions are male-dominated in terms both of their membership as well as their leadership. A survey of fifteen of the largest trade union federations reveals that only one has a woman as its president; she was also the only woman office bearer in the federation (PILER Survey, 1991). The situation in plant-level unions is hardly different, with the almost total absence of women in the trade union structure. In the PILER study overall, only ten factories had unions, nine of which were in the multinational sector. In the unionised factories, out of the total number of workers employed (2759 men and 1446 women), only 160 women were members of unions, concentrated in the pharmaceutical and electronics industries. There were no unions in the other industries. Only fifteen women were office bearers, but none of them held the main office of President or General Secretary. Male industrial workers demonstrate feudal attitudes towards women, and do not view or treat women as their equals.[8] Indeed, the men find it difficult to accept women as co-workers, and they tend to keep women out of daily union activities.

In addition, established trade union organisations and their leaders tend to keep away from sectors where women are employed because of the very low level of financial contributions affordable by the workers in these industries. The high incidence of victimisation[9] by management in these sectors, and particularly in the garments and food industries, requires lengthy legal and mobilisational effort by the unions, and also reduces the incentive for these organisations to invest time in these workers. Such a situation obviously makes it extremely difficult even for the male workers to unionise. Women workers are therefore doubly disadvantaged.

It is not surprising therefore that in the survey, most women workers did not even know what a trade union was, and the researchers had to explain the concept of trade unions and the right to collective bargaining before continuing the discussion. In the discussion, it was interesting that 46 per cent of the women surveyed expressed the need for a separate union, while only 23 per cent of the control male group felt this need. In Karachi, there was greater support expressed by women for a separate women's committee within the union, than for a separate union. The opposition by men to women having their own unions indicated that they saw these as a potential threat or source of inter-worker conflict. The acknowledgement of joint struggle by women and men expressed in the need for a women's committee in Karachi could be due to the lesser rigidity of *purdah* ideology in Karachi, compared to the Punjab.

STRATEGIES FOR ORGANISING

We have seen earlier that the problems faced by the women workers are at the following levels:

– Problems faced as workers;
– Problems faced as women;
– Problems faced as citizens.

Organisations which address these issues range from trade unions and community organisations to welfare-oriented women's organisations such as Pakistan Women's Association (APWA), to Women's Resource Centres such as Shirkatgah and Aurat Foundation, to pressure groups such as Women's Action Forum (WAF). We have already discussed the limitations of the trade unions. As for the community organisations, they are even more exclusively male preserves. The women's organisations are established and run mainly by upper-class women, and have not as yet brought the concerns of working women onto their agendas. However, all these organisations do in some ways provide services, such as legal information and advice, for women in general.

RESEARCH IN ACTION: FORMATION OF THE WOMEN WORKERS CENTRE

In the group discussions mentioned earlier, the workers in Karachi made very interesting comments and suggestions regarding new organisational forms. Given the inadequacies of the existing trade unions and their way of functioning, some workers mooted the idea of a separate women's committee for every trade union, while others went even further to suggest separate trade unions for women. They were unanimous on the need for trade unions. However, the process of unionisation could not be initiated and sustained without an external support system which was capable of providing the necessary information and skills, as well as mustering the required legal, financial and institutional support during the crucial formative stages. It was also realised that the existing trade unions could not and need not be by-passed. It was necessary to create a link with them while concurrently making concerted efforts to transform their present attitudes towards women. It was also decided to make use of the services provided by existing women's organisations, and to link with them as part of a broader movement for women's rights.

The Women Workers Centre was formed as a strategic support group, based outside but closely connected to the trade union movement on the one hand and the women's groups on the other. The Centre was to act as an educational, mobilisational and lobby group for the workers. A Steering Committee was constituted with representation from PILER, Aurat Foundation, Applied Socio-economic Research (ASR), Women Lawyers' Association, Human Rights Commission of Pakistan, Women's Action Forum (WAF) and Shirkatgah. It was decided to base the Centre initially in the office of a sympathetic trade union federation, so that the women responsible for running the centre could benefit from the practical knowledge and experience available in the federation. Such a location would also influence the trade unions positively in support of women workers.

The Women Workers Centre is now over two years old. It has two sites and is staffed by a group of five women, some of whom were part of the original survey team, and were subsequently trained for a period of six months in labour law and trade union administration before they started work for the Centre. The Centre staff have also had the benefit of visiting various women's groups in the Indian cities of Delhi, Ahmedabad and Bombay. The Centre is engaged in a number of activities. It brings out a monthly newsletter for women workers, organises educational classes for women workers, produces relevant documents in Urdu, and acts as a referral agency for women with personal or family-law related problems. The

Centre also helps individual workers in cases such as illegal deduction of wages, old age pension benefits and illegal termination of services. Most important of all, the Centre is actively involved in supporting formation of trade unions by women workers, identifying and training potential organisers, and providing necessary support services. A detailed example demonstrating the nature and extensiveness of some of this support is given here:

The garment factory under consideration here is situated in the New Karachi industrial area. It employs around 300 workers, of which over 90 per cent are women. It produces cotton gloves and shirts for export. We came into contact with the workers during the survey. There was no union in the factory. The management was extremely repressive towards the workers: the workers had to take permission from the supervisor even to drink water or go to the toilet. The workers were sacked for the flimsiest of reasons. The workload was too heavy, while the wages were abysmally low. Not a single worker was issued an appointment letter. Illegal deductions from wages were a common occurrence. The management punished the workers like schoolchildren on trivial grounds. Punishments included keeping one's arms raised for long periods or standing in the sun. The factory manager would tell the women that the factory was similar to the home, and he was only admonishing them like a father would do to his daughters. For a long time the workers endured this humiliating treatment. At one point a group of three women, two sisters and a friend, decided to act and started looking for avenues for changing their situation.

During this period, in December 1988, an elected government had come to power after eleven long years of military dictatorship. The three women workers found their way to the Chief Minister's office in Karachi and lodged a complaint against the management. The Chief Minister ordered the Labour Department to take action according to law. The management was compelled to issue appintment letters to the workers. However, while handing over the letters, the factory manager told the workers that after the issuance of these letters, they would have to appear frequently before the courts and the Labour Department officials for the redressal of grievances, and that the management could not guarantee their safety or chastity in the event of such visits. Most of the young women became frightened and they tore up the letters of appointment in front of the management.

The management then incited the workers against the three women who were responsible for the official intervention which resulted in the issuance of appointment letters. In June 1989, the management was able to entice a co-worker to level false charges of theft against the three. In spite of their rebuttal of the charges, the management dismissed them without even fulfilling the legal obligation of instituting an impartial enquiry and affording them a fair chance of defence.

By that time, the Women Workers Centre had been established and the three women approached it for assistance. The Centre filed a case on their behalf before the Labour Court. After the case against the management had been filed, one of the women, Bano, became actively involved in working with the Centre. She kept in regular touch with the workers of the factory and took keen interest in helping them. Slowly, the workers realised what the management had done and they began to respect and respond to Bano. In interaction with the Centre, the idea of forming a union gradually gained ground. Finally, in June 1990, 62 workers assembled at the Centre office with the intent of forming a union. The Centre, as well as the Secretary General of Muttahida Labour Federation (MLF), who was fully involved in promoting the objectives of the Centre, doubted whether the workers were sufficiently prepared or trained to sustain a union by themselves. The workers were therefore advised to wait for a while, and educate themselves in labour law and trade union administration before they actually formed the union. Their attention was drawn to the very strong possibility of reprisals by the management, the corruption of the Labour Department, and the hardships they were likely to encounter. However, once mobilised, the workers were determined to go ahead with their decision and the union was formed. This was just the beginning of a long battle for the exercise of a right guaranteed by the Constitution of Pakistan, the ILO Conventions and the labour laws of Pakistan. The battle continues to date.

It is important to detail some of the main problems confronted by the workers in this regard, as it will highlight the importance of a support structure such as the Women Workers Centre in sustaining the resistance of women workers, once they decide to stand up to the gross injustices meted out to them by management in violation of the law of the land. According to the law, a trade union is only recognised as a legal entity after its registration with the Registrar of Trade Unions. Upon receipt of the application for registration of the Union under discussion, an official of the Labour Department informed the management. The management then immediately entered into a deal with the officials and obtained a copy of all the documents. The management went to a Civil Court, which in fact has no jurisdiction over labour matters, and obtained through dubious means a Stay Order against the registration of the Union. The Civil Court did not even bother to hear the workers' case for a period of five months. The Stay Order was finally vacated in March 1991. In the meantime the Centre, with the experienced advice of the MLF, was able to get the union registered, albeit with a changed name. The management began victimising the members of the union. The Centre arranged for a lawyer to fight the Stay Order, and to obtain an injunction from the National Industrial Relations Commission (NIRC) barring the management from taking any illegal action against the members of the union, with an intent to coerce them into leaving the union. While these cases were still pending before the respective Courts, the management further intensified its campaign against the Union. In yet another example of the manipulation of law through the alliance of repressive capital and the corrupt state machinery, the management succeeded in getting a pocket union registered, thus blocking the way for the genuine union of the workers to be recognised. To counter this move, the Centre applied on behalf of the union to the Registrar to hold a referendum in the factory to determine the CBA union. Under the influence of the management, the Registrar expressed his inability to do so, on the pretext of the existence of the Stay Order of the Civil Court. The same Registrar, however, did not feel constrained not to register the pocket union while the Stay Order was in force. After the vacation of the Stay Order a fresh application for the determination of the CBA was filed by the union. However, in violation of labour law, the Registrar accepted an application for the registration of yet another pocket union. The Registrar then informed the union of his inability to oblige the union with their application for a referendum until the application for registration of the new union had been dealt with.

Meanwhile, to break the morale of the members, the management declared a lay-off (suspension of production) in the month of March for a period of 14 days, during which the workers are paid only half their wages. This was a severe economic blow to the workers whose wages were already very low. This action was followed by a concerted campaign against the office bearers of the union and against the Centre, who were painted as responsible for all the problems of the workers. The agents of the management went around workers' homes spreading rumours of permanent closure of the factory and termination of their services. However, the workers were kept informed of developments through regular meetings organised by the Centre. The workers were also called together and informed about the illegal nature of the lay-off and appropriate strategies were discussed.

Once again, the Centre filed a case before the NIRC against the unfair labour practices of the management and was successful in obtaining a comprehensive injunction forbidding the management from resorting to any future lay-offs or other coercive action. In 1991, some workers approached an ethnic-based party, the MQM (Mohajir Qaumi Movement

[Migrants National Movement]), in the hope that the ethnic network would help them in their struggle. However, they discovered that the Managing Director of the factory had made large donations to the party, and there was thus no response to their demands from this quarter. They decided to continue on their own to build a class-based organisation.

More than nine months after the formation of the union, the management continues with its illegal blockade. However, both the workers and the Centre remain firm in their resolve to fight to achieve the recognition for the union, probably the first women workers' union in Pakistan.

The Centre was able to generate financial resources from various trade unions and donor agencies to provide for substantial legal fees during this continuing and drawn-out legal battle. It has also been able to support the dismissed workers in order to sustain their resistance. Clearly this battle, which is still not concluded, could not have been sustained by the workers alone, given their vulnerability in the face of such pressure.

In addition to work-related issues such as those noted above, the Centre has assisted with other issues and problems facing women workers. For example, the Centre has helped with divorce cases for some women workers who, while being the sole earners in the family, had been subjected to untold miseries by their husbands. By taking its activities to the working-class neighbourhoods, the Centre has been able to initiate a dialogue between workers belonging to different industrial sectors who otherwise hardly come into contact with each other, as well as between factory-based industrial workers and home-based, self-employed women workers. The Centre hopes to evolve an appropriate organisational form which could include women workers from all the different sectors of the economy. It also strives to bring the unionised, the non-unionised, the permanent and the non-permanent categories of workers together in educational workshops and seminars to highlight their common problems and destinies.

The Centre has remained in constant touch with women's groups and has tried to bring issues such as the imposition of the Hudood Ordinances, the Shariat Bill and other discriminatory measures against women, onto the agenda of women workers, as well as taking the problems facing women workers before women's organisations and groups.

Women workers are confronted with problems which have a class dimension, a gender dimension and also a broader human dimension. These cannot be dealt with by one single strategy or one specific form of organisation. There is need for a multidimensional approach encompassing all the different requirements of women workers in appropriate forms of organisation.

External support structures such as the Women Workers Centre can play a significant role in the struggle of workers for the fruition of their organisational efforts in a hostile environment. However, for such structures to be really effective, they must have the capacity to draw support from existing organisations of the workers: trade unions on the one hand and the women's movement on the other.

NOTES

1. In the 1981 Population Census, of the 25.8 million women in the age group 10 years and above, only 0.8 million, or 3.2 per cent are shown as 'working' or 'looking for work'.
2. The factories covered in the survey constituted 4.8 per cent of the total number of registered factories in the industrial sectors concerned, and the total number of workers employed therein came to around 1 per cent of the total number of workers in those sectors.
3. The choice to restrict the sample to production workers in registered factories only was made because these categories were likely to be governed by most of the labour laws relating to the right to organisation, minimum standards of working conditions and terms of employment as well as the laws relating to various welfare benefits. Such a choice would provide insights into the existing situation of relatively stable sections of industrial workers, and give some evidence of the state of the implementation or non-implementation of the existing laws. The registered factories are divided into three sectors: private, government and multinational.
4. It is a paradox of Pakistani society that there are women who are leaders of some unions. For instance, Karachi Shipyard and Engineering Works Union is headed by a woman, as was the Steel Mill Union at one point. However, like women in politics such as Benazir Bhutto, their position is derived more from their family and party connections than from acceptance by the membership of a woman representing them.
5. Details of these bills are contained in 'Worker's Rights in Pakistan' in Fredrich-Ebert Foundation, 1991.
6. Federal Bureau of Statistics, *Women in Pakistan*, 1985, pp. 251–4, cited in PILER Survey, 1991, p. 39.
7. In a study conducted by the Aurat Foundation in 1988, food manufacturing emerged as the largest employer of women (Aurat Foundation, 1989). However, the recent trend seems to be towards garments, which is an export industry. In 1990, the Garment Manufacturers Association of Pakistan stated that they employed over 500 000 workers, of whom close to 70 per cent were women.
8. This conservatism is further strengthened due to the fact that most of the workers are migrants who belong to ethnic communities which are very conservative in relation to women.

9. A woman-specific form of such victimisation is the threat of sexual violence.

REFERENCES

Aurat Foundation. 1989. 'Female Employment in Lahore District'. Unpublished Report.

Fredrich-Ebert Foundation. 1991. *Rights of Workers in South Asia*, New Delhi.

Government of Pakistan. 1991. *Pakistan Labour Gazette, 1990–1991*, Labour Division, Islamabad.

Hafeez, Sabeeha. 1981. *Metropolitan Women in Pakistan*, Royal Book Company, Karachi.

Hafeez, Sabeeha. 1983. *Women in Industry*, Women's Division, Government of Pakistan.

Mumtaz, Khawar and Farida Shaheed. 1987. *Women Of Pakistan: Two Steps Forward, One Step Back*, Vanguard Books Private Lahore.

PILER Survey. 1991. 'Female Industrial Labour Force in Pakistan 1988–1990'. Unpublished Report, PILER, Karachi.

World Bank. 1989. *Women in Pakistan: An Economic and Social Strategy*, World Bank, Washington, DC.

5 The Contribution of Feminist Training to the Democratisation of Labour Unions
Cecilia Olea Mauleón

The 1980s constitute one of the most important decades for understanding Peru's history. In this decade, elected governments followed one another without interruption, and the economic crisis caused extreme deterioration of the living conditions of the population. In the same period, the development took place in Peru of a most violent terrorist group, comparable only to the followers of Pol Pot.

But also during this decade, the women's movement developed and consolidated, especially in its popular and feminist branches. Women's organisations appeared in the urban space earlier, together with migration, and had their expression also during the 1970s through communal organisations. But in the 1980s, new expressions of popular and feminist actions became evident.

THE WOMEN'S MOVEMENT

The popular women's movement organised to face the effects of the economic crisis in a collective way. For example, the Communal Kitchens began to provide a collective answer to the food supply problem. Organised around fifteen to fifty families, communal kitchens save time, as duties that were formerly assumed by women in individual families are now developed by groups of women in turns. Thus, women have time for activities out of their homes, and the wholesale purchase of food supplies reduces costs.

The Glass of Milk Committees appeared as an answer to a local governmental proposal during the Izquierda Unida period (1984–6), as part of the Emergency Programme in Nutrition and Health. This programme benefits children, and at present, around 7500 Committees are active.

These organisations represent a new practice for women. In a space

151

external to private households, the preparation of meals is no longer an individual but rather a collective task. This represents an organisation and division of work that is radically different to that within households. This new organisation must be made precise and explicit, with the establishment of rules that are external to the individual, but internal to the group. The massive way in which the groups operate require rules, instances and spaces, which act directly to regulate women's participation in the organisation as such, and only indirectly to the preparation of meals. This has constituted a space for socialisation and interaction with other subjects such as NGO promoters and feminists, and also as a space of dialogue with the Church and the State.

Thus, women's responsibility towards their families and their children's health and future became a source of energy and action that has permitted them to break with traditional patterns. It has permitted them to enter the public sphere and even, in the last five years, to pass from protest to proposal, and to become active participants in proposing social policies. For example, in 1987 the National Co-ordinator of Communal Kitchens elaborated a proposal whereby urban family consumption was linked with land production, i.e. this was a joint food and agriculture development proposal.

This process has also enabled women to recognise for themselves the significance of gender. The interchange of experiences, transcending their immediate space, has enriched them and facilitated the development of a new potential beyond that of the household. It has also enabled them to gain self-esteem, as well as political and social knowledge and strength.

However, this process has not been an easy one, and has been marked by contradictions and rejections. On the one hand, lack of confidence, and on the other the attempt by others to manipulate and in some cases the rejection of communal organisations. Contradictions have also been found within families: all the women have had to struggle within the family to have their roles as leaders understood.

The feminist stream has also had important developments in this decade. From small protest groups which appeared in the late 1970s, feminist groups have incorporated the role and demands of women in the social and political agenda. From the struggles for the right to organise autonomously and for the defence of reproductive rights of women, and from gender consciousness and conscientising, feminist groups now design public political proposals in favour of women. The feminist movement in this decade gave impulse to legal proposals such as the acknowledgement of sexual harassment in labour legislation, the creation of women's police stations, and the participation of women in national and local electoral processes. The rapid growth of feminist collectives and centres and the actions carried out by them have contributed to sensitising public opinion and to placing the issue of women on the agenda of several policy-making social and state institutions.

The complex development of the women's movement has resulted in women being recognised as active political participants. It is an achievement that aspects of daily life that were formerly considered private, such as nutrition, health, protection against violence and domestic ill-treatment, and child survival, are now seen as subjects of social policy. Women's police stations have been created, decrees have recognised the Glass of Milk Programme and the Communal Kitchens, and therefore these are now considered within the State Budget.

Women have also created a complex organisational network with a massive and centralised structure that has developed a new institutionality which contributes to the democratisation of the social and political spheres within the country. In the last months, the popular women's movement has been a leader in the rejection of Sendero Luminoso's terrorist actions, and has thus become a prime target for Sendero's actions.

The popular movement, organised basically towards subsistence, has transcended these communal actions, and is now raising political issues and putting forward proposals. The association of women within these organisations has created a space in which they begin to question roles traditionally assigned to them, sometimes resulting in the raising of gender-specific demands.

THE LABOUR UNION MOVEMENT

During the 1970s, the labour union movement in Peru showed substantial development, from both quantitative and qualitative points of view. The movement was successful in going beyond the struggle for better working conditions. The movement became the nucleus which linked with other institutions representative of civil society, which joined forces with labour unions in order to confront the military regime. As a result of these actions, power was transferred to civilians.

The movement developed within the framework of class-oriented trade unionism. Workers were acknowledged as subjects who enjoyed rights. Radical action based on direct opposition was the response to the managers' clientele-forming and authoritarian practices: far from involving bargaining, the dynamics of the movement implied the imposition of workers' interests. Within the frame of classist trade unionism, the working collective was perceived as a homogeneous whole: no distinctions were recognised within the movement, disagreements were interpreted either as dissidence or betrayal, or as an attempt to institutionalise hierarchical divisions.

A number of converging factors accounted for the rise of this strong movement. The country was heading towards a breaking-off with the oligarchical state. Economic growth enabled the government to meet workers' demands for better wages and better working conditions. Enthusiastic young men and women who were striving for justice were incorporated into the industrial workforce. In the factories, they came into contact with leftist activists who carried out proselytism within labour unions.

During the 1980s, however, the economic crisis, the consequent decrease in industrial jobs and the ensuing recession narrowed the field of union action and weakened the labour union movement.

INDUSTRIALISATION AND WOMEN

Women started to join the workforce in significant numbers during the 1960s, during a period of industrial growth and diversification. Their incorporation was subject to a sex bias: while men had access to all fields of industry, women only had access to certain fields: those of tailoring, food industries, laboratories and electronics.

Female labour was restricted to certain spaces and certain functions as a result of sexual segregation within the productive sphere, and as a consequence of the fewer opportunities for promotion offered to them. Women were hired to carry out less skilled jobs and they were confined to restricted areas. Women account for only 10 per cent of the total industrial working population. In factories, an external rhythm was imposed on women and they became subject to a greater level of physical and hierarchical control than men. Due to the functions that they carried out, female workers were subject to a higher level of competitiveness than men. In the field of tailoring, where female labour is as high as 90 per cent, piecework is the rule: this acts as an incentive to competitiveness and hinders solidarity.

The labour union movement was also built on the basis of a sexually-biased structure. The number of female union leaders was quite insignificant even in predominantly female industrial fields. It was only in 1982 that a Secretariat of Female Affairs was created in the largest Trade Union Association in Peru, the Confederación General de Trabajadores del Perú, (CGTP). The creation of this division had no repercussions at the level of grassroots organisations.

Women's participation in unions is basically conceived and experienced as the offering of support: the roles assigned to them in trade unions are always related to the services they can provide, and they include the social work secretariat, the economy secretariat, the drawing up of minutes and file-keeping.

FEMINIST STRATEGIES IN THE LABOUR UNION MOVEMENT

We have shown above that the women's movement in its popular and feminist streams developed greatly in the 1980s. The growth and actions of the Flora Tristan Centre, a non-governmental feminist organisation founded in 1979, have been part of this movement and this period. In 1982, when this particular project began, Flora Tristan Centre had organised its work around four programmes: Information and Culture, Urban Development, Legal Advice, and Women and Work. From these programmes, actions were carried out together with other streams of the women's movement, in relation to society as a whole.

We have based our objectives around activities in relation to women and work in the areas of promotion, training and advice to women workers. The experience accumulated by the Centre, as well as its presence in the public arena, has provided the conditions to get to know the working world from women's perspective and to organise women workers further. The project with women workers was implemented by a multidisciplinary team, formed both by researchers and social empowerment workers. The objectives and strategies have varied through time (the project was initiated in 1982 and is still being developed) according to the achievements and difficulties presented.

Our goals have been the following:

a) To carry out research on the life and work of female workers in the field of industry. To map the structure of industry, pointing out the positions which women hold within industrial organisations.

b) To open up a space for reflection and a space where women can communicate with other female workers.

c) To get the organised labour movement to acknowledge demands which are specific to women, and to incorporate these demands in the actions they carry out and the proposals they set forth. We believe this is a contribution towards the democratisation of the labour movement.

d) To identify problems and to articulate gender-specific demands within the field of labour; to suggest alternative courses of action and to draw up proposals aimed at solving those problems.

e) To contribute to the articulation of the different branches of the women's movement.

In order to achieve the above-stated goals, we outlined the following strategies:

a) To analyse data on female employment, and to conduct in-depth interviews with female and male workers and employers.
b) To identify women's specific labour demands. To determine the pertinence of each demand, taking into account the country's social and political situation, the situation of the trade union movement, and that of the women's movement.
c) To organise and train female leaders in areas connected with gender and class, and in the area of leadership.
d) To produce appropriate educational support such as brochures, primers, videotapes and bulletins. To encourage discussion about female workers and their demands in the political and academic milieux, and at the level of public opinion.

The methodology applied depended on acknowledging the interaction of the two acting subjects involved: female social empowerment workers and female workers. Ties between them are strengthened by taking into account both differences and similarities in life experiences and knowledge. This implies a climate that elicits the opinion of female workers, and where social empowerment workers are not the only persons who express their points of view.

This educational process is aimed at raising the critical consciousness of the women who participate in it. It has been designed to offer them key elements so they can create strategies aimed at reactivating and revaluing labour union action.

The knowledge which women have accumulated has to be set down, made explicit, rendered collective and framed according to useful categories that stem from gender theory, so that the particularity of women's experiences can be explained and built upon.

We have attempted to create a pedagogical situation aimed at guaranteeing the active expression and the socialisation of life experiences, a situation that facilitates and stimulates the analysis of 'everyday reality' by resorting to broader and more abstract categories. The idea is that the woman who participates becomes the subject of her own training, and is capable of pinpointing and analysing the factors that determine her life.

The experience and knowledge owned by each subject is recovered in order to raise the subjects' capacity as individuals and to modify existing conditions. We intend that the processes of synthesis and acquisition of new knowledge bestow unity and generality on different partial experiences by connecting them to more global analytical categories. This pedagogical proposal has taken different shapes according to the demands and needs of the acting subjects involved.

SOCIAL EMPOWERMENT

Social empowerment takes place during the process which female workers experience both at individual and group levels. Factories are visited on a permanent basis, and we take part in several union and non-union activities. This enables us to grasp the climate within the organisation, and to understand female workers' needs and concerns. This also constitutes a privileged information source for proposing topics for reflection, and for advice, consultancy and training. This also allows us to create and strengthen ties that transcend those that originate during project activities. It enables us to get to know and to be a part of the everyday world of the women and men we work with. Trust is built and a two-way and easygoing communication is established.

Workshops

The workshops, open to groups of 10–15 participants, are the most suitable tool for raising individual consciousness and for dealing with subjects that affect only certain groups – the presence of pro-violence groups within trade unions, for instance. Issues connected to conflict resolution within trade unions are also discussed.

Courses

Around 100 male and female workers attend courses where the processes of industrialisation and labour union activities are discussed. The information conveyed in these courses covers areas such as legal instruments available to workers and techniques for devising strategies for labour union functioning. The fact that the information each participant brings is shared, and thus becomes more public, enables workers to learn from experience and to articulate new demands they may later address to the union and to the management.

Day-long Reflection and Comradeship Sessions for Female Workers

These sessions are the most important action in the framework of our strategy. These are attended by over 100 female workers, both leaders and union members. They bring their children to these sessions and a parallel programme is organised for them. This kind of meeting is a total novelty in labour union organisation. On two occasions, several Interunion Commissions of Women were formed as an outcome of these meetings: their goal was to draw up documents containing the most important demands which female workers recognise as their own.

From Individual Consciousness to Action

At the first stage of implementation of workshops, the women themselves explained the way in which they perceived their participation in the working world. They explained how they understood their role as producers, and the different shapes taken by resistance to work discipline. They analysed how they experienced the trade union, why they participated in the union, and what hindered their participation. The links between the productive and the reproductive worlds were also discussed.

Until the staging of these workshops, women had not had a formal space in which they could gather, and where they could socialise their experiences as women and as workers. They were able to identify individual problems and to acknowledge them as collective problems. Until that time, female workers perceived the union as a tool for solving problems related to working conditions and wages, and not as a space where they could gather as women. Thanks to the workshops, women were able to revalue their participation in the union from a different perspective, and they were able to recognise the importance of a space and time of their own.

Through a period of seven years participating in different workshops, female workers have discussed a variety of topics that give shape to their lives. They have spoken of their fear to participate actively (to speak in public) in union gatherings, and of their fear of being used for political purposes or otherwise manipulated.

Women have also discussed the difficulties they experience with their partners. They have seen themselves in this new light as subjects and objects of violence, and they have even shared their strategies aimed at transforming the terms of their relationships at home. Consequently, the development of workshops implied the opening up of a new space that transcended the limits of labour unions as such.

The successful implementation of workshops where female workers in the electronics industry participated (1982–3) demonstrated the need for extending this experience to workers in other fields. We took into account the women's situation both as producers and as responsible for household work. This led us to organise the day-long reflection and comradeship sessions. We invited women from the four fields of industry where female labour is significant. Workshops constitute until this day a different space: neither the factory nor the union. Sessions are held in out-of-town facilities that offer relaxation and recreation. This is an aspect which workers value highly, since it breaks the stressful dynamics to which they are subjected day after day, especially given the extent of the economic crisis and the increase of violence. The environment contributes to breaking through the cult of sacrifice and suffering which exists in Peru, a cult to which persons of working-class culture are no strangers.

The day-long sessions have provided a space for interaction between professional women (lawyers, doctors, sociologists and psychologists) and women workers. This space does not resort to the mediation of party politics, a practice which was characteristic of the 1970s. In these sessions, as noted above, workers from different factories interact. This is quite important, especially if we consider that during the past years, organisations which group unions (*federaciones*) have not been functioning. In certain cases, attendance at day-long sessions has acted as an incentive to reactivate associations that link different unions. This was the case in the fields of food preparation, laboratories and tailoring.

The Women Workers' Petition Committee

At the time power was transferred after the elections held in 1985 and 1990, several committees were formed in order to draw up proposals, which were submitted to the national Body of Legislators. The first committee was created in July, 1985 and female workers in different factories drew up a petition. The drawing-up of the petition opened a space of interaction where professionals whose field of specialisation was labour policies met with leaders of other branches of the women's movement and with women workers. Female workers were able to broaden their frame of reference during these gatherings. They gained information on comparative legislation, and they carried out research on the organisational experiences of female workers in other countries. Over a period of three months, they articulated demands which were more connected to the role of mothering than to their roles as workers. The changes they proposed were aimed at having more leisure time to raise their children.

When this process was completed, the women discussed these issues at union level. They later organised a new gathering of female workers where the original proposal was revised. Immediately afterwards, they contacted representatives in order to discuss these issues. This was a totally new experience for the women who participated in the Petition Committee. This was the first time they had access to Parliament, and representatives listened carefully as they voiced their proposals. It was a time of meeting for politically and socially active subjects. As part of the campaign, the media were contacted in order to have an impact on public opinion. The living and working conditions of the female workers were debated, not only from the perspective of complaint, but also from the perspective of the proposal set forth by these women.

The committee's lobbying efforts were successful, as some of the proposals became laws. One of these was for the special payment workers are entitled to if they work for a period of 25 or 30 years for the same employer. The most important achievement was that sexual harassment was included *as a fault of the employers* in the Law regulating labour relations. Long debates accompanied this victory, and female workers were able to discuss these issues openly for the first time. The discussions stressed the specificity of being a woman in the world of labour.

The experience gained by this particular group of women transcended petition-related activities. The group became the team in charge of organising events in commemoration of special days that were particularly significant for the working women's movement, such as International Woman's Day, Labour Day and Mother's Day. The women were active in the feminist movement also.

A second Committee of Women Workers was created in 1990. The document they presented included deeply-felt demands related to wage policies, employment policies, working conditions, occupational health, occupational safety, hygiene and industrial safety, social security and working women's rights stemming from their status as mothers. These included, among others, child-care, leaves of absence in the case of sickness of their children and an hour for breast-feeding.

As opposed to the situation of the 1985 Committee, the women who participated in this new committee showed a higher degree of consciousness of being producers. The demands they articulated are connected to the productive world, to the improvement of working conditions and the defence of employment. They even challenged the sexual segregation of jobs and they proposed their demasculinisation. Two factors account for this change: their identities were shaped in the process of participating in the activities organised by the women's movement on the one hand and, on the other, they were prompted by the threat which the economic crisis imposes on female employment.

BECOMING UNION LEADERS

Most of the participants of the Working Women's Petition Committee created in 1985 were soon to become union leaders. They assumed responsibilities in union jobs that had been controlled by males traditionally: General Secretariat, Defence, and Organisation.

The presence of women in labour union leadership imparted a new dynamic to it. Women demanded training so that new leadership would be able to take on their duties in an efficient manner. Unlike male leadership, women resorted more to negotiation in order to solve labour and union conflicts. They recognised the importance of communication between leadership and union members, and of unity and interunion co-ordination, and they created the appropriate channels that guaranteed such communication.

The presence of women in labour union leadership demanded a combination of training for leadership skills on the one hand, and advice and consultantship to labour union organisations on the other. This implied working with men who at the beginning were reluctant to receive advice at a feminist centre. They were even afraid of entering the institution's premises. For us, this meant discussing gender issues with men, which in turn implied unveiling the ways in which gender bestows power on males but restricts their power as well.

After the men's initial reluctance was overcome, excellent levels of communication followed. We analysed with them issues related to gender identity as well as political aspects connected to the situation of labour in the country. The climate of trust that was built up enabled men to speak about certain aspects of their lives which included work expectations and relationships with their partners. We even discussed issues such as free sexual choice and abortion, which were topics banned from the labour union sphere.

RESULTS

The actions we carried out gave rise to a new collective within the labour union movement: that of women workers. The active presence of this new collective implied the acknowledgement of heterogeneous subjects within the framework of labour unions, a crucial step towards the democratisation of labour union activities. The creation of a space of socialisation and exchange of opinions and experiences broadened the frame of reference of the labour union movement, and thus contributed to identify appropriate interlocutors for each specific demand.

Training was successful in recovering certain aspects for labour union dynamics and in introducing new aspects as well. Among these we must point out recreation and play, key aspects for the expression, consolidation and development of working-class culture.

By fostering the interaction of female workers with persons from other institutions which are active in the women's movement, we contribute to the process of linkage and networking in the women's movement, and to the creation of a women's movement within the workers' movement.

The groups of female workers relate as an autonomous collective to other interlocutors: the women and men that work with them, union leaders, labour union associations, other movements and the state itself. Those who are members of the workers' collective may or may not assume responsibilities within the union. They have a space for development within and outside the labour union movement; the union is no longer their exclusive frame of reference as the cllective of women, the feminist movement, is becoming a new frame of reference for them. This guarantees their freedom of choice and enables them to establish political alliances in a concrete way that responds to their own interests. When the situation of women in industry has been discussed, female workers have been able to articulate proposals and have devised participation strategies of their own. This *modus operandi* is closely linked to the commitment towards change in the labour union movement. Women now enjoy several spaces that are not mutually exclusive.

PERSPECTIVES

The achievements of women during the past years have been parallel to macrosocial processes which point increasingly towards the fragmentation and division of labour union movements. In the case of labour unionism, new neoliberal economic policies and the pressure towards more flexible employment policies are altering the material foundation upon which the consciousness of being a worker relies.

General recession in industry challenges the organic reproduction of the workers' movement. Massive lay-offs, shutdown of factories and changes in work legislation are a challenge to a weakenened labour union movement, and are especially a challenge for women workers.

The presence of pro-violence groups that are striving to have representation in the workers' movement further complicates the scene. These groups appear at a time when social contradictions are at a very acute stage, and when political crisis is rampant. They present themselves as the only persons who can guarantee a coherent and effective response to workers' demands. The broad socio-economic crisis within the society makes the incipient working women's movement also vulnerable to these groups.

The problems which we now face belong to different levels. At the theoretical level, we face the challenge of reconstructing a collective frame of reference which takes into account the manifold ways in which women work. At the level of practical politics, we have to provide elements aimed at defending and guaranteeing industrial employment for women. One of our priorities is to participate at the policy-making level, where industrial policies are designed.

Support to labour union organisations and to gender-specific consciousness-raising must be prioritised. These are needed to guarantee the existence of institutions to act as mediators between civil society and the state, and to prevent the chaos which threatens the labour union movement. We are also involved in providing economic consultancy for the implementation of alternative income generating strategies and job-creation strategies for women who have been forced to leave the industrial sector, so as not to waste the professionalisation which they acquired after years of experience in industrial jobs.

It is vital to continue organising groups of women workers, even among those that have left the industrial sector. In this way, we hope to contribute to create channels that will link these groups with other organisations and expressions of the women's movement.

6 Philippine Trade Unions and the Challenge of Gender

Jurgette A. Honculada

Industrialisation in the contemporary period has come to acquire a specific meaning for the Third World, or more precisely the Less Developed Countries (LDCs), which share a common legacy of colonialism that has bred structures of elite politics, the dominance of transnational corporations and economic dependency, along with an invidious cultural imperialism, all in the name of economic development whose zigs and zags have impoverished and marginalised growing numbers of its peoples.

This chapter first briefly traces Philippine economic development strategies and secondly, examines their impact on women's work in industry over the past two decades, in relation to the formal and informal workforce, more particularly in the phenomenon of home-based or sub-contracted work. Thirdly, the chapter looks at the efficacy and adequacy of trade unions in organising women and addressing their demands, and at the influence and support provided by the women's movement and feminism. Fourthly, it probes the role of gender and the interplay of class and gender in efforts to organise women workers from the formal and informal workforce. Finally it offers some conclusions and recommendations.

ECONOMIC DEVELOPMENT STRATEGIES AND THE FEMALE WORKFORCE

The Philippines broke free from over three and a half centuries of Spanish colonial domination in 1896 after generations of struggle, only to be subdued by superior and rampaging American military forces. Thus did the country come under the sway of Pax Americana, its economy and political system grooved more firmly to the needs of American capital as an agricultural base and dumping ground for American surplus goods. Free trade was neither free nor equal. In the first decades of the twentieth century, Philippine exports to the United States grew 32 times, while American exports to the Philippines multiplied 92 times (Shoesmith, 1986).

Moreover the Philippines sold cheap and bought dearly, resulting in an annual trade deficit of Pesos 273 million in 1949. The shift from subsistence to cash crop production for export at grossly unequal terms of trade led to growing impoverishment in both city and countryside, prompting government to embark on import substitution industrialisation (ISI) in the 1950s (Shoesmith, 1986).

ISI, the local manufacture of previously imported goods, in fact raised the manufacturing sector growth rate to over 14 per cent in the early 1950s, but by the 1960s it was clear that such growth could not be sustained. This was due to at least three factors: a narrow market base, the import-dependent character of this industrialisation, and growing US dominance in manufacturing and other sectors abetted by ISI, wittingly or unwittingly (Shoesmith, 1986). In response to a worsening balance of payments deficit, import controls were lifted and the currency devalued. These moves only served to raise costs of debt service and imported production inputs, on the one hand; and cause a massive outflow of dollars through capital and profit repatriation, on the other hand. In spite of increased US investments, by the late 1960s basic economic problems persisted such as the growing trade deficit, unemployment and underemployment. Hence the decision to shift to export-oriented industrialisation (EOI) as an economic development strategy.

EOI, it was claimed, would spur industrial growth through manufacture for export of labour-intensive goods. Production would not be constrained by a narrow domestic market or tight foreign exchange; and there would be massive generation of jobs. EOI came hand-in-glove with the rise of transnational companies (TNCs) in the 1960s and their increasing need to globalise production to offset declining profits caused by rising labour costs in advanced industrialised countries. Globalised production would farm out the more labour-intensive processes to the Third World where cheap labour abounded. And what labour was cheaper than female labour; perceived as docile, content with lower wage levels and dispensable?

This set the stage for massive entry of women into manufacturing in Third World countries including the Philippines, initially concentrated in export manufacturing or free trade zones. Women workers thus suffered from the conjuncture of the social, sexual and new international divisions of labour (NIDL): social because the majority of these women came from the rural and urban poor; and sexual because their labour largely reflected domestic work, drew lower pay and experienced poorer conditions relative to men. Export-oriented industrialisation and the NIDL meant, at best, light manufacturing for the LDCs, and the production of consumer rather than capital goods. Female labour forms a high proportion of the workforce in electronic, garment and textile production, as well as in footwear, toy manufacturing and food processing. In October 1990, women made up 8 185 000 workers or 36.32 per cent of the labour force of 22 532 000. This figure includes those working as well as those looking for work (National Statistics Office). In the formal sector in 1988, employed women comprised 36 per cent of the total employed in all industries. Employed women formed 45.2 per cent of workers in manufacturing (Philippine Development Plan for Women, 1989). In the informal sector a significant percentage were women in domestic outwork also called sub-contracting or home-based work.

Home-based workers in the Philippines are roughly estimated at seven to nine million. They form a significant part of the informal economy, estimated to contribute at least 30 per cent of economic activity. In 1981 there were estimated to be 450 to 500 thousand home sewers in the garment industry, and 214 thousand in the cottage industry (Vasquez, 1989).

The garment industry in fact had its origins in low-key cottage industry production of embroidery and infant wear from the 1950s through the 1960s. With the advent of EOI, garment production for export hit the $107 million mark, peaking at over $500 million in 1981. The oil crisis of the early 1980s, global economic recession and the political convulsions of Marcos' last years combined to halt business expansion, hitting the garment industry, among others, hard. Sub-contracting of garment production for export was a consequence of this, which received active encouragement from the government as a means to stem the grave problem of unemployment. The arrangement worked well for garment exports reached $600+ million and $800+ million in 1986 and 1988, respectively, peaking to over $1.6 billion in 1989 (Salud, 1989). Not only does home-based work cut down on costs; it also fragments the workforce, thus making unionising difficult, if not impossible.

Home-based garment workers are basically of three kinds: the labour-only sub-contractee who works on materials supplied by the sub-contractor at pre-agreed-upon rates, and is paid upon completion of production at a designated time; the sub-contractee who provides both materials and labour, bound by a market contract to sell only to the sub-contractor; and the micro-entrepreneur homeworker who provides materials and is free to sell to anyone although preference is for guaranteed purchase. Of over 600 combined respondents in two surveys of homeworkers in 1984 and 1989, 53 per cent belonged to the first category, 30 per cent to the second and 17 per cent were small entrepreneurs (Vasquez, 1989).

The major problem of homeworkers is the piece-rate system of wages, or wages paid by output depending on size, design and material worked with and reflecting peak or low demand seasons. Although quality must be up to factory standards, there is no guaranteed wage: this constitutes the primary form of exploitation of homeworkers (Vasquez, 1989). A home sewer could earn 10 cents for a baby dress tagged at $12 in US department stores. Other problems relate to the widespread lack of written contracts, which places homeworkers at a disadvantage, work time whose apparent flexibility in fact disguises an insidious twinning of paid work and housework, and work space which is commonly cramped, poorly lit and subject to external disturbance. When home tasks and work deadlines conflict, either or both suffer, resulting in great stress for the homeworker and a high rate of rejects, further reducing income.

Belonging to the informal economy, homeworkers lie beyond the pale of labour standards and other legislation. Thus, there is no agency to turn to for work-related complaints and illnesses. Lastly, the majority of homeworkers have no access to credit, training, marketing and product development which in the medium and long term can help free them from dependency on the sub-contracting system.

FORMS OF ORGANISING WOMEN WORKERS

Organising Women Workers in the Formal Economy

The organisation of women workers in the formal economy must be viewed within the broader context of the labour movement or trade union movement. The Philippine trade union movement is fragmented into five centres, over 150 federations and national unions with various structures and sizes (some with only a few hundred members). The labour force currently stands at over 23 million of which roughly half is either unemployed or underemployed. The official unemployment rate is 13.5 per cent (National Statistics Office).

Workers belonging to unions comprise less than 10 per cent of the labour force, that is to say over one million are unionised. Workers covered by collective bargaining agreements number considerably less, between 600 000 and 800 000. Figures are imprecise partly owing to rapid turnover in union representation and continuing retrenchments that worsened beginning late in 1990.

Unionism in the Third World has always been beset by external difficulties such as vast numbers of unemployed (undermining security and wages of those employed), repressive labour legislation, corrupt labour department officials and paramilitary violence, apart from the practice of runaway shops. All this added to internal weaknesses among workers such as individualism, opportunism and lack of self-confidence, largely account for the low rate of unionisation in the country.

Among 620 216 union members registered with the Bureau of Labour Relations in 1985, women comprised 25 per cent of the total membership. A survey of 116 independent unions and one federation in Metro Manila in 1985 indicated that 15 529 workers were union members out of a total of 26 648 workers. (It can be surmised that casual workers, contract workers and apprentices accounted for the high proportion of non-union members.) Of the total number of union members over half (51 per cent) were in the manufacturing sector; half in this sector were women. Total female membership among the 15 529 union members showed over 43 per cent but the profile of women in union leadership positions tells a different story. Out of 330 female union officers in the same survey, 34 per cent served as board members, 19 per cent were treasurers, 16.6 per cent secretaries, 11.5 per cent auditors, 6.6 per cent vice presidents, 6.3 per cent press relation officers and only 4.8 per cent assumed the union presidency (Philippine Development Plan for Women, 1989). The sexual division of labour governs union leadership here as elsewhere.

An informal survey of labour centres and unions in mid-1989 (undertaken by Labour Research and Education Network, Inc.) reveals the same phenomenon: male dominance in union leadership, particularly in executive decision-making. In four labour centres – Trade Union Congress of the Philippines (TUCP), Kilusang Mayo Uno (KMU), Lakas Manggagawa Labour Centre (LMLC) and Federation of Free Workers (FFW) (although a federation the latter may be considered a quasi-centre because of its size), 92 per cent of the combined national executive board and national executive council positions were occupied by men and only 8 per cent by women. Among seven unions or federations (six of which are affiliated to the above-mentioned centres), men held 78 per cent of the national executive positions and women 22 per cent.

These figures are doubly remarkable in that from the middle to the late 1980s, women had formed a significant percentage of the formal workforce (36 per cent in 1990); and that in the geographical and occupational sectors represented (Metro Manila and manufacturing) women represented a significant percentage of the workforce, at least half in manufacturing and higher in electronics, garments and textiles which abound in Metro Manila. Finally it must be noted that most, if not all, of the seven unions surveyed were progressive unions as distinguished from 'yellow' unions which defend company interests more than they do workers'. What explains this gender gap in unions: women at the base but not at the top; women as support (treasurer, auditor, secretary) but not as executive? The corollary question is: are unions the most effective forms of organising women workers, given their low rate of involvement and participation?

Historical and social reasons account for the subordinate position occupied by women in the unions. Women in pre-colonial Philippines enjoyed a relative gender egalitarianism as evidenced in their right to trade and pass on property to offspring and in the lack of stigma attached to children born out of wedlock. Spanish colonialism changed all this, reducing women to the roles of wife, mother, and church devotee. Half a century of American neocolonial rule unlocked doors for women through universal public education and the emergent bureaucracy and industry that required their skills and labour, albeit in limited numbers.

But entry into the public spheres of school and work did not bring gender equality but rather the double burden, for the production–reproduction divide remained as entrenched as ever. Women were responsible for housework and child-care while men earned the bread; and even when women ventured into paid work, the domestic burden was primarily theirs. While paying lip service to gender equality, bourgeois culture rode on women's subordination in society. Dependent capitalism introduced labour as a commodity. With the dualism of woman as madonna or whore carried over from Spanish feudal culture, a specific class of women developed for sexual servicing. The double exploitation on account of class and gender held true not only for prostitutes but also for the majority of Filipinas as well. For women workers this meant not only low pay, but also lower pay vis-à-vis male counterparts for their work outside home was considered an extension of domestic labour. It also meant being concentrated in low-skilled and low-prestige production work as against higher paid and higher-placed positions for men. It further meant being subject to sexual harassment and exploitation in the workplace.

Male dominance that infused society and culture was also reflected in the labour movement, its ethos, self-image and structures. Historically the early workforce in sugar and rice mills, logging camps and sugar plantations was largely male, but the advent of export-oriented industries in the 1970s ushered in women in large numbers. The labour movement, however, remained intractably male-oriented in its priorities and programmes. Women were indeed at the base of the labour movement, but they were not a critical mass. Thus their numbers did not translate into gender solidarity and gender power.

The Women's Movement and Union Feminism

If the issue of gender were solely left to the unions, it might be a case of 'too little, too late'. Fortunately women in our collective past and present are helping us recover the imperative of gender. Spanish colonisation failed to completely obliterate the female principle from our historical consciousness. The *babylanes* or priestesses who healed, counselled and, on occasion, led rebellions, have come alive as role-models for young Filipinas as they seek a persona that redefines the barriers of private and public, and as they negotiate emotional and work arrangements that are mutually supportive rather than conflicting.

Keeping historical continuity with the babylanes and heroines are the activists of the various waves of feminism in the country: the suffragettes in the 1930s who fought for the vote, the women professionals in the 1940s and 1950s who struggled for equal space and recognition, the activists of the 1970s who wanted a whole new world; and the rainbow of feminists in the 1980s and 1990s, heir to the rich tapestry of the past, on surer footing but also facing more profound challenges.

Union feminists have come to feminism through various routes, or, more often, a combination of these. As local union officers they experience inequality first- or second-hand through insensitive male peers or unreasoning and brutalising spouses. As federation staff with some exposure to feminist writings, they see the reality of gender oppression in the lives of women workers. As radical activists they find socialist theory and practice wanting on the question of gender. In any case, feminist theory (which is by no means monolithic) provides the categories with which to frame and re-read the reality. Thus the women's movement, or more precisely, feminism, has touched women in the unions, and has been touched by them.

Interviews with 16 women, most related to unions and half coming directly from unions and federations, have yielded parallel tales of earnest organising and conscientisation of women by women. Highlights of the interviews include the gender profile of members and leaders, and representation of a gross disregard of gender issues. These unions and federations have a high percentage of members from the garment industry, around 90 per cent in two organisations.

As shown earlier, female membership ranged from 38 per cent at the labour centre level to 40–50 per cent at the federation level and 80–90 per cent at the alliance or local level. Female leadership however constituted a low 12 per cent to 20 per cent and 37 per cent to 50 per cent at the top and medium levels, respectively. This explains the common complaint about men's insensitivity to gender issues. One interviewee recounts that 12 years ago, pregnant women members were simply told by unions, 'You get pregnant so often, we'd better look for a replacement'. Male union leaders had no practical knowledge of maternity benefits guidelines. Women had to press for seats for garment sewers. There was no support either for women officers at the local level who had to make up such excuses as overtime work or a birthday party to attend union activities, risking spouse-beating if found out. Husbands, boyfriends and fathers objected to female participation in union leadership because of the perception that a woman's world revolved around the home, church, school, market and factory; unions were a man's world. Thus the interviewee decided to form a separate organisation along with other women.

Interviewees from a major labour centre said a women's department had existed for 11 years, mostly for show, until women raised the issue of real participation and pushed for a formal structure, not a token one, to represent women. A women's organisation has been formed within the centre whose specific thrust is education and training for women.

Interviewees from the two alliances represented observed that a female organiser cannot focus on both trade union and women's organising, for the former is already demanding work. One other interviewee stressed that the gender issue becomes stale within a context of predominantly male leadership. Interviewees from both organisations recognised that activating women and forming a core female leadership is difficult: they are distracted at seminars and meetings, thinking of the shopping, laundry and housework awaiting them. Representing left-of-centre political tendencies, both alliances organise mainly on class-based issues. However, women's participation is not developed or sustained for gender-related reasons: the double burden, objection of husband or family or cultural blocks. One garment local faced a leadership crisis when 90 per cent of the officers, who were single, got married: they either left or took lower positions such as shop steward.

So the women in these unions and federations started organising, confronting the male leadership, forwarding resolutions on affirmative action, organising seminars and forming study circles. One interviewee felt an inter-local alliance could join the efforts of women in various locals for greater weight within the federation. The alliance is envisaged to be within the federation, but will generate its own dynamics to develop and push women into the leadership and to raise gender demands. Two other interviewees proposed a women's institute to help provide for education, training and other needs of women workers, but also to show to alliance men that women are capable of founding and running their own structure. Without this men would not take the women seriously, even if the men had undergone gender sensitivity training.

Finances are a weak point, and thus far the above initiatives are hampered by a lack of committed funding from local sources; foreign funds are fine for as long as they're there. The 12-year-old women's organisation affiliated to a federation suffers from very low dues and can only undertake limited education and organising.

Affirmative action in the form of resolutions for guaranteed education and seats on the executive for women and guaranteed funding for activities have either been treated in a patronising way ('approved without thinking') or have been rejected precisely because male leadership had comprehended the import of such action. Where a visible core of female leadership has developed, or where finances are held separately, part of the male leadership feels threatened and asks, 'Why do you want to break away?' The feeling among women is that while union structures are not completely closed to them, neither are they that 'open'.

Organising Home-based Workers

PATAMABA (National Association of Home-based Workers) was formally launched in May, 1991 with 200 delegates representing 2000 members, mostly engaged in sewing, from 13 towns. PATAMABA's major advantage is continuing support from its 15-year-old parent organisation, with 25 000 members, KABAPA (Association of the New Filipina), which is largely rural-based, many of whom are community leaders. Home-based work proliferated in the early 1980s among many KABAPA areas, but it was not until the late 1980s that its various initiatives in research, co-op building and income-generating projects (with some ILO assistance) melded organisationally.

KABAPA has various guidelines on how to form and run organisations, co-operatives, budgeting and the like which has greatly helped in PATAMABA organising. Other favourable conditions included a rising global interest in home-based work, inspiration provided by SEWA in India, and support from some top labour department officials. PATAMABA leaders have undergone training along with paralegal training, the latter with assistance from academe. There have been setbacks such as the temporary failure of a co-op project that sold dusters at P5 apiece instead of the P1.50 market price because 'the objective is that the homeworkers earn and not that the project profits'. Market research and credit supports are but two of the components necessary for the organisation to succeed.

A KABAPA supporter was of the opinion that income-generating projects and co-ops are not the whole answer to the problem of home-based work; intervention at the level of government is necessary in terms of legislation and executive policy. KABAPA-PATAMABA has teamed up with colleagues in the state university, the labour department and Congress to draft a bill that seeks to define homework, set down terms and conditions of work, provide social security benefits and ensure the right of self-organisation. The bill is certain to face rough sailing in Congress, but at least the first step has been taken towards meaningful and comprehensive legislation on home-based work. The draft bill seeks to do away with or reduce sub-contracting.

Another crucial area is research including research on the garment and textile industries: how to ensure viability apart from export markets? There also is talk of possible interco-op exchange, for instance rice traded for goods produced in the city. Research must also examine the relationship between the formal and informal sectors both at macro and micro levels. In Cebu in central Philippines, for instance, male rattan furniture workers bring home rattan chains for their wives to sand. Framing however remains a male task and earns more than twice the rates for sanding. Women themselves have accepted this gender division of labour, saying 'If we take on that task (framing), what will our men do?'

The informal sector, and home-based work in particular, has long been a netherworld for organising, self-empowerment and legal protection. PATAMABA is showing that painstaking work, an indomitable will, a fine sense of timing, gender solidarity and a lot of help from a lot of friends (to be sure the difficulties are multitude) can make inroads into that netherworld.

One other example of an alternative route to organising women must be shared. The Livelihood Revolving Fund for Women (LRFW) seeks to integrate income generation with organising and consciousness-raising, targetting groups of 5–10 women.[1] How does LRFW relate to the question of organising women workers? Apart from the fact that this concept will be tested among groups of women workers this year, this initiative combines organising and education with generating the wherewithal. Women's organising in unions often gets bogged down on the issue of funds (whether truly or as mere excuse).

The programme meets this need head-on and has other strengths as a model for organising women. As the person most responsible for project conceptualisation and administration observes:

1. Union women's committees need not depend on the union for crumbs.
2. Its social responsibility component with a built-in social fund can provide for social services such as child care; and women can themselves generate the needed resources.

3. The project can develop a power mechanism or base separate from
    the union.
    (Interview with Karina David, Executive Director of Harnessing
            Self-Reliant Initiatives and Knowledge, Inc. (HASIK))

All this is not meant to develop separatism, but rather to help women build
their self-worth in the community and to change the conditions of their
lives in quickly tangible ways. This can proceed parallel to, related or even
integrated with union organising. It breaks the bind of women not getting
far in unions since there are no funds for activities for reasons such as
men's insensitivity to women's needs. It breaks the possible non-utility
of consciousness-raising seminars *ad infinitum* without clear organising
targets.

Are unions the best way to organise women workers? The answer is yes
and no. Yes because unions remain the prime instruments of the working
class to defend and advance its interests: to opt out of unionism is to miss
the mainstream. Having said that, we know that unions are capable of a
fractured vision: unions can turn on their narrow needs and definitions and
ignore whole sections of humanity, their co-proletariat included. Unions
initially, intermediately and finally may leave no time and space for women.
Thus women need their own organisations and structures as part of, but
also apart from, unions.

Within unions there is a need for women to have their own time and
space, through women's committees, affirmative action, education and
training geared to women, and federation-based women's alliances. But
outside unions or related to them, there is need for women's support
structures such as legal clinics, women's crisis centres, health centres, and
women's organisations. (Political parties are largely elite-dominated; there
is as yet no base of experience to say definitively how open they are to the
gender issue.) The point is that organising women workers starts with a
core that provides mutual sustenance and support for members, and from
which initiatives flow and structures are set up. The core must move into
the leadership so the gender issue will impact on all aspects of union life.
At the same time, union women need the broad women's movement to
help sustain them.

GENDER, CLASS AND AUTONOMY

Women workers have been spurred to union involvement, or at least,
membership, primarily through class-related issues of low pay, long hours,

heavy quotas, intolerable and unsafe working conditions. But in the past few years parallel with the growth of feminist consciousness, gender has increasingly become central in stirring women's consciousness, moving them to industrial action and social protest, enlarging their vision of the future and sustaining their participation in union activities.

This has been made possible by a political economy that in the first instance needed the massing of women workers in industry albeit light manufacturing or plain assembly work; and, in the second instance, their being thus gathered under conditions which violated their humanity and their gender.

The Philippine labour movement ranges in political persuasion from right to centre to left-of-centre to extreme left, but there is a consensus among various women leaders that women need to be activated and mobilised for their own and the union's sake. The depth of understanding of gender and class, and the interplay between them, varies from union to union. The national democrats as exemplified by Kilusang Manggagawang Kababaihan (KMK) and some affiliates of Kilusang Mayo Uno (KMU) would tend to emphasise class or anti-imperialism; while most left-of-centre unions would maintain that gender and class are equally important. (Remember these are the women's views; the men think rather differently.) Nevertheless, there is grudging recognition of the significance of gender across the unions. The linkage between class and gender comes easily for home-based workers who are at the bottom of the sub-contracting ladder, at whose apex lie the multinational companies (MNCs) and TNCs.

TRAINING WOMEN WORKERS: FEMINIST METHODOLOGY IN ACTION

The framework and substance of women's seminars have slowly evolved, initially drawing from some concepts and key issues in Western feminism, but eventually claiming and enriching the same for Filipino women. Thus a basic women's course might have all or most of the following topics: women's situation, sex and gender, socialisation and sex-role stereotyping, history of women's oppression in the Philippines, principles of feminism.

The situationer provides an overview of women in various classes and sectors in the country, zeroing in on women workers. Sex and gender (or nature and culture) shows that sex is biologically determined but gender is a cultural construct and can therefore be changed. Socialisation probes the range of institutions (which includes the family, church and religion, school, media) as they stereotype boys and girls into distinct roles. History traces the roots of gender oppression in the country, and feminist principles deals with basic demands such as equal pay and equal opportunity. Law as an instrument of gender oppression, and the need for legal reform and advocacy, is another area of concern. In the course of the seminar key concepts emerge such as the sexual division of labour, subordination/patriarchy, gender inequality and discrimination, violence against women, and autonomy.

These are not highly abstract concepts for women workers and female union staff, but realities they face daily. As one woman organiser observed:

> The trade union agenda is easier . . . to overcome one's timidity, inferiority feelings, for instance. But gender? Personal change is too deep and difficult a process. How does one change culture which seems to have become nature?

But the question of gender proved unrelenting: why did women come to meetings with a black eye? Why did working mothers have to lock their children at home the whole day? Why did women vanish from the picketline? She came to the conclusion: 'Once the gender issue is resolved, the union issue will also be resolved'. Gender discrimination is experienced in the workplace through higher pay rates for men; or in the union through the sexual division of labour – men as executive, women as support staff. Sexism is uncovered in sexist ads, child-rearing practices as portrayed in commercials, pop songs that celebrate *machismo* (as in *Babaero* or womaniser, or such lines as 'your legs daze me'). Gender violence is seen in a continuum with vulgar jokes at one end and rape, wife-beating and child sexual abuse at the other. The traditional view of wife-beating is that it is a male right. Some women workers with their own incomes may be less subject to physical violence but do suffer from emotional harassment, being made to feel guilty for perceived neglect of home and family. The marriage contract is understood to mean woman saying to man: marry me, feed me and I will cook for you, keep house for you (even if I also work outside the home).

Sexual harassment in the workplace frequently takes the form of trading sex for promotion, higher pay, or simple favours such as being able to buy and sell while at work or suffering no penalty from tardiness. The ratio of one male superior for every 100 or more female subordinates also encourages sexual exploitation. In garment enterprises, roughly half of the workers may be married. There is a high incidence of single parenthood from failed relationships and such women may become *kabit* (or someone's 'woman') to augment income. While many don't like trading sex for advantage, they don't consider this sexual harassment. Unions are also guilty of sexism in the practice of some male organisers (single or married) of having 'a girl in every local' as an organising strategy; or because 'we men have our needs'. Or women workers' complaints about vulgar jokes that are trivialised by male union officers: 'Anyway talk can't get you pregnant, besides it's just a joke'. A common complaint seems to be the practice of male security guards (when women guards are absent) of 'chancing' or even 'feasting' (*nagpiyesta*) on women's bodies during inspections. (There have been rare reports of lesbian security guards 'chancing'.) In one extreme case, male guards paraded a worker's panty on the charge that it was pilfered from the company.

To the union's credit, local officers (including the male executive) confronted management on the issue. The learning methods developed (both original and borrowed) have been very creative.[2] Openness and self-disclosure (the latter to the extent possible) are crucial for the success of seminars for the personal is indeed political. 'Shape me' exercise asks participants to symbolise themselves through coloured paper cut-outs.[3] The revelations and rich reflections that follow would not have been evoked through simple verbalising. An Activity Profile lists a woman's tasks at home and at work; comparative male and female profiles may be drawn up. 'Fantasy of Eve' is an exercise in reverse sexism, asking participants at the end whether this is their vision of the future. *Web chart* starts with a single 'why': why were you late to work? and keeps on asking why until a whole web of women's dilemmas and difficulties emerges. *Image theatre* freezes a scene in a woman's daily life and asks whether injustice is reflected in the scene, and how the women would want it changed, without the participants speaking. Gender stereotyping is portrayed through role play. Feminist principles are evoked simply by asking, 'What are the negative/positive images you associate with feminism?' Or alternatively, 'What are your fears and hopes with regard to women's liberation?' This gives the opportunity to quickly debunk images of feminists as bed-hoppers, bra-burners, women with nothing better to do. Songs that reflect the new culture are contrasted with sexist tunes, e.g. compare the earlier lines quoted with, 'A woman is not just a wife or a friend but also a comrade'.

Women's health is also seen as a central issue, often in conjunction with reproductive rights (the National Federation of Labour is one of the few unions with a full programme on health), which is the other related half of sexuality. In this predominantly Catholic country, fertility is not an easy subject to tackle; and tackling the subject of sexuality is like treading on thin ice, so we tread ever so lightly. Skilled and competent resource persons are called on to handle these sessions which usually include sexual learning and practice and surfacing participants' views on such issues as divorce, abortion, hetero- and homosexuality, all of which relate to the concept of bodily integrity. The concept of autonomy requires knowing oneself and one's body, hence the importance of discussing sexuality, particularly where sex is still equated with procreation and the childless woman is regarded of little value. Or where sex is deemed a wifely duty 'or else he may go after someone else'. If time allows, 'time travel' or *guided imagery* takes participants back in time through some form of hypnosis. It is a process of helping women begin to face themselves, their long-repressed traumas, their fears, their hang-ups, their demons. It is cathartic but also full of pain, and a number of women always end up sobbing. Later, sharing in the group is optional. One woman, estranged from her husband, spoke of this scene: running for the bus and always missing it, prompting her to cry out, 'What have I done to deserve this? Why does life always pass me by?' In another group a participant was moved to share the secret she could no longer bear: a sadistic husband who brutalised her and once even took a woman home.

Autonomy is emerging as a key concept that gains meaning at various levels, personal and organisational. One way to counter guilt feelings over alleged neglect of domestic duties is the 'I' imperative: one owes it to oneself to attend seminars, meetings, to develop friendships outside home. This forces the question: is there an *I* to begin with? Women then begin to appreciate the need for time and space for themselves, the need to try to create options where none exist: to marry or not, to have a child or not. A small but growing number of women workers in manufacturing (but also plantations and, I suppose, services) are quite clear about not wanting to marry but, making the decision doubly remarkable, wanting to have a child whether adopted or biological. As one of them put it, 'marriage is too much of a gamble'; and they have the evidence of domestic violence and failed marriages before them. (Another problem: 'My parents would beat me if I had a child without marrying', one woman said.) Financial independence, working (from the ages of 16 or 18) has also brought emotional independence. Relationships, yes, but based on mutuality and equality which are rather hard to come by. This explains the appeal of lesbian relationships for a few because here, conflicts can be thrashed out peacefully and not through the fist. Feminist unionists (and even those not quite) frequently negotiate household arrangements with spouses or partners to achieve, or approximate, equality inside and outside the home.

Autonomy also takes organisational meaning when women develop a structure; be it a core group, committee, or full-blown organisation; within or related to the union or federation. They keenly recognise that autonomy is merely hot air without one's own funds, hence the importance of such experiments as LRFW to generate resources for women not contingent on male goodwill and charity. A parallel level of meaning is the autonomy of the women's movement (women of various sectors and classes banding together on common demands) *vis-à-vis* the broader political movement or political parties.

Thus far, change seems to have most taken place at the personal plane, as it should in the first instance: in being more aware about men and relationships, in cringing at sexist jokes or discomfiture at exclusive language, in an enhanced self-image, in greater involvement in union activities such as seminars and mobilisations.

But change must also take place structurally through viable and vibrant women's committees and inter-union alliances that press for mainstreaming of gender in unions: through more women in leadership, more grievances and collective bargaining agreement (CBA) proposals with a gender dimension (e.g. sexual harassment, parental leave, child-care) so that union negotiations do not simply entail men in the union talking with men in management and disregarding women's issues. This will require basic changes in the way a union organises, conducts seminars and other activities.

Lastly, we tackle the imperative of 'men must change too'. More specifically, gender conscientisation or sensitivity training for men in which modest initiatives have been taken. It proceeds from the recognition that while men may be victimisers, they are also victims and stand in need of salvation. They are not allowed to cry, they must rein in their emotions; so they die from heart-attack instead. The bare fact is of course that there can be no women's liberation without men's liberation.

A handful of these seminars have been undertaken thus far with both trade union and mixed (NGO and TU staff men) groups with very creative methods employed, including a card game that is too detailed to explain here. There is less confrontation and more an attempt to hold up a mirror with which to objectively view gender inequality and subordination. Feedback from the men has been very positive, e.g. rubber tappers who drew up activity profiles for themselves and the wives whom they described as 'doing nothing' were speechless at the volume of housework the women did and promptly asked, 'How can we solve this?' It is a truism that the method is the message. One feminist tells the tale of how gender conflict was sown (or perhaps exacerbated) in an urban poor community with a women's module given without regard to sensitivities in the community. One group of women did not know how to handle the anger they were developing towards their menfolk, which in turn provoked the men. Conflicts ensued, the education effort boomeranged, the women turned around and said this is not for us, it only creates trouble. Glib as it may sound and hard as it may be to achieve in reality, gender solidarity means not only sisterhood among women, but also friendship and community between men and women.

CONCLUSION

The process of industrialisation, or more precisely, the new international division of labour and globalised production, has had contradictory consequences for the massive numbers of young (and middle-aged) women plunged into the formal and informal sectors of the economy. While they are doubly exploited as part of the labouring poor and as women, socialised production creates the opportunity for collective action and collective learning.

Trade union education has largely focused on common issues in the workplace and political education, such as it is, that deals with political and economic analyses and strategies. Such education is inadequate to confront gender contradictions in the workplace, at home and in the unions.

A small but growing critical mass of women, organic union leaders, feminist staff women, are putting forward analyses and raising issues that make gender a central demand in and out of unions. There is a need to deepen and develop the substance and methodology of gender education as basic, not specialised, education in the unions. Gender is to be taken in interaction with class and other oppressions and the basic homework of field and library research must be done to show these conjunctures. To hold up one contradiction, such as class or gender, as paramount and primary is reductionism and worse, idolatry of an insidious kind. This primary contradiction dogma impoverishes reality.

The gender education that is being undertaken is by no means widespread. It has to become part of the norm and for this there must be changes in ways of organising and other union structures. Support structures must be created so the tasks of reproduction can be lightened for both women and men; these include child-care centres, community cafeterias and laundries, and the like. Time and energy saved can go to quality time for the family, creative personal development, union and political activity.

Our vision of the future must include the macro: genuine industrialisation and an economy that meets the needs of its people for jobs, food and shelter. Not daily backbreaking work and a patriarchal culture that turn young women prematurely grey, and force them to choose between work and family, union and husband. This vision must also confront the problematic of home-based work.

The young female activists of the 1970s were right: there is a whole new world to win. This is also the message borne by women workers thrust willy-nilly into the process of industrialisation as they seek to transform their unions. But in the 1990s that message comes with the cutting edge of gender: feminise politics, feminise unions. Or, in the words of some of them: when you solve the problem of women's organising, you solve the problem of union organising. There is no other alternative.

NOTES

The writer wishes to acknowledge the help of Virginia Teodosio, professor at the University of the Philippines School of Labour and Industrial Relations, in preparing this paper.

1. Now in its first year of operation, LRFW covers over 100 women's groups in 40 provinces and was made possible by a Peso 5 million grant from the Office of the President. Careful conceptualisation (by feminists with a track record in organising) drew on experiences here and abroad: a review of the local '5/6' loan system and the Grameen Bank in Bangladesh and their high repayment rates, a study of past livelihood projects and their weaknesses, and one year of pretest and refinement. The project is backed by three networks with a total reach of 700 NGOs and co-operatives. One network is each tasked with marketing, monitoring and evaluation, and fund management and secretariat functions.

    Among the many elements that account for the project's success is speedy processing (proposal and feasibility study are done in questionnaire form to unburden women), weekly repayment, group fund to develop the discipline of saving, social responsibility fund to instill community values and make visible the value of women's labour. The base unit is deliberately kept small for more effective group discipline and support and building of social values. Consciousness-raising is done through sessions with related NGOs and other more informal ways. The issue of gender also emerges as when women's double burden must be shared by husbands at the risk of project failure.

2. Editors' note: A handbook for gender awareness trainers and facilitators has subsequently been published in the Philippines. The book, *Usapang Babae: Gender Awareness through Theatre Arts, Games and Processes*, was published in Manila in 1992 by the National Commission on the Role of Filipino Women. It is positively reviewed in the *Asian Women Workers Newsletter*, Vol. 13, No. 1, Jan. 1994.

3. 'Shape me' is an exercise in self-representation through shape and colour. Participants cut and shape coloured pieces of paper into symbols that reflect themselves. The author has used this exercise with different groups of women union leaders and has found it very enriching and revealing of the subjective

182   *Confronting State, Capital and Patriarchy*

and objective situation of a growing number of women workers and union staff women who may not have heard at all of feminism but who, in conscious thought and unconscious dreaming, reject the 'no choice' and 'no win' situation that was the lot of their mothers and grandmothers.

REFERENCES

Philippine Development Plan for Women 1989–92. 1989. Manila.
Saludo, Noemi. 1989. 'The Garments Industry: Its Rural Women Homeworkers', Manila.
Shoesmith, Dennis (ed.). 1986. *Export Processing Zones in Five Countries*, Caritas Printing Training Centre, Hong Kong.
Vasquez, Noel. 1989. 'Issues and Problems of Rural Women Homeworkers in the Philippines', Manila.

7 Urban Working-class Women: The Need for Autonomy
Rohini Hensman

Women workers are women, and they are workers; in theory, it should be possible for *all* their rights as women workers to be fought for through the women's liberation movement and the trade union movement. Yet if we look at the case of Bombay, India, where both movements have been very vital and active, it appears that the interests of women workers have been, ultimately, passed by. More specifically, in the organised industrial sector, where most of the better employment for women is to be found, thousands of women's jobs have been lost. If there is any expansion in industrial employment for women, it is in the unorganised sector, under very inferior terms and conditions. In other words, women remain a cheap and disposable part of the labour force, *despite* struggles for women's rights by both the trade union movement and the women's movement. This chapter examines the reasons for the continued marginalisation of women workers, on the basis of case studies of the pharmaceutical and food industries in Bombay.

METHODOLOGY

In 1982, the Union Research Group (URG), an independent collective supplying bargaining information to Bombay unions, was asked by some employees' unions to investigate the effects of the automation of packing lines in these two industries, since it was apparently leading to increased workloads on the one hand and so-called 'surplus staff' on the other. As the packing lines were staffed mainly by women, two women in the URG, Sujata Gothoskar and I, undertook this assignment. We also took the opportunity to find out more about the facilities these women workers enjoyed, the problems they suffered, and the history of how they got to be where they were.

The plant-level unionists in most of the companies we approached did their best to help with our study. Where the union was strong, it was able to arrange interviews for us in working time, and in some instances also plant visits, so that we could observe the women at work. In other cases, we had to interview the workers in the factory canteen or union office during the lunch break or after work; and where even this was not possible, we visited the women at home and interviewed them there. We explained to the workers we interviewed that the URG would be bringing out information bulletins comparing the situation in the various plants we were studying, and that this information could be used either to improve their own conditions, if they were at a disadvantage, or, if their own conditions were satisfactory, to improve the situation of less fortunate workers. In every case, we were met with interest and co-operation by the workers, who were often eager to talk about their work experiences. This at first surprised us, given that the work was usually monotonous, if not downright unpleasant; but it is not really surprising if we recognise how important a part of their lives this occupation was. There were also some interviews with supervisors and managers.

The initial interviews with women workers on the nature of their work and the way in which it had changed over the years were carried out with one woman at a time describing the packing line which she worked on. There was no structured interview schedule, but standard questions were asked, i.e. a description of the machinery and operations performed by the staff, past and present; the production output, past and present; any other changes (e.g. in the packing materials); problems and suggestions for improvement (e.g. fatigue, bottlenecks, under-staffing, inappropriate machinery, etc.). We also asked about maternity benefits, crèche facilities, and women's involvement in the union and struggles.

After the investigation was over, a small meeting of women union activists was held. The discussion was completely unstructured and free-ranging, after we had presented a summary of our findings. Out of it came suggestions for improving conditions for women workers, which we incorporated into the final reports which were carried in two information bulletins and also summarised in a one-page report called 'Making the Workplace a Better Place for Women'. The summary was then discussed with groups of around five women in each factory. These discussions were structured only in the sense that they were around the points contained in the report; apart from that, the women simply picked up the points which had taken their interest, which were not necessarily the same in each factory, and of course also varied from woman to woman.

The women workers who participated in the discussions were a mixture of younger and older, married and unmarried, but with a preponderance of middle-aged married women. In some cases, the male unionists who had helped to organise the discussions wandered in and out, or sat in on part of them. Their contributions have been marked with an (m). Whereas the earlier set of interviews had been aimed at documenting the actual situation in the factories, past and present, these discussions were aimed at exchanging ideas and opinions, with the aim of finding ways to make the workplace a better place for women, and were therefore more on the 'action' side of the research.

The discussion below is limited to the pharmaceutical industry, but similar trends were apparent in the food industry.

TRENDS IN WOMEN'S EMPLOYMENT IN PHARMACEUTICAL COMPANIES

We found that over the past 10–20 years there had been extensive automation on the packing lines; less commonly, there had been reduction of packing materials and simplification of the process, or speeding up and reduction in line strength even without the introduction of new machinery. The combined impact of these changes was a tremendous increase in production and a clear reduction in line strength.

However, the process of automation was uneven between different factories, some of which had reached much higher levels of automation than others; different lines in the same factory; and different operations on the same line. It was often the case that earlier operations like filling, sealing and labelling were automated, while later operations like carton-packing and especially case-packing remained manual. Where this happened, there were complex effects on both effort and line strength. Generally, the number of people engaged in the operations which had been automated declined, and the effort required for these tasks also declined, although sometimes workloads increased due to the allocation of an excessive number of tasks to one operator, or due to badly-designed machinery. Further down the line where tasks remained manual, however, there might be an increase in the number of operators and, where this was insufficient to offset the increase in production, a greater level of effort as well.

Thus where only the earlier operations were automated, displaced workers could be redeployed further down the line, and the strength of the line as a whole might be unchanged. However, when packing itself became automated, the consequences were more far-reaching, because line strength as a whole was drastically reduced. Where there was a large reserve of temporary workers, they were generally terminated at this point. The same could not be done to displaced permanent workers, because in the plants we surveyed, unions had included in their agreements with management a clause that automation would not lead to retrenchment.[1] So instead of being retrenched, the 'surplus staff' were shunted from line to line and given the worst jobs – a procedure which created such a sense of frustration and insecurity that many of those subjected to it were later willing to accept voluntary retirement schemes. In other cases, management simply waited till workers retired and then left the vacancies unfilled. Overall, jobs were being lost, either through early retirement or through natural wastage (Union Research Group, Dec. 1983).

However, these changes did not have the same impact on women and men. Gender segregation of jobs, with jobs in manufacturing and maintenance departments monopolised by men while women were concentrated in labour-intensive jobs like packing and visual inspection, meant that the bulk of the jobs which were disappearing were those which had earlier been done by women. But the loss of women's employment was greater than what would have been expected from this process alone; even in the jobs which remained, women were being replaced by men. There could be no question of the tasks, once automated, being less suitable for women than they had been before. Indeed, many of the women pointed out that with automation, the work had become easier and less hazardous than before. For example, manual capping and sealing of bottles was a strenuous operation requiring muscular movements of the arm or leg several thousand times a day, whereas the automated operation involved mainly machine-minding and filling caps into a hopper. Understanding why women were being replaced by men in such jobs requires an examination of other changes which had been taking place.

When these companies started from the late 1940s onwards, a large number of young unmarried women straight out of school were recruited to work on the packing lines. Although the Factories Act of 1948 already prohibited night work for women, this was irrelevant because only day shifts were being run at this stage in the jobs they were doing. Legislation on maternity benefits and workplace crèches (which were required by the Factories Act to be provided for children up to the age of six, where 50 or more women were employed) was evaded by dismissing women when they got married. The pharmaceutical employees unions began taking up this issue in the late 1950s, and when in 1961 a woman employee was dismissed on getting married, they took up the case legally and pursued it up to the Supreme Court, where they finally got a judgement outlawing the so-called 'marriage clause' in 1965.[2]

The campaign against the clause involved various forms of militant agitation, including demonstrations, processions, and public fasts, in which women played a leading role. Subsequent campaigns for maternity benefits and workplace crèches were also spearheaded by women workers (P. H. Rohini, 1991). By 1983, women working in most of the chemical and pharmaceutical companies we studied not only had job security, and pay and benefits equal to those of men, but also enjoyed additional facilities such as protection from night work, 12 weeks' fully paid maternity leave for two deliveries, and workplace crèches for their children under the age of six (Union Research Group, Feb. 1984).

This is the background to the decision by many companies to stop recruiting women even for the jobs they formerly did. In the case of Hindustan Lever, the policy was begun as far back as 1952, whereas in companies such as Pfizer and Roche Pharmaceuticals it was more recent, and associated with the process of modernisation.[3]

PREJUDICE OR CALCULATION?

In view of the fact that a similar process of displacement of women by men had earlier occurred in the textile industry (Morris, 1965; Chhachhi, 1983; Kumar, 1983; Savara, 1986; Westwood, 1991; Standing, 1991), it becomes relevant to ask: are employers and managers inherently prejudiced against women?[4]

Managers whom we interviewed said they had stopped recruiting women for the following reasons:

'Women only work for pin money; they are not serious about their jobs.'

'When we first employed women, we thought they would be docile and easy to manage; but after the union was formed, they have become as bad as the men.'

'Women are absent every time someone in the family is ill; they have to be paid maternity benefit and provided with a crèche.'

'The new machines have to be used on a shift basis, and women can't work shifts.'

(Union Research Group, Feb. 1984, p. 28)

Some of these answers do betray prejudice. We found, for example, that in most cases the contribution of women to the family income was vitally necessary in order to maintain an acceptable standard of living. Nor was it true that women flitted in and out of employment and were unserious about their jobs. Most of those we met had worked 15 or more years in the industry and had no thought of leaving until retirement. It was true that women were more likely than men to stay at home to look after a sick relative, especially a child, but this did not necessarily mean that their rate of absenteeism was higher than that of men: a high proportion of absenteeism was related to alcoholism, which affected only men. The exclusion of women from most of the skilled and better-paid jobs also indicated prejudice on the part of managers – a prejudice which in most cases was shared by male workers.

However, it is not by any means prejudice alone which has resulted in the large-scale displacement of women from the organised industrial sector. Restructuring has not left male employment intact, nor has modernisation. Factories which stopped recruiting women decades ago as well as those which never had women employees have more recently stopped recruiting men. Moreover, closures and industrial disputes have been used by employers in order to achieve a more rapid expulsion of labour. Thus in the aftermath of the Bombay textile strike of 1982, tens of thousands of male textile workers lost their jobs, as did hundreds of male workers at the Hindustan Lever factory during and after the lockout of 1988–9. We therefore have to examine the loss of women's jobs in large-scale industry in the context of management strategy as a whole, their constant attempt to cut costs and search for a more flexible workforce.

Most of the answers given by the managers we spoke to displayed a hard-headed capitalist rationality. When women were initially recruited to most of these factories, they had appeared to be cheap labour which was also exceptionally flexible due to their supposed docility and the possibility of dismissing them on marriage. However, once they were unionised, not only did these advantages disappear, but new disadvantages became apparent. The necessity to provide women with maternity leave and crèche facilities for their children made them more expensive to employ than men; the ban on using them for night work made them fatally inflexible at a time when increasing automation and the pressure for more intensive use of machinery was leading to the spread of shiftworking. Moreover, women seemed to pose greater resistance to increasing workloads: in Hindustan Lever, where until 1965 four women worked on each soap-packing machine, management had to remove the women and replace them with men in order to reduce the number to three workers per machine; and in Parke-Davis, women workers who were dissatisfied with the male union leadership ultimately elected their own leadership to undertake go-slows and other militant actions aimed at reducing workloads. Given these developments, it made good economic sense for employers to stop recruiting women into organised industry.

In fact, the lack of prejudice against women as such has been amply demonstrated by management responses to male workers who have posed resistance to demands for greater automation, increased workloads and greater flexibility. In companies like Voltas, Pfizer and Hindustan Lever, where unions have fought for years to preserve some control over the work process, managements have used various methods to reinforce their own control over production and secure workforces which were both cheaper and more flexible. These include:

1. Transfer of part or all of a factory's production to a new unit in a 'backward' area using non-unionised labour. While this enables a company to avoid paying the relatively high wage-rates of organised labour in Bombay, the more important consideration, perhaps, is that this strategy enables it at one blow to introduce the latest technology and new work practices without the headache of having to negotiate these changes with a highly organised workforce capable of disrupting production – with go-slows, boycott of machinery, and even sabotage – if the changes are carried out unilaterally and arbitrarily.

2. Decentralisation of production by sub-contracting to small units: from the standpoint of managements, this achieves lower wage costs; much greater flexibility of numbers, since workers in the ancillary units have no job security, can be laid off at will, and are not even on the company payroll; and greater bargaining power *vis-à-vis* workers in the main plant, since production no longer depends solely on them. Putting out work to homeworkers – sometimes families of factory staff – has been another way of achieving decentralisation of production.

3. The use of workers with inferior employment statuses – temporary, casual and contract workers – alongside permanent workers in the main plant. This enables managements to get the same work done at a fraction of the cost, and to terminate the services of those workers without any legal complications. The practice of transferring production from organised to unorganised workers is by no means confined to these industries or to Bombay. For example, in Coimbatore in 1951, 79 per cent of cloth production was in the organised sector, but by 1981 this had declined to only 38 per cent. Meanwhile, production of cotton cloth in the low-wage decentralised powerloom sector grew by 8.7 per cent in the 1950s, 10.6 per cent in the 1960s and 8.0 per cent in the 1970s (Baud, 1983: 31–2). Most interesting was the relationship between the mills and the powerlooms:

Four out of six composite mills in the Coimbatore sample have adopted powerloom units in and around Coimbatore . . . SIMA, the millowners' association, is helping set up powerloom centres by way of SITRA (the research organisation financed by SIMA), so that powerloom producers have access to technical advice on machinery and cloth production. . . . All these factors taken together show a clear indication of great interest by the mill sector (especially the composite mills) in subcontracting out their production to the decentralised sector, where income levels for producers are lower than those for mill workers, and labour legislation does not apply.

(Baud, 1983: 60)[5]

In the Calcutta bidi industry, a similar pattern can be observed:

In our 1976–77 study of unorganised sector workers in Calcutta . . . we found that in the bidi rolling industry men and women did identical tasks; but men got Rs 8/– for 1000 bidis plus a daily dearness allowance while women got only Rs 3/– per 1000 bidis. There was no perceptible difference in the work since payment was strictly by results after a check for quality. However, while essentially the work was the same, the main difference from the point of view of employers was that men worked in bidi factories while women did the same work at home. In fact this industry of Calcutta was at the time of that survey in a process of transition and employers were increasingly putting out the work to cheap female labour because men workers in factories had got organised and had obtained an officially fixed, fairly reasonable piece rate for the work. Over the next few years, the industry has increasingly shifted production to home-based women workers and can now be regarded as a women's occupation which apparently justified the payment of the significantly lower piece rates.

(Banerjee, 1984: 6)

Finally, up to the 1970s, all operations in the fish processing industry in Kerala were carried out in the organised sector. However, cost-cutting competition between big exporting companies resulted in decentralisation of the industry: canning and freezing continued to be done in large units employing mainly men and a few women who worked as graders, while peeling and cleaning, highly labour-intensive operations, were transferred to the unorganised sector employing an almost entirely female workforce. The estimated number of women peelers was around 25 000, whereas the number of workers in the organised sector was only about 2000. The militancy of trade unions also led to a similar decentralisation process in

Kerala's cashew and coir industries, again generating jobs in the unorganised sector (Kabeer, 1987: 77–9).

We see, then, that management policy has not been aimed specifically at reducing female employment. On the contrary, in all the examples cited, decentralisation of production resulted in a net *increase* in female employment, since women were more strongly represented in the unorganised sector. The changes are an outcome of the employers' search for a cheap and flexible labour force, and it is because of their peculiar characteristics that women workers in large-scale industry have been hardest hit in terms of loss of employment. We would argue therefore that the reduction of women's employment in factories in the organised sector is primarily due *not* to patriarchal ideology but to the need to maximise capitalist accumulation.[6]

WHY WOMEN WORKERS ARE AT A DISADVANTAGE

We need to look more carefully at the reasons why women are at a disadvantage in the labour market in order to understand why the organisational strategies used until now have been inadequate to alter the situation substantially. Some of these factors affect male workers as well, but it becomes strikingly apparent that women *as workers* are crucially affected by conditions which go far beyond the workplace.

1. The existence of the unorganised sector adversely affects both men and women, but women more than men. In India, the growth of the unorganised sector has not been spontaneous, but rather has been encouraged and fostered by government policies such as soft loans amounting to subsidies, tax benefits, and exemption from labour legislation. The main justification for these policies is that they increase employment by enabling and encouraging small entrepreneurs to invest in labour-intensive production. There are many reasons to doubt that small units necessarily create more employment. It has been pointed out, for example, that much of the production in the unorganised sector is either directly owned by big capital, or is producing for it (Banerjee, 1981: 282–5; Holmstrom, 1984: 114, 110). In other words, if this production were not carried out in the small-scale sector, it would *have to* be done in the organised sector. Moreover, in many cases decentralised production does *not* use more labour-intensive technology than centralised production (Banerjee, 1981: 286; Holmstrom, 1984: 151); there are many instances where savings in capital are achieved not by using labour-intensive technology, but by cutting down on overheads and providing inferior working conditions.

Indeed, far from creating more employment, the longer working hours and greater intensity of labour which can be enforced on unorganised workers may mean that *fewer* jobs are created than would be the case if the same production were carried out in the organised sector.

Even if it can be shown that *some* small-scale units do increase employment, this is no justification for denying basic rights to the workers in this sector. Although trade unions have hardly taken up this issue in any serious way, it is ultimately their task to abolish the system of virtual industrial apartheid which produces a vast stratum of underprivileged workers. Obtaining equal legal rights for workers in the unorganised sector and fighting to implement them would also be in the interests of workers in the organised sector. The existence of an underprivileged section which can be called upon to do the same work under inferior conditions is a constant threat to the jobs of organised workers, and drastically undermines their bargaining power; managements know this only too well, and use the situation to their advantage by sub-contracting work to the unorganised sector, both in order to get it done more cheaply and flexibly, and in order to break the resistance of their organised workers. If, on the other hand, workers in the unorganised sector had equal legal rights and were organised to obtain them, this threat would not exist.

2. The complete absence of any social security system also adversely affects both men and women, but in different ways, due to the gender division of labour in the home. Since all social security functions fall on the family, men have an extra financial burden, because the primary responsibility for supporting relatives who are unemployed or too old, too young or too sick to work falls on them. Women, on the other hand, burdened with the care of those who need it as well as the necessity to earn, are put at a severe disadvantage in the labour market. The absence of social security also has many other disastrous social consequences, including the proliferation of child labour, begging, prostitution and crime. Trade unions in other countries have fought for and won social provision of both financial aid for those who cannot work, and care for those who need it (state-funded nurseries, for example), and this suggests that the same could be done in India although, once again, this is not an issue which has been taken up in any serious way.

3. Combined with the lack of social security, the predominant system of marriage puts women at a further disadvantage. Since it is a son who is supposed to support his parents in their old age while a daughter is lost to her parents when she marries, most parents for purely pragmatic reasons prefer to get education and employment for their sons rather than their daughters. Moreover, both unmarried and married women are often

subjected by their families to restrictions on their mobility, and this results in their suffering a whole range of disadvantages at work, from being unable to participate in trade union activity to being pushed into homeworking at abysmal piece-rates. Some of these problems of oppression within the family have been taken up by the women's movement, which, however, has yet to tackle them in a systematic campaign.

4. Violence against women and sexual abuse are major factors restricting the mobility of women and putting them at a disadvantage in the labour force as well as in the trade union movement. These are issues which the women's movement *has* taken up strongly; perhaps with little success so far in actually *reducing* the violence and sexual abuse, but with considerable success in making them more visible and raising them as social issues. The successful campaign by the Forum Against Oppression of Women for 24-hour women's compartments in local trains in Bombay, for example, asserted the right of women – many of whom are working women – to travel late at night without fear of sexual harassment and abuse.

5. Lastly and most crucially, women are at a disadvantage in the labour force due to the gender division of labour. In an earlier period, trade unionists had in many cases assumed that wage work for women was supplementary, or even altogether unnecessary if they had access to a male wage (Chhachhi, 1983: 41–2; Standing, 1991: 147–9). In the modern pharmaceutical industry, on the contrary, struggles against the dismissal of women on marriage and for maternity benefits and crèche facilities were based on the premise that women have a right to remain in employment even when they have access to a male wage. However, women continue to face discrimination due to the gender division of labour, both in the workplace and in the home. In the workplaces covered in the study, women are still concentrated in labour-intensive occupations which are being destroyed by mechanisation and automation; where the division of labour has altered, it has been a case of men taking over what were previously considered to be women's jobs rather than the opposite. The demand for equal opportunities for women in training and skilled jobs has hardly been raised.

Even more significant is the gender division of labour *in the home*: the notion that housework and child-care are entirely the responsibility of women, even if men may sometimes help. A survey carried out in Bombay and Kanpur showed that the domestic division of labour was extremely rigid, with women doing virtually all the housework and child-care or taking responsibility for it even if they had full-time jobs. Asked whether her husband helped her with the housework, the wife of a railway worker responded, 'Ask him! It would be a great help even if he poured out his own water from the *matka* (earthen pot). When I'm ill, bedridden, he does cook. He cooks very well. But I have to wait till I fall ill before I taste his cooking.' (Rohini, Sujata and Neelam, 1984: 108–10, 74)

It is this division of labour which results in the fact that men have no entitlement to crèche facilities or (except for a few days in some cases) paternity leave; while on the other hand they can be called on to work on continuous or semi-continuous shift systems without being given shorter working hours or more than a few rupees shift allowance to compensate for the inconvenient hours, because it is assumed that they have no responsibility for child-care or work in the home. It results in the fact that in a country where there is massive unemployment and new technology is spreading rapidly, the statutory working week is still a long 48 hours, leaving little time for domestic work (Union Research Group, Feb. 1984, Sept. 1984, Nov. 1986). Completing the vicious circle of discrimination against women is the fact that lack of time off for trade union work combined with the domestic division of labour makes it impossible for most women to participate actively in trade unions and ensure that their interests are being served.

WHAT CAN BE DONE ABOUT THE GENDER DIVISION OF LABOUR?

When we had a discussion with women trade union activists, they were unanimous that abolishing the protection, facilities and benefits won by women workers and trade unions in an earlier period was *not* the answer. Instead, they proposed the abolition of gender stereotypes which on the one hand exclude women from many jobs, and on the other hand make it appear that housework and child-care are unsuitable for men. A one-page summary of these points from the discussions in four pharmaceutical factories, when taken back to women workers in the various factories, produced some interesting and instructive discussions: extracts are quoted and analysed below: (male unionists are indicated by an '(m)')

Child-care and Housework

'It's the mother who takes most of the responsibility for children, and they are more attached to her.'
'That depends on the man. My husband helps a lot with looking after the children, and they are very much attached to him.'

'After delivery a woman needs to have someone to help her; usually it is the mother or mother-in-law.'

'My husband took three months' leave when I had my first child, and he used to do almost all the work in the house.'

'In this country, there isn't much sharing of work between husband and wife. In other countries it's different.'

'If a man wants his wife to work outside, he should help with the children and the housework.'

'Even though I'm not married, I have to work so hard after going home, carrying water, cooking, making chapatis, etc. – while my brother just comes home, throws his clothes in a corner and sits down. There's a limit to what a girl can do!'

This issue was extensively discussed, although the opinions expressed were quite diverse. Perhaps the predominant attitude was a kind of resigned acceptance of the fact that at least in India, men were not much use in the house at most times; a few women seemed to find this situation natural, and a few (both married and unmarried) iniquitous, but most simply took it for granted. One or two strongly felt that men should, and in some cases did, have a relationship with their children which was comparable to that of a mother. It was apparent that in normal situations, most of them had got used to coping with their double workload, whether willingly or unwillingly.

However, the institutionalised sexism of the workplace set up made no allowance for abnormal or crisis situations, and a majority of women were critical of this. Most of them felt it was wrong that a man should not be able to get paternity leave to help in the home when a baby is born, or to bring children to the crèche when a wife was dead, ill or worked in a place where there was no crèche. Clearly, these were situations where the normal coping strategies did not work; many were speaking from experience of problems which they or their friends or acquaintances had faced.

This is a much less radical point of view than one which argues that men should take an equal share of household responsibilities; it argues merely that men should not institutionally be barred from playing such a role if there is an acute need for them to do so. Interestingly, the few male trade unionists who responded to this question were sympathetic to this point of view, most of them having either themselves experienced or known other men who had experienced problems in such situations. Discussion on the issue led to a more clearly positive assertion of its necessity.

(We): 'Do you think men should get paternity leave at the time of the birth of their children?'

'What for? What would they do at home?'

'It's not necessary.'

(We): 'Aren't they needed at home to look after the other children while the mother is in hospital? Or to help out after she comes home?'

'There's not much they can do to help at home – they're not used to it. Of course my husband did everything – marketing, cooking, even bathing the baby – but that's very rare. Most men wouldn't do all that.'

'It's true they should help – now that women go out and help with the earning, men should also help with the work in the house.'

'And it's true that women need some help in the house after a delivery. It's not always the case that there's some other relative to help out, and they may not have servants either.'

'Yes, they should get something – not as much as two weeks, but maybe, say, ten days.'

'Yes, they should get ten days.'

(As a male committee member comes in) 'You should ask the men this question . . . What do you think, should men get paternity leave?'

(m): 'Of course men should get paternity leave!'

However, companies flatly refused to consider such arguments, even under extremely tragic circumstances. This suggests that they felt, perhaps correctly, that allowing even one bereaved male employee to bring his children to the crèche could be the thin end of a wedge which split apart the whole strategy of phasing out crèches and maternity benefits.

There is a possibility here of a joint struggle by male and female workers for paternity benefits and crèche facilities for men, and this struggle could in turn lead to a more extensive questioning of the gender division of labour in the home. But it would be an important issue for only a small minority of men; for most it would be minor or even irrelevant; and for some, even the more limited issue would be threatening. For men to bring children to the crèche was perceived as undermining their masculinity – comments on this ranged from, 'they would be afraid of being laughed at,' to 'men are too shy to carry the children to work'.

Working Hours

'It would be good if working hours were shortened. The morning is not so much of a problem, but we should be able to get home earlier in the evening.'

'What with work and travelling, we don't get any time to spend at home with our families.'

'When we first got our Saturdays off, 45 minutes were added to all the other days. But since then, with all this automation, production has increased so much that they can very well afford to shorten working hours.'
'If others are working an 8-hour day with a 5-day week, we should also be able to do that.'

The issue of shorter working hours was raised only in two of the factories, which had longer working hours than the others. The omission of this issue from other discussions, and the way it was raised in these, suggests the importance of what is seen as normative: the idea that if others can have shorter working hours, why not we? This, of course, is the basis of much trade union bargaining, and one purpose of comparative information published by the Union Research Group was to facilitate such bargaining. The argument brought up by another woman – i.e. production has increased so much that employers can well afford to shorten working hours – is also a crucially important one from a trade union and class standpoint. The purpose of new technology, from the standpoint of capital, is to get more and more production from a smaller and smaller number of workers, thus leading to overwork for some and unemployment for many more. The potential benefits of new technology for workers (lighter workloads, improved working conditions, shorter working hours, etc.) can be realised only if trade unions fight for them. We found, in general, that women workers felt much more strongly on these issues than men, and thus took a more correct class standpoint; the reason for this, however, was usually the extra workload, fatigue and responsibility they experienced due to the domestic labour which fell on them as women.

Job Segregation and Promotions

'The jobs in manufacturing are heavy jobs – even the lighter jobs, like tablet compressing, are alternated with heavy ones. Women can't do these.'
'And this work is done in shifts. We can't work in shifts, can we?'
'Women don't work in the engineering department either. The work is not suitable for them.'
'But they do work on the capsule-filling machines. Even that is heavy.'

Differential grading and pay was a problem in only one workplace, and aroused so much anger that we could imagine that the situation would soon change. Where men and women doing the same work were graded and paid differently, the inequity is so obvious and simple that it seems to be an issue which figures high on the agenda of most unions; this was in fact the only workplace in our sample where it still had not been resolved. It is interesting that the male unionists who tried to justify the difference did so by arguing that women were in fact doing a less skilled job, which was sharply disputed by the women involved.

> (m): 'We introduced the Senior Packers' grade so that everyone can get a promotion after 15 years of service.'
> 'There are some cases of more junior boys being promoted over the heads of more senior girls. The machine operator on one line has put in only five years of service whereas some of the girls have put in 20 years of service or more. Naturally they feel bad about it.'
> (m): 'But they get promoted to the Senior Packers' grade which has the same salary scales as the Skilled grade.' (According to the collective agreement it hasn't, however.) 'We don't have a machine operators' grade as such. Men who operate machines are promoted to the Skilled grade.'
> (We): 'Are there any women in the Skilled grade?'
> 'No.'
> (We): 'But don't women operate machines?'
> 'Of course we do!'
> (m): 'But not continuously. And when they do operate machines, they get paid an allowance for it.'
> 'No, no, we don't get any allowance for operating machines.'
> 'And there are some women working continuously on machines, but they don't get the grade nor an allowance.'
> (m): 'But that is because we don't have a machine operators' grade.'
> (We): 'What is the difference between a man in the Skilled grade who operates a machine and a woman in the Packers' grade who operates a machine?'
> (m): 'The skilled worker knows how to look after his machine, set it up, repair it and so on.'
> (At this point the male unionists left for a meeting.)
> (disgustedly) 'They're just the same as management on this point!'
> 'Women operators look after their machines just as much as men do. We can also set up machines and do minor repairs. And major repairs are done by mechanics, even if the machine is operated by a man.'
> 'Men and women do the same work, exactly the same, only women don't get the grade.'

There were no cases where women had tried to get 'women's' jobs up-graded on the grounds that they involved more skill than they were credited for. Watching the women at work, we could see that many of the manual jobs required considerable dexterity and speed which, however, were not recognised as skills. There was a tendency among the male workers to belittle the working capacities of women workers, both physical and intellectual, and one could anticipate that any demand for the upgrading of jobs done predominantly by women would meet with considerable hostility from many of the men.

There was job segregation in all the workplaces we studied, but it had never been taken up as an issue. The women themselves had widely differing attitudes to it: some seemed to take the division of labour in the workplace as natural and necessary, while others argued that women not only could do but actually did some of the tasks which were traditionally supposed to be a male preserve – without, however, getting the grade or pay for it.

Union Work

'If there are women in a department, some places on the committee should be kept for them.'

'It's necessary to have women representatives on the committee. But they also have problems.'

'Here we may be leaders, but at home we're not leaders! If I ever have to stay late for a meeting, I have to prepare for it and give notice two days in advance.'

'If women have problems representing their interests in the union in any other factory, I would like to help them.'

'Getting time off for union work is very important.'

This issue was raised in only one of the four workplaces. The women who did feel that this was an important issue also felt that there were problems for women who wanted to be involved in union work, both at home and in the workplace. Older women unionists told us that the involvement of most women in union work fell off when they got married and had children, mainly due to lack of time but in some cases also due to opposition from their husbands. This was a kind of vicious circle, because it meant that union work tended to become more and more a male preserve and to develop an atmosphere alien to women, and this in turn discouraged women from participating even when they had time to do so. Women workers in the workplaces we studied were all union members, but few were committee members and hardly any were office bearers. They were strongly in favour of unionism as such, but rarely felt that they could play an active part in running the union. It seemed to us that for women to get involved in union activity, changes from two sides were required: changes in the home, to release the women from part of the burden of domestic labour and give them more freedom; and changes in the union to make its structure and functioning more suitable to the needs of women.

THE ARGUMENT FOR AUTONOMY

There is nothing extraordinary about the wide range of opinions expressed in these discussions. What is extraordinary is that these issues had never been systematically discussed by these workers before, far less taken up and fought for as demands. The gender division of labour is, theoretically, an issue which could be taken up by *either* the trade union movement *or* the women's movement, yet neither has shown much interest in it. Why?

There can be no doubt that the trade union movement has won a great deal for women workers; the conditions enjoyed by the women we interviewed were incomparably better than those of women in the unorganised sector, in terms of job security, wages, benefits, working conditions, working hours and so much else. Not only as workers, but as women too they had gained from the outlawing of sexual harassment, the provision of free workplace crèches, and fully-paid maternity leave.

Nonetheless, the trade union movement has developed as a male dominated movement, and therefore even where it has fought for women's rights, it has done so from a masculine standpoint: equal pay for the same work, but not for work of equal value; the reservation of 20 per cent of jobs in all industries and services for women (called for by AITUC since 1966 (Savara, 1986, p. 80)), but not for an equal opportunities policy; protection and benefits for women, but based on the assumption of a rigid domestic division of labour. All these leave untouched a hard core of male privilege, loss of which would be perceived by most male workers as unthinkable. Even some less radical demands which move in that direction but which could be seen as being in the immediate interests of men too, such as paternity leave, crèche facilities for men, and shorter working hours, tend to be seen as relatively unimportant and are easily dropped from the charter of demands. Of course it is true that in the long term, shorter working hours would reduce fatigue and create more employment for both men and women; that men too lose out from the domestic division of labour and would gain from its abolition; that abolition of job segregation and implementation of equal oppurtunities in the workplace would create a stronger and more united workforce; and that the trade union movement would be revitalised and enormously strengthened if women workers could be fully active within it. In this sense, these are not simply women's demands but working-class demands. But this is not how they are perceived by the dominant male section of the trade union movement; and so long as women workers have no alternative means of struggle, they are condemned to see these issues constantly pushed to the bottom of the agenda in some cases, and out of it altogether in others.

In other words, the attempt to fight against the gender division of labour entirely from within the trade union movement as it exists today is doomed to failure; only a working women's movement which is autonomous of the trade unions can do this. This does not mean a movement which is separate from the trade union movement. On the many issues which are of common interest, it can fight within or alongside existing unions. But it does mean that when unions refuse to take up gender issues or drag their feet about them, women workers do not simply have to give up, but can go ahead with their campaign or struggle while continuing to pressurise the unions to take them up too. There is no assumption here that the labour movement cannot be transformed into one which truly represents the interests of the working class as a whole instead of being a male-dominated one; only that this transformation cannot be achieved solely from within the existing unions.

A similar dynamic operates with respect to the women's movement. The women's movement in India has taken up issues of sexual exploitation and violence against women, and these are obviously issues which are of vital importance to working-class women. Yet it has never taken up the gender division of labour very seriously. Perhaps in this case too, there are historical reasons for the failure. The movement has developed, especially in urban areas, under the leadership of middle-class women who do not face the problem of the gender division of labour in the same acute form. They are able to afford commercial crèches and domestic servants to help out with child-care and housework, and the occupations they engage in are not subject to the same rigid job segregation. And we must admit that in this case too, there are advantages for many middle-class women in a gender division of labour which forces large numbers of working-class women into domestic service. And as in the case of male trade unionists, there are difficulties involved in fighting against a system from which you derive immediate benefits, although in this case we are talking about class privilege rather than male privilege. In the long term, abolition of the prevailing system of domestic service would be beneficial to all women; but in the short term, it would undoubtedly cause a great deal of inconvenience and even hardship to most middle-class women.

When we question the gender division of labour – which after all appears to be the most 'natural' and universal one – we are, if we follow through the logic of our thought, questioning the basis of all social divisions of labour. A system where working-class women do all the housework while middle-class women do higher things is every bit as unjust as a system where women do the housework while men do higher things. If you fight against the latter you must, for the sake of consistency, fight against the former; and this is not something which the women's movement as it has developed up to now is equipped to do. Once again, an autonomous working women's movement is required: i.e. one which can work within and alongside the existing women's movement on issues of common interest, but can also act independently to combat aspects of the gender division of labour which the latter has not been interested in taking up. It does not follow that the women's movement cannot be transformed in such a way that it will combat all oppressive aspects of the social division of labour; only that such a transformation will require a shift in the social base of the movement, and that this cannot be done solely from within the existing movement.

It seems that only working-class women would be likely to see this issue as being unambiguously *their* issue, because it is only they who have *nothing to lose* from the abolition of the system. Women workers in large-scale industry, unorganised sector women workers, and working-class housewives all suffer in various ways from being burdened with the entire responsibility for domestic labour and excluded from large areas of employment. Acting as a combined force which is autonomous of the trade unions and women's movement, and yet active within them, they could campaign against all forms of the gender division of labour, and the ideology and institutions which perpetuate them. They could also press the trade unions to take up issues such as the rights of workers in the unorganised sector and the provision of social security benefits. And their participation in campaigns against sexual violence and oppressive family relationships would immeasurably increase the impact hitherto made by the women's movement. At the point where working-class women feel that their interests are adequately represented both within the labour movement and within the women's movement, they could dissolve themselves as an autonomous force. But until then, there is a need for autonomy.

NOTES

1. An example of a 'no retrenchment clause' from one of the factories in our sample (Pfizer) is as follows:

    The Management assures that as a consequence of improved mechanisation and on the introduction of the use of the computer there will be:
    a) no retrenchment;
    b) no reduction in the complement; or
    c) no adverse effect on grade or salary
    of any workmen in Accounts or IBM Department or any other department.

2. The 'marriage clause' was a clause in agreements which stated that women would be dismissed when they got married. In some cases, management carried out this policy without actually incorporating such a clause in the agreement.

3. According to unionists in Hindustan Lever, the reason that management ceased to recruit women in 1952 was that they wished to phase out maternity benefits and crèche facilities.

4. I have used 'prejudice' in the dictionary sense of 'a judgement or opinion formed beforehand or without due examination'. Such prejudices would include, for example, the judgements that women are not serious about their jobs, have a higher rate of absenteeism than men, or are incapable of doing skilled jobs. These judgements are formed *before* examining the actual evidence, which in fact indicates the opposite. This reflects the operation of patriarchal ideology.

5. See Chhachhi, 1983, for a similar process in the Ahmedabad textile industry.

6. The needs of capital and the needs of patriarchy are separable, if not always separate. The need of capital is accumulation, the production of surplus value, and it will strive to achieve this even at the expense of the patriarchal subordination of women, if necessary. It is therefore essentially gender-blind. For example, it will use women in the labour force if they are cheaper and more flexible than men, and will use men if they are cheaper and more flexible than women. It does not follow however that individual employers or managers are gender-blind; it is quite conceivable that they can act against the interests of capital under the influence of patriarchal ideology. For instance, to the extent that job segregation results in the best person not being chosen for a job, it can be detrimental to the accumulation of capital; nonetheless it happens all the time due to prejudice on the part of employers, management and workers. However, if women are replaced by men on some jobs in the organised sector, and women are preferentially recruited for the same jobs in the unorganised sector, this cannot be due to prejudice based on patriarchal ideology. There is a different logic operating here – that of capital accumulation. There are two distinct sets of power relations operating: those of men over women on the one hand and of capital over labour on the other. The exercise of capital's power over labour can (and does on some occasions) reduce the power of men over women, especially within the family; but capital can and does use patriarchal power to reinforce its own power by using the ideology of domesticity in order to get a

supply of cheap labour. There is no simple coincidence nor any simple contradiction between the two.

REFERENCES

Banerjee, N. 1981. 'Is Small Beautiful?', in A. Bagchi and N. Banerjee (eds), *Change and Choice in Indian Industry*, Centre for Studies in Social Sciences, Calcutta.

Banerjee, N. 1984. 'Women's Work and Discrimination'. Paper presented at Conference in Bogota, Colombia.

Baud, I. 1983. *Women's Labor in the Indian Textile Industry*, Research Project IRIS Report No. 23, Tilburg Institute of Development Research, The Netherlands.

Chhachhi, A. 1983. 'The Case of India', in W. Chapkis and C. Enloe (eds), *Of Common Cloth: Women in the Global Textile Industry*, Transnational Institute, Amsterdam.

Holmstrom, M. 1984. *Industry and Inequality – The Social Anthropology of Indian Labour*, Cambridge University Press, Cambridge.

Kabeer, N. 1987. *Women's Employment in the Newly Industrialising Countries*, Report prepared for IDRC, Institute of Development Studies, Sussex.

Kumar, R. 1983. 'Family and Factory: Women in the Bombay Cotton Textile Industry, 1919–1939', *The Indian Economic and Social History Review* 20, No. 1, Jan.–March.

Morris, M. D. 1965. *The Emergence of an Industrial Labor Force in India*, University of California Press, Berkeley and Los Angeles.

Rohini, P. H. 1991. 'Women Workers in Manufacturing Industry in India: Problems and Possibilities', in Haleh Afshar (ed.), *Women, Development and Survival in the Third World*, Longman, London and New York.

Rohini, P. H., S. V. Sujata and C. Neelam. 1984. *My Life is One Long Struggle: Women, Work, Organisation and Struggle*, Pratishabd, Belgaum.

Savara, M. 1986. *Changing Trends in Women's Employment: A Case Study of the Textile Industry in Bombay*, Himalaya Publishing House, Bombay.

Standing, H. 1991. *Dependence and Autonomy: Women's Employment and the Family in Calcutta*, Routledge, London and New York.

Union Research Group. 1983. 'Automation and Redeployment on Packing Lines: Need for a Union Strategy', *Bulletin of Trade Union Research and Information*, Dec. No. 3.

Union Research Group. 1984. 'Women's Employment in Industry: A Challenge for Unions?' *Bulletin of Trade Union Research and Information*, Feb. No. 4.

Union Research Group. 1984. 'Benefits and Bonus', *Bulletin of Trade Union Research and Information*, Sept. No. 5.

Union Research Group. 1986. 'Leave and Working Hours', *Bulletin of Trade Union Research and Information*, Nov. No. 9.

Westwood, S. 1991. 'Gender and the Politics of Production in India', in Haleh Afshar (ed.), *Women, Development and Survival in the Third World*, Longman, London and New York.

8 Women Organising for Change in Caribbean Free Zones
Leith L. Dunn

This chapter examines the experience of Caribbean women organising in export production enclaves for industrialisation, called free zones, free trade zones (FTZs) or export processing zones (EPZs). The majority of the foreign companies who invest are transnationals, who are encouraged to invest by offering them an attractive package of incentives aimed at reducing their production costs and maximising their profits. The incentives are wide-ranging but the most attractive aspect is the offer of cheap non-unionised labour, which in the majority of zones is female.

The chapter presents findings from a research project examining the impact of export-oriented industrialisation (EOI) as a development strategy in Jamaica and the Dominican Republic. The structure and characteristics of EPZs are outlined as they represent the *modus operandi* of transnational companies and illustrate how the new international division of labour impacts on workers. These factors influence employment practices and present limitations and challenges for organising free zone workers.

The rationale used for organising is to advance the social, political and economic development of workers, as well as their quality of life. As the majority of workers are women, the chapter also assesses whether employment offered by transnationals in free trade zones can help women meet their practical and strategic gender needs. It is assumed that national economic development is a necessary condition for the advancement of workers and as such, organising should also aim to meet national needs.

The chapter examines the case of two groups of free zone workers in Jamaica and the Dominican Republic who have managed to organise themselves, despite the constraints of working in the zones. Their experience is used to extract common lessons that relate to organising in this particular context. These are then used to analyse the issue of building gender sensitivity in traditional and new trade unions, which could encourage greater participation of women in the trade union movement.

Jamaica and the Dominican Republic are selected because their economic crisis epitomises the situation of many developing countries who use the EOI strategy as a solution. They also lead the Caribbean region in using the strategy. Both are among the world's most highly indebted countries with foreign debts in excess of US$4 billion each. The World Bank and IMF have provided support to expand the FTZs in both countries. In so doing they hope to boost foreign exchange earnings to help debt repayment and employment opportunities. Thousands of jobs have been created through investment by transnational corporations. The impact is limited however because of the structure of transnationals, the types of industries that have been introduced in the FTZs which have few linkages with the domestic economy, and the effects of structural adjustment programmes, which are largely inflationary and impact negatively on the poor. Together these place considerable constraints on women's scope for organising as well as their own development.

The framework used for addressing the issue of women organising in the process of industrialisation, is that of Moser (1989) and Molyneux (1985). Moser's framework for gender planning was developed from Maxine Molyneux's conceptualisation of women's interests, strategic gender interests and practical gender interests. Whereas Moser uses the framework for planning, the general framework, used more in its original conception of women's practical and strategic gender interests, appears useful as an objective for organising. As such, women would organise to meet their practical and strategic gender interests and needs. Loosely defined, practical gender needs relate to women's ability to survive and fulfil their reproductive, productive and community-managing work. Strategic gender needs relate to women's empowerment, their participation in decision-making and the establishment of a society that facilitates more equitable relationships between men and women.

It is suggested that free zone jobs are more likely to enable women to meet practical gender needs and are important because increasingly, many women are the primary breadwinners for their families. Jobs in the free zones also enable many of the workers to achieve some level of economic independence. The constraints of assembly production and the economic conditions imposed by structural adjustment, however, limit their ability to use these jobs for personal development and meeting strategic gender needs. Their time to organise in pursuit of these goals is extremely limited, and this is further undermined by the strong anti-union climate in the zones. The culture of traditional male-dominated trade unions also presents limitations. The case studies argue the need for a new type of organisation which reflects and responds to women's multiple roles and needs. They also address women's cross-class alliances as an important aspect of organising.

The chapter has three sections. A brief introductory overview provides a framework for examining the issues. The two case studies are then presented, and parallels drawn where applicable. The chapter concludes by highlighting some of the common issues and strategies that relate to women organising.

INTRODUCTORY OVERVIEW

Export-oriented industrialisation (EOI) has incorporated the region's countries into the new international division of labour, with a resulting expansion of industries that are linked to the global economy. These industries are operated mainly by transnational companies (TNCs) which mass-produce consumer goods for the world market. They use assembly-line production that is labour- rather than capital-intensive and requires low levels of skill. EOI has become a popular development strategy because its effects have enabled the Newly Industrialised Countries (NICs) of South-east Asia to prosper. The development effects related to EOI include: the potential of earning foreign exchange, the transfer of technology from foreign to local companies, employment for large sections of the economy that have low levels of skill, stimulating the expansion of the local manufacturing sector by establishing backward and forward linkages between foreign companies and the domestic economy, developing local managerial expertise required for competing on the international market, and retaining earnings from foreign investment that can be used to provide capital for national development. Sub-contracting to local companies to fill large export orders exposes them to new technologies and comes under the broad concept of technology transfer, which is one of the development effects of EOI.[1] The underlying assumption is that workers who are exposed to the practices of foreign companies will acquire the industrial skills, work ethic and the attitudes necessary for establishing successful and viable indigenous manufacturing industries. Over time this will increase the capacity of developing countries to compete globally.

In the Caribbean, the transnationals who invest tend to be involved in industries that require low levels of skill, pay low wages and employ mostly women. Emphasis is on light consumer goods including clothing and textiles, footwear, sportswear, toys, games, and to a lesser extent, data processing and electronics. Data processing industries involve women keypunching information from payrolls or airline tickets into computers for immediate dispatch to the US, which is the main source of this type of business.

Many developing countries start their EOI strategy with low-skill industries in the hope of moving 'up-market' to attract industries that require higher levels of skill, and also to set up their own industries. Even if they do, however, the global trend is that manufacturing industries that are more technologically advanced and require higher levels of skill, rarely employ women (Joekes, 1986).

FACTORS LIMITING ORGANISING IN EXPORT PROCESSION ZONES

Characteristics of the Zones and the Structure of Transnationals

Transnational companies (TNCs) are by definition companies that operate in more than one country. Dunning (1971) defines a TNC as a:

> separately identifiable vehicle of international activity [which] embraces, usually under the control of a single institution, the international transfer of separate, but complementary factor inputs, viz equity capital, knowledge and entrepreneurship – and sometimes goods as well. . . . The second unique quality of direct investment is that resources which are transferred are not traded, they are simply moved from one part of the investing enterprise to another. (1971: 16)

He further notes that they operate in more than one country. The vertical and horizontal integration of TNCs has created a new international division of labour in which production is spread across the globe and combined at their convenience to maximise profits.

EPZs are special export production enclaves that facilitate the operation of transnational companies in a developing country. They are located near to air or sea ports to facilitate the movement of goods into and out of a country and are a convenient mechanism for administering the wide range of incentives offered to foreign investors. The same facilities are sometimes extended to companies located outside the zone who produce for export.

EPZ/FTZ incentives generally include exemption from customs and other duties, unrestricted repatriation of profits, good communications systems, subsidised infrastructure, cheap credit, cheap labour, and an anti-union climate. A government's commitment to export investments and the country's political stability are also important factors. Given our focus on organising, we will address the issue of cheap labour as an incentive.

In the Caribbean, as in other parts of the world, FTZs are characterised by the employment of young women usually below the age of 25 years.

Most work in garment assembly which is very labour intensive and requires low levels of industrial skills, which are rarely transferable to other industries. Employment is unstable as it fluctuates in relation to the state of the North American economy, the main destination for exports. Skills are specialised as they apply to one operation of the whole assembly process (e.g. joining sleeves or doing buttonholes). They are not easily applied to other sections of the process and many women never learn to sew a whole garment. Retrenchment represents difficulties in an industry where accuracy and speed determine earning levels. Jobs are repetitive and monotonous with few prospects for career development. The wage structure is exploitative to the workers who only get bonuses if they achieve production targets.

Working conditions in some export assembly industries are hazardous to the health of workers. Findings from research on working conditions in the EPZs in Jamaica indicate that the major health problems affecting workers are: back pains, respiratory problems from overexposure to steam irons, stress from working at an intense pace for long periods, headaches, kidney and bladder infections from retaining urine for long periods, sinus problems and allergies from the dust and the materials used (Dunn, 1987). In the electronics industries, soldering microchips over a prolonged period leads to intense eye strain because of the close work involved.

In a situation where thousands of people use common facilities, the situation of canteens and bathrooms is often cited as a problem in the literature. These facilities are often inadequate for the large volume of workers who use them, and this sometimes creates conflicts among the women, who are placed in a very competitive environment. Forty-five minutes or an hour is a very limited time to allow thousands of workers to have their lunch, line up to punch their time sheets and return to their work station. The resulting competition to rush for lunch does create conflicts, and it is a common sight in both countries to see a mass exodus of free zone workers leaving the factory, to then stand or sit on the ground to eat lunch. The size and number of canteens is usually inadequate to handle the volume of workers, even with a staggered lunch-time.

Workers in both countries have complained of needing written permission to use the toilets and being limited in the frequency and duration of visits. In the Dominican Republic, some workers reported the removal of toilet doors in some factories which managers rationalise as a way of reducing theft. Also related to the suspicion of theft is the practice of body searches on leaving and entering the free zones. In the Dominican Republic there were reports of women being searched by males and facing sexual harassment.

Together, these characteristics help to create a work environment which is competitive and conflictive rather than co-operative. In addition to jostling to use bathroom and canteen facilities in a limited period as cited above, the work structure places women in competition with each other. They compete to produce more than their peers, earn more or have access to other non-monetary incentives such as electrical equipment (e.g. fans, blenders, irons, television sets, hair dryers etc.). The discipline required for assembly-line production also creates stress and tension in the work environment and this sometimes contributes to violent confrontations between workers, and between supervisors and workers. Dismissals for fighting at work are not uncommon.[2] This climate is not conducive to creating harmony and group cohesion which are important for organising.

The International Debt Crisis and Structural Adjustment

In addition to the specific characteristics of transnationals and the structure of free zones, the debt crisis and structural adjustment policies also present limitations to the labour movement and the climate for organising. Structural adjustment policies in both countries place additional burdens on women which limit their time to organise. Currency devaluation, which is a common feature, reduces production costs for foreign investors and makes exports cheaper. Devaluations however have the undesirable effect of making imports, including raw materials for local production, and essential items for health and education, more expensive. Trade liberalisation is introduced to increase the availability of imported goods on the domestic market. This however forces local producers to compete with cheaper imports, some of which are mass produced with subsidies. The removal of price controls on basic food items serves to increase the cost of living for the poorest, which is the category in which most free zone workers fall in both countries. Workers complain of having to spend more time looking for essential food items that are cheaper, which has the effect of reducing the time they could spend on organising.

Tight wage controls to curb inflation have the effect of reducing the standard of living of the poorest members of the community. High interest rates to make credit expensive and curb spending also limit alternatives for any improvements in the standard of living of the poor. Drastic cuts in social expenditure and other areas that are not considered 'economically productive' increase the burden on women particularly, who have the main responsibility for attending to the sick. Privatisation of state sector investments has also been encouraged to reduce their involvement in the economy, and stimulate the private sector to fill the gaps.

Women bear the brunt of these policies in Jamaica and the Dominican Republic, as they have to fill the gaps created by cuts in social spending. These activities further limit their time for organising to address practical and strategic gender needs. Increasingly, free zone workers, like many professionals and small business entrepreneurs, have joined the informal sector to supplement their wages. This helps them to meet the increased costs for transportation, food, housing and other items. Ironically, some of their efforts at local production (e.g. sewing garments) are constrained by competition from foreign imports which they also produce.

The combined effect of these policies increases social tensions, and creates an industrial relations climate that favours non-unionisation as increasingly more people join the largely non-unionised informal sector. It could be argued that investment incentives such as infrastructure, utilities, labour, duty free access to markets, unrestricted repatriation of profits, tax holidays and tax exemptions represent export production subsidies which could have been used to increase wages and boost local production. These policies are also changing the character of trade union demands as workers struggle to secure their jobs rather than lobby for improving wages and working conditions.

Caribbean women workers continue to fulfil their productive, reproductive, and social management roles, but with less time for essential rest, and fewer opportunities for getting together to address their problems collectively and lobby for changes which could improve their quality of life.

Internationally Recognised Labour Standards

It is important to note the rights of workers as outlined by the International Labour Organisation. A rationale for organising is to ensure that employers comply with these minimum standards, which include the right of association, the right to organise and bargain collectively, the prohibition on the use of compulsory labour, a minimum age for the employment of children, and acceptable conditions of work with respect to minimum wages, hours of work, and occupational health and safety.

CASE STUDIES

Introduction and Methodology

The case studies present findings from a participatory research project with women working in free trade zones in Jamaica and the Dominican

Republic, which has contributed to strengthening organisations of free trade zone workers. The women learn about their situation collectively, and increase their self-confidence and their problem-solving skills. Participatory research is more likely than traditional research to empower women, making them the subjects rather than the objects of research. The climate of fear among free zone workers, the strong anti-union attitudes among some managers, and the tight security in and around the zones, do not facilitate large quantitative surveys. Findings from interviews as well as information gleaned from workshops, meetings, and a wide range of documentary sources are therefore used as the basis of information presented.

Caribbean Women: Roles, Status and Aspirations

Caribbean women have always worked. During slavery, after emancipation and in the post-independence period, they have been an essential part of the cash and non-cash economy. They have consistently played an important role in the family and the community, managing and organising to meet collective needs. Patterns of women's integration and involvement in the paid labour force reflect the historical and colonial legacy of the region. Industrialisation has expanded women's participation in the labour force and increased the range of job choices open to them.

In the Caribbean, women make up more than half of the region's total population of 26.4 million. Education has been seen as an important route for social mobility and data presented by Anderson and Gordon (1987) indicate that in recent years, there is a growing trend of more Jamaican women being enrolled in the University of the West Indies than men. Women are also more likely to make more use of training opportunities than men. However, their level of income compared to that of men is disproportionate, especially among the working class. Gordon's National Mobility study (1989, p. 78), concludes that although employment opportunities for Jamaican women have expanded in the post-war period, and there has been some social mobility at different levels of the society, the position of women relative to that of men has not greatly altered. He notes that although women made up half the workforce in 1984, a third of those who could, do not participate in the workforce; this compares to one fifth for men. In unemployment, 39 per cent of women were unemployed compared to only 16 per cent of men.

In general, the data show that despite their best efforts to get an education or acquire marketable skills Jamaican women are still at a disadvantage.

This is an important issue around which to organise. During the 1970s, the Jamaican government passed laws during the Manley administration guaranteeing women equal pay for equal work, and paid maternity leave for three months. The Status of Children Act was also passed which abolished the distinction between children born inside and outside of marriage. Fathers are therefore legally bound to support all their children, but despite this some women have trouble getting child support, and are the main source of income for their children. For many of the free zone workers interviewed, this was a major problem.

Gordon's and Anderson's findings are supported by Elssy Bonilla (1990: 208) who used documents prepared for the IDB by Mayra Buvinic and Molly Pollack, to look at the situation of working women in Latin America and the Caribbean. The article gives a more global perspective of the region's female labour force which the IDB estimates at 40 million in 1990. Using health, education, birthrate, employment and social equality as the bases for comparison, the situation of women in Jamaica was regarded as 'good' and female participation in the labour force was 45.7 per cent in 1990. Data from the Population Crisis Committee indicates that Jamaica ranks third after the US and Canada on the status of women and the gender gap, measuring life expectancy differentials between men and women. The situation in the Dominican Republic, on the other hand, was classified as 'poor' and it ranked eighteenth out of the 25 countries in the region. There, women's participation in the labour force was only 15 per cent in 1990.

The analysis offered by the report is that paid occupations of the majority of women are of a 'low level of productivity' and therefore provide limited income. The reasons offered are women's lack of access to important factors such as capital, technology training and land, as well as their double burden of paid and household work, and inadequate training. The report however confirms that there have been advances in women's status during the post-war period as a spin-off of the 'modernisation' process. This includes women having greater participation in the workforce, greater knowledge and access to birth control and as such having fewer children. Women are also more likely to be urban-based and have a longer life expectancy than their mothers.

Despite these gains which some women working in the free zones share, the reality is that they have virtually no time to get the education or the skills they require for a better life, neither do they have access to the capital and credit required to raise their 'level of productivity'. Time to organise is also limited.

WOMEN ORGANISING IN THE DOMINICAN REPUBLIC

Development of Free Trade Zones

The Dominican Republic (DR) is the second largest Spanish-speaking country in the Caribbean, covering 48 442 sq. km. It has a population of 6.8 million (1988) with a labour force of 2.8 million of which 12.6 per cent are involved in manufacturing. The DR is rated as a lower middle income country with infant mortality at 7.5 per thousand, life expectancy at 64.1 years and a literacy rate of 69.4 per cent (1981). GDP per capita is US$1509 (1988).

Free trade zones have been promoted in the DR during three distinct periods. The first was initiated with the passing of Law 4315 in 1955, which provided the legal framework for establishing commercial and industrial free trade zones. Very little happened for the next 14 years however and in 1963, Law 38 was passed which legally created the free zone in Puerta Plata. Again, there was very little follow-up.

The second phase of free zone development was between 1969 and 1983. Industrial Promotion and Incentive Law 299 was passed in 1969 to promote industrialisation through import substitution. Special credit and foreign exchange facilities were provided to ensure importation of raw materials for these industries at cheap rates. During this period, the first free zone actually built was in La Romana in 1970 under Law 3461. It was set up by Gulf and Western which had major interests in sugar and tourism. Under an agreement with the state, they agreed to operate the zone for 30 years and then pass it on the state. Under Decree 4369 of 1971, a free zone was established in San Pedro de Macoris and operations began in 1973 under the management of the Industrial Development Corporation. In 1974, under decree 4369, the Santiago free zone was established and began operations in 1975. It was run by a non-profit corporation, involving the state and the national private sector. During the 1970s, several other companies were established outside the free zones, but were given special designation as 'special free zones'. Most of these were involved in agro-industrial production.

Business developed fairly rapidly and things went well until a shortage of foreign exchange led to the establishment of a parallel market. The authorities allowed some areas of the economy to operate under the formal system and others to operate under the parallel market. This policy was used selectively to stimulate some areas of the economy. The free zone was given the priority of using an exchange rate of one dollar to one peso to cover local costs such as salaries, rental and utility costs. This policy effectively subsidised the operations of the foreign companies because the exchange rate was kept artificially high. During the same period, however, neighbouring countries also hit by world recession, high interest rates, and the oil shocks of 1973 and 1979, devalued their currency, thereby giving the Dominican Republic strong competition in the area of foreign investment. The government passed Law 69 in 1979 to promote export-oriented industrialisation. One of its main provisions was that non-traditional exports would be able to benefit from the parallel market, but the free zones were not included under this provision.

The government signed an agreement with the International Monetary Fund in 1982, which led to the devaluation of the peso, and an understanding that the country would give priority to export promotion. To boost this initiative, Decree 895 was passed in 1983, which formally established the National Council of Industrial Free Trade Zones. This state organisation brought together representatives from companies operating in each zone as well as representatives of the various industrial groups operating in them. In the same year, a non-profit company was formed bringing together the state and the local private sector to build a free zone in Puerta Plata, giving life to the legislation approved 20 years before.

This marked the third phase in the development of free trade zones in the Dominican Republic. Since then, many more zones have been established and there are currently 19 spread over the country. Eight of these are privately owned, seven are public, and the others are publicly owned and privately managed. The zones vary in size from 20 000 sq. ft. to 2 500 000 sq. ft. of factory space, and currently operate between two and eighty businesses each. According to the National Free Zone Council, there were 259 companies in operation in 1989 (Yung Whee Rhee *et al.*, 1990, p. 30). The Independent Workers Central (CTI) estimates this figure at 340 companies employing 120 000 workers, 75–80 per cent of them women (anon., 1991).

Investment and Incentives

Eighty-nine per cent of the free zone companies are transnationals and of this number, over half are from the US (52 per cent); 19 per cent are from the newly industrialised countries (Korea, Taiwan and Hong Kong); 17 per cent are wholly owned by Dominicans; 6 per cent are joint ventures and another 6 per cent are from other nationalities (Germans, Canadians, Panamanians and Puerto Ricans) (Yung Whee Rhee *et al.*, 1990, p. 14). The range of goods produced in 1989 included clothing and textiles (66 per cent), footwear (12 per cent), electronics (6 per cent), food and cigarettes (3 per cent), jewellery (2 per cent), pharmaceuticals (2 per cent), furniture (1 per cent) and others (8 per cent).[3]

The range of incentives offered to foreign investors include: lack of foreign exchange controls and free repatriation of profits; rapid investment licensing procedures; income tax incentives; and access to foreign exchange for imports of raw materials and machinery. They gain access to imported capital equipment, and raw materials duty-free, and to locally produced inputs at world market prices, without duties, complex procedures and delays. Foreign investors also have access to investment finance, access to non-tradable inputs at competitive prices, high-quality living conditions for export workers, and favourable labour code provisions (Yung Whee Rhee *et al.*, 1990: 27). Transnationals do not pay any duty on patents, or municipal charges. They do not pay production and export costs, except for petrol. Local companies get a 75 per cent exemption on rentals as well as on production and export duties for the first five years, and 50 per cent for the remaining years (de Moya Espinal, 1986: 4–6).

The climate for investment is also considered favourable because successive governments have maintained the same policy, and there is relative political stability. The deteriorating economic situation also favours investment because there are large numbers of unemployed people (24.8 per cent unemployment and 40 per cent underemployment) who are relatively well qualified. According to Abreu *et al.* (1989: 115), the industries that come to the DR are labour intensive, with most of them having labour as approximately 50 per cent of production costs. In 1988, the basic salary was 2.60 pesos an hour, averaging a monthly wage of 500 pesos a month. This was equivalent to (US$) 41 cents an hour which was 87 per cent lower than the amount paid in the US, for only a slightly lower rate of productivity (Abreu *et al.*, 1989: 115–17).

Labour Laws

The labour laws of the country provide the following guarantees for all workers: freedom of association, the right to organise and have collective agreements, freedom from forced labour, and acceptable conditions of work in respect of minimum wages, hours of work, health and social security. These rights are guaranteed by section 502 (B) (7) of the law relating to business passed in 1974 and reformed in 1984. Laws 2920 and 4505 guarantee these laws. Additionally, the Dominican Republic is a signatory to international labour codes such as Code 87 and 98 of the International Labour Organisation (ILO). Laws in the US also establish the right of workers to organise. The reality in the Dominican Republic contrasts sharply with this, however.

History of the San Pedro de Macoris Free Zone Trade Union

The expansion of free zones in the Dominican Republic during the 1980s was accompanied by equal determination on the part of workers to struggle against the wages and working conditions which were the norm in several factories. Efforts to establish a union were intensified in November 1987 after a three-months-pregnant employee of Clover Company, in the San Pedro de Macoris Free Zone, was kicked by a Korean supervisor. The woman, Rafaela Rodriguez, lost her baby. There were massive demonstrations and this incident became the focal point around which workers in the San Pedro de Macoris Free Zone rallied to demand better wages and working conditions. Workers occupied the local offices of the Labour Secretary and there were mass meetings in the zone. According to Elida Segura, one of the founders of the union, 'Over 2400 workers participated in the inaugural assembly that formally established the union'. The union now has more than 4000 affiliates and is growing stronger daily.

Many workers know about the union, but out of fear or ignorance do not join because it may cost them their job. Some, however, come to the union after they are dismissed. This was the experience of the General Secretary of the San Pedro de Macoris Free Zone Workers Union, Myra Jiminez. She is only 19 years old, but is confident and articulate with several years' experience as a worker.

In 1988, workers in the American Sport clothing factory went on strike to demand better wage and working conditions, especially in relation to forced overtime. The work-stoppage lasted several hours, and a few days later there was a witch hunt to identify those 'suspected' of being union members. Several workers were dismissed. Prior to this, another Korean factory, Tejidos Internacional (TISA), laid off 20 workers. This factory was reported to be a regular violator of the labour codes because it employed many minors. There was a lot of tension between workers and management, which threatened to lay off the entire workforce, alleging problems with their electrical generators. The dismissals were not authorised by the Labour office and the workers protested but also tried to reason with the company's representatives. According to Myra, 'There was no way of explaining that trade union militancy in this country is not a crime; factory owners upheld the dismissals despite all the protests and all the explanations'.

Among the other disputes that came to public attention was that of the Suprema Manufacture company, where four workers were dismissed 15 days after a strike which was called to get colleagues who were unjustifiably dismissed reinstated. The attitude of some foreign company executives was that they would prefer to relocate their factories and machines to another country than allow unions to operate.

In July 1990, about 200 workers occupied the offices of the Ministry to press their demands that the union be recognised. The fledgling union in San Pedro de Macoris has received support from the Independent Workers Central (CTI), one of the 11 trade union blocks that exist in the Dominican Republic. The CTI has helped to expose the working conditions in the free zones at the national and international level through the ILO. The AFL-CIO has also demanded respect for labour laws. Late last year the government bowed to national and international pressure and declared that trade unions could organise in the free zones, and finally recognised the San Pedro de Macoris Free Zone Workers Union. This is the base for establishing a national union of affiliated trade unions from the other zones.

Myra's story exposes the less glamorous and successful side of the free zones. She began working there as a machine operator when she was only 14 years old and in her first job, many of her colleagues were girls younger than herself. Some factories specialised in employing minors and paid them less than the minimum wage. They, like other workers, were strip-searched to check for possible theft. Many employees, including Myra, worked in the day and continued their schooling at night, hence the popularity of the phrase among free zone workers, 'leave in the dark – return in the dark'.

Many workers live in communities far from the zone and travel long distances to get to work, so they have a very long day, starting as early as 4 a.m. to get to work by 7 a.m. An estimated 1000 workers live in Consuelo, approximately half an hour's distance from the zone. They pay 12–15 pesos daily for transport alone. This is about a third of their daily wage, which is the equivalent of US$3–4. Others who live further away in places like Santa Fé, often have to wait three hours to get a lift because there is no transport. Workers who live in surrounding 'bateyes' travel long distances, partly on foot because transport is very poor.[4] Those living in the 'barrios' (depressed communities) surrounding the zone also pay a lot for transport, and have to scramble to get into the overcrowded mini-buses that ply the route. Poor transport is a common problem which affects the ability of women to organise, as they need to know how they will get home after work or meetings. At present, transport is unreliable, inadequate, irregular, costly and uncomfortable.

Myra worked in a number of factories in the zone and reports that she was dismissed from her job at Camisas Dominicanas in 1989, because she joined other colleagues in demanding that production quotas be adjusted. After she was dismissed she went to the union that had been operating but was not recognised by the authorities. After a few months she was elected General Secretary and has been at the forefront of delegations, campaigns and petitions to the Ministry of Labour to get the union legally registered. The first request for registration was made on 24 November 1987, a few weeks after the inaugural assembly of the union.

The Struggle for Unionisation

Myra and others have been arrested a number of times in the struggle to get the union recognised. She and other free zone workers report that names of trade union activists or those suspected of being activists are identified on a data base at the Computer Centre of the Association of Industrialists. This information is circulated to all the companies within the zone and these workers are denied employment. Being a union member, wanting to form a union or even talking about unionisation is considered by many company managers to be a crime worthy of dismissal. Hundreds of complaints are lodged with the Labour office by workers alleging that this was the motivation for their dismissal.

Although the laws guarantee workers the right to organise, and the government has affirmed this right, the attitude of many company representatives is still anti-union. The views expressed by Angel Castillo, President of the Association of Free Zones in San Pedro de Macoris, were similar to those voiced by the President of the National Free Zone Council, and attributed to Mr Castillo's counterpart in the Santiago Free Zone.[5]

When asked for his response to the government's decision to allow trade unions to organise in the free zone, Mr Castillo admitted that labour laws have always existed, but companies in the free zone have always managed to ignore them.[6] He said he was not opposed to unions *per se*, but those linked to political parties, as these were, can disrupt production if, for example, there is a dispute with the government. This was detrimental to business in the free zone because failing to meet deadlines means lost orders for goods.

ORGANISING STRATEGIES

Building Links in the Factory

Myra and Elida Segura, a founding member of the union, shared their experiences of organising to build the union. They, and a core of other union members, establish personal contact with women at work, during lunchtime or on the bus from work. They share personal experiences about work, family and life in general. These contacts form a basis for building trust and friendships.

Elida worked as a supervisor in a garment factory, and was fired for being a union activist. She was blacklisted and since then has been denied employment in the zone. There was a point at which the police were called if she appeared anywhere near the factory. With two children to support and no regular source of employment, life is extremely difficult for her. She firmly believes in the principles that the union represents, however, and is determined to continue supporting the struggle for better wages and working conditions.

Elida explained how she organised women at work. In the factory, work is organised in sections and each section has a supervisor, who functions as the group leader. The supervisor is responsible for helping the section meet or exceed production targets and this is done through domination, coercion or co-operation. The supervisor can play an important role in building a union. The women in her section were high producers, usually exceeding their quotas. She motivated them by building a human relationship with them, encouraging them, developing a team spirit and pride in their section. From her already meagre wages, she also provided her own incentives which included inexpensive cakes, sweets or drinks to reward the group when they had achieved or exceeded their assigned production targets. Occasionally, the group also pooled their pesos and celebrated birthdays or special events together, usually with their children. In keeping with Dominican culture to marry at the age of about 17 or 18, almost half the women workers are married or in established relationships and have children. By supporting each other and providing solidarity and friendship they became strong and increasingly acted as one body. About a third of these women are the sole breadwinners for their families and have a lot of problems in common. These seemingly small acts helped to build cohesion within the group and cement a bond among the women.[7]

Building Links in the Community

Relationships established at work were extended by personal visits to each other's homes at nights and on weekends. In building the union in the early days, these casual visits became more formalised and house meetings were organised in several communities. There, problems were discussed and support in the form of advice and assistance was given. Myra and Elida report lightheartedly that sometimes they attended as many as five meetings in one night, returning home in the early hours of the morning with sore feet and broken shoe heels, but having to report for work the following morning.

The sacrifice was worth it because these contacts helped to improve communication and establish friendships across a wide cross section of workers and factories. Poor working conditions and other common problems that the union needed to address were identified. Committees were then set up in the communities which met regularly or more frequently if there were urgent problems. The union leaders attended these meetings, which helped to strengthen the groups and to plan strategies for addressing problems. For example, they report that at the height of the struggle to form the union, a woman was beaten in the Royaltex factory, where Elida last worked. Although this was one of the smallest factories, it had the reputation of having the largest number of violations and the most militant workers. Despite threats from the factory owners and the Secretary of Labour, employees continued meeting in the communities to plan their strategy, which included organising pickets.

These meetings away from the watchful eyes of management provide an important space for workers to express themselves more freely. There is always the danger of spies however. Some workers report activities to the management, as they see their advancement linked to establishing friendships with management and carrying 'news' to them. The presence of spies contributes to the atmosphere of fear, as being linked to trade union activity or branded a 'troublemaker' usually leads to dismissal.

The fear is real because the struggle to survive is hard. Structural adjustment policies and lay-offs in the traditional male employment sectors place an additional pressure on women, who then become the main breadwinners, but usually at a lower wage. Tensions are inevitable on the domestic scene as roles are reversed, and domestic violence is also part of the reality that women face.

Attending some of these community meetings in the last two years provided insight into the daily lives of women workers, their problems, fears and aspirations. Some problems relate to their multiple roles as workers, mothers, partners and trade unionists. Their expectations of a new kind of trade union are also revealing. One left full of admiration and inspired by their pride and determination.

The kind of union many would like is one which would help them to achieve both strategic and practical gender needs. They want a union that will serve their interests that relate not only to wages and working conditions, but also to their personal development, their well-being and their security. On a practical level, they want a union that sees the need for improved transport to and from work especially late at night and over long distances. It would also struggle to eliminate sexual harassment and the sexual division of labour in the workplace. It would help them to deal with domestic violence, some of which is directly and indirectly related to their role as workers. They need a union that can lend support to their struggle for child-care facilities and child maintenance.

In a macho society like the Dominican Republic, the women want a union that will value their ideas and contributions in areas other than administrative work and arranging food for events. Women interviewed revealed that many feel intimidated by the confrontational style of traditional, male-dominated unions, which may be less effective in dealing with free zone managers. A more negotiating style would be more effective in improving wages and working conditions, yet reduce the risk of dismissal.

Decision-making structures within male-dominated unions tend to reinforce traditional cultural practices that prescribe special roles to women (e.g. administration) and do not always ensure that women have equal status with men. Women tend to be in the minority in trade unions, and changes are therefore needed to encourage more women to become active members, giving them a higher profile and more involvement in leadership positions. The atmosphere in traditional unions increased women's feelings of insecurity and made them reluctant to speak up in meetings. Even in the San Pedro de Macoris union, which has both male and female members and female leadership, it was noted during meetings attended that some men tried to dominate discussions, and the leadership had to ensure that women also got a chance to share their problems.

In addition to the internal group dynamics of leadership and participation, other factors affecting women's willingness to become involved include the times at which meetings are held and their frequency. Women's participation is affected by their multiple roles. Children attended some of the meetings, and women reported that they helped each other in organising child-care in communities or at meetings. Women mentioned that they found it easier to attend outings where they could bring their children and families.

Building Links with other Unions

Through the Independent Workers Central (CTI), the San Pedro de Macoris Free Zone Union has been receiving assistance for legal aid, education and organising work. Much of this was acquired through Fenazucar, which represents workers in the sugar industry and other sectors. With massive retrenchment in the sugar industry, some of Fenazucar's members have been working in the free zone, and thus the link was established. This has been an important organisational base, as these workers have many years' experience of trade union activity. However, the union is male-dominated, although women are involved. It has shown its commitment to being more sensitive to the needs of women by including them more consistently, involving them more in leadership positions, and at Fenazucar's 6th Congress in February 1991, a women's section was formed. Women trade unionists have also been participating in the network of women trade unionists in Central America and the Caribbean, established through ILO training programmes.

Fenazucar has been very supportive, and there have been tangible successes. In 1990, the government finally conceded the right of free zone workers to organise a union, and the female-led Free Zone Union was finally recognised. These events have strengthened both Fenazucar and the CTI, which mobilised international support for the free zone workers' struggle. The plan is to organise workers in other zones around the country and form a national union of free zone workers.

The relationship between Fenazucar and the St Pedro de Macoris Free Zone union has been positive, although their approach is different. Fenazucar's style is confrontational and based on class struggle, which presents some constraints for the free zone environment. Although some demands have been met, many workers have lost their jobs. It would be unfair, however, to attribute this solely to the union's style of negotiating. For many women it is their first experience of involvement in any kind of organised struggle for their rights, and some would prefer to suffer in silence.

Building Awareness and Class Consciousness

The issue of class struggle raised above, is related to class consciousness. Discussions with Fenazucar representatives indicate that in their view, there is an absence of working-class consciousness among the free zone workers. This contrasts sharply with the position of sugar workers which is the core of the union's membership. The free zone women's previous work experience has been either in the home or in unorganised sectors. As such, they have had fewer opportunities to develop awareness of their class as a group, except as poor people.

Interviews indicate that the women, especially the poorer ones, are more likely to see themselves as individuals working at the free zone to earn a living, than as a group of industrial workers who share a common experience and who need to join forces to change their situation. When asked what they would like to be doing if they were not working at the zone, many indicated that they really wanted to set up their own business (sewing, hairdressing, grocery trading, etc.).[8] Over a number of visits, however, it was noted that there is a growing awareness of common problems that industrial workers face, and a decreasing perception that such problems are personal.

A major challenge to organising to improve wages and working conditions is the need to create class consciousness and solidarity in a manner that does not alienate workers. Myra and Elida both noted that women have a different style of trade unionism from men, and that there is need to affirm this when organising within the free zone. Both women are militant, work very hard but also bring sensitivity and warmth to their work. They represent models of the new breed of women trade union activists. They are bright young women, economically poor but with high aspirations to improve their education. They are committed to working for improvements in the working conditions of free zone workers, particularly women. In a culture that values fashion, these militant women blend in as they conform to the dress code of their peers (within their economic limitations), and wear modern, attractive styles. They understand the need to create awareness among the women but approach it patiently and in a non-judgemental way that will build women's confidence. Myra, Elida and other women interviewed recognise the need to balance basic survival and family responsibilities with trade union work. They can only relate to the struggle for better wages and working conditions if they can directly link it to their daily struggle for survival.

Even while building links with other unions, these trade union leaders have learned to discriminate between different types of unions. In the DR, they reported on the competition they face from what they refer to as 'yellow' unions. These tend to be conciliatory and try to pacify workers rather than mobilise them for action. In sharp contrast to leaders like Myra and Elida who work full-time but receive no regular salary, 'yellow' union leaders receive large salaries of 3000 pesos a month, plus transport and a per diem when they travel. In Myra's union, contributions from members are used to pay for transport costs and related expenses for leaders to attend meetings, but are insufficient to guarantee regular wages.

Building Alliances with other Groups

In addition to building links with other unions and learning from them, women's efforts to organise also depend on the support of other community groups such as the church. The Free Zone Union meets in church and school buildings and whereas this is a major help, it is not always reliable, as the building is not always available when they need it.[9]

Support of other groups is also needed to do basic administration and accounting. The union has no office and has to operate from members' homes, which means families finding space to accommodate papers and the normal clutter of any organisation. The women share a manual typewriter to do their correspondence.

The support and goodwill of the women's movement is vital. Organisations like CIPAF and Ce Mujer have published information on the situation of women working in the free zone (Pineda, 1990). Other non-governmental organisations supporting community development in the country also focus on the issue and have contacts in the free zones. These are important resources that enhance the process of organising. Establishing a more consistent and organic link between these organisations and the women's union would be mutually beneficial. Although many of them are of a different class background, they want to support the union's struggle through, for example, collaboration on socio-economic research, awareness building, and media training. What they learn from the union members in return will enhance the quality of their work, while enabling them to understand the issues better.

The Media

Publicity around the free zones has played an important role in bringing much-needed changes and has helped the process of organising free zone workers. Articles and publications from organisations such as those mentioned have helped to create public awareness of the issues, and points to the importance of the media as an organising strategy.

Fenazucar has, as a deliberate strategy, helped the union to handle the media and bring common problems to public attention through news releases and special articles in the press based on interviews. This aspect of the union's organising experience has been very successful. Since 1987, their efforts have helped to raise public awareness about working conditions, provide an alternative view of the free zones which are usually portrayed as economic successes with no disadvantages, and have increased people's physical access to the free zones. The union has helped to publish articles on issues such as the practice of some companies to make wage deductions for Social Security but not pass them to the government. The result is that workers are unable to get state benefits when they most need them. The embarrassment associated with such exposés creates pressure for change. These issues raise public awareness and have been the focus of public debate.

An important organising strategy is therefore knowing how to use the media to publicise issues. Mobilising members of the media for demonstrations has helped to guarantee essential publicity. Myra, for example, is now publicly known as a result of media exposure and handles the press like a professional.

Institutional Strengthening

Even with the support of other trade unions and community organisations and a knowledge of how to handle the media effectively, the process of organising to advance the struggle of free zone workers will be seriously constrained by a union that is weak internally. A 'recipe' for institutional building and forming a strong and democratic union is emerging from the stories of Myra and Elida, interviews, union meetings and other documentary sources. The process starts with a small core of committed people who establish personal contacts, build trust and friendships which can lead to greater group solidarity and group size.

Institutional strengthening relates both to creating a formal structure as well as prioritising demands and finding an appropriate way of handling them. The union needs an office and basic equipment as well as materials for education work. The volume of complaints is usually far greater than the union's capacity to address them. Complaints are investigated and priority given to cases typical of common problems. These are then processed for arbitration and legal action. The latter is costly and has so far only been possible with support from sympathetic lawyers in the community and limited international support. The strategy is important, however, as such cases establish principles, build workers' awareness of their rights and increase union membership.

Other common problems that could form the basis of campaigns include the non-payment of overtime; low overtime rates and dismissals for refusing to do overtime at short notice. The arbitrary increase of production quotas is also a common complaint, as is the issue of industrial health and safety. Some workers complain of health problems from handling dangerous products, but companies are reportedly unwilling to offer compensation. Workers feel that unjust dismissals without compensation are common because of inadequate monitoring by the Secretary for Labour. They cited cases of workers being coerced into signing dismissal letters that included untrue allegations.

Training for Organising

Based on observations and discussions with union members, it would appear that organising and institutional strengthening is enhanced through training. Basic training related to workers' rights and responsibilities must be complemented by programmes to strengthen administrative and organising skills such as developing clear objectives, planning and implementing effective strategies for changing working conditions in the zones. Leadership training for members is a priority to ensure continuity of the organisation. Skills in doing action-research and disseminating the findings through education programmes, are necessary as well as the techniques of developing data bases for effective campaigning on wages, for example. This requires information on production costs, company profits, and cost of living indices in the country. Negotiating skills are also necessary, including ensuring good communication within the membership. Training in decision-making, consensus-building, conflict resolution and organisational development are vital to building an effective union, but are particularly important because the structure of work puts women in competition with each other.

In planning training programmes, the Free Zone Union already has certain factors in its favour. The majority of women working in the zones tend to be of a higher educational level than the national average although they have lower levels of education than women working in local industries. (See CONSA study, 1989.)

Following the trend in Latin America and the Caribbean in recent years, women in the Dominican Republic have an increasingly higher level of education (Baez, 1983). It is therefore likely that this higher level of education will be accompanied by increased social and economic expectations as well as a wish to exercise more control over decision-making and to assume leadership positions. These factors could enhance the potential for organising. There are reports of teachers and women with university degrees applying for jobs in the zones because the level of pay in local industries is so low. Their level of education would understandably add to their frustration at work because most jobs can be learned in three months. This leads to a de-skilling process that Duarte (1986) refers to as 'educational proletarianisation'.

Training can include participation in union programmes as well as exchanges with groups of workers in other parts of the world to share experiences. Establishing contacts within the 'global factory' is strategically important in building worker solidarity, given the tendency for transnationals to move jobs to countries that offer more 'competitive' wages.

In summary, therefore, organising free zone workers in the Dominican Republic is limited both by the structure of transnational enterprises, the production culture of the FTZs and by the economic crisis which places additional burdens on women. Despite this, there are opportunities and the experience of the San Pedro de Macoris Free Zone Workers Union clearly demonstrates this. Among the factors influencing their success to date are the presence of strong committed leaders, who have developed a strategy of building personal contacts at work and strengthening them in the community at different levels. Networking with other unions and support groups including the media, has contributed to the union being recognised by the government after three years of hard work. The educational level of the average worker increases the union's potential to advance both practical and strategic gender needs of this group of women.

WOMEN ORGANISING IN JAMAICA

Background

With an area of 10 962 sq. km, and a population of 2.4 million (1988), Jamaica is the largest English-speaking island in the region. It is considered a 'middle level' country with infant mortality at 13.2 per thousand (1984), life expectancy at 73 years, a literacy rate of 73.1 per cent (1982). GDP per capita was US$1843 in 1988 dollars. The labour force in 1987 was 1.1 million of which 24 per cent were unionised and 14.4 per cent were involved in manufacturing. The average minimum wage is US$98 monthly (Schoepfle, 1989, Table 3).

Women and Labour Struggles

Jamaican women played a vital role in the labour struggles of the 1930s which led to the creation of trade unions and contemporary political parties. They are part of the rank and file in both movements, but are less evident at the leadership level. Women are at the forefront of demonstrations and the two main political parties have their core of strong militant and often physically large women, fondly referred to as 'the Fat Brigade'. There are elements of this militant tradition among young women employed in the free zones, and they have had some limited success in changing working conditions there.

History of Free Zones in Jamaica

As part of the government's commitment to the 'industrialisation by invitation' strategy, incentive legislation has been in place since the 1950s. This includes: the Industrial Incentives Act (1956); the Export Industry Encouragement Act (1956); the Factory Construction Act (1961); and the Jamaica Export Free Zone Act (1982) (Dunn, 1987, pp. 10–11). The Kingston Free Zone Act was passed in 1980 but was superseded by the 1982 Act. By the early 1970s, Jamaica led the Caribbean in assembling garments for export (Schoepfle and Perez-Lopez, 1990: 6).

The development of the free zones in Jamaica can be divided into two distinct periods. The first phase started with the establishment of the Kingston Free Zone in 1976 as a warehousing and trans-shipment facility and the second started in the 1982/1983 period as part of the government's strategy to pursue export-oriented industrialisation. Existing warehouses were converted for assembly operations, but are uncomfortable without cooling.

Investment and Incentives

The incentives offered to foreign investors include: 100 per cent tax holidays on profits; minimum customs procedures; duty free concessions for importing capital, raw materials, equipment and consumer goods for the export industries; and unrestricted repatriation of profits. The government provides infrastructure and utilities at competitive rates and the zones are a major source of foreign exchange earning. This is accounted for by foreign exchange payments made by transnational companies and other investors to the Central Bank to pay for the rental of factory space, goods and services purchased locally and payments to local residents for goods and services supplied. The Kingston Free Zone Co. estimates that between 1982 and 1988, a total of US$80.9 million was transferred to the local economy.

As was the case in the Dominican Republic, there was an expansion of the zones in 1982, which marked the second phase of their development. This was financed by the Port Authority and two World Bank loans of US$13.5 million and US$18.8 million (Kingston Free Zone Co., 1989a: 7; Diamond and Diamond, 1989: 3–5). Data provided by the Kingston Free Zone Co. indicate that the Caribbean Development Bank also provided a loan of US$6 million in 1986 (Kingston Free Zone Co., 1986: 3).

Since 1982, the pace of Kingston Free Zone expansion has been rapid. Employment increased from 210 in December 1980 to over 11 000 in December 1987, with some 19 registered companies operating on approximately 670 000 feet of factory space. Decline in the international garment industry in 1988, the International Stock Exchange difficulties and local unrest were blamed for a 40 per cent fall in employment at that time in this sector to 6656 employees. This figure rose to 13 000 in 1989, showing fairly wide fluctuations in employment. Since 1986, some 95.1 per cent of all free zone companies are involved in garment assembly, and thus free zones are almost synonymous with garment manufacturing. In 1989, free zone companies accounted for 50 per cent of Jamaica's apparel exports and 28 per cent of total exports (Kingston Free Zone Co., 1989b: 2–3). In addition to the Kingston Free Zone, there is GARMEX, also in Kingston, Spanish Fort, located near to Kingston, the Montego Bay Free Zone on the north coast, Hayes Industrial Estate in Clarendon on the south-east coast, and Yallahs Industrial Estate on the east coast. In addition, free zone status has been granted to some factories in Trelawny, producing garments for export. There is a clear policy to introduce the zones to rural areas as well as the main cities.

The major source of investment in terms of volume and value comes from the United States, and this accounts for about half of the companies, most of which are involved in garment assembly. The second largest source of investment comes from Hong Kong. Other investors are from Canada, India and Hungary, as well as a number of joint venture companies involving Norway and the US. There are some twin plant investments with Puerto Rico in which part of the goods are assembled in Jamaica and the rest in Puerto Rico for re-export to the US. Most of the goods produced in the free zones are for the US market, but other destinations include, Canada, West Germany, Denmark, Hong Kong, Grand Cayman and CARICOM.

Most of the garments are produced under Tariff Schedules (TSUS) 806 and 807 now known as 9802.00.60 and 9802.00.80.[10] This means that pieces of the garments are cut in the US and assembled in Jamaica for re-export. Some 807 exports in 1989 were valued at US$139.1 million, and were made with fibres containing 70 per cent US fibres (Schoepfle, 1989, Table 1 in Appendix). Garments are also designed, cut and sewn in Jamaica under Cut Make and Trim (CMT) arrangements. They use more local skills but attract more duty on entry to the US, and are subject to quota restrictions. Jamaica also benefits from Lomé and Caribcan.

Most investment is in light manufacturing, mainly garments (jeans, underwear, T-shirts, sweaters etc.) but also includes some animal feed ingredients, food products, pharmaceutical products and ethanol. All except the ethanol production are labour intensive, making use of the large unemployed labour force. According to Wedderburn/Women's Action Committee (1990, p. 43), the value in US dollars of garments exported from Kingston, Montego Bay and GARMEX free zones in 1989 was US$118.25 million. Of this amount only US$26.8 million was retained in the local economy in the form of workers' wages, statutory deductions and company expenses for electricity, telephone and water. The balance leaves the country as company profits.

Labour Laws and Labour Standards

The Labour Relations and Industrial Disputes Act (LRIDA) outlines regulations of all workers' rights, and includes free zone workers. The LRIDA also provides guidelines for workers, management and government on issues such as organising work sites, conflict resolution and negotiating agreements. The Jamaican Constitution specifically provides for the right to form or join a trade union, and the right to organise. It also obliges the government to protect trade unions. The Constitution does not address the issue of forced labour, but the government is a signatory to the ILO Convention which prohibits compulsory labour. The Juvenile Act and the Education Act prohibit the employment of children except by parents, and there are no reports of children working in the zones. General enforcement of these laws is difficult, however. Wages guidelines limit increases to 10 per cent to control inflation although settlements are negotiated freely. The 10 per cent constraint is a major problem because of structural adjustment policies. In 1990, the minimum wage for garment workers was increased to J$130 which is equivalent to US$16 weekly. Most workers take home J$250–300 per fortnight (US$31–4), which is half of what they need for minimum survival. When work is available, some production workers earn up to US$126 a fortnight, but this is not the norm.

The minimum wage law provides for a 42-hour work week and overtime pay. Most employees work a basic eight-hour day, with an extra half-hour for lunch (e.g. 7 a.m.–3.30 p.m.), and a few hours' overtime if necessary. The law provides for nine days holiday leave in the first year, and two weeks after one year's service. The Factory Act requires all factories to be registered and stipulates regulations for fire exits and occupational health and safety standards. With budgetary constraints the Ministry of Labour is not able to monitor this regularly. Employers are also required to pay social security, worker's compensation and severance pay. About 25 per cent of the workforce is unionised and trade unions are an important part of economic life.

ORGANISING FOR CHANGE IN THE KINGSTON FREE ZONE

During 1986 and 1987 free trade zones took centre stage in the national media. There were several demonstrations around the issue of wages and working conditions, and the unions demanded their right to organise in the zones. Traditional trade unions have been discouraged, but in some factories managers have set up workers' councils to discuss problems and improve industrial relations. In the Kingston Free Zone there is only one company that is unionised, Lawrence Manufacturing, and this preceded their entry into the zone. Efforts to establish unions within the zone have been firmly resisted by the companies, who at the height of the protests formed the Free Zone Manufacturers Association.

Notwithstanding the strong resistance to trade unions in the Kingston Free Zone, some unions have tried to get representational polls, but with little success. During one of the largest demonstrations in the 1986–7 period, one of the largest unions tried to take over the demonstration, led some of the women to their offices, and tried to register them quickly. This was firmly rejected by the women who became very suspicious of the union's intentions.

JTURDC/CUSO Study

In response to this situation, a national study (Dunn, 1987) was commissioned by the Joint Trades Union Research and Development Centre (JTURDC – an umbrella group for the five major trade unions) and CUSO, a Canadian development agency. The study investigated allegations of abuses related to wages and working conditions in the Kingston Free Zone, compared this with conditions in the local garment factories producing for export, and recommended changes.

A participatory methodology was used that involved various national groups and sectors in the study. Workshops were held with garment workers inside and outside the free zone. Findings were shared widely with women workers and published in the national press. A graphic exhibition of the life of a free zone worker, Fay, was prepared and taken to different parts of the island and shared with women workers, trade unionists and the public at large. A record of the struggles to organise the union were recorded in a scrapbook of newspaper clippings between 1986 and 1987.

CUSO facilitated the participation of the main researcher in a conference and exposure visit to the Philippines in 1986. The conference was sponsored by the women's programme of the International Council for Adult Education (ICAE) and entitled 'Micro-Chip Technology: Its Impact on Women Workers'. It facilitated the exchange of organising experiences among workers, academics and activists and helped to build an international solidarity network. The experience of workers in the Bataan Free Zone was recorded in slides by the researcher and shared with women workers in Jamaica in workshops, which also used drama as a tool for analysis and organising. Honor Ford-Smith of Sistren Theatre Collective co-facilitated these workshops.[11]

The study was done at the height of the struggle, which was a challenging exercise because of the fear of being identified with a union, and the level of media attention. Interviews were done in the communities in which women lived, as permission was not given to do them in the Kingston Free Zone. Some were held at the St Peter Claver Church in Western Kingston. Women workers there have since established their own organisation to improve their situation, which is discussed later.

Media Campaign and Public Enquiry

Media exposure fuelled further publicity. Women organised public demonstrations to expose problems in the Kingston Free Zone. These issues became the subject of public debates, campaigns, newspaper articles and calls to popular radio phone-in programmes. The government finally established a Commission of Enquiry into the free zones to test allegations and make recommendations. Several organisations were called to present evidence before the Commission. This included the trade unions and the free zone managers. Among the organisations presenting evidence was the Women's Action Committee (WAC), a broad-based group of seven individuals and 15 organisations concerned about the free zone, which was formed as one of the recommendations of the JTURDC/CUSO study. The St Peter Claver Free Zone Women's Group and Sistren Theatre Collective, both grassroot women's groups which have been very active in the campaign to change conditions in the free zones, also made presentations.

The Report of the Enquiry confirmed many of the allegations of violations, and made most of the same recommendations that the JTURDC/CUSO study and the Women's Action Committee had previously made. The WAC continues to be an effective lobbying group, and in 1990 published a booklet for free zone workers outlining their rights and responsibilities. WAC works closely with the Client Services Committee of the

Kingston Free Zone Co., and as a result many improvements have been made in wages, working conditions and general facilities.

This experience shares many similarities with the Dominican Republic. There is clear evidence of the media's important role in building public awareness and pressure for change. There is also evidence that women workers resist in similar ways by organising demonstrations, and forming alliances with other women's groups.

Another experience which is similar, though different, relates to the importance of establishing organisations outside the zones and within the community. The following section relates the case of free zone women establishing their own organisation within the community to address a particular problem, that of housing.

Women Organising: St Peter Claver Women's Housing Co-operative

Given its proximity to the Kingston Free Zone, many workers live in the Waltham Park community which is part of the large inner city area Western Kingston. In response to the level of media attention on conditions in the zones, the St Peter Claver Roman Catholic Church did a community survey in 1987/88, targetted at women working in the free zone (Anderson, 1988). Priests and nuns visited homes in the area and invited the women to the church to discuss their problems. Regular meetings were organised, with resource persons invited to give them advice on problems. Over a period of several months, a small group was formed which later expanded to include a core of about 45 women.

The group called themselves the St Peter Claver Free Zone Women's Group and became an important source of support for the women. It served as a regular forum for sharing problems related to work and life in general, as well as discussing events in the Kingston Free Zone. Coping strategies were also shared, as the women faced similar problems regardless of the factory in which they worked. The group also became an effective network for other women in the community to get jobs. As in other parts of the world, free zone jobs are acquired through friends and relatives already working there. Information on vacancies is shared and passes for interviews acquired and passed on to prospective candidates. This served as a valuable network in the community, which has a higher than average unemployment level generally, but particularly among young women, many of whom are single parents.

The women decided to upgrade their skills through sewing classes, basic literacy, mathematics and English in the evenings and on weekends. Personal development workshops were organised on issues such as parenting, sexual violence, grievance procedures, and budgeting. Many women in the community registered in the sewing class to increase their chance of success when applying for free zone jobs. The group became active in the women's movement, joining the Women's Action Committee and the Association of Women's Organisations in Jamaica (AWOJA) for example. Social events played an important part in building the group as they gave rare opportunities for outings with their families and a chance to see places that were previously inaccessible. For example, they went to the National Pantomime during one Christmas holiday. This popular and hilarious farce, as well as parties to celebrate birthdays or Christmas treats for the children, provided opportunities for learning to organise small projects in preparation for bigger ones, and learning team work. It is interesting to note that like those in the Dominican Republic, these women find it easier to relate organising to their productive, reproductive and community managing roles. Their involvement in organising of a more political nature included the national campaign to increase the minimum wage.

The motivation for organising a more formal structure that was aimed at addressing problems more effectively emerged from the regular meetings. They eventually concluded that many of their problems related to poor housing and they decided to form a housing co-operative for women, run by women. Hurricane Gilbert, one of the century's most violent hurricanes which devastated Jamaica in September 1988, provided further impetus to address this problem. Many free zone workers lost their already precarious accommodation and were forced to share the already overcrowded facilities of relatives and friends.

Some of the hurricane relief supplies for shelter were channelled through the group, which helped to identify those in the worst situation. With the help of the church, they contacted the Department of Co-operatives and the Church's Co-operative Credit Union and CUSO, the Canadian Development agency that had co-sponsored the Women in Industry study. There was already a link with CUSO because a number of the women had been interviewed for that research project and had participated in some of the workshops and meetings.

CUSO, as part of its support for the programme, provided a Canadian volunteer with experience of housing co-operatives in Canada to work with the group over the next two years. The two organisations and the volunteer trained the women to organise the housing co-operative, which was formally registered on 26 January 1989. The volunteer worked with an understudy, a bright, articulate and ambitious free zone worker who had been fired. She was appointed as the group's co-ordinator when the volunteer withdrew and manages the programme from the church's office. This again shows the similarity between the Dominican Republic and Jamaica case. Leaders of both groups have become involved in organising and were subsequently fired. The groups are supported by the church, and in the latter case, they helped in contacting international agencies for financial assistance.

Debt Swap

These efforts were quite successful, and in a relatively short time, the group was able to get support for their training programme as well as contributions which they used to arrange a debt swap through CIDA, the Canadian Development Agency. They received a grant of J$2 233 631.40. In brief, they arranged to purchase an agreed amount of the Jamaican government's foreign debt at a rate cheaper than the official rate, using the foreign exchange they had raised from international donors.[12] These funds were matched by CIDA and the total amount used to repay a portion of Jamaica's foreign debt. In exchange, the Bank of Jamaica paid the co-operative the equivalent amount in Jamaican dollars.

The funds were used to purchase and renovate eight houses in the community, ensuring that although two families still shared kitchen and bathroom facilities, there was less overcrowding. These eight houses now accommodate 16 co-op members and their families, and plans are underway to expand the programme to create another 50 units.

Priority was given to co-op members in the most precarious housing situations, particularly those with children. Interviews with the women indicate that the experience has helped them to develop personally as well as organisationally. Having access to comfortable, affordable housing has given them and their children much-needed security. For some, it is a dream come true. In addition to the physical comfort, many enjoy the power of owning and having control over their household. The houses are jointly owned by the co-op members, but only women can become members. This guarantees them shelter in the event of separation from their partners.

Impact on the Women

Their new status has given the women more confidence and according to them, they have become more articulate and assertive in standing up for their rights at home and at work. They have learned the discipline of running an organisation, purchasing and managing properties, building participatory structures, negotiating skills, reflecting on their experience and planning for the future together. In 1990, they produced a video documentary about their experience entitled 'We Run Things'. This has been shared with other groups for information and to animate group discussions. Articles about them have been written in the press and they use the media to raise issues. They too have learnt how to handle the media as an important strategy for organising.

Building Links with other Groups

An important part of their strategy has been to collaborate with other organisations working on similar issues. The co-op's involvement in a joint campaign with women's groups and trade unions to improve wages and working conditions in the zones, their participation in the Women's Action Committee, giving evidence at the public enquiry, and speaking from their own experience, has raised their profile and they are now an important reference group on free zone issues, regularly consulted by groups locally and internationally. The group has also helped to produce other videos, such as that made by the UK-based charity, Christian Aid, on the impact of the debt and structural adjustment on women in Jamaica (1991).[13]

Advocacy

The experience of the St Peter Claver Women's Housing Co-operative represents another method of organising for change within the context of industrialisation. They are not a trade union in the traditional sense, neither do they purport to represent a broad cross section of free zone workers. However, they play an effective advocacy role at a national level by collaborating with a number of other organisations and the trade union movement to introduce changes in the free zones.

There have been tangible successes to date. The litany of abuses that were regularly publicised during the earlier period has abated. Conditions are still not ideal, but the industrial climate has improved considerably. The group monitors events closely, and responds publicly to voice their opinion. A recent case of this was the public repudiation of a free zone manager's views about pregnant free zone workers.

Through participation in the Women's Action Committee and collaboration with the Bureau of Women's Affairs, the Co-op has helped to improve the industrial climate at the Kingston Free Zone. The number of canteens has increased, and health facilities, transport and security have improved. Asian supervisors who used to be a major source of complaint now have access to an orientation course to acquaint them with Jamaican culture, which better prepares them to relate to the Jamaican workforce. Increasingly, more Jamaican supervisors are employed, which eliminates the cultural conflicts that previously occurred.

Gender Solidarity

Changes in the Kingston Free Zone are in part due to gender solidarity. The Chairperson of the Free Zone Administration's Client Services Committee is a woman who has experience of industrial relations and a long history of working with the free zones. Close liaison between herself and the WAC has helped to improve working conditions. Here again a parallel can be drawn between this approach and the one proposed by the women in the DR. Instead of confrontation as the only strategy for seeking improvements, these women on both sides have tried co-operation and collaboration as they negotiate for changes that ultimately serve the interests of the workers, the manufacturers and the government that wants to keep investors happy to retain their business. Talking to some of the women on both sides, it is clear that this is not an easy alliance, but there is respect and a commitment to improve the situation of women workers.[14]

There are also reports that a number of the managers (the women particularly) have been supportive of the process and have in turn tried to introduce changes that benefit their workers while not harming production. An example of this is arranging weekly shifts to allow women to leave early one evening to handle their domestic affairs. Similarly, in cases where there have had to be temporary lay-offs because of reduced orders, some have staggered the workforce to provide more women with jobs, albeit at a reduced level.[15]

Through their participation in other organisations and their education and campaigning work at different levels, the St Peter Claver Women's Housing Co-operative provides a model for organising at the community level, which for many women is less threatening than a traditional trade union. Being involved makes many of them feel part of a process for changing the situation of free zone workers and this gives them not only a sense of purpose, but also a new-found power in finding that in tangible ways they can influence their future. In its own way, the Co-op is helping a number of women to meet their productive, reproductive and community managing roles. Their participation is part of the process of developing their organisation and is helping to prepare a new cadre of women leaders, and this is creating a climate for meeting some of their strategic gender needs.

CONCLUSION: LESSONS FOR ORGANISING

The *Concise Oxford Dictionary* (1981: 719) defines organise to mean 'furnish with organs, make organic, make into living being or tissue; to form into an organic whole, enrol as members of a formal body e.g. trade union; give orderly structure to, frame and put into working order etc.' The case studies and experiences described above suggest that the concept has to be expanded to include a whole network of relationships that can enable groups of free zone workers to realise their full potential and improve their quality of life and that of their families.

As the definition takes form, there is evidence from the two case studies that the element of furnishing the group with organs, and making it a living being takes place at two obvious levels. The first is through building membership and helping the group take on a life and dynamic of its own. This makes the case for institutional strengthening that was developed in the DR case study, but is equally applicable to the Jamaica case. This process involves building social solidarity and creating cohesive organisations that understand the social, economic and political context within which they operate. To avoid alienating members, participatory structures are needed to enable people to work through issues and collaborate on the basis of consensus. Ideally, this should lead to a coherent political strategy that can guide programmes for social change, in the factory and in the zones.

This type of organisation contrasts sharply with traditional trade unions, some of which have lost their spark and need new life. The new unions play an important role as catalysts and as models of a new kind of organisation. They strengthen gender sensitivity and empower members, recognising women's ability and need to participate equally with men.

Given the size and importance of the trade union sector in Jamaica, as in most countries, it is strategically important for the large-scale traditional unions and the new unions to find ways of working together. Communication and education programmes must be able to make workers aware of their rights and responsibilities, but also improve their capacity for social, political and economic analysis. This provides a scientific basis for understanding the economy and their particular industry which is essential for bargaining.

Organisations of women workers have to ensure that their *modus operandi* builds members' confidence and provides practical support to reflect the various social roles that women occupy. This involves the struggle for crèches and more equitable sharing of domestic and social maintenance responsibilities among members of the family. There is need to find strategic ways to influence members of the society (including women) to change attitudes and actions which work at present to oppress women.

Summary

Against the background of the information presented, the EPZs and the EOI strategy have an important impact on the economies of the Dominican Republic and Jamaica and the women working in them. Undoubtedly, thousands of jobs have been created, giving large numbers of women the opportunity to be more independent. This has to be seen as a short-term solution, however, whose scope is limited by the type of industries that invest and the impact of the structural adjustment policies, which in general defeat rather than promote economic development. Expansion of the local manufacturing sector which is considered an important objective of the industrialisation process is limited by the structure of transnationals, and the inability of local companies to provide the quantity and quality of raw materials needed.

Transnationals benefit most from the EOI strategy and are creating a new kind of colonialism based on wage slavery, which increases workers' motivation to organise groups to defend their interests. Countries like Jamaica and the Dominican Republic seem likely to occupy permanent positions at the bottom ranks of the global factory with few possibilities for rising to more highly skilled types of industries and investments as was the case with the NICs. Within the current global recession it is unlikely that these 'economic miracles' can be duplicated.

In sharp contrast to this picture of doom are women's efforts to organise, creating political space to do so. Their strong actions for survival are helping them to use the structure, patterns and rhythm of the FTZ work environment to organise. They use their limited time to build networks and form alliances in their struggle to pursue their own development.

NOTES

1. See L. Sklair, 'Shenzhen: A Chinese "Development Zone" in Global Perspective', *Development and Change*, 16, 4, 1985, pp. 571–602. See also L. Sklair, *Assembling for Development: the Maquila Industry in Mexico and the United States*, Unwin Hyman, London 1989; and L. Sklair, *Sociology of the Global System*, Harvester Wheatsheaf, London 1990.
2. Interviews with free zone workers in Jamaica, August 1990 and in the Dominican Republic, February 1991.
3. Source: National Council of Free Zones, quoted in Dauhajre *et al.*, 1989, p. 72.
4. Bateyes are communities of Haitian migrant workers and Haitian-Dominicans who traditionally worked on sugar plantations. With diversification of the industry, many now work on plantations producing export crops, in construction and in the free zones. Living conditions in the bateyes are very poor, and in the more isolated bateyes, they are treated like slaves, with their freedom severely restricted. Sanitation is very poor, with 500 residents sharing a bathroom, and this influences how they use the bathrooms in the free zone. Overcrowding, high unemployment and a very low standard of living create an abundance of social problems in the bateyes. Workers reported problems of prostitution, rape and incest. Many women feared for their daughters who they had to leave unprotected to go to work, and the very long day increased the risk.
5. Interviews with Mr Castillo and the President of the National Free Zone Council in February, 1991. Similar views were attributed to Mr Castillo in an article in El Nacional of 7 August 1990 by Vianco Maritinez (p. 15). He was quoted as saying that, 'the political trade unionism that we have here, wants to blow the free zone problems out of proportion, when in reality these problems are insignificant'.
6. Reports in the Dominican Republic are that this decision was made after considerable pressure from local unions, the AFL-CIO and the International Labour Organisation. The country stood the chance of losing their CBI status if they did not respect labour laws and did not improve their treatment of Haitian migrant workers, most of whom work in the agricultural and construction sectors, although many of the women work in free zones.
7. The Group Dynamics school in Social Psychology establishes a correlation between workers' perception of leadership style, group cohesion and job satisfaction. In a study of Jamaican media workers, this relationship was confirmed (see L. Dunn, 1986). Other studies have confirmed this relationship, and it stands to reason that the same would apply to these workers.
8. Interviews with free zone workers in San Pedro de Macoris, February 1991.
9. In February, for example, the meeting had to be relocated at short notice. In the time it took to arrange an alternative site, some workers left. However, those who relocated were extremely patient.
10. Source: News Release from United States International Trade Commission of 27 December 1989.
11. Sistren Theatre Collective is a group of primarily working-class women who have used drama as a tool for analysing community and women's

issues. They have consistently highlighted the situation of free zone workers in their workshops and plays, and are a major force behind 'Sister's Celebration'. This is a six-year-old tradition, celebrated on International Women's Day, and takes the form of a cultural show. Popular artistes present songs in praise and support of women and each year a different group of women in Jamaican society is honoured. One of the most successful 'Celebrations' was held in 1987 and honoured free zone women. The female compere, Fay Ellington-Smith, intersperses facts and commentary about the women being honoured. This and the choice of songs and other items on the show, builds awareness about issues that those being honoured face, in a lively and entertaining celebration.

12.   Debt swaps are done between debtor countries and international creditors. Creditors are willing to release debt papers for a fraction of the original value in situations where it seems likely that the full amount plus interest will not be repaid. In this way they recover some of their money and the debtor agrees to pay a local organisation the equivalent in local currency.

13.   Film entitled 'Jamaica, No Problem?', Christian Aid, 1991. That organisation has supported the St Peter Claver Free Zone Women's Group and the Co-operative since 1987.

14.   Individual interviews with Mrs Beverly Dunkley, Chairperson of the Free Zone's Client Services Committee; Ms Selena Tapper, CUSO's Caribbean Field Director (a Jamaican); and Ms Lisetta White, President, St Peter Claver Women's Housing Co-op, August 1990.

15.   Interviews with free zone women and WAC members, August 1990.

REFERENCES

Abreu *et al.* 1989. 'Las Zonas Francas Industriales: El Exito de una Politica Economica', Centro Internacional para el Desarollo Economico, Santo Domingo.

Anderson, P. and D. Gordon. 1987. 'Economic Change and Labour Market Mobility in Jamaica: 1979–1984'. Paper presented at the First Conference of Caribbean Economists, Jamaica.

Anon. 1991. 'Las Zonas Francas y Los Trabajadores en Republica Dominicana', Santo Domingo (pamphlet).

Bonilla, E. 1990. 'Working Women In Latin America', in *Economic and Social Progress Report*, IDB.

CONSA. 1989. 'Zonas Francas y mano de obra feminina en el Caribe: el caso de la Republica Dominicana', (mimeo).

Dauhajre *et al.* 1989. 'Las Zonas Francas Industriales', Santo Domingo.

de Moya Espinal, F. 1986. 'Las Zonas Francas Industriales y las Empresas Multinacionales: Efectos economicos e impacto sobre el empleo en la Republica Dominicana', Working Paper No. 46, ILO, Geneva.

Diamond, W. H. and D. B. Diamond. 1989. *Tax Free Zones of the World*, Vol. 3, Matthew Bender and Co, New York.

Dunn, L. 1986. 'Perception of Leadership Style and Group Cohesion: Their Influence on Job Satisfaction'. Unpublished Masters Thesis in Sociology, University of the West Indies, Mona.

Dunn, L. 1987. 'Women in Industry: A Participatory Research Project on Garment Workers in Jamaica', Joint Trades Union Research and Development Centre/CUSO, Kingston (mimeo).

Dunning, John H. 1971. *The Multinational Enterprise*, George, Allen & Unwin, London.

Gordon, D. 1989. 'Women, Work and Social Mobility in Post-War Jamaica', in Keith Hart (ed.), *Women and the Sexual Division of Labour in the Caribbean*, Consortium Graduate School of the Social Sciences, Kingston, pp. 67–78.

Joekes, S. 1986. *Industrialization, Trade and Female Employment in Developing Countries*, INSTRAW, Dominican Republic.

Kingston Free Zone Co. 1986. 'Free Zone Contribution to the Domestic Economy', (Company Document).

Kingston Free Zone Co. 1989a. Report of the Kingston Free Zone Co. (Company Document).

Kingston Free Zone Co. 1989b. 'Kingston Free Zone'. A report prepared by the Research and Development Division, 31 January.

Molyneux, M. 1985. 'Mobilization without Emancipation? Women's Interests, the State, and Revolution in Nicaragua', *Feminist Studies* 11, No. 2, Summer, pp. 227–55.

Moser, C. 1989. 'Gender Planning in the Third World: Meeting Practical and Strategic Gender Needs'. Paper submitted to *World Development*, 1989.

Pineda, Magaly. 1990. 'La vida mia no es facil: la otra cara de la zona franca' (My life is not easy: the other side of the Free Zone), Colección Minerva Mirabal, CIPAF, Santo Domingo.

Schoepfle, G. K. 1989. 'Labour Standards in Export Assembly Operations in Mexico and the Caribbean'. Paper presented at the North American Economics and Finance Association Meetings, Atlanta, Dec. 29 (mimeo).

Schoepfle, G. K. and J. F. Perez-Lopez. 1990. 'Employment Implications of Export Assembly Operations in Mexico and the Caribbean Basin'. Commission for the Study of International Migration and Co-operative Economic Development Working Paper No. 16, January.

Wedderburn, J. 1990. *Rights as well as Jobs for Women in the Garment Industry*, Women's Action Committee/CUSO Caribbean, Kingston.

Yung Whee Rhee *et al.* 1990. 'Free Trade Zones in Export Strategies', World Bank, September (mimeo).

9 Asian Industrial Women Workers in the 1980s

Loh Cheng-Kooi

The focus of this chapter is on the changes which have occurred in relation to Asian women workers, particularly in the last decade of the 1980s during which a new women workers' movement has emerged in the region.

As early as the 1960s, Asian countries have undergone a process of export-oriented industrialisation, beginning in East Asian countries such as Korea, Taiwan and Hong Kong. By the 1970s, the South-east Asian countries of Malaysia, Philippines, Indonesia and Thailand were adopting a similar pattern followed later by countries such as Sri Lanka, Bangladesh and Pakistan. This pattern of industrialisation encouraged foreign investors to invest in these countries, and large industrial areas, better known as free trade zones (FTZs), were set up for predominantly light industries such as electronics, textiles, garments, shoes and plastics. One of the main attractions for investors was the promise of cheap and abundant labour. This was made viable by the massive recruitment of young, single women generally under 20 years of age who had come from the rural areas and provinces to work. From the management viewpoint, these young girls were ideal as they were not only dexterous and nimble-fingered at their work, but their exposure as first-time wage earners also meant that they were unorganised, seemingly docile and easily controlled.

After several decades of industrialisation, the scene of thousands of factory women workers going to and from work is a familiar sight in many cities in Asian countries. Statistics indicate that women workers today comprise 30–40 per cent of the workforce in the manufacturing sector, a very significant increase. In the past decade this young workforce has matured into women in their twenties and thirties. While the working conditions in these factories remain exploitative – low wages, poor working conditions, job discrimination, etc., the picture of the docile, unorganised woman worker is clearly changing. Today, it is not uncommon to read about women workers going on strike for better wages or fighting back against retrenchment. These women are prepared to struggle for a better situation. They are realising that unless they actively choose to participate to change their own conditions, these will not change. The docile woman worker is being transformed into one who is actively becoming aware of herself and her rights in society.

I shall examine aspects of the ways in which the organising strength of women workers has evolved, how women workers are presently defining their own struggles, and the impact of these changes on the labour movement and its future prospects.

THE STRUGGLE FOR DEMOCRACY AND THE EMERGENCE OF WOMEN WORKERS' ACTIVISM

The emergence of women workers' organisations is linked to the intensification of the broader struggle for democracy, especially in the Philippines and South Korea. Women workers had been actively involved in the struggle to set up democratic trade unions in the late 1970s in South Korea. However, there was soon a backlash due to repression by the management and the state. In addition a number of serious problems emerged within the leadership of the unions. Women workers faced specific problems: a number of women leaders were forced to give up their activism due to marriage as a result of social pressure, domestic duties and child-care; and unmarried women leaders who could not cope with personal problems dropped out. This led to serious reflection amongst women activists about the specificities of women's subordination. When the labour movement became active again in the mid-eighties, the KWWA was formed to take up the particular issues of women workers (CSIS/CAW, 1985). As a woman organiser stated:

> We felt that the issue of women's rights was not being taken up seriously by our Welfare Association, even though we had our own women's section. The enormous personal and social problems encountered by working women were not being catered to. To us, democratic rights, human rights and women's rights are all on the same platform when we talk about genuine democracy. There is need for us to form our own separate organisation to take care of women workers' needs.
>
> (CAW, 1988: 50)

Similarly in the Philippines, from 1975 onwards, militant organisations began to organise around workers' issues and challenged the Martial Law Regime, and in 1980 the KMU was formed. Although concerned women labour organisers began to raise women's issues in 1979, it was only in 1984 that it was decided by women labour organisers and women trade unionists in the newly-formed Women Industrial Workers Alliance (WIWA) to establish a Women Workers' Movement (KMK), which would mobilise unionised as well as non-unionised women workers. The KMK is now one of the largest mass organisations of working women.

Other factors also played an important role in the highlighting of women's issues in the 1980s. The 1970s and the 1980s were marked by the growth of non-governmental organisations (NGOs) in many Asian countries in response to the deteriorating socio-economic conditions in these countries. Concerned citizens began to get involved with the people's movement, and numerous groups of social concern focusing on issues related to peasants, workers, human rights and overall development sprang up. The women's movement too began to take shape in these countries in the 1980s as women began actively to challenge traditional patriarchal Asian values and norms. Women's groups were set up ranging from consciousness-raising to campaigning around issues such as wife-battering, health, and reproductive rights. The women's movement called for recognition of women oppression in Asian societies and argued for the need for autonomy to take up their specific struggles.

Repressive labour policies also forced the emergence of alternative forms of organising as well as involvement of wider sections of society in movements. As organising of any form was severely repressed in the FTZs by management, abetted by the state, labour activists continued to look for alternatives to organise these women workers. In the meantime, the women workers themselves were involved in broader social movements in their own countries, and different forms of women workers' participation began to occur. At this point the women's movement did influence the fledgling women workers' movement: by the mid-1980s, the women workers' organisations that were formed had called for recognition of the specific problems faced by women workers, namely both labour *and* women's problems. This was a clear departure from the earlier situation when women workers were participating in demanding their rights only as workers. One can locate the specific organising for women workers only from the 1980s onwards.

At present, one can broadly categorise several types of groups and/or organisations which cater to women workers:

1. Labour centres: these centres have largely been started by the churches or NGOs since the 1970s. They have been crucial in providing the initial services for women workers in the industrial zones, where any form of organising was prevented. These centres were seen as providing social welfare services for the large numbers of women workers, and were therefore allowed to function. Besides serving as a drop-in place for women workers to come together socially, these centres also provide legal counselling, as

well as educational training on workers' rights. Legal counselling and educational activity formed important aspects of service as workers began to realise their rights as wage earners. The centres operate on the basis that women workers have been exploited, and therefore services are geared towards conscientising them towards their rights as workers. The gender aspects faced by women workers are often not dealt with.

2. Women workers' centres: these centres arose in the 1980s, started by women activists or former women workers who had been retrenched as a result of their activism. Set up specifically to cater for women workers, their activities range from basic skill training and literacy classes to conscientising programmes. The aim has been to bring women workers together, and to build their confidence towards being aware of themselves as women as well as workers. Though still small in number and limited to localised work, these centres do provide the space for women workers to come together to share and work out their problems.

3. Trade unions: despite managements' efforts to thwart attempts to form trade unions, in recent years there has been an increasing number of company trade unions formed through relentless action by women workers. The tendency though is to elect men into the leadership positions. Attempts to get women to take up key leadership roles have been slow. However, in areas where there is strong support, women have been able to take up key trade union positions. This has been an important development for the women workers' struggle, as the type of issues that are taken up by women-dominated unions tend to be more women-worker oriented than merely more general issues of wages and other economic demands.

4. Women workers' organisations: the most important change has been the formation of autonomous women workers' organisations. These organisations were formed and led by women workers themselves, and therefore have the potential to define their own agenda. In Asia today, there are already two national women workers organisations, one in the Philippines – Kilusan ng Manggagawang Kabaibahan (KMK) – and the other in Korea, the Korean Women Workers' Association (KWWA). Elsewhere there are other less comprehensive efforts to form women workers' organisations, such as the Hong Kong Women Workers' Association (HKWWA). The two broad-based organisations have been actively lobbying for women workers' issues. When KMK was formed in 1984 and the KWWA in 1987, they had called for the recognition of women workers' specific problems as both workers and women. These autonomous small or mass-based groups reflect a significant change, since they are often led by women workers themselves who saw the need to come out separately to provide an alternative perspective for the women workers' struggle.

THE GROWTH OF A WORKING WOMEN'S MOVEMENT

There are several factors which have resulted in the growth of a working women's movement. Firstly, there is now a greater number of women who are taking up the work of organising. As the interests of women workers extended from mere concern to identifying strategies whereby something had to be done, organising efforts of women workers began to take place. Earlier labour organisers were primarily men who were organising women workers on their rights as workers, to be part and parcel of the labour movement. These days, the organising work has been taken over by women themselves, be it women activists or former women workers. As women themselves enter into organising work, their involvement inevitably leads them to question the women's aspect of women workers' lives, and they are forced to confront these issues when they are organising them.

In contrast, traditional male labour organisers and trade unionists, experienced in mobilising workers to fight primarily for wages, are often unfamiliar and insensitive to the gender aspect of women workers' lives and working conditions, which time and again has proved to be an obstacle towards their organisation. Discussions with several male organisers who have been involved with organising women workers, revealed that it is not so difficult to mobilise women workers to go on strike. For instance, a Thai male organiser stated,

> In fact women are very tough and are prepared to take drastic actions when the necessity arises. They are always prepared to be in the forefront of the strike. The main difficulty lies in trying to sustain their activism after the strike action. They simply go back to their former situation and stop being active.
>
> (Asian Women Workers Newsletter, 1990)

Until today, this very organiser, in spite of successfully organising several strike actions involving women workers, has failed to make any inroads towards building women workers' groups.

The presence of both men and women organisers in organisational work has enabled women organisers to be more openly critical of the male chauvinist attitudes of their male colleagues. In this way, male organisers to a large extent are forced to recognise the women's aspect when organising women workers. Whether they take action on it is another story, but it has led to male organisers being more sensitive to women workers' needs.

With women as organisers, there has also been a change in the organisational methods used to work with women workers. Women organisers have been emphasising a 'women's way of organising' in the centres and with the groups with which they are working. The emphasis of the organisers has been to create confidence and self-awareness among the workers, both as women in society and so that they better understand their position as women workers. These activities often take the form of participatory methods which involve theatre workshops and use of audio-visual media. This contrasts greatly with educational programmes undertaken by labour centres which only stressed educating women workers on workers' rights and the role of trade unions. Training by women workers groups discuss issues of women's oppression in society and the double burden, as well as economic issues and general rights of workers. Trade unions are limited to developing only workers' consciousness, while women workers' groups have managed to highlight the gender aspects of women workers' consciousness.

Another important development has been the openness of women workers' organisers to work with women activists of women's groups and vice versa. When women's groups were first formed, there were accusations that these groups were middle-class and not grassroot-oriented, and many people, including women workers' organisers, could not understand the need for separateness. This wall of suspicion is gradually breaking down as women workers' organisers are beginning to realise the importance of taking up the gender dimension in their work. Women organisers are finding that issues such as wife-battering, the double burden and health raised by women's groups are also problems suffered by women workers. Similarly, the urban women's groups are trying to break down their isolation, and on many occasions have come out in support for women workers' struggles. Women's groups have been able to utilise their resources to publicise and give support to women on strike, whether for better working conditions or for specific issues such as maternity laws or sexual harassment. Events such as International Women's Day are often jointly commemorated by both groups. During such occasions, demands which are raised are related to the needs of working women, such as the availability of better day-care centres, as well as to general discrimination against women and a call for an end to violence against women.

The biggest change comes from the women workers themselves. Earning a wage, living communally with each other, away from their families and learning to survive independently – all these have helped them to mature and grow away from the protective environment from which they originally came. Their own experiences through years of fighting for better wages and unionisation, while gaining little ground to articulate and fulfil their needs as women, taught them that they have to fight their own battles.

Hence the determination by women workers' leaders to start their own groups and organisations, and prioritise their needs. When the Korea KWWA was inaugurated in 1987, one of the first things they did was to set up a Women Workers' House, in which they run a day-care centre, provide laundromat services to save time on washing, and conduct women leadership courses and educational programmes on women workers' issues. Shortly after the Philippines KMK was formed, it put forth 11 specific demands of Filipino women workers including equal pay, guarantee of women's full participation in gainful employment, and the elimination of discrimination against women due to sex, age and marital status.

MOVING BEYOND WAGE ISSUES

Given the above perspective, the demands of the working women's movement have gone beyond the fight for better wages and working conditions. While there are still strikes constantly taking place which deal with the issues of low wages and bad working conditions, increasingly the struggles by women workers have taken up women-specific issues. Issues such as better maternity protection, equal pay for equal work, and job discrimination are some of the specific demands of women workers. Other examples include women workers fighting for transport facilities for night shiftwork in Pakistan, and Japanese women taking their employers to court against job discrimination. In Sri Lanka, when a few women workers were raped when returning from night work, a campaign by the Church, local activists, and women's groups was launched to demand better security for the workers. Women workers are defining their own immediate needs and demands.

Unfortunately, specific issues affecting women workers are issues that male-dominated trade unions or labour organisers hardly take up. It is only where women-dominated unions or women workers' organisations exist that these issues have been raised. The battle to take up issues pertaining to women workers continues to be the concern only of women workers' groups. The national level mass labour movement still tends to see issues affecting women workers as issues that are restricted to women workers' groups and there is little attempt made to integrate these issues into the mainstream as part and parcel of the labour movement.

Even now, the change is still slow. Recently in Manila, Philippines, there was a breakthrough when some unions won paternity leave for workers. But this success was due to the perseverance of women unionists. 'If members and officers of the unions had all been males, paternity leave might still have been a dream today', stated Perlita Serrano, chairperson of KMK. Male unionists are more concerned with economic demands or with problems such as quota systems and overtime than with anything else. Women unionists, on the other hand, have been increasingly aware of their rights as women, redoubling their efforts for better working conditions. Perlita Serrano points out further that:

> Pushing for women's issues during the collective bargaining agreement (CBA) negotiations can be heart-breaking. At first stage, women's issues are up on the list of demands in the CBA, but they are the first to get thrown out when things are not going well in the negotiations. Like when a union was made to choose between a rice subsidy and maternity benefits, they took the rice subsidy, of course.
>
> (Sol Juvida, Women's Feature Service, 1990)

Nevertheless, issues such as additional maternity benefits, choice of work during pregnancy, menstruation leave, day-care centres for workers' children, and stiffer penalties for sexual harassment are vigorously being pursued in CBA negotiations by women trade unionists.

CHALLENGING TRADE UNIONS AND BUILDING ALLIANCES: THE CHANGING SCENARIO

Women workers' groups, though organised autonomously, continue to maintain a link with the trade union movement which is showing a greater interest in women workers. This stems from the fact that today women workers have proven their own capability, and have often criticised their male counterparts for their lack of interest in taking up women workers' issues. However, in spite of this change, women workers' organisations cannot become complacent since male support is not always forthcoming. Often women workers have to battle with their male colleagues who see women workers' concerns as a 'deviation'. The labour movement expects women to follow their (male) agenda, with those economic and political demands which they define as priorities. For instance, in 1988 when the KMK launched their national maternity campaign to demand improvement in maternity leave benefits, they had to battle with resistance from their male colleagues in the KMU (May 1st Movement), who saw their national labour economic demands as far more important than the demand for maternity leave. Similarly, when KWWA was trying to establish its own separate organisation, criticism came from their male colleagues who saw the move as splitting the labour movement. Today the accusation of being 'deviationist' still remains, as there are still many male trade union leaders who do not recognise women's issues as important, or do not see the need to take these issues up.

This kind of relationship with the labour movement is an unequal one, since women workers' organisations have fully supported the labour movement in the struggle for their demands. May Day celebrations are marked by the active participation of women workers. Trade union federations have no hesitation in mobilising women workers to participate in a general strike, yet are reluctant to take up demands raised by women workers' organisations. The Korean KWWA have been successful even in mobilising the wives and children of male workers who are on strike to participate together with their husbands. The wives and children shout slogans and wave banners in unity with their husbands. But the scene after the strikes remains the same: the husbands are the breadwinners and the women are the housewives. KWWA is also consciously trying to change the husbands' attitude so that they participate in household work, while encouraging the wives to participate in community affairs outside the home.

The KMK continues to work via women's committees in the unions, and exerts pressure to see that women's issues are raised in Collective Bargaining Agreement (CBA) negotiations. For instance, they plan to introduce a bill in Congress on paternity benefits. The arguments during CBA negotiations for paternity leave stressed that 'a husband's support is needed by the wife during childbirth, especially when there is no household help nor relatives around' (AWWN, 1991). These demands begin to lay the basis for changing the sexual division of labour in the household and establish the joint interests of working women and men in this area. In 1992, women workers in Hong Kong were joined by their male counterparts in their petition for full paid maternity leave. In addition, the male workers who supported the petition, used the occasion of Father's Day to demand 14 days' parental leave, saying that paternity leave was necessary for fathers to take care of their wives after delivery and to do the housework (AWWN, July 1992).

Such actions should make a great difference to the trade union movement which expects that both the men and women be active in the labour movement, yet has given insufficient attention to issues directly affecting the workers' families as a whole. Today, many active women workers' leaders are forced to perform the miracle tasks of working full-time as activists and running homes, doing housework and child-care. For many women with children, the Asian extended family of mothers and mothers-in-law plays an important role in temporarily resolving the dilemma of child-care responsibilities of activists' families. For other women activists, the choice has been to remain single in order to continue to be active. Few fortunate activist women workers are able to continue their activism with the help of supportive husbands.

Given the necessity to apply continuous pressure on male colleagues and the trade unions in general, women workers' groups have had to build links and draw support from other women's organisations. These new formations have been linked from their inception with women working in other sectors as well as with other more broad-based organisations. KMK, for instance, has chapters of agricultural workers, co-ordinates with other service centres such as the Women's Centre in Metro Manila, and is linked with GABRIELLA, a coalition of different women's organisations in the Philippines.

A significant development in recent years has been the establishment of linkages at a regional level between workers in Asia. Apart from regional conferences and workshops, a number of exchange visits have led to the building of closer ties between women workers' organisations in the region. In 1993, four Korean women organisers from the Korean Women Workers' Association United (KWWAU) visited the Self Employed Women's Association (SEWA) in Ahmedabad, India. As the number of women workers in the informal sector and home-based work increases, KWWAU found the work done by SEWA inspiring for their future plans to extend organising efforts in this area (AWWN, July 1993). In May 1993, an exchange was organised between Thai labour activists, including women unionists, organisers, NGO activists and the KMK. The Committee for Asian Women has played an important role in facilitating these linkages.

PROSPECTS FOR THE FUTURE

The past decade has shown the potential and the capability of women workers to surge forward to define their own agenda. The issues they have organised around and the methods of organisation chosen have challenged the divisions between factory work and community work, women as workers and women as wives, and strengthened the link between women's rights in the labour movement and the struggle for democracy. It is crucial that this movement is sustained so that it can continue to provide the space for women workers to evolve their own methods and ways of organising and struggling for their own issues. Women workers have shown that they are capable of being in the forefront of struggles and taking up their own specific needs and issues. The experience of KMK and KWWWA shows that women workers' issues cannot be isolated from the mainstream of broader labour issues. Their growth has challenged the trade union movement and forced transformations at the level of organising structures.

However, even as women workers continue to be wooed by the labour movement to participate actively in strike actions and general strikes, there is still not enough acceptance that the struggle for democracy has to begin with both men and women workers' needs. The importance of sensitising the men in trade unions is therefore of urgent importance. Unless male-dominated unions begin to allow women into leadership positions, not only in female-dominated sectors of industry but also in national congresses and federations, women leaders will continue to battle to put their needs on the agenda. The patriarchal values operating within trade unions and their leadership needs seriously to be challenged and taken up. It is not only a question of women workers sensitising their male counterparts, but also trade unionists themselves should take the initiatives to change their attitudes and take an authentic interest in understanding women workers' struggles. The understanding of women workers' issues can be concretely integrated into the many training and educational programmes organised regularly by trade unions. The power of trade unions lies in the fact that they are the legal entity for workers' organisation and negotiations. Women workers' organisations can only facilitate the building of a power base for women workers' needs and demands. Therefore it is vital that the labour movement recognise their role in supporting women workers' struggles and needs in the movement.

While the emergence of the women workers' movement in Asia today is indicative of significant changes and provides hope for the long-awaited realisation and recognition of women workers as women as well as workers, there is however an ever-present threat that these gains will also be set back in the fast-changing socio-political climate in these countries. The new women workers' movement is part of the broader people's movement in the Philippines and Korea, where women workers are actively participating in the national struggles. There is a danger of prioritising national struggles above women workers' own demands, unless the leaders themselves are aware of the necessity of balancing women workers' needs with the struggle for democracy.

The flight of capital by foreign investors also threatens the existence of this movement. There has been massive retrenchment of workers in the Philippines and Korea as capital has moved to countries where workers are less organised. In other situations such as in Hong Kong and Taiwan, plant closures have also occurred as even cheaper labour is found in other Asian countries. All these developments make the women workers' movement extremely vulnerable. Nevertheless, hope lies in the transformation of women workers, who through a relatively short period have made important gains and shown their capabilities to struggle as women and as workers to regain their dignity.

REFERENCES

Committee for Asian Women. 1980–93. *Asian Women Workers Newsletter*, CAW, Hong Kong.
Committee for Asian Women. 1985. *Industrial Women Workers in Asia*, CAW, Hong Kong.
Committee for Asian Women. 1988. *Beyond Labour Issues*, CAW, Hong Kong.
Committee for Asian Women. 1990. *Moving On: Education in Organising*, CAW, Hong Kong.
Committee for Asian Women. 1992. *When the Hen Crows . . .*, CAW and KWWA, Hong Kong.

10 Women Working Worldwide: A Case Study

Linda Shaw

Women Working Worldwide (WWW) is a group of women in Britain concerned with the employment, pay and working conditions of working women internationally. This chapter uses the experience of Women Working Worldwide as a case study of women's networking and information sharing, and looks at some of the tangible results of a sustained programme of work in areas of its concern over a period of more than seven years.

Women Working Worldwide focuses on three main industries which employ large numbers of women: clothing, textiles and micro-electronics. Our aim is to support the struggles of women workers through information exchange, international networking and public education. These are familiar terms to those involved in international work, but how do they translate into tangible actions and what role can an organisation such as Women Working Worldwide play?

The organisation is composed of mainly white middle-class, educated women who are not employed in the industries specified above. The ideal is for women who are organising themselves to have ready access to innovative means and strategies for collectively improving their position. WWW is not a source of such first-hand experience, but we can facilitate links and information exchange; our position of relative privilege helps us to do so. We accept these limitations and use the resources available to us to further the exchange of women's experience.

The wider context is clear for, as in so many industries in the 1980s, companies controlling clothing, textiles and micro-electronics operate across national boundaries and through international processes of marketing, sub-contracting and investment. The interdependence of women in relation to the textile and garment industries, for example, is established not only through the internationalisation of production processes but also through women's role as major consumers (particularly in the North) of clothing. If women workers in these industries are to organise to improve their conditions at a local level they must know the international context and if consumers wish to make informed choices they also need to understand the nature of the internationalisation of the clothing industry.

In this context, WWW initially held a highly successful conference in 1983 called 'Women Working Worldwide' which was attended by researchers, workers and organisers in the three industries of textiles, garments and micro-electronics. The overwhelming conclusion of the conference was the need to co-ordinate the exchange of information through a network of women and organisations working on or around these industries. Out of the conference came the present day WWW, taking its name from the conference title. Our first practice of our stated aims was writing and distributing the conference report. To date, 2000 copies have been sold or given free around the world. Since such conferences are attended by few shop-floor workers, distributing the report went some way towards making the conference's very real and pertinent conclusions on the state of the industries more accessible to others.

From the starting point of the 1983 conference, we have been building up a considerable number of contacts. This has been a slow and gradual process. Other contacts have been made through attending conferences ourselves and by holding public meetings for researchers and activists visiting the UK from developing countries in which these industries are important. Our close links with organisations involved in international development have also been a valuable source. The idea is to have up-to-date lists of contacts in all areas of the industries in both First and Third Worlds: workers, community groups, women's groups, trade unions. However, to maintain contacts, bulletins or updates need to be sent out regularly in order for new groups of women to contact us easily. This work is severely limited by lack of person power and financial resources. Nevertheless, the network we do have has formed a basis for the exchange of practical requests for information.

WWW has two regional centres which work autonomously: a Manchester-based group that concentrates on the garment and textile industries which employ many local women, and a London group which concentrates on different aspects of the micro-electronics industry. We feel focused activity is more likely to see tangible results, and most recently the London group has produced a book entitled *Common Interests: Women Organising in Global Electronics*. This is a compilation of interviews and testimonies, focusing on the women who work in the electronics industry worldwide. They talk about how they organise as workers and as women, giving vivid descriptions of shop-floor life, speaking about health hazards and sexual harassment, and relating their situation to the wider concerns of women.

The Manchester group's project, 'The Labour Behind the Label', was designed to explore the links between women as producers and consumers of the textile and garment industry, aiming to build up international contacts and develop educational materials for use in community and women's and labour movement (see below). The projects have been quite different from each other in the way they have been carried out, but they share the common aim of the exchange of information between women about women and their conditions of work and how women are taking action to improve them. Discussions with individuals and groups of women have greatly influenced perspectives and plans. There is a clear demand from Southern women to Northern women for solidarity.

WOMEN IN THE INTERNATIONAL TEXTILE AND GARMENT INDUSTRY: THE LABOUR BEHIND THE LABEL PROJECT

The Labour behind the Label Project was intended to develop both the networking and educational aims of WWW as outlined above. In particular, we sought to develop strategies which addressed the fact that women were both a major part of the workforce in these industries but also were significant consumers. Women's NGOs (non-governmental organisations) face particular funding difficulties especially in the UK: funding was only obtained for a single full-time worker for two years. In addition, not many UK-based NGOs deal specifically with employment issues from an internationalist perspective (outside the formal trade union structure). Consequently, few models and developed strategies existed. In the remainder of this chapter, we consider the development of the Manchester project – its successes, problems and some of the wider implications raised for the processes of women's networking concerned with employment-related issues. Linked to this was the aim that the project could also investigate the kinds of role consumers could play in improving conditions for workers in the textile and garment industries. Do organisations such as WWW have a specific contribution to make?

Regional Context

Manchester is located within the north-west of England – an area famous for its long association with the textile and garment industry, particularly the cotton-spinning and weaving mills of Lancashire. These have traditionally employed considerable numbers of women workers, but there have been severe job losses during the last 20 years. During the period from 1980 to 1983 approximately 130 000 jobs in the industry nationally were lost and over 30 000 jobs in 1991/2. Local newspapers provide a stream of stories concerning local plant closures. This year, several major garment factories have gone into liquidation. In this climate of uncertainty and job loss, it is hardly surprising that the UK-based textile and garment trade unions, and many of their shop-floor members, adhere strongly to a policy advocating protection for the domestic industries via trade barriers and control over imports from the developing world. Third World women workers are perceived as docile, unorganised and as a direct threat to UK women workers' jobs. In this context networking and campaigning around women's employment issues from a broad internationalist perspective has many complexities and difficulties. However, it is also true that women in the UK textile and garment industry, as throughout the world, are paid low rates, endure bad working conditions and insecurity of employment. Wage rates and conditions, jobs and training have been declining in both quantity and quality in the UK.

Networking and Campaigning Strategies

Underpinning this work in a regional context has been the development of a sound and extensive data base on the industry internationally. In addition to the simple accumulation of data, it was found that the role of networking organisations such as WWW was important in providing channels of communication between the more academically-based research and the information and concerns developed by grassroots activists. This has been especially important around information relating to the practice of homework/outworking and to consumer issues. For the former, although some work has been done on this practice (Mitter, 1986; Allen, 1987) much needs to be done, especially in Europe to put this quintessentially invisible women's work on the agenda for change politically. WWW has been part of an alliance of activists and academics campaigning with homeworkers and able to provide information concerning actions of Third World women in organising in the informal sector from which we have clearly much to learn in the West. The success of the Self Employed Women's Association in Ahmedabad, India has been a very important example. In addition, our data bank and contacts have been used by the local and the national media (newspapers and television) as a resource on the textile and garment industry. Finally, and not the least important, has been responding to demands from women workers in the Third World for information concerning UK-based multinationals employing them.

Effective networking has provided a firm foundation for the work of the project. As WWW is not a membership organisation in the sense that obtaining a large and growing membership has never been a primary aim of the group, it has been a priority to develop effective contacts locally with a wide range of organisations in the north-west concerned with the industry, with development issues and with adult education. These contacts have been constrained by the limited time and energy available, although we consider this work crucial. It provides a sound framework within which our international contacts and visitors can have a maximum impact within the local community. Our contacts with trade unionists and with black/ethnic minority communities have proved particularly valuable. In the international context, although we have other contacts, work was done in further developing links with groups in south and south-east Asia. In the context of the north-west this is especially relevant since many women working in the industry are British and also of Indian, Pakistani and Bangladeshi extraction.

A valuable experience in the importance of these interlocking networks and the concrete gains that can occur from them is illustrated in our involvement with the struggles of Filipino garment workers. There has been a long history of contact between WWW and the workers at a garments plant located in an Export Processing Zone outside Manila, a plant which is ultimately owned by a UK garment multinational. In September 1989, we heard from the women workers that the factory had been suddenly closed down apparently to avoid paying a wage increase deriving from a new ordinance concerning minimum wage rates. They wished for further information concerning the company, publicity for their case, and asked for action in the UK in support (e.g. a boycott of the factory goods, letters of protest). This WWW undertook to carry out as far as we could and we notified our UK contacts, raised the issue at local union branches, leafleted outside a local store, etc. In January 1990, the local office of the Transport & General Workers Union contacted WWW with regard to the Filipino women workers. After discussion with the union, women union members in the region decided to campaign on behalf of the Filipino workers during International Women's Week. In the light of this decision, WWW together with Philippines Support groups in the UK were able to arrange the visit of the woman who was president of the plant union to participate in the week of action. WWW also provided the administrative back-up and fund-raising capacity to make the trip a successful and productive one. Extensive press and media coverage was obtained locally and nationally. Meetings were also arranged with a variety of different groups including UK development agencies, black women as well as trade unionists.

This direct personal contact between women workers was invaluable. In particular, British workers were able to see that Filipino workers were not docile 'cheap labour', but are capable of developing and sustaining a high level of organisational activity from which British workers have much to learn. The impact of the Filipina union leader's visit to the UK was still remembered and discussed many months afterwards. In the labour movement, for example, although the need for greater international solidarity is much emphasised, in practice international contacts occur usually at the 'higher' male dominated levels of the organisation. The developing of international networks between groups and individuals from diverse backgrounds cannot be formally quantified. However, the experience of WWW, especially in relation to the Manchester-based project, shows that given adequate funding/commitment, tangible results can be obtained.

Educational Work

Educational work has been one of the key aims of the project, and it was decided to produce and print materials and resources. There was almost nothing published for the non-academic reader which looked at women in the international textile and garment industry in an accessible and friendly way. Consequently both an exhibition and a teaching/resource pack were planned. Developing the exhibition was seen as a way of presenting textual and photographic images in a striking and enjoyable way for a wide audience. Following its initial display, the exhibition was to be available for hire.

The work in developing the materials was done in partnership with the National Museum of Labour History in Manchester. This enabled WWW to call on professional resources and skills, and for the museum to develop their collection concerning women workers. The topics covered ranged from changing fashions, as well as Gandhi's visit to Lancashire in the 1930s, to photos of contemporary women garment workers in Sri Lanka. Threading through these different topics was the theme of women organising to improve their situation whether it be in Lancashire or India. The exhibition ran successfully for over two months at the museum and was used extensively by local schools. The Local Education service in Manchester developed a teaching pack for schools on the exhibition using text and images from the exhibition itself. Children from the ages of 7 to 18, as well as women trade unionists, visited the exhibition. To date, the exhibition has been shown in Manchester, Northern Ireland, Amsterdam and Denmark.

Based on the exhibition, a resource pack is also being produced which can cover the same issues in more depth. The form and development of the material was influenced and guided by a series of seminars, lectures and discussions undertaken by the project worker – these involved work at both a university level, trade union education classes, and work with students such as an Asian women's sewing class. Although any single text cannot hope to meet all the needs of such a diverse audience, feedback and experience proved invaluable especially when developing an understanding of the role of women as major consumers of clothing. It is intended that the pack could be used in various stages of education, by church and community groups and within trade union education programmes.

Free Trade or Protectionism?

One further and important aspect of the work of the project has been looking at the patterns of international trade in the industry. International trade in textiles and garments is regulated by a special agreement called the Multifibre Arrangement. In essence it restricts the imports of goods from developing countries to developed countries. Introduced in 1974, it was intended as a temporary measure providing time to enable industries in the North to restructure in order to face successfully the challenge of cheaper imports from the developing world. This temporary measure has lasted for over 15 years.

In the face of continuing job loss and lack of investment, British trade unionists have seen the retention of import protection as crucial. The debate is a complex one but has often developed into simple for or against positions by trade unionists, industrialists and consumer agencies. In considering their contribution to the debate, WWW concluded that there was very little proposed which took fully into account the special importance of women's relation to the industry. WWW has submitted a paper (see Appendix) to the relevant agencies outlining our specific position on this critical issue. Developing a position somewhat removed from a full protectionist stance is not a popular one with many sections .of the British trade union movement and a problem which other development education agencies have had to face. For example, Derry Development Education centre faced such difficulties when they published A Derry Shirt Tale which tackled the issue of 'competition' between Irish women garment workers and women workers in developing countries. There is often considerable hostility to individuals or groups who do not assume a full 'protectionist' stance.

During the two years of the project no easy way was found to resolve this tension. This has not been aided by the UK situation where substantial investment in the industry, retraining for the workforce has not been a realistic agenda politically. Challenging received notions such as protectionism is not easy for groups such as WWW, nor can it be seen to have much impact. It remains important though to provide alternative perspectives and to continue to question whether the specific needs of women as workers are being addressed in the Multifibre debate. In this case, for example, a local newspaper covered our perspective when the matter was being debated in national parliament. Despite differences, individual members of WWW have continued to be and work as trade unionists in the region and have considered the developing of links with trade unionists as one of the most successful outcomes of the project.

Consumer Awareness

One of the more encouraging developments has been the rapid growth, not simply in the UK alone, of consumer awareness with a 'green' agenda and by association with a growing emphasis on potential consumer power. A concern with the environmental impact of products has not always included an equivalent concern with the health and safety and overall working conditions of those engaged in production.

WWW has participated in networks and campaigns in the UK which have been a major factor in persuading a major UK garment retailer, Littlewoods, to adopt a code of practice for its garment suppliers which goes some way towards trying to ensure decent working conditions for garment workers internationally. As far as we can ascertain, this is the first example of a major retailer issuing a code of practice for its suppliers and as such is highly significant. Its impact cannot be effectively assessed, however, since the resources are not available to provide adequate monitoring of the implementation of the code.

The adoption of Fair Trading Charters for clothing retailers has special implications for the UK, where in practice six or seven large retailers control the domestic market for knitwear and clothing. This is in contrast to many other European countries where small independent retailers control a much larger section of their domestic markets. WWW will be looking in the future to participate in any further campaigns around these issues and to develop effective evaluation of their effectiveness. We have developed links with the Clean Clothing Campaign in The Netherlands who have adopted this approach in their strategy for change.

Demand for the textile and garment industry exhibition and the forthcoming resource pack have indicated that providing accessible information on the industry is also needed. The exhibition has proved a particular success in being shown to a wide range of groups. Most importantly, it presents information in an enjoyable way. Some of the younger visitors from schools, for example, certainly enjoyed making as much noise as possible to simulate working conditions in a noisy cotton mill in order to understand the impact this might have on the hearing of women weavers. For the project, it also illustrated the importance of looking at working conditions in an international context, as the similarities in conditions for women workers inside and outside the workplace in both the North and the South became apparent. Outworking seems particularly pervasive. These similarities can provide a useful focus for organising – as conditions worsen for many women workers in the UK with increasing flexibilisation – the strategies already adopted by women organising in the South became more and more relevant.

The projects in London and Manchester have learnt much about the value of joint efforts and co-ordinated actions. Discussions with individuals and groups of women have influenced plans for future work. The shape of future programmes is not clear yet but will continue to be in response to the demand from Southern women for solidarity – not charity – for example, through campaigning and educational work in Europe on aid and trade policies and the role of transnational corporations.

APPENDIX

Submission on the future of the Multifibre Arrangement to the hearing organised by the Socialist Group in the European Parliament and the European Trade Union Committee for Textiles, Clothing and Leather.

From Women Working Worldwide: Textile and Garment Project

The MFA or free trade are the two options currently being offered to women textile and garment workers in Europe and the developing countries. Neither option meets the needs of women, neither the needs of European women, nor the needs of women in developing countries.

The MFA has not prevented women in Europe losing jobs in the textile industry because of the introduction of new technology. This new technology is hitting women harder than men as jobs are redesigned to be more 'technical' and are then designated as more suitable for men on the grounds that women lack technical aptitudes. The MFA has not prevented women in Europe in the garment industry losing job security and decent rates of pay and working conditions, as homeworking, sweatshops and casualisation increase. The MFA cannot protect women workers against the instability of exchange rates and interest rates.

The MFA has not prevented women textile and garment workers in developing countries being forced to work exhausting hours in unhealthy conditions, unable to organise and campaign for improvements because of denial of trade union rights. It has not prevented multinational companies from closing down plants where workers have, against all the odds, managed to get organised; and resiting in new areas in which there is no previous experience of factory work for women.

But free trade would not address the needs of women workers either. It would lead to large job losses in Europe, with no guarantee that market forces would create replacement jobs of the right kind, in the right place. It would probably lead to an expansion of jobs in developing countries, but with no guarantees that these jobs would not be exploitative; and no guarantees that internationally mobile forms would not play one developing country off against another, moving from Hong Kong to Thailand to Bangladesh.

What about women as consumers? Wouldn't free trade be good for them, leading to falls in the price of clothing and textiles? But there is no guarantee that free trade would lead to price falls – it might boost the profit margins of large retailers instead. More and more consumers are, in any case, concerned about more than the price of what they buy. They are concerned about the product's effect on the environment, and about the effects of its conditions of production on the health and human rights of the workers who provide the labour behind the label. Women can see that a narrow concern with getting the lowest price as consumers tends in the long run, in a roundabout but inexorable way, to undermine the rights and conditions that they want to enjoy as workers. Women are more and more concerned with the impact of what they buy on the quality of life.

Is there an alternative to renewal of the MFA or free trade? We think there is. Instead of trying to hold back international restructuring of the industry (like the MFA), or turning over international restructuring to market forces (like free trade), we could try to devise a strategy for the planned restructuring of the industry.

The strategy we envisage would have three components:

1. Phased run-down of the MFA.
2. Introduction of the social regulation of sales of textiles and garments.
3. Planned regeneration of European regions formerly devoted to textiles and garments.

The Social Regulation of Sales of Textiles and Garments

The basic principle of the social regulation of sales is that no textile or garment product should be marketed in Europe that does not meet certain quality standards with respect to the conditions of its production. *These standards must apply to goods produced within Europe and not just to imports – there is no reason to suppose that unacceptable conditions of production occur only in developing countries.*

Absolute standards for conditions of production should include health and safety; rights of workers to overtime pay, redundancy pay, maternity leave, sickness benefit; rights of workers to organise; facilities for workers to organise.

Different levels of economic development mean that it is not feasible to set absolute standards for hours of work and wages. Relative standards for hours of work and pay would need to be set related to each country's norms.

The standards would have to be met at the *enterprise* level. It is no use just examining what legislation a country has on the statute books. In many countries the law may not be implemented.

Large retailers, large wholesalers and multinational companies and firms sourcing abroad, could be given responsibility for checking their sources of supply, not just for the quality of the fabric and stitching, as they do now; but also for the quality of conditions of production.

Much more stringent labelling requirements could be introduced so that consumer products carry not just a brand name, but also the name of the parent firm, the country of origin, whether the conditions of production just meet or exceed the standards set. That way companies could compete on their record as providers of high-quality conditions of work and not just high-quality products.

Activist groups which are already campaigning for the social regulation of sales on environmental, ethical and solidarity grounds could be funded to monitor the extent to which manufacturers, wholesalers and retailers were meeting their obligations. We expect that women would play a prominent role in this. There is no need to construct a huge bureaucracy in Brussels, though existing national inspectorates for health and safety, labour legislation, etc. in Europe would need to be strengthened.

Regeneration of Former European Textile and Garment Areas

This would need to be planned in conjunction with local authorities and backed up by a European fund. Some types of textile and garment production would still be cost-effective in Europe and would be able to meet the social standards outlined above. But some would undoubtedly not.

We would like to emphasise the particular needs of women workers which such regeneration should take into account. Women need employment close to their homes, or much better transport systems, because of domestic duties. They need adequate, publicly provided day-care facilities for children – and for old people. They need training which allows them to break out of a narrow range of stereotypically female jobs. More part-time work in fast-food outlets is not the answer for skilled machinists. There is a danger that women's employment is taken less seriously by policy makers; and that women's unemployment becomes invisible as married women are discouraged from further job searching. It is essential that any process for planning regeneration should explicitly address the differing employment needs of women and men, and not assume they are identical, or that women's needs are less.

Conclusion

We think that the three-pronged strategy outlined above would provide a basis for meeting the needs of women both as workers and consumers, in both Europe and the Third World.

If you would like to discuss theses ideas further please contact Linda Shaw, Women Working Worldwide – Textile and Garment Project, Department of Sociology, University of Manchester, Manchester M13 9PL, UK. Telephone 0161–275–2515.

REFERENCES

Allen, S. and C. Wolkowitz. 1987. *Homeworking: Myths & Realities*, Macmillan, London.

Elson, D. and R. Pearson. 1989. *Women's Employment and Multinationals in Europe*, Macmillan, London.

Enloe, C. 1989. *Bananas, Beaches and Bases: Making Feminist Sense of International Politics*, Pandora Press, London.

Mitter, S. 1986. *Common Fate, Common Bond: Women in the Global Economy*, Pluto Press, London.

Women Working Worldwide. 1991. *Common Interests: Women Organising in Global Electronics*, Available from WWW, PO Box 92, 190 Upper St, London N1 1RQ, UK. £8.00 (including postage and packing).

Women Working Worldwide, Exhibition and Resource Pack. 'The Labour Behind the Label'. Available from Women Working Worldwide, Dept of Sociology, University of Manchester, Manchester M13 9PL, UK.

Part III – Work is Where You Find It: Organising from Home and Community

This final part focuses on initiatives and campaigns away from the factory floor, among homeworkers, traders, and other groups of workers in the informal sector. Issues, networks and organisations from household and community extend to and confront state and international constraints, yet provide alternative routes to support women workers.

The part opens with the chapter by Rudo Gaidzanwa, which brings out the multiple roles and responsibilities, and perceptions of women as mothers, family providers, and as citizens. Ideologies of domesticity underscore the activities of a group of Zimbabwe women, whose eminently appropriate labour of crocheting is used to create products which are saleable in wider Southern and South African markets. Through networks established with women traders of the surrounding countries, the Zimbabwe women receive shelter, trading bases and outlets. Regional sales goods, electronics and other much-desired products replace foreign exchange as currency, and the traders work as necessary through or outside the formal regulated import/export system, as permitted or possible. As the traders' patriotism and morality are called into question by the state, the women are able to counter through reference to their obligations as mothers, wives and kinswomen.

In the subsequent chapter, Mairo Bello discusses the effects upon women of the Structural Adjustment Programme in Nigeria. Government programmes for women have been slashed with the economic crisis, while at the same time, women workers in the formal sector are being retrenched in disproportionately larger numbers than men. Women throughout the country are required to take on responsibilities such as health care and educational costs, previously assumed by the state. Focusing particularly on the activities of Women in Nigeria, a nationwide NGO for which she is a state co-ordinator, Bello demonstrates how the organisation has done research and shared information in relation to the effects of the economic crisis on women in urban and rural areas, and has then acted to improve women's situation. In the areas of credit, training, and political action, WIN is supporting and conscientising women workers, and is seeking to maintain and expand its proactive role as a forum and site of mobilisation for women.

Using data from detailed and extensive research which she carried out, Young ock-Kim discusses the characteristics of industrial homeworking in South Korea. Young demonstrates that women tend to take up homeworking through lack of viable alternatives, given limited child-care facilities, and women's socially defined and expected responsibilities. She points out the exploitative nature of homeworking in South Korea, and that homeworkers often work hours as long as full-time formal sector employees. The women contend with low wages, long hours, poor and often unhealthy working conditions, but are not conscientised or organised to effect changes in these conditions. Indeed, Young points out that the homeworkers' very existence can be and is used as a foil by formal sector employers against demands by their employees for improvements in their own wages or working conditions. Young suggests that the optimal outcome would be the abolition of industrial homeworking in South Korea, and the emplace-ment of the necessary facilities to permit women to take up formal sector employment. Recently created neighbourhood workshops may serve as midway structures between the isolation of the individual homeworking situation, and the factory context. Young notes, however, that the homeworkers' best source of redress must ultimately come from their own organising efforts.

In India, considerable work has been done in organising women outside the formal employment structures. Nandita Gandhi's chapter, the final chapter in this part, centres on the new unions and organisations which have been created specifically for these workers, or have been available to and supportive of actions by the workers. Gandhi opens her chapter with a history of the involvement and ideology of traditional trade unions and parties in relation to women. Particularly in the 1980s and 1990s, inde-pendent unions have focused on the significance of the informal, or un-organised, sector, as the main site of women's work and of extreme exploitation. Gandhi gives an extensive and compelling picture of the initiation and growth of these and of women's organisations in creating new groups, processes and strategies in working in and with the unorgan-ised sector. The relationship between union and women's groups is complex, ranging from hostility to indifference to active support and respect, and changing over time and sometimes in relation to particular issues. Some issues, such as job reservation, retrenchment and wages, have been taken up jointly or serially by organisations, using different strategies.

Organisational links are created in various ways, including through dual or multiple memberships. Through actions of solidarity, whether on a long-term or one-event basis, the strengths of the different organisations (political, membership, particular perspectives, etc.) can be brought to bear in improving women's situation in the workplace, wherever that may be, the community and the home.

11 The Ideology of Domesticity and the Struggles of Women Workers in Zimbabwe
Rudo B. Gaidzanwa

This chapter deals with the issues pertaining to ideologies of domesticity in Zimbabwe, state policies and industrialisation. It is based on research that has been conducted amongst women, both waged and unwaged. The chapter deals with research conducted after independence in 1980. It outlines briefly some of the legislative, social and economic policy changes instituted after independence. The chapter then focuses on ideologies of domesticity and how they are handled by women in different circumstances in the process of making a living for themselves and their dependants.

In order to understand the policies of the post-independence government of Zimbabwe, it is necessary to outline the priorities and preoccupations of the populations that had to be serviced by the government. The nature of the post-independence government itself also has to be discussed so as to make clearer the reasons for the policy choices made after 1980. Independence was supported by the majority of the black population, which had relatively poorer land, menial jobs and very little security in their everyday lives. The struggle for liberation was led by elements of the black petit bourgeoisie whose life chances were frustrated by the white, racist, capitalist regimes that ruled Zimbabwe during its colonial history.

The bulk of the black population resided in the rural areas, except for the labour migrants, predominantly male, who worked as wage labourers in the mines, towns and in the households of the settlers. The major economic activity for the black population was agriculture which was practised by most of the black peasantry at little beyond the subsistence level. Only a few master farmers and small-scale commercial farmers managed to produce agricultural surpluses consistently enough to sell to the grain marketing boards or privately within the rural areas. As different studies of women's employment show, women have tended to be employed in subsistence agriculture and small-scale enterprises which yield very low incomes in rural and urban areas (Helmsing, 1991; Mkandawire, 1983; Moyo *et al.*, 1984; and ILO, 1986).

It is within this context that the ideologies of domesticity prevalent in Zimbabwe prior to, during as well as after colonialism have to be analysed. Pre-colonially, Shona and Ndebele economies were mainly agricultural with hunting, gathering and animal husbandry being undertaken to diversify the food base for most households. Within this situation, the division of labour was premised on age, gender and skill. There were specialist roles for both men and women. Some women became midwives, spirit mediums and healers. Amongst the men, there were metal workers, hunters, healers and entertainers. These specialists were not necessarily emancipated from performing the work that their gender was expected to take part in. However, their participation was reduced or substituted for by other members of their households and kin.

The domestic realm tended to be dominated by women and girls who were responsible for the house and home-based tasks such as cleaning, cooking, food processing and preparation. Women were also participants in agricultural production as mothers, wives and daughters within households. A woman was responsible for ensuring that her children had enough to eat; this she did by helping her husband to work on the land. There was also an internal individualisation of land-use rights within households, and in this division of land-use rights, a wife and mother had control over her own land whose produce she could dispose of as she willed.

At marriage, a woman was usually accompanied by a younger sister or niece whose role was to help the new bride with housework such as washing dishes, pounding meal and running errands. For a woman to excel domestically, she had to be able to attract relatives' daughters and sons who would help her with chores as well as with agricultural work. Thus, excellence in the domestic realm was premised on the control by a woman over agricultural produce from her own field and over the labour of young women, boys and girls who could be relied upon to perform chores that would free the woman from the more repetitive maintenance work in the house. In this way, the woman could concentrate on the more socially, politically and nutritionally profitable tasks such as growing food and producing valued craft goods.

THE COLONIAL CONTEXT

The advent of colonialism changed the social and economic set-up within which women could fulfil their roles in relation to domestic labour and subsistence production. The alienation of the land from the black population, and the migration for wage labour by young men thrust a greater burden on the older men, women and children who were left behind in the rural areas.[1] They had to perform the agricultural tasks such as land clearing and ploughing which had previously been performed by younger men within households. Thus, the rural women found it more difficult to excel at their domestic tasks because they had to put in more work and time in agriculture. The situation of those women who were exposed to Western education through the missions and women's clubs in the rural areas was worsened by the imperatives of domestic excellence which were derived from the values of the white settler women, who had black domestic and agricultural labour to help them in their own households.

Among the settlers, the women were expected to play a leading role in the house as housewives. They were not expected to work in the fields amongst the farming population. Farmers' wives concentrated on tending the animals, the labourers and the wives and children of the labourers in cases of sickness. Amongst the settlers on the mines and in the urban areas, the women were supposed to supervise the domestic workers who performed most of the cooking, cleaning and child-minding tasks. The white women who came into the colonies to undertake wage work in their own right were the missionaries who were teachers and nurses. Most settler women came out to marry and become wives of colonial functionaries in the different sectors of the economy. Outside their households, settler women were supposed to take part in philanthropic activities, most of which consisted in teaching skills such as cooking, cleaning and decorating houses in the British style. Given that most of the black women, both rural and urban, did not have the wherewithal to lead this type of life, it was not possible for most of them to excel in the approved domestic style of the settlers.

It is necessary to explore the ways in which the ideologies and practices of domesticity changed from the vantage points of different categories of black women in Zimbabwe. Amongst the nascent black middle-class women whose husbands were state functionaries such as teachers, clerks, policemen and low-level administrators, the ideal of domesticity was modelled on that of the settler (Weinrich, 1973). These functionaries often had access to subsidised housing which was built on Western lines. The houses often had a kitchen, sitting room, one or two bedrooms and a shower. Often, these houses were not electrified and were very small. They also placed men and women within the same living and sleeping areas, and this led to the rearrangement of the traditional spatial relationship between men, women and children. The women in these households were in some cases professionals themselves, and this placed their incomes in a higher bracket than those of other people who were wage workers. These women were in a better position to try to approximate the domestic ideal advanced by the settlers. These families were able to buy cheap Western-style furniture, food and clothing. They were also able to use traditional fostering arrangements to acquire access to the labour of their poorer kin's children who then played the same or modified roles that domestics played in the settler households.

The nascent middle-class women could become housewives, especially in those cases where they were not professionals themselves. They could accumulate prestige from their ability to approximate a Western lifestyle. The major departure from the pre-colonial domestic ideal was the fact that the new black middle-class women were only able to approximate the ideal of domesticity on the basis of their dependence on their husbands' incomes. This is so, given that in most of the cases it was the husbands who were the employees of the state rather than the wives. Thus, the women became dependent on husbands' employment and income in order to achieve excellence in the expressed ideal of domesticity in their social stratum within the colonial order.

It is important to note that there was a recomposition of the gender roles of black males as a result of their participation in domestic labour in settler households. The employment of black males in domestic labour in the colonies was partly due to the fact that in patrilineal societies such as those of the Shona and Ndebele in Zimbabwe, it was not acceptable for women to leave their agnatic homes and attach themselves to settler households where there was a possibility of them consorting with their white male employers or their black male employees outside the bounds of custom. Amongst the settlers, the black men were defined as non-human and therefore ineligible for relationships with white women. These circumstances combined to create the conditions necessary for the domestication of the black men in household labour as cooks, cleaners, gardeners and babyminders. Correspondingly, the black women who were the wives, mothers and daughters of these men were 'masculinised' by virtue of the labour that they inceasingly performed since their men were away in wage labour.

Despite the increasing importance of agricultural work for black rural women, they were not emancipated from the traditional or the Western ideals of domesticity. In fact, both ideals of domesticity began to hang heavily on their shoulders. They were still expected to feed their children in the absence of the men who had migrated for wage labour. Women's organisations that were dominated by white middle-class women, such as the Women's Institutes and The Federation of Women's Clubs, spent their time and budgets teaching black women how to be 'better' housewives.

The black women were supposed to acquire the valued Western goods through the wages of their husbands. These goods consisted of agricultural implements, food, furniture and brick houses. Given that these goods were adapted for a Western climate and lifestyle, it was onerous for women to keep them clean and to maintain them. For example, cloth-covered chairs attracted and retained dust and needed constant cleaning and shaking. Concrete floors needed constant mopping, polishing and shining. Enamel pots and pans needed more water to keep them shiny. The maintenance demands of these goods increased the work of women and girls within households since the work was labour-intensive and time-consuming.

In the agricultural realm, the use of ploughs and better hoes extended the area of land that needed to be weeded. The introduction of hybrid seed, pesticides and fertilisers which were sent by labour migrants to their wives meant that more work was needed to realise a good harvest. Thus, the rural women found themselves struggling to approximate two different ideals of domesticity. The women were encouraged to form women's clubs by philanthropic settler women who worked through chiefs' wives, local school teachers and nurses. Apart from producing good harvests, the black women were expected to keep spotless homes and have clean, well-nourished and healthy children.

It was difficult for most of the rural women to realise these ideals of domesticity simultaneously or separately. During the colonial period, land became increasingly depleted of nutrients, scarce and unproductive. Increasing levels of investment became necessary to sustain agriculture beyond mere subsistence. Both the Western as well as the Shona and Ndebele ideals of domesticity became difficult to achieve for the peasant women. It became necessary to purchase food supplements through the wage incomes of the male migrants. Thus, the conditions that underpinned the traditional ideals of domesticity were increasingly eroded while the new Western ideal was not achievable for women who were peasants. The levels and types of domesticity that were possible were increasingly premised on the dependence of the peasant women on their migrant men. To this extent, the black women were moving closer to the white ideal of domesticity in terms of dependence on men's incomes, while at the same time the ideal could not be realised given that the incomes of black males could not equal those of white men.

On the other hand, the white women were freed from the more onerous burdens of their ideal of domesticity by their ability to enlist the labour of black men and, later, black women within the settler households. The time that accrued to the settler women was used to crusade for a lifestyle that would lead to the domestication of more blacks in white as well as black households.

POST-INDEPENDENCE ZIMBABWE

The advent of independence and changes in legislation had an impact on this situation in various ways. The new government enacted the Legal Age of Majority Act in 1982. This act made all Zimbabweans majors at law when they reached the age of 18. Previously, black women had remained minors throughout their lives because customary law was interpreted to that effect during the colonial era. The Sex Disqualification Removal Act (Chapter 339) provided that women had the same rights as men to hold public or civil office as long as they had the same qualifications as the men. Through the Minimum Wages Act of 1980, employees were to be paid the same wages for equal work regardless of age, sex and race. Previously, black people had been paid less than whites for almost all types of work, and black women were disadvantaged on the labour market because they were treated like temporary workers who worked to supplement their husbands' incomes and were not primary earners. Thus, they had to reapply for their jobs after leaving for short periods to have babies or for any other reasons.

The Labour Relations Act of 1985 among other things entitled women to paid maternity leave and retention of their job-ranking on their return from maternity leave. This act also protected workers from arbitrary dismissal. It replaced the Industrial Conciliation Act that had suppressed and exploited black labour during colonialism by prioritising industrial peace, that is, lack of militant labour action.

These legislative changes affected waged women in various ways. The equal pay legislation coupled with the minimum wage legislation spurred employers to retrench their labour whenever possible. Paid maternity leave for women made women less attractive as employees because the wage bill for employers rose when they employed women of childbearing age as permanent workers. Thus, while the legal situation of women in the labour market improved, their real situation and prospects for employment in the wage sector deteriorated in the long term.

USING DOMESTICITY TO ADVANTAGE: CROCHET TRADING IN ZIMBABWE

It is within this context that this chapter will analyse the experiences of a group of women who are involved in unwaged work in Harare. In total, there were ten women whose economic histories and strategies were examined in depth in the first phase of the study. Four of the women had been laid off their waged jobs in a textile factory after independence because the government had stipulated a minimum wage in the textile industry. The factory owner reacted by retrenching most of the unskilled and semi-skilled workers and threatening to relocate his enterprise in Botswana where there were no minimum wage regulations.

The ten women gravitated together when they started producing crocheted items such as tablecloths, bedspreads, doilies and dresses. They also knit thick sweaters which are popular among Western tourists. Four of the women are married to wage workers. Three are divorced and two are widowed. The tenth woman is a single mother. All the women have children whom they send to school, feed and clothe, and all of them were involved in cross-border shopping activities in Botswana and, lately, South Africa. The trading patterns of these women is indicative of the kinds of strategies being taken up by many other women in Zimbabwe, who are seeking to use what skills and resources are available to them, within the constraints of Structural Adjustment, to the best advantage of themselves and their dependants. The following exposition describes the expansiveness and regional nature of the trade, the consequences this trade has had on state and capital, and the state responses which have ensued.

Crochet skills have traditionally been extended to women as part of the home economics training that black women get in the school system in Zimbabwe. These skills are supposed to help the women to make the meagre incomes of their husbands go further and to beautify their homes. These skills have been used by the black women involved in this research for commercial purposes. The articles that they produce are of limited utility to the women who make them because their homes are not suitable for these items. The crocheted bedspreads are usually suitable for a double bed and in most high-density residential areas, the homes are not big enough to take a double bed, a dining table that can seat at least six diners, a lounge suite for six or seven people and three or four small coffee tables. In most working-class homes, there are usually some small children and grandchildren as well as kin who have to be accommodated. Thus, the furnishings and working-class lifestyles are not compatible with lacy drapings that need frequent cleaning and intensive care. The logical market for the crochet products are the middle classes in Zimbabwe as well as outside it.

In the early 1980s, there was a booming market for the crochet goods of the women who had crochet skills. This was due to the fact that independence heralded the expansion of the middle classes through the employment of blacks in the government and private sector. The Zimbabwean middle classes were interested in furnishing their homes in natural fibres and materials in keeping with the new yuppie and ecological chic that placed higher value on hand-produced and natural fibre goods. The cotton crochet goods fitted the bill perfectly. However, the Zimbabwean market quickly got saturated as more women with crochet skills tried to cash in on the boom. The middle-class women who were enterprising started buying the crochet items for resale outside Zimbabwe, and some tried to diversify the items produced in order to keep up with the fads and fashions abroad. However, it was clear that there were cheaper textiles from South-east Asia in Europe and this limited the potential for market expansion in Europe and the United States of America.

The limited market posed a dilemma for the women, because they found it difficult to branch out into other economic activities. Wage work was increasingly difficult to find for unskilled female workers. Investment in industry tended to be directed towards substituting labour with machinery. Unemployment was increasing while the economy was sluggish and therefore incapable of absorbing primary, secondary and vocational school graduates. Small trade was not very lucrative because people's incomes were dropping in real terms as the economic recession intensifed in the 1980s in Zimbabwe. The research report produced by ENDA with World Bank sponsorship in 1991 has outlined the problems that beset women in different informal sector activities in Zimbabwe.

Crochet work was convenient for the women because they could produce various items at home as part of their domestic chores. It is acceptable for women to knit, sew and crochet while chatting with neighbours. What was originally conceived as an enriching leisure activity for middle-class housewives could be turned into a commercial venture by working women who were displaced from the wage labour market and the peasant economy. Crochet work could be carried out with the help of children within the household. Children were enlisted in the winding of thread from cast-off cotton items. The involvement of children ensures that mobile little children are kept off the streets and are under the observation of their mothers constantly. Crochet work can be interrupted while other household chores are performed. It is also possible for two or more women to work on the same item, especially when there are rush orders from customers.

In most areas, market places have been designated for traders in vegetables, crochet items and other small crafts in Harare. Women can sell their items at these markets. Women may spell each other at selling points so that it is possible for a woman to sell the goods of other women on specific days while the owners of the items are free to conduct other business away from the market. Thus, it is possible to combine crochet work with all other types of work within the households (see also Helmsing, 1991 and ENDA, 1991).

Given the flexibility and convenience of crochet work for women, it was quite difficult for women to come to terms with loss of income from crochet production. The women sought ways of expanding the market for crochet products. The shortages that developed in the economy in the late 1980s provided the impetus for women to explore ways of exploring new markets. People started going to Botswana to buy scarce items such as cars, office machinery and luxury electronic consumer items. A shopping trip to a neighbouring country entailed getting a holiday allowance from a commercial bank. The commercial bank has to get permission from the reserve bank to allocate foreign currency to a traveller who, presumably, was travelling for holiday purposes. Before independence, only middle-class people, mostly whites, ever made use of this facility. But as shortages became widespread, even working-class people started to use this facility.

In order to realise an amount of foreign currency large enough to buy enough items to sell, travellers began to take as many dependants as possible in order to buy saleable items. Children were particularly useful for this purpose since they are also entitled to a part of an adult's allowance. As long as a person has a passport and an itinerary, he or she can apply for a holiday allowance. It became the practice to hire friends and relatives to travel so that their holiday allowances could be used by the person who sponsored the shopping trip. This facility enabled people to procure scarce goods for their own use, especially cars. However, it was also lucrative to buy car spares, office machines and electronic goods for resale to the middle-class consumers who could afford to pay high prices in local currency for these goods.

The crochet women also joined the shoppers in order to realise the profits from cross-border trade. For them, it was difficult to use cash for currency conversion purposes because they could not accumulate large amounts of disposable cash at any one time. The government clamped down on the number of holiday trips that any individual could make so that now, only one holiday trip can be made in a six-month period. Thus, the women had to devise alternative ways and means of obtaining currency to buy saleable items in Botswana. On the local end, all they needed was a return train ticket.

The solution was to buy a cheap ticket to travel and take a large volume of crochet goods which could be sold in Botswana and South Africa. In these countries, payment could be realised in hard currency which could then be used to buy the scarce and valuable goods for resale. There was still the issue of accommodation that needed to be resolved for the shoppers. Paying hotel bills could be prohibitively expensive in the country that was being visited. Hotel bills could absorb a large proportion of the money realised through the sale of crochet products. Thus, alternative accommodation arrangements had to be made so as to conserve foreign currency.

In the case of the women who shopped in South Africa, they found that quite a lot of working-class South Africans were curious to find out about life in independent African countries. The exchange rates between the currencies was favourable to the South Africans and the Batswana. It was therefore possible for the women to make reciprocal arrangements for accommodation so as to minimise cash outlays on board and lodging. The women could then realise their travel aims without spending large amounts of cash on accommodation. Thus, a lot of the shopping women dispensed with the need for dealing with commercial and the reserve bank altogether. They no longer had to use cash in Zimbabwe in order to buy foreign currency. Their reciprocal hospitality arrangements actually saved Zimbabwe a lot of foreign currency! At the same time, they were able to ameliorate the shortage of consumer goods that were desired by the middle classes. These shoppers actually managed to take the pressure off the government, which was failing to regulate the economy in ways that satisfied the consumers of all classes, particularly the working class.

STATE RESPONSES

The reaction of the government's various bureaucracies is instructive in the way it illuminates the differences in perceptions about what is legitimate in eking out a living. From the strategies adopted by the shoppers, most of them women, it became clear that women, particularly those of the working classes, were able to read the financial markets very easily. When the currency of Botswana became stronger than that of South Africa where the scarce goods were manufactured, the shoppers switched to South Africa as a shopping country. The same reciprocal arrangements were adopted by the crochet women in South Africa. South Africa is much larger than Botswana and the market is therefore bigger. The Zimbabwe government was embarrassed by the opinion of it that its citizens were expressing with their shopping habits! South Africa was a world pariah, and it said a lot that ordinary Zimbabweans were willing to go to South Africa to shop. There was some vehement denunciation of shoppers by government officals who cited the drain on foreign currency by shoppers as reprehensible. The shoppers were also denounced as unpatriotic, unsympathetic and subversive of the liberation struggle in South Africa. The shopping women were accused of prostituting themselves for currency and accommodation in the countries in which they travelled. They were searched thoroughly, and in some cases, roughly, since they were suspected of attempting to smuggle in goods or evade import duties and taxes on the items they brought in. In March, 1991, a female Deputy Minister for Political Affairs appeared on television protesting against the internal searches being conducted on women by customs officials at one of the country's border posts. The shoppers have also complained of having their goods stolen or fraudulently confiscated by customs officials.

ISSUES OF CLASS AND GENDER

There is a class element to the whole issue of shopping for scarce goods outside Zimbabwe. It is closely tied to the responses to the economic crisis by different categories of the population. The working classes in Zimbabwe cannot afford to pay heavy fares to shop in politically acceptable places such as London or Paris. They therefore have to carry the burden of the country's political stance, should they decide not to shop in South Africa or Botswana. A sizeable number have refused to carry this burden, thus forcing the public political stance of the government to be debated openly. It is true that the products from South Africa are manufactured with the aid of cheap and grossly exploited black labour. At the same time, it is important to recognise that the shoppers also attempt to fulfil their domestic obligations to feed, clothe, educate and maintain their dependants in the face of spiralling consumer commodity prices, health and education fees and unemployment of adult men and women. The poor who shop in South Africa have chosen to survive in a manner that is politically embarrassing to those members of the middle classes who benefit from the way in which the economy is presently handled.

Ironically, the economic crisis has helped to develop entrepreneurship among the crochet women in ways that were not intended by those who extended crochet skills to them. The economic crisis has helped to generate an atmosphere within which alternatives to wage labour can be highly lucrative. Thus, hustling and dealing have become attractive and respected to some extent. Those people who are unable to obtain jobs no longer blame the 'system' as much as they used to, because there is always the possibility of discovering a lucrative hustle which can be made to pay off with a one-off injection of capital.

Simultaneously, everyday life has increasingly become criminalised because of the red tape that surrounds official transactions necessary to procure the goods and services that are necessary for the conduct of everyday life. Even those people who are waged now have an incentive to convert aspects of their jobs to income generation. The shoppers have been joined by waged people such as school teachers, nurses and other professionals whose jobs do not afford them facilities to travel to Europe and the United States of America.

What has all this to do with the ideologies of domesticity that were discussed earlier in this chapter? In the first place, the proletarianisation of men has been premised on the domestication of women within as well as outside the rural households. This chapter has indicated that the content of this domesticity has encompassed agricultural as well as housework in the rural areas, while in the urban areas, domesticity involves the commercialisation of handicraft skills that were originally intended to enhance the aesthetic and material lives of the households served by the women who possess these skills. In the urban areas, domesticity also has a sizeable housework component.

Among the women in the crochet study, divorce, single parenthood, widowhood and the unemployment of some of the husbands of the women eroded the expected and assumed underpinnings of this domesticity. When a husband has deserted, died or become unemployed, the content of a particular woman's domestic role changes. She has to provide the cash that is needed to purchase the day-to-day necessities within her household. If she or her husband is not able to do so, she cannot perform her domestic role of cooking, feeding and managing her household by proxy, that is by hiring a substitute or by doing the work herself.

Among the crochet women in the study, their domestic roles had to expand to accommodate their shopping trips. These women necessarily had to find substitutes for themselves, and these substitutes performed most of the household labour such as caring for the children, cooking and cleaning. The husbands of those women who were married could not travel for or with the women because the skills and arrangements surrounding the crochet trade were defined as domestic ones which could only be undertaken by women.

It became increasingly clear that for the households in which these women survived, the relative immobility of the women could not be maintained. There necessarily had to be a redefinition of the spatial reach of domesticity. In all the households of these women, none of the men had ever been outside Zimbabwe – it was the women who had more knowledge of the politics, economics and social arrangements in the neighbouring countries. This is an interesting development, given that at the beginning of colonisation and urbanisation in Africa, it was the men who migrated first and acquired knowledge of the new cultures and customs of the towns, mines and farms. For the women who ostensibly are the housewives, their horizons have expanded beyond those of the men in their households who are expected to be wage labourers in a space that is bounded by the borders of Zimbabwe.

The crochet women are sharing their housewife roles with their proxies, who are waged domestic workers or kinswomen who take care of the household when the crochet women are away. At the same time, there is a limit to the number of shopping trips that can be made to South Africa because of the visa requirements for that country. There are no visa requirements in Botswana, but the pula of Botswana is stronger than the Zimbabwean dollar and the consumer population in Botswana is poorer and much smaller than that of South Africa. Thus, the levels of industrialisation in the Southern African countries as well as the differences in the costs of labour for producing manufactured goods are having an impact on the ways in which the women are reacting to industrialisation in Zimbabwe.

It is also important that government efforts to stop the shoppers tend to use the ideologies of gender and domesticity against the women. By implying that women do not know much about politics, and that they get into illegal transactions and prostitution while they are conducting their business, the message is that these women are housewives who really do not know much about the world outside their households. The stereotype of the housewife is that she is insulated from all but her hearth and home and does not really care and should not care about the world outside the house. In the case of the crochet women, they use the content of the stereotype to produce their wares, to sell them within as well as outside Zimbabwe and to justify their ability to do this in terms of caring for their children's welfare above all else. Thus, even though these women are in the import–export trade, they still express their participation in it through the ideology of domesticity which is palatable to those who have power over them within as well as outside their households. Similar reactions to women's entrepreneurship have been noted in Ghana, Nigeria and Zambia where during times of economic hardship, the intensification of competition between men and women in commerce, retail and other economic activities is played out in the realm of gender debates about women's neglect of their domestic roles or their unseemly behaviour which negates their mothering and wifely roles.

THEORETICAL AND STRATEGIC ISSUES: STATE, CLASS AND GENDER

The relationship between women and the state is very important in this discussion. The erosion of the state and its declining effectiveness in the provision of basics such as food, shelter and health has created an atmosphere that stimulates the development of individualised strategies for survival and accumulation. The decline of the state and the services that it can deliver provides the impetus for the creation of the second economy which can facilitate the provision of scarce goods and services for those who need and can pay for them in diverse ways. In the case of the shoppers, they cannot turn away from the state altogether even though the state is tardy and increasingly inefficient in providing them with services such as passports, birth certificates and registration documents. Thus, there is still a need to engage with the state in order to procure the necessary documentation for participation in lucrative economic activities.

The issues of patriotism and citizenship also become problematic in this case. In Zimbabwe, the middle classes can afford to shop in politically acceptable places, thus escaping the label of 'subversive', while the poorer sections of the population cannot escape this label, given that they can only afford cheap bus or rail fares to Botswana and South Africa. The burden of political correctness is borne by the poorer people, who are most affected by the economic decline of Zimbabwe. The form and content of patriotism in its symbolic and material forms is important, and in this case the ruling classes can indulge in symbolic patriotism by not going to or shopping in South Africa while on a material level, Zimbabwe continues to trade with South Africa on a national basis.

The class and gender struggle that is manifesting itself in the economy is exemplified by the interface between the state and the shopping women who, in effect, are involved in import–export trade. The restriction of the types of goods individuals can import, the increased bureaucracy in the application for documents and currency, the vaginal searches and the public vilification of the shoppers as unpatriotic and subversive of the South African struggle are all manifestations of the state's attempts to limit access to the services of the state only to those people who are defined as acceptable by state functionaries. The monopoly of access to foreign currency by the middle classes is no longer enforceable on racial or income grounds by a black government. This partly explains why it is increasingly being articulated in terms of patriotism and support for the struggle for the liberation of South Africa. This 'political' articulation of male, ruling class interest in monopolising the access to and use of foreign currency is supposed to be effective in discouraging shoppers from going to banks to apply for foreign currency allowances for their shopping cum holiday trips.

The struggle between the state and the shoppers culminated in the allocation of foreign currency to a trading concern that is run by the state so that it can import 'trinkets'. The thinking behind this move was that the shoppers buy trinkets and use up precious foreign currency to do so. Logically, it followed that the official importation and sale of these 'trinkets' would undercut the market for the shoppers, thus chucking them out of business. The wisdom of this move is questionable, based as it is on a very partial understanding of the import–export trade in Zimbabwe.

The move by the state illustrates its concern with restricting access to foreign currency by the ordinary waged and unwaged Zimbabweans who are struggling to evade proletarianisation. It is an important turn in the gender debate between the state and working women in Zimbabwe and it illustrates the state's understanding of what women should or rather, should not do in pursuing survival and enhancing incomes for their households. Thus, the state and ruling class interests are becoming less and less reconcilable with those of working women who survive through resale of commodities that are in demand amongst middle-class people in Zimbabwe. The type of entrepreneurship that has arisen as a result of the structuring of the economy is not acceptable because it allows poorer people to use the same resources that the emerging black bourgeoisie and the established white capitalists are competing for in the economy.

It is therefore very important to realise that the struggle for survival is effectively pitting working people, in this case poorer women, against the state and in competition with the established and emerging bourgeoisies in ways that were not anticipated in the initial economic arrangements that provided for holiday allowances for the middle classes in the pre-independence era. The entitlement felt and now effectively made use of by these women has demonstrated the limits to the exercise of citizenship rights and the class nature of definitions of patriotism in the context of economic decline in Zimbabwe.

It is also important to point out that even ordinary demands for and exercise of citizens' rights and the attempt to fulfil domestic obligations now pit women against the state, where the state is unable or unwilling to shoulder the burden of provision of services such as food, shelter and clothing for its citizens. Thus, the fulfilment of domestic obligations by women is closely tied to the state and the ordinary services that people have grown to expect from it. Where there are very few jobs and very little land for women to work on, women of the working classes may collide with the state in their attempt to fulfil and live up to the ideologies of domesticity which may have developed under different conditions in the economy and the polity.

For the purposes of organising, the ways in which the crochet women have to deal with bureaucracies make it very difficult for concerted action to be taken by the women. People are loath to reveal their hustles, and this isolates individual women when they are harassed by officialdom. It is also interesting to note that the unwaged women have managed to politicise the issue of body searches at border posts and to push the local authorities to revise and repeal those bye-laws that discriminate against the economic activities of small-scale entrepreneurs, a significant proportion of whom are women in urban and rural areas.

It is also necessary to note that the government has tended to stigmatise the poorer shoppers while ignoring the expenditure of foreign exchange on luxury goods such as whisky, microwave ovens, video and audio equipment by middle-class travellers who do not face the same degree of hostility from the bureaucracies. This selective harassment of women and the undercutting of their livelihoods reveals a class aspect to the gender and survival struggles currently taking place in Zimbabwe in the arena of entrepreneurship under conditions of economic hardship.

From the research conducted with crochet workers, it becomes evident that there is great need to strengthen women's rights and to establish the legitimacy of women as entrepreneurs as well as mothers, wives and relatives of men. This is particularly the case since the path of wage work seems to be limited for ensuring women's economic self-sufficiency. Freezing women into one-dimensional roles as housewives or mothers is clearly not realistic or conducive to their success in ensuring and safeguarding their livelihoods. It is obvious that women's entrepreneurial roles are not viewed by them as incompatible with motherhood and other roles. Thus, policy-makers need to understand women on their own terms as the first step towards assuring their survival. If this does not happen, the state will have to settle for a long period of struggle with working women. This struggle might alienate the state from working people generally, and undermine the legitimacy that it neeeds to survive in the long term.

It is necessary to compare the Zimbabwean experience with that of women involved in itinerant trading activities in other parts of Africa such as Nigeria, Zambia and Zaire, which have also undergone economic problems. This may help to indicate the likely direction of changes in the activities of itinerant traders, state responses and the possibilities for organising women to secure their livelihoods in ways that are sustainable in the long term.

NOTES

1. The work of Elizabeth Schmidt presents examples of some of the ways in which the colonial state, local political leaders and male household heads shared and furthered interests which restricted women's mobility and economic possibilities within particular contexts in Zimbabwe. This work demonstrates also early examples of women's resistance to curtailment of opportunity, movement and access to resources. In this present chapter, however, the class referent is particularly significant, a focus not always clear in Schmidt's work.

REFERENCES

ENDA. 1990. 'The Informal Sector in Zimbabwe: The Role of Women.' Harare.

Gaidzanwa, R. 1984. 'The Policy Implications of Women's Involvement in the Informal Sector', *MISS*, Journal of the Ministry of Manpower Planning and Development, Vol. 3, No. 3, April.

Gaidzanwa, R. 1988. 'Rural Migration and Prostitution' in *UNESCO Report on the Causes of Prostitution*, Madrid.

Helmsing, A. J. 1991. 'Non-agricultural enterprise in the communal lands of Zimbabwe', in A. J. Helmsing and N. D. Mutizwa-Mangiza (eds), *Rural Development and Planning in Zimbabwe*, Gower Publishing Co., Aldershot.

Hunt, N. R. 1990. 'Domesticity and Colonialism in Belgian Africa: Usumbura's Foyer Social, 1946–1960', *Signs*, Vol. 15, No. 3.

ILO. 1986. 'Women's Employment Patterns: Discrimination and Promotion of Equality in Africa. The Case of Zimbabwe.'

Mkandawire, T. 1983. 'The Informal Sector in the Labour Reserve Economies of Southern Africa with Special Reference to Zimbabwe', ILO, Lusaka.

Moyo, N. *et al.* 1984. 'The Informal Sector in Zimbabwe: Its Potential for Employment Creation', Department of Economics, University of Zimbabwe, Harare.

Mutambirwa, S. 1989. 'Entrepreneurship and Small-scale Enterprise Development for Women in Zimbabwe', ILO, Lusaka.

Schmidt, E. 1992. *Peasants, Traders, and Wives: Shona Women in the History of Zimbabwe, 1870–1939*, Heinemann Educational Books, Baobab Books and James Currey; Portsmouth, NH, Harare and London.

Weinrich, A. K. 1973. *Black and White Elites in Rural Rhodesia*, Manchester University Press, Manchester.

World Bank. 1987. 'Zimbabwe. A Strategy for Sustained Growth.' November.

12 Women Organising under the Structural Adjustment Programme

Mairo V. Bello[1]

The purpose of this chapter is to highlight the impact of the Structural Adjustment Programme (SAP) on Nigerian women in the formal and particularly the informal sector, and examine the responses of the state and of the women. Women and children have suffered the worst impact of SAP, with women in various classes and categories affected differently by the policies and consequences of the SAP.

The economy of Nigeria has gone through many changes in the last 20 years. The recent economic crisis has come with a package of economic recovery measures, the SAP, introduced into the economy in the 1986 presidential budget speech. While there have been opportunities for a tiny minority to enrich themselves, for the majority of workers and peasants things have never been so bad. Women in the rural areas, the main focus of this chapter, have found themselves burdened by worsening landlessness, indebtedness, unemployment and underemployment of their husbands and male kin, and an increase in local conflicts. In additional, children and women are more malnourished, diseased, and demoralised among both the rural community and the urban poor. The issue for the women of Nigeria therefore is not just a matter of livelihood, but rather of survival.

Women have been organising and reorganising themselves through political and economic actions to respond to the changes in the economy. This is despite the fact that they are rarely taken into consideration when policies are formulated, nor do they have a say in the implementation of those policies. The chapter begins with a description of the changing Nigerian economy, and gives some background to the introduction of the SAP. The economic activities of women under the SAP then become the focus of the chapter, particularly in relation to how women have been able to respond to the constraints of changing economic policy and conditions working and acting together. In this context, we centre especially but not solely on the input and impact of the organisation, Women in Nigeria, and upon the need to relate research, policy and action in seeking to improve conditions for women, and thus for the citizenry more broadly.

ORIGINS OF THE NIGERIAN ECONOMIC CRISIS

Nigeria's integration into the world capitalist system through the institution of colonial rule assisted in the subjection of its economy to the capitalist system of development. During the crisis of the 1970s, the Nigerian economy was insulated from the crisis. While the OPEC oil price increase of 1973/74 exacerbated the crisis in most African countries, Nigeria benefited as an oil exporter. The quadrupling of oil prices in that period generated a change from the agrarian basis of accumulation in Nigeria to that of crude petroleum. Petroleum exports, which accounted for only 10 per cent of the country's export earnings in 1962, rose to 82.7 per cent of export earnings in 1973 and, during the second half of the 1970s, peaked at between 90 and 93 per cent. By 1980, the country was producing 2.05 million barrels of oil per day. The massive oil earnings were used to finance the expansion of the country's industrial sector, commercial enterprises, numerous agricultural projects and the construction of many infrastructural facilities. This massive expenditure was instrumental to the rapid development of the Nigerian petit-bourgeoisie, the expansion of the foreign corporate presence in the country, and the growth of state capital to an unprecedented level.

While the windfall from oil exports led to a considerable expansion of the economy, it did little to increase the country's self-reliance. If anything, the country's dependence on external sources for crucial inputs and various commodities increased, as shown in Table 12.1 below. The structure of the country's import substitution industries entailed a high import profile for machinery and spare parts. Importation of machinery and transport equipment increased by 121 per cent during 1976–81, while that of capital equipment grew by about 156 per cent in 1974–9 and by 28 per cent in 1979–81. The importation of consumer goods and food items into the country also underwent rapid growth. The importation of manufactured goods increased by nearly 50 per cent in 1976–9, and nearly doubled again by 1981.

The first indication of the 1970s crisis in the Nigerian economy came in 1978 when, in the face of a world oil 'glut', the Obasanjo administration sought to maintain the country's revenue by raising the posted price of oil by two per cent. This resulted in a boycott of Nigeria's oil by customers with access to cheaper sources of supply, including the spot oil

Table 12.1　Imports by End Use at Current (1983) Prices
(N million) (N1 = US$1.40)

	1974	1975	1976	1977	1978	1979	1980	1981
Consumer goods								
1. Non-durable								
a) Food	166.4	353.7	526.7	912.6	1004.1	1040.1	1416.8	2198.3
b) Textiles	31.5	81.3	65.0	38.9	41.9	73.2	92.4	202.6
c) Others	173.6	353.5	476.7	612.1	720.5	705.8	567.4	822.0
2. Durable	65.8	191.3	282.0	421.7	370.2	380.7	473.7	674.1
Sub-total	437.3	979.8	1350.4	1985.0	2136.7	2199.8	2550.3	3897.0
Passenger cars	97.0	220.3	261.0	297.4	350.1	169.7	206.1	1316.9
Capital goods:								
Cap. equipment	490.0	1137.0	1515.0	2129.0	2529.8	1576.0	2228.0	2661.3
Tran. equipment	129.0	371.1	729.6	1013.0	1233.8	988.7	1770.2	1818.7
Raw material	519.0	903.0	1094.0	1543.0	1880.1	1115.7	2166.9	3038.5
Fuel	55.4	100.2	175.0	128.6	156.7	116.4	173.4	187.2
Sub-total	1289.7	2731	3774.6	5111.0	6150.5	3966.5	6545.3	9022.6
GRAND TOTAL	1727.0	3711	5125.0	7097.0	8287.2	6106.3	9095.6	12924.0

Source: National Economic Council Expert Committee Report on the State of the Nigerian Economy, 1983.

markets. The effect was recession during 1977–8, when there was a decline in the country's oil output from 2.10 million barrels per day in 1977 to 1.57 million by February 1978. In the circumstances, Nigeria's import bill, which had been accelerating at a rate of 40 per cent annually and stood at a staggering N1 billion a month by May 1978, could no longer be sustained. The country suffered a balance of payments deficit of about N1.3 billion. Also in the 1977–8 period, industrial production increased by only 3.9 per cent as against 19 per cent in 1976. The public debt had reached N5001.1 million in December 1977. However, by 1979, Nigeria's foreign exchange account had a reserve of N3 billion, rising to N5.6 billion in 1980.

It was against this background of an apparent improvement in the economic situation that the civilian government of Shehu Shagari was inaugurated in October 1979. The advent of the Shagari administration coincided with a dramatic increase in the international price of oil, rising from $14.90

a barrel in 1978 to $33 per barrel in 1979 and $44.40 in 1980. This in turn led to a dramatic increase in government revenue. With this favourable development, the import controls introduced in 1978 were removed by the Shagari administration. When the price of oil suddenly collapsed in the world market towards the end of 1981 and early 1982, a crisis of immense proportions, much more severe than the relatively mild one suffered in 1977–9, hit the Nigerian economy.

The crisis quickly spread to all sectors of the economy. Unable to bring in the required levels of raw materials, many Nigerian manufacturing concerns collapsed. It was reckoned that about 50 per cent of Nigeria's import-substitution factories folded up as a result of the crisis. Also, an acute shortage of consumer goods and food items developed as importers were no longer able to bring in commodities. As a result, the rate of inflation rose astronomically. As manufacturers and commercial companies closed down, a large number of workers were laid off, leading to a grave unemployment situation in which, for the first time in Nigeria's history, many university and high school graduates, including female graduates, were unable to find jobs.

The crisis also led to a debt problem for the country. In 1983, for example, the repayment of principal and interest on the public debt rose to N1.3 billion, an increase of 72.2 per cent compared with payments in 1982. The debt service ratio jumped from 8.9 per cent in 1982 to 17.4 billion in 1979 to N22.2 billion in 1987. The increase in 1983 alone was N7.2 billion. As the crisis escalated, basic social services collapsed, the agricultural sector underwent further decline, the construction boom in the economy ended, and infrastructural facilities deteriorated rapidly. The severity of the crises compelled response from the state.

THE MARCH TOWARDS STRUCTURAL ADJUSTMENT

In a bid to contain the escalating crisis, the Shagari administration announced a set of austerity measures through the Economic Stabilisation Act of April 1982. It marked the beginning of the country's march towards structural adjustment. The thrust of the Act was unmistakably monetarist. It called for a massive imposition of import restrictions, monetary controls and cuts in public expenditure. Compulsory advanced deposits for all importers, ranging from 25 to 50 per cent, were imposed on a wide range of commodities. The government also began negotiation with the IMF for a loan of $2.5 billion under the Extended Fund Facility (EFF).

The Buhari regime accepted the broad outlines of the December pre-coup budget of the Shagari administration. In line with the general intent of curtailing public expenditure, the regime further reduced the 1984 current expenditure by 15 per cent, and capital expenditure by 15.6 per cent. Monetary and credit guidelines were established for industries, financial institutions and general commerce. There was also a massive purge of the public service, aimed mainly at cutting the public service to size and making it manageable; wage-earning women were not spared in this purge. A plethora of levies and special taxes were also introduced. The Buhari regime also continued the IMF negotiations started by its predecessor for an EFF loan of $2.5 billion. However, very little headway was made in the bargaining; a stalemate soon developed as neither the government nor the IMF was ready to budge on the points of disagreement.

Yet clearly, the Buhari regime had all the credentials to qualify for an IMF loan: it had agreed to reduce grants, subventions and loans to parastatals, suspended federal loans to state government, massively reduced public expenditure, controlled wages, retrenched workers and allocated 44 per cent of state revenue for debt repayment in 1984 as the debt crisis escalated. Indeed, the measures taken by the government had reduced the budget deficit from N6.2 billion in 1983 to N3.3 billion by 1984. However, the regime was unable to agree with the Fund over the latter's insistence on the devaluation of the naira, removal of the petroleum subsidy, liberalisation of trade and an across-the-board privatisation of public enterprises. As a result, no agreement with the IMF was concluded: Nigeria's debts could not be rescheduled and blocked lines of credit were not re-opened. In the midst of this, the repressive tendencies of the regime increased, alienating virtually all sections of Nigerian society, including workers, students, press, and professionals. An atmosphere conducive to the overthrow of the regime developed and, on 27 August 1985, the regime of General Buhari was toppled.

The new government was dissatisfied with the stalemate in the negotiations with the IMF and declared its determination to break the deadlock. To do this, the regime needed the broad support of Nigerians, since the IMF conditionalities would seriously erode their living standards. In an attempt to judge the public mood, the Babangida administration decided on 2 September 1985 to declare a national debate on the IMF loan. In the course of the debate, it was clear that the vast majority of Nigerians were opposed to the IMF loan and its conditionalities. But while the debate was still on, on 1 October 1985, the government declared a state of National Economic Emergency. This was to last for 15 months. Under this

Emergency, a general pay cut for both civilian and military employees was introduced, ranging from two per cent to 20 per cent.

Although at the end of the national debate the government decided to reject the IMF loan, it proceeded through the 1986 budget to articulate and implement a SAP, which is based on IMF conditionalities.

The SAP has several objectives, most important of which are to: restructure and diversify the productive base of the economy in order to reduce dependence on the oil sector and imports; achieve fiscal and balance of payments viability; lay the basis for sustainable growth with minimum inflation; lessen unproductive investments in and improve the efficiency of the public sector; and intensify the growth potential of the private sector.

The official aim of the programme – economic reconstruction, social justice and self-reliance – is hardly different from previous statements of economic policy. What distinguishes it, according to one economist, is its comprehensive breadth, much greater depth, and radical determination.

The major policies aimed at achieving these objectives have been devaluation of the naira through the SFEM; trade and payments liberalisation; tariff reform to promote industrial diversification; deregulation to promote greater reliance on market forces; removal of subsidies, especially on petroleum products; rationalisation and privatisation of productive enterprises; strengthening existing demand management policies; and adoption of measures to stimulate production and broaden the supply base of the economy.

Some institutions were especially created to help achieve some of these objectives, at the cost of many millions of naira. These include the National Directorate of Employment (NDE), intended to encourage and train young school leavers in various trades with a view to making them self-reliant; the Directorate of Food, Roads, and Rural Infrastructure (DFRRI); and the Mass Mobilisation of Social Justice, Self Reliance and Economic Recovery (MAMSER). Both DFRRI and MAMSER seek to raise citizen awareness and were intended to stimulate production.

Increasingly, Nigerians are becoming aware that the SAP has failed to bring about even the beginnings of economic recovery to the country. A close reading of the President's 1990 budget speech reveals that some four-and-a-half years since the introduction of SAP, the economy has continued to deteriorate. It also became abundantly clear that all the sacrifices occasioned by SAP have failed to reduce the debt which crushes our economy – a stated main objective of SAP when it was introduced in 1986. Yusuf Usman has identified the areas of deterioration of the economy as follows:

1. The rate of growth of the GDP declined;
2. Industrial capacity utilisation declined;
3. Severe inflationary pressures were experienced;
4. High interest rates discouraged long-term investments;
5. Transport costs increased significantly;
6. The naira depreciated markedly; and
7. Urban unemployment increased at a disturbing rate.

(Usman, 1990)

Usman (1990) contends that Nigerians can ill-afford to ignore these budget plans whether or not they get implemented, because the ritual of the annual budget has 'lost any pretence at public accountability', addressing as it does only what the government will spend, and not what has been earned.

WOMEN ORGANISING AROUND THE DEBATE ON SAP

Women's organisations are also well-aware that the government only talks of 'starting to witness positive signals of an enduring turn-around' (I. B. Babangida, 1990). From the onset, women did not allow themselves to be left out of this very important debate; they knew that the end effect would tell on them and their children. Various women's groups protested and sent delegates to the government to register their protests against the IMF loan:

- Women in Nigeria (WIN) met on many occasions, sent out press releases, sent delegates to the government, and issued communiques in protest against the IMF loan and its conditionalities.
- The Nigerian Labour Congress Women's Wing condemned without reservation the loan and its conditionalities.
- The market women also acted. In some states the women closed down their stalls, refusing to sell or buy, and marched collectively to the government house to register their protest.

All these protests ultimately were to no avail, in terms of subsequent government policy and action. However, they were relevant in terms of giving notice to government of the vocal and active presence of these groups of women, who intended to respond jointly to threats to the livelihood of their members through formal representation and action. With the introduction of SAP, as is often the case, women are worse off and bear the brunt of the adverse situation. But in order to detail further the economic situation of women, it is necessary to outline the areas of work in which they engage.

ECONOMIC ACTIVITIES OF NIGERIAN WOMEN

Nigerian women are engaged in a broad range of economic activities. Their activities can be divided into four main categories: manufacturing, production, public services, and small-scale enterprises. Some of the enterprises found in the production and manufacturing sector are farming, agro-linked activities, handicrafts, garment manufacturing, pottery, weaving and spinning. Those found in services are traders, caterers, hairdressers, street food sellers, and transporters. Some women are in the civil service and professions such as medicine, law, banking, engineering and architecture.

The economic projects undertaken by many Nigerian women are in small business enterprises. In the majority of these cases, the businesses are expansions of the women's domestic responsibilities and skills. They serve as a form of self-employment in the absence of alternative gainful employment or regular working hours away from domestic duties. The small-scale enterprises are flexible and less restrictive than employment elsewhere, which may also require education, experience and training prerequisites which most women lack. This notwithstanding, Nigerian women are increasingly participating in larger manufacturing and distribution business sectors, mostly as unskilled labour. In the rural areas, most entrepreneurs are engaged in trading mainly in local agricultural commodities. In the urban areas, women are involved in the operation of small retail businesses such as fruit and vegetable selling, running market stalls, kiosks, and dress and cap-making. Women also manage retail shops, increasingly participating in non-traditional fields for women such as the wholesale business, management of private ventures, and contracting. The SAP has propelled women into the area of contracting. They now actively seek access to government contracts which they sell for a percentage of the gross value (from 10 to 15 per cent) for a quick monetary turnover. The areas most women concentrate on are providing supplies and furnishings, but increasingly enterprising women are competing for building contracts, mainly in the housing industry, and are slowly carving out a place for themselves in this arena. Access to such work of course also implies access to much more substantial funds and to networks which are not open to the majority of Nigerian women.

SAP AND WOMEN WORKING IN THE FORMAL ECONOMIC SECTOR

The role of Nigerian women in the formal economic sector, though significant, has been accorded little or no recognition. In the area of domestic production, women's activities are defined as unpaid labour and therefore distinct from other productive activities such as agriculture. It has been stated that 75 per cent of the agricultural work in Nigeria is done by women under 'strenuous conditions and with primitive tools . . . and their role in [this] and other sectors of the economy is taken for granted and tends to be ignored in the computation of their contributions to the GNP' (Obasanjo and Mabogunje, 1991). The authors regard this as deriving from the fact that in the formal or 'foreign derived economic model women constitute less than 20 per cent of wage labour whilst in agriculture they are the exploited victims of male middlemen' (Obasanjo and Mabogunje, 1991).

Women workers can be found in most professions, but the majority of women are unskilled workers, and so are found in manufacturing companies doing manual jobs such as packing, arranging, wrapping and generally putting finishing touches on manufactured goods. Constraints such as lack of education and professional training also militate against the women in the organised formal sector: they were among the first workers who suffered retrenchments and lay-offs when the SAP and its conditionalities were introduced into the economy. Because the women working in this sector are mostly unskilled workers, employers do not hesitate to fire them as soon as there is any crisis in any organisation. There has also long been a notion that women take too much time off their jobs, or fall sick too frequently, and/or go on maternity leave. In the Nigerian case, as soon as the crisis started, employment was dealt a severe blow. During 1980–3, about one million workers were estimated to have been retrenched from the industrial sector, and at least one third of these retrenched workers were women.

Most of the women who lost their jobs had no choice other than to join their sisters in the informal sector and also engage in petty trading or food processing. However, it must be noted that many women who work in the formal sector, work also in the informal sector. With wage freezes, devaluation of the currency, and uncertain employment prospects in the formal sector, working only in the formal sector is often insufficient for a woman to feed herself and her family, and also does not provide sufficient funds to *improve*, rather than only to sustain, her situation.

It is through research that the realities of this 'double (or, in this case, triple) burden' of formal and informal sector work, are shown to be added to the already heavy constraints of combining domestic obligations and income-earning labour. For example, WIN carried out research in the urban and rural areas around Kano. Of the 300 women interviewed in the WIN survey, about 50 per cent were primarily in manufacturing and production, 30 per cent in the public service, and 20 per cent in small-scale enterprises. Of these women, 30 per cent were in both public service and small-scale enterprises, and 40 per cent in both manufacturing and small-scale enterprises. Another 30 per cent were in manufacturing, public services and small-scale enterprises. Thus, *most women engage in more than one economic activity.* Only one per cent of the survey sample were working only as housewives.

SAP AND WOMEN IN THE INFORMAL ECONOMIC SECTOR

The informal sector is comprised of individuals trading or organising petty businesses to make a profit for their survival. The informal economic sector is dominated by women and makes a significant contribution to the continuing economic growth of the country. A number of advantages have been advanced for the informal sector, such as the provision of opportunities to create (low cost) jobs for rural and urban dwellers who do not have the skills to compete for scarce formal sector jobs, and the creation of a virtual training ground for entrepreneurs where innovations are conceptualised and introduced at low cost to the entrepreneur and the country, using local materials. Work in the informal sector provides women with an opportunity to earn a cash income as well as a chance for personal and professional development, and success can create wealth and raise the quality of life for the entrepreneur and her dependants in particular, and the community and country as a whole. As enterprises in this sector are usually initiated and funded from the resources of the enterpreneurs, this saves the state capital; the state gains additionally as products can also ultimately earn much-needed foreign currency by providing products for sale on foreign markets. Other levels of society also benefit, as the informal sector also provides services and products for the formal sector and the higher income groups.

However, many of the much-vaunted advantages do not come to fruition in Nigeria because of the problems faced by the women who constitute the majority of the informal sector, because also of the self-exploitation which is implicit in the informal sector, the difficulties of finding funding, and the fact that the profits accrued may well be marginal, or lacking altogether.

The boost that the SAP was supposed to bring to the agricultural sector did not transpire, and the naira continued its downward spiral. As the prices of essential goods skyrocketed, the rural sector, largely farming-based, suffered a crisis. Less money was available for local produce, nor was local produce necessarily supported or sought. Twenty women mat-makers, respondents in a local survey, said that they could not make as many mats as before, nor could they sell them as readily as before: this was due to the introduction into the market of plastic mats. The women of Isari Village saw this as 'men doing a women's job' and depriving them of a market. One hundred and fifteen respondents said that they do not get their cooked food sold any more, so they now cook less and because of the high cost of ingredients, they now make less profit (Chamo Isari Village Survey, 1991).

In addition, through policy and planning which is not gender-sensitive, areas where women have had access to informal sector earnings may be lost to them, as is discussed below.

AGRO-INDUSTRIAL POLICY AND INFORMAL SECTOR LABOUR

Government policy is rarely gender-neutral; it may or may not be gender-sensitive. The description given here of the situation of women in the rice-producing industry, based on research by a Kano WIN member, Sindi Medar-Gould, demonstrates how women's access to particular forms of income-earning activity has been removed through government policy which did not take gender constraints facing women into consideration. It must be noted, however, that it is questionable whether an affirmative policy towards women informal sector workers would have been forthcoming in any event, given dominant discourse assuming the need to support (male) breadwinners.

In the rice-producing industry, one group of women which has suffered the backlash of unfavourable government policy is the rice processors. They have either been totally displaced or have suffered from a severe economic downswing. The women tell of the hardship ensuing from the advent of SAP, which has brought small-scale rice mills into their local-ities, and of the battle to keep life and limb together under strict economic constraints. Normally one would not associate agro-industry with the in-formal sector. However, in the Islamic north of Nigeria where women are secluded, this is very much the case since the women work from home, often employing other women and children in the process.

As the government structurally adjusted itself, one of the clarion calls was for 'self-sufficiency'. With a view to achieving this self-sufficiency in rice production, the government offered incentive packages to various states to embark on rice production. This encouraged intending farmers by providing both technical and financial assistance. Pioneer rice-processing mills sprang up in various rice-producing areas of the country. In Kano State alone, around fifty small-scale mills were introduced in various local government areas between 1987 and 1989. Prior to this, rice paddy had been locally processed by the rural women, using simple traditional methods for parboiling, drying, husking, winnowing and de-stoning. The introduction of small-scale mills into what was the stronghold of women workers showed immediate adverse effects on women's employment and income levels, for the mill-owners entered into direct competition with the women by charging the same fee as the hand pounders. Since the mill is considered time and labour saving, and better at polishing, the loss of customers was felt at once.

Agro-processing such as for the grain and groundnut industries is not only labour saving; it is also labour replacing, and as such can absorb only very few women, especially since the vast majority of women in the informal sector work from home. Since small-scale rice mills were introduced into the Kano rice-producing area, the connected activities which employed rural women have been marginalised, displacing the female labour force and adding to the problems of the rural women. None of the government strategies for self-sufficiency in rice production (i.e. to bring more land under cultivation; to provide irrigation facilities; and to promote research and development in rice production) include women as a concern. As the economic squeeze becomes tighter, more and more men are moving into traditionally female-dominated employment areas. Men are setting up road-side parboiling processes on the doorstep of the mills and diverting the trade which would normally find its way to the women. (For further information, see Medar-Gould, 1990.)

Research has also been carried out more generally in the rural areas, for it is not possible to act effectively to ameliorate women's situation, without having a clear picture of the difficulties they face. Thus, research was carried out in several local villages. From this work, it became clear that another group of women suffering from SAP are women farmers, who cannot afford to farm on their lands due to the escalated costs of grains, fertiliser and labour. They now resort to letting their lands and seek to work as hired hands to other farmers during planting and harvesting seasons (WIN Research in Gabari and Chamo villages, Kano State, 1990).

RESEARCH, POLICY AND ACTION: THE EXAMPLE OF ACCESS TO CREDIT

For effective and relevant action, it is necessary to link such action with research. All of the women in the research sample, without exception, complained of lack of access to credit and lack of starting capital. All, whether they sold groundnut oil, cooked food, made mats, parboiled rice, sewed wrappers or sold salt and tomatoes, were of the opinion that an infusion of money would bring some relief to their condition.

In order to highlight and bring more information and response in relation to this area of concern, a seminar on credit for women was held in July 1990. The seminar brought out the discrepancy between the law as enunciated and as practised, as it relates to women. The seminar also showed that Nigerian women generally find it difficult to obtain loans from banks for their business.

Creditors put forward a variety of reasons or rationalisations why women are usually refused credit facilities, such as the assumptions that women can effectively manage in their homes but not in business because they are too emotional; that women cannot keep reliable accounts and are therefore high risks in handling loan money; and that real estate collateral offered by women is unreliable for security. In the event of separation, death or divorce, the security might be threatened. A woman has to obtain her husband's consent even where the property is in her name.

Difficulty for women to obtain access to banks may also be traced to lack of educational skills needed to prepare business plans or to interact effectively with the banking sector. Because of lack of necessary information and difficulty in obtaining loans from banks, women generally resort to informal means for financing their business. These are usually from personal savings, from relatives and friends. Failing this, some may resort to pawn-brokers or to tontine arrangements. Tontine (called in Nigeria, among other terms, *asusu* or *adashe*) may be organised by a group of individuals who agree to pay a certain amount into a common fund. The total is collected in rotation each month by members. A woman may belong to a few tontines simultaneously. Such financing arrangements are only good for small businesses and may not be suitable for business expansion or for that involving serious venture capital.

Efforts have been made to provide more credit to Nigerians via government as well as non-governmental institutions. For example, the People's Bank was established in 1988 by the Nigerian government to solve these problems. This is one of the various programmes introduced into the economy to cushion some of the hardship of SAP on Nigerians and reduce the suffering of the masses. The bank gives small-scale loans, and women are supposed to have full access to these credit facilities. But women, and especially rural women, still have problems in obtaining this assistance, since they are expected to apply for these loans in groups. In addition, cultural and religious practices compel many of the Muslim women, particularly in the north, to stay in purdah.

Financial assistance by the government and non-governmental organisations (NGOs) is also extended to women to help in promoting their various trades, and covers commercially viable projects undertaken by women's groups. WIN Kano has assisted women in seeking access to credit, in an expanding local programme. A WIN chapter was established in a local Kano village in 1990, and the scheme is now operating very successfully. A total of five villages in five local government areas now participate, and it is planned to extend the service as soon as funding is available.

The scheme was begun by advancing a hundred naira to 25 women from each village, which they had to repay at the rate of ten naira a week. Every week, ten more women were able to borrow. There is a service charge of N1.50 per person a week, which the women used to open a bank account in the name of each village chapter. WIN hopes that eventually they will accumulate sufficient money to satisfy the demands of all the women of the villages. Started with 12 500 naira and 125 women, 30 000 naira is now in circulation among 300 women. The scheme has been so successful in Kano State that at a subsequent national WIN Co-ordinating Committee meeting, other states were asked to put it into operation.

Along with the loan scheme, WIN Kano has accepted the responsibility of getting the village organisations registered with the state social services department, and with helping the women to arm themselves with the skills necessary to make their businesses more viable. To this end the group helps with seeking out lenders, filling out applications, writing letters of complaint about such things as access roads, lack of electricity, potable water, and letters of solicitation for donations. Research, policy and action are the three legs of ongoing response to improving women's situation – and we know, from our cooking stoves and our hearths, that a tripod is the sturdiest and most secure foundation for our activities.

NIGERIAN WOMEN ORGANISING

Nigerian women are organising around their own interests, interests which are sometimes separate from, and sometimes indistinguishable from those

of the community at large. This organising ranges from doing the necessary research to establish, analyse and suggest relevant policy responses
and local and state procedures to deal with issues brought out through that
research; to creating fora such as seminars, workshops, and local-level
meetings to further discussion and suggest possible action; to activities
which reflect and respond directly to the problems various categories of
women face.

The SAP has aggravated the already precarious position of women in
the Nigerian economy: they are now so preoccupied by matters of daily
survival that they have little or no time to organise for political participation. Yet through the work of NGOs such as WIN, women are becoming
progressively aware of the link between economic production and political
power. Consequently, along with the move to organise labour, there is a
parallel movement to agitate for political participation both at local and
national levels. In Kano State, for example, women from the Nigerian
Labour Congress and the rural organisations are running for Government
House and the House of Assembly. It is believed that with proper representation, the informal sector of the economy will become more vibrant
and sustaining. The leaders of organisations in this sector are solidly behind
the female candidates, for they see them as a kind of force for survival.

At the federal level, a National Commission for Women has been established. The National Commission for Women reflects the recognition by
the Nigerian state that the time is ripe for women to be encouraged to play
a more visible role in the nation. It is also a recognition of the contribution
of Nigerian women to the nation. A nation that neglects its women and
takes them for granted or hides them in purdah, no matter its wealth in
natural resources, cannot achieve a position as a leading world economic
power. The establishment of the National Commission for Women may
seem a beginning of effort to actualise the United Nations Resolution of
1975, which called on its regional commissions to give special attention
to programmes and projects which promote the integration of women in
development. But groups such as Women in Nigeria have taken up the
task of organising and conscientising the toiling women of Nigeria, deep
into the rural areas, long before the National Commission for Women was
inaugurated, and they continue in these efforts today.

For example, the 1990 budget unleashed a series of disastrous measures
for the rural populace, and for the rural environment. Chief among these
were the rise in the poll-tax and in the price of kerosene and cooking gas
(166.6 per cent and 100 per cent respectively) (Usman, 1990). The poll-
tax, already implemented in neighbouring states, is supposed to serve
as a vehicle for greater revenue mobilisation for rural development, but

according to Usman (1990), this and the increased fuel costs mean that a considerable amount of trees and shrubs will be cut down and used for firewood. WIN has tried to make the connection between SAP and the decline in rural rehabilitation real to the women, so that in political campaigns the women will be more equipped to challenge politicians on these urgent matters of community interest.

CONCLUSION

The devastation wrought by the SAP clearly cuts across all sectors of the Nigerian economy. Women, though organising to meet the challenges, are hampered by a lack of essential infrastructure. However, if the present economic recovery programme is to be successful, in the sense that all human resources are to be fully mobilised for self-reliant growth, then planners and policy-makers must develop strategies to promote the equitable participation of women in the industrial growth of the Nigerian economy, and to advance economic democracy. Moreover, for many Nigerian women, personal income-generating activities are crucial for their family's well-being.

The introduction of SAP, which heralded the present high level of inflation, has resulted not only in the displacement of female workers, but also in the loss of essential goods and services. Money for female-based programmes has become exceedingly scarce, resulting in the reduction of those programmes. The importance of national policies to promote women's participation gains additional significance when it is realised that Nigerian women constitute over half of the economically active population. We in Nigeria have become convinced by circumstances of the wisdom of tapping the potential of our women, by reducing the problems which hinder their progress.

It is incumbent on Nigerian women to unite in positive action to change their situation. This is possible through action within non-governmental organisations, through lobbying government for legislative and other changes, through the workplace, through the community and in the home. In this context, it is vital to continue to combine research, policy and action in our ongoing efforts to ameliorate the situation of Nigerian women.

NOTES

1.   This chapter is a contribution from Women in Nigeria, Kano State Branch.
      Mairo Bello is presently Co-ordinator of WIN, Kano State.

REFERENCES

African Leadership Forum. 'Farmhouse Dialogue on Women and Development.'
Babangida, I. B. 1990. Annual Budget Speech.
Central Bank of Nigeria. 'Report on the Impact of the Better Life Programme on
   the Rural Economy of Nigeria', Lagos.
Mdachi, F. B. 1990. 'Women in Business'. Paper presented at a Workshop for
   International Federation of Business and Professional Women, Lagos.
National Economic Council Expert Committee. 1983. 'Report on the State of the
   Nigerian Economy', Lagos.
Obasanjo, O. and A. Mabogunje (eds). 1991. *Elements of Development*, A4 Pub-
   lications, Lagos.
Oclo, Esther. 1990. Address at a Workshop for International Federation of Busi-
   ness and Professional Women, Lagos.
Olukoshi, Adebayo. 1989. 'Impact of IMF – World Bank Programmes in Nigeria',
   in Bade Onimode (ed.), *The IMF, the World Bank and the African Debt: Volume
   2: The Economic Impact*, Zed Books, London.
Otu, Deborah O. 1985. 'Nigerian Rural Women: Access to Social Amenities.'
   Paper presented at the Fourth Annual Women in Nigeria Conference, on Rural
   Women in Socio-economic Development, Ilorin, Nigeria.
Sunday New Nigerian, 3 July 1988.
Usman, Y. B. 1990. 'The 1990 Budget and our Future.' Paper delivered at Bayero
   University, Kano State, Nigeria.
WIN, Lagos State. 1989. Paper presented at WIN Conference on Women and the
   Transition to Democracy.
Women in Nigeria. 1989. Communique from WIN Conference on Women and the
   Transition to Democracy.

OTHER SOURCES

Medar-Gould, Sindi. Survey on the Effects of SAP on Women in the Rice-
   processing Industry, Yadakwari village, Kano State, July–September, 1990.
Women in Nigeria (WIN). Survey of Chamo, Chaichai, and Sai, Diribo and Gangur
   villages, Kano State, Nigeria, December 1990.
Women in Nigeria (WIN). Survey of Conditions of Women in the Urban and Rural
   Areas, Kano State, Nigeria, 1990–91.

13 Homeworking in South Korea[1]
Young-ock Kim

Those who are familiar with poor areas in Korean cities have noticed that women are involved in various forms of income-earning activities, mainly in the poorly-paid, informal sector. In particular, a substantial portion of the married women labour force is shown to be subject to homeworking, a paid work carried out in the home.

However extensive women's involvement in homeworking may be, this industrial outworking at home has been hidden from public view and little attention has been paid to the analysis of this labour process: it has been for long ignored or portrayed as peripheral. Literally, homework appears to fade into the domestic realm and it is not seen even in the eyes of homeworkers as real.

One purpose of this study is to try to make homeworkers visible as workers. The socio-economic niche of homeworking activities is identified in the chains of sub-contracting, and the working conditions of homeworkers are specified based on the results of the empirical investigation. This work is intended to draw the attention of activists and scholars to the difficulties faced by homeworkers, and thus to contribute toward improvement of the lives of these women.

The orthodox Marxist approach to the issues of female labour has been regarded as sex-blind.[2] This criticism is very relevant: the importance of the household and the domestic milieu as factors which condition women's participation in the labour force needs to be stressed in any discussion about homeworking. The second part of this chapter is devoted to discussion of the ideological background which serves to generate and reproduce homeworkers. The influence exercised by the ideology of domesticity and women's definition of their roles as mothers/wives within the domestic sphere is specified. Following this, possible strategies are outlined to remove homeworkers' social and political isolation, especially in relation to initiatives for organising.

The presentation of empirical data and the corresponding conclusions are preceded by a brief discussion of the concept of homework. Homeworkers are generally defined as persons working at or from home for payment of some kind under a variety of contractual arrangements.

307

There is an assertion that homeworkers should be acknowledged as self-employed entrepreneurs or independent contractors (S. Dakahuji, 1972: 129–59). Homeworkers may be independent contractors trading on their own account in the sense that they could exercise control over the pacing and timing of work, with full or partial economic ownership of the means of production. In practice, however, their obligations to the supplier and conditions of employment are those of employees. The supplier establishes the hours of work through the times set for the delivery and collection of work and payment by the piece.[3] Thus, their earnings are limited not by their willingness to work, but by the availability of work and the allocation of work with different piece rates. The means of production which they own, such as tools and machinery, are generally low-cost at best, a second-hand sewing machine or an iron.

METHODOLOGY

Manufacturing firms, especially small-scale firms, have experienced a drain of labour and difficulty in recruiting on-site workers in South Korea since the late 1980s.[4] Increasing numbers of young unmarried women prefer working in the service sector to manufacturing, and the number of young women in factories has decreased. Very few young unmarried women tend to be involved in homeworking, which provides much lower remuneration than on-site working.

In the empirical investigation, the research subjects were confined to presently- or ever-married women residing in poor areas of Seoul. We selected areas designated as poor by the Seoul Municipal Government. In these areas approximately 110 000 households were distributed among 103 blocks of unequal but known size. A sample selection of cluster samples with probabilities proportional to size[5] was employed in order to produce an equal probability in selecting 20 sample blocks.

The total number of presently- and ever-married women under 66 years of age in these selected sample areas was 8050. Among them, 438 women were recorded as homeworkers. Of these, 415 women homeworkers were interviewed. Interviews with the remaining 23 homeworkers could not be completed due to refusal or long-term absence. A questionnaire covering all 415 women was used to collect data on family income, labour relations and attitudes relating to homework. A second questionnaire (usually accompanied by open-ended interviews) was applied to a selection of 10 women in order to achieve detailed information about instability and health hazards of homework, as well as occupational histories.

Interviews with employers, managers and workshop proprietors involved in industrial outworking were conducted in order to investigate sub-contracting arrangements. Official statistics of firms fail to provide direct information about the scope of firms employing homeworkers. Only the Report on Mining and Manufacturing Survey (Economic Planning Board, 1987) listed 'the cost paid for contract work'. On the assumption that this cost of small-scale firms of five-to-nine employees should be the labour cost for employing homeworkers, we selected industries in which the rate of that cost to the total production cost was high. As a result, major labour-intensive manufacturing industries of textiles, garments, leather products, and toys and dolls were selected. However, many firms were difficult to study due to their reluctance to speak about sub-contracting relations. We managed to interview primary firms of outwear knitting, shirt-making, luggage-making and toy-making. These represented the textile, garment, leather products, and toys and dolls industries, respectively. Interviews with agents situated at different levels from the top of the chain to the bottom were conducted wherever possible: interviews with 11 firms altogether were completed.

The household survey on the economic activities of married women and the working conditions of homeworkers was carried out from 25 June to 27 July, while the firm survey was carried out from June to September 1989.

THE EXTENT AND CLASSIFICATION OF HOMEWORK

Although women homeworkers are easily observed in urban poor areas in South Korea, it is not an easy job to show the extent of homeworking empirically. This is largely because of the very nature of that work, with dispersion of work places as well as a floating employment situation.

Many people who work at home are unlikely to reveal this fact to researchers. Since homeworking for the most part belongs to the underground economy, homeworkers may fear that revealing the existence of such work may result in negative consequences, such as taxation or loss of work. More critical difficulties come from the fact that the employment status of homeworkers varies with the supply of the work. For example, the research subjects in this study were operationally limited to married women who had participated in homework during a reference week. Those who worked at home two weeks earlier but not in the previous week because the homework was intermittent or irregular were excluded.

The results of our survey give some idea of the density of homeworking

Table 13.1   Percentage of Homework by Industry

Industry/per cent/number of homeworkers in survey	Kinds of homework
Textiles 42.4% (176) and garments	sweater stitching (37), suit stitching (26), machine sewing of suits (24), making bed clothes (15), machine sewing of hats, outer socks, scarves (12), machine knitting (11), removal of thread from hat, sweater, etc. (11), hand knitting (9), stitching of hats, outer socks, scarves (8), hand embroidery (7), machine embroidery (4), sewing Korean costume (4), other (8)
Leather 14.7% (61) products and footwear	machine sewing of luggage (15), knotting of jogging shoes (11), fixing buttons or other accessories (9), accessories (9), removal of thread (6), machine sewing of jackets (5), machine sewing of boots (5), machine sewing of gloves (5), leather pasting (5)
Fabricated 7.5% (31) metals, machinery and equipment	electronic component assembly (16), electric component assembly (14), other (1)
Paper and 5.8% (24) paper products	making paper bags (16), packing paper products (4), wrapping of wooden chopsticks (3), other (1)
Food and 4.3% (18) beverages	garlic-peeling (14), treating dry fish (2), other (2)
Others 25.3% (105)	trinket assembly (32), toy-making (17), pasting (17), artificial flowers (14), other crafts (9), wig-making (5), other (11)

in urban poor regions, though these results should be interpreted with caution. These factors mentioned above may result in underestimation of the extent of homeworking. The number of homeworkers in poor districts of Seoul was 5.4 per cent of the total married women, and 9.4 per cent of the total married women in the labour market at the time of the survey. Thus, about one in ten working women in low-income urban areas was engaged in homeworking. This portion of the workforce is too substantial to be ignored.

The products produced by homeworkers are incorporated by firms into their final product. Table 13.1 shows the wide range of miscellaneous activities in which homeworkers of our survey are involved. These industrial outworking operations, despite their differences, have a number of common characteristics. The major similarity is that all are industrial rather than artisanal activities, representing a single stage or sub-process in the creation of a final product for the market such as pasting, sewing a piece, assembling and putting together. It results from a specialised division of labour, made possible by a fragmentation of the labour process which exemplifies modern industrial production.

Most homeworkers said that they started to work after either a simple demonstration by the supplier/intermediary or a half-day-long training session in workshops. That is, this work involves intensive manual labour in tasks that are highly specialised and monotonous, which nevertheless require only a minimum of formal qualification and a minimal need for quality control. Interviews conducted with homeworkers confirm this fact. Therefore, these parts of the production line can be shifted to homes, and piece-work can be controlled easily even though these parts of the production process are physically separated from the overall process.

These assembly-type operations have proved difficult and/or costly to mechanise further, and thus homeworking has fulfilled a function outside the work of the mechanised manufacturing industries (K. Hirota, 1969). Homeworking is extensive in the labour-intensive manufacturing industries in South Korea.

Changes in the political and economic situation of South Korea which have affected the extent and relations of sub-contracting must also be mentioned. First of all, domestic and foreign markets have become increasingly unstable due to exogenous variables such as oil shock, floating exchange rates, and severe competition in foreign trade since the late 1970s. Trends in fashions and seasonal changes contribute to this instability as well. Industry has looked for a new flexible labour force which can be readily dismissed and re-employed according to the ups and downs of the market.

As a domestic factor, Korean workers have become more conscious of their rights, and the general level of wages has increased with the active civil rights movement and labour movement since the middle of the 1980s. Employers in labour-intensive manufacturing industries have experienced difficulties in attracting a sufficient number of full-time workers, partly because of the low pay, and partly because of the employers' inability to manage their labour force.

Sub-contracting has become extensive in the manufacturing industry. Of small- and medium-scale manufacturing firms of 300 employees or less, sub-contracting firms accounted only for 17.4 per cent in 1970, but this figure increased to 19.7 per cent in 1976, 37.7 per cent in 1982, and

48.1 per cent in 1987 (Korean Federation of Small Business, 1988: 320–25). Textile and garment industries in particular resorted to sub-contracting; firms in textile and garment industries paid 12.1 per cent of total production costs to outside workers in 1987, compared to a 6.2 per cent average in all industry. In the case of small-scale textile and garment firms of five-to-nine employees, this figure accounted for 24.8 per cent of total production costs in 1987, most of which was probably paid for homeworkers.

As much evidence shows, homeworking has developed as an integral part of the industrialisation process of South Korea within the orbit of the world market economy. Dependence on homeworking will, therefore, survive and even prevail as long as low-wage labour in the home is in good supply.

THE SUB-CONTRACTING CHAINS

According to M. Roldan (1985: 258), the chains of sub-contractual relations into which industrial homeworkers are integrated are made up of enterprises of different sizes: multinational corporations producing commodities directly for the market, factories producing these types of final products or components, small workshops, and the intermediaries who supply the inputs. This is more or less true in the South Korean case also. Based on the results of the firm survey, this part of the chapter is devoted to specifying the ways in which homeworking is incorporated into sub-contracting links, with an emphasis on the impetus of employing homeworkers.

Sub-contracting in Shirt Manufacturing

A big firm (H), with more than 600 workers, has been producing and exporting men's shirts to the United States of America, Canada, etc. This firm has faced difficulties in managing workers since trade unions became more militant. Firm H stopped increasing production lines, relying instead on sub-contractors for excess orders, or for cheap items. As of 1988 it carried on transactions with about ten sub-contractors.

Firm D, with 100 workers, is one of such sub-contractors, and it has managed to cope with order fluctuation through expanding transactions with other primary companies besides firm H. As seen in Figure 13.1, firms H and D both utilise homeworkers for the removal of bits of thread. The machine which automates the process of removing bits of thread is

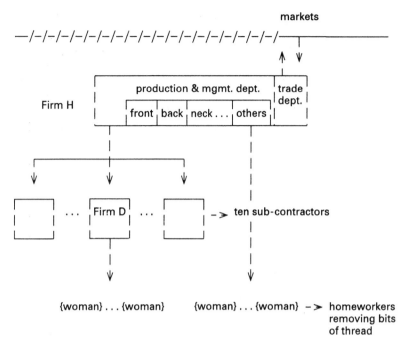

Figure 13.1   Sub-contracting Relations (Firms H, D)

quite expensive, and firm D totally depends on homeworkers for this process. There is a manager in charge of recruiting homeworkers, distributing raw materials to homeworkers, and collecting the finished products.

Although both firms report that the major impetus behind the workforce of homeworkers is flexibility and the avoidance of militancy of organised workers, it is clear that cutting costs is also an important goal. The present piece-rate for removing bits of thread for one shirt is 18 won (2.4 pennies). When homeworkers do this work for ten hours a day, they usually complete 250–300 pieces and earn 4500–5400 won a day. If they worked the same number of hours in a factory, their daily wage would be 6600 won.[6] By substituting on-site workers with homeworkers, contractors and sub-contractors can reduce the wage by 1200–2100 won per worker per day.

Employers can reduce not only wages but also allowances for holidays and sick leave, bonuses, pensions and welfare expenses and overhead. As Table 13.2 shows, the labour cost of in-workers reflects several kinds of expenditure. Since homeworkers are paid at best the 'fixed' wage, they make about half the factory worker's rate (57.3 per cent).

Table 13.2   Average Monthly Labour Costs of Manufacturing Workers

	Units: 1000 won	Per cent
Fixed pay	227	57.3
Overtime	57	14.3
Bonus	49	12.5
Pension	22	5.6
Legal welfare	7	1.8
Other welfare	25	6.3
Goods	3	0.8
Job training	4	1.0
Other	25	6.3
Total	396	100.0

Source: Ministry of Labour (1988), *A Report on Labour Costs per Workers*, p. 26.

Sub-contracting in Outwear Knitting

This category shows similar results with the earlier category in terms of sub-contracting structure and motives for recruiting homeworkers. Firm A, a sub-contractor, produces finished goods by employing a minimum number of experienced skilled workers, utilising homeworkers in part of the production process.[7] It is important to note in the case of firm A, that skilled homeworkers are paid far less than their counterparts in on-site factories.

For example, one woman in the survey had worked for a garment factory for seven years prior to her marriage. When her second child was born, she started taking in homework making buttonholes with a special sewing machine, which requires skill. Working around 63 hours a week, she could manage to earn 300 000 won per month. The starting wages of skilled workers of firm A working 56 hours a week was 300 000–400 000 won. The homeworker's hourly wage (1190 won) accounted for 67–87 per cent of the wages of her counterparts in firm A, whose hourly wages were 1340–1790 won. Thus, the employer of firm A can save anywhere between 20 per cent and 40 per cent on homeworkers.

Although most homework requires a minimum of formal training, firms are now increasingly depending on skilled homeworkers such as machine sewers and knitters for more complicated work processes. These women are recruited from a pool of ex-workers formerly employed by these firms.

A significant minority of homeworkers, relatively skilled, were found to work for the firms at which they had previously been employed as in-workers.

Sub-contracting in Luggage Manufacturing

Firm C was established in 1984 with 70 manufacturing workers, but in 1987 closed down its factory due to increasing labour costs and trade union activity. Furthermore, there had been seasonal fluctuation. The total quantity of outside orders usually increases from May to August and decreases in winter. Since then, this firm has operated like a big retailer. All products are exported to the USA and France.

At present firm C deals with seven sub-contractors including firms K and L regularly, and also deals periodically with 10–13 sub-contractors. Although firm K is the largest firm among the sub-contractors, it employs only 11 full-time workers, These include three sewing-machine technicians, two semi-skilled mechanics, four sewing-machine assistants, and two persons in charge of managing homeworkers. The production processes of this firm consist largely of parts sewing, manual jobs and completing whole products from cut-out pieces. Homeworkers are used for both manual jobs such as pasting accessories and skilled jobs such as machine sewing of bag straps. Some of them act as intermediaries recruiting homeworkers in peak seasons, while also doing their own homeworking. Firm K has maintained inventories just sufficient to meet current demand to solve the problem of irregular and fluctuating orders, and to reduce labour costs.

One reason for firm K to recruit more homeworkers is to cut costs. The manager and owner of firm K explained the mechanism to decide homeworkers' piece rate: if an in-worker completes 1000 pieces per hour, a homeworker is assumed to do 1150–1200 pieces per hour. This firm profits about 100 000 won per month per homeworker.

Evidence from the firm survey showed clearly that homeworking is an integral part of a total labour process involving all levels and phases of the capitalist production of a final product. The primary impetus behind this home-based workforce is to cut costs. By hiring homeworkers, the employer of firms D, H and K paid only for the work done, not for any lag-time between projects. Thus, firms were very efficient in the pursuit of low-cost production for export.

'Remaining flexible' was most often mentioned, followed by 'reducing costs'. In fact, many firms have moved to a two-tiered workforce of core and peripheral workers in order to cope with variations in the volume of

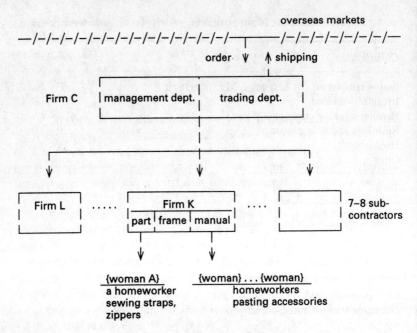

Figure 13.2   Sub-contracting Relations (Firms C, K)

orders without cost to the company. While the core consists of full-time waged employees just sufficient to meet current demand, the peripheral rings consist of workers hired under casualised conditions; the workforce can be reduced, expanded or redeployed according to demand.

Labour-intensive industries in South Korea have faced growing pressures and organisation from their workforce and general reduction in the regular workforce due to the relatively poor working conditions,[8] as firm D among the firms surveyed confessed. These industries have reduced or even closed down production lines and resort to domestic outworkers. Work at home may have been intended to be a supplement to full-time work, but it is now increasingly used as a substitute for full-time labour.

WORKING CONDITIONS OF HOMEWORKERS

The location of homeworking as the lowest links of this total sub-contracting chain gives a rough idea about working conditions. The empirical results do not counter this expectation. When questioned about the most unsatisfactory aspect of homework, as shown in Table 13.3, five problems were

Table 13.3   The Most Unsatisfactory Aspects of Homework

Classification	Number (%)
Low wage	119 (28.6)
Irregular workload	96 (23.2)
Harmful working environment	67 (16.2)
Rush jobs and time pressure	64 (15.5)
Hard labour	52 (12.6)
Other	16 (3.9)
Total	414[*] (100.0)

[*] One non-respondent was excluded.

cited: a) low wages; b) irregular workload, c) harmful working environment (excessive noise, dust, and bad odour from synthetic glue); d) rush jobs and time pressure: and e) the hard labour. These constitute the fundamental characteristics of most homework.

Low Income and Long Hours

All the homeworkers were paid at piece-work rates. The respondents of this study displayed wide variation regarding piece-rates. For example, one earned 0.6 won for bending one ring for luggage accessories, while another earned 15 000 won for weaving a roll of silk cloth, which took four or five days. The average wage of the homeworkers corresponded to 26.3 per cent and 52.8 per cent of the average wage of male factory workers and married female factory workers, respectively. Among homeworkers, machine sewers earned the highest wages, 194 000 won a month, while the garlic-peeling workers earned the least: 47 640 won a month.

However, it is not meaningful to compare monthly wages of homeworkers with factory workers because total working hours of homeworkers may also be shorter than those of factory workers. As shown in Table 13.4, the average hourly wage of the respondents was 627.4 won which was 77.7 per cent of the wage (807.7 won) of married female factory workers.

Homeworkers' wages are calculated by multiplying the piece-rate by the number of items. Payment by results establishes an immediate connection between payment and pieces produced. Their work and intensity of work are determined by it, and the low piece-rates make long hours essential.

Table 13.4   Statistics for Homeworkers versus Factory Workers in
Manufacturing Industries

Classification	Avg. age	Working hours per day	Days per month	Monthly working hours	Monthly income (Won)	Hourly wage* (Won)
Men workers in manufacturing factories (married or unmarried) **						
	32.3	9.57	25.1	240.2	398 511	1 659
Married women workers in manufacturing factories **						
	38.9	9.77	25.2	246.2	198 782	808
Married women homeworkers in manufacturing ***						
	35.3	7.74	21.6	167.2	104 894	627

*   Wage per hour = monthly income/monthly working hours.
**   Source: Ministry of Labour (1987), *Report on Occupational Wage Survey*, pp. 1910–11.
***   Source: Average data of 415 homeworkers of our survey.

Although homeworkers are paid by piece-rates, the wages are not paid daily or immediately after goods are delivered to sub-contractors. Most of the respondents (82.3 per cent) received wages once a month, since sub-contractors tended to pay homeworkers only after they were paid by primary firms, usually at the end of a month. Thus homeworkers are often subjected to their wages being overdue. During the in-depth interviews, homeworkers said that payments were often three to five days delayed.

Homeworkers work on the average 7.7 hours a day for 21.6 days in a month. The average monthly working hours correspond to 67.9 per cent of those of married women in factories in 1987. But 32.3 per cent of the total number of home-based workers in the survey work at least eight hours daily, and 25 days a month. This means that a third of homeworkers work as much as married female factory workers. One of the prevalent images of homeworkers is that they are part-time workers who spend their time mainly caring and cleaning, with little time for homeworking. However, in terms of the number of working hours, these women are actually far more than part-time workers.

The freedom to fit paid work around housework and child-care is believed to distinguish homework from other kinds of paid employment. It is clear from our data that this scenario is misleading. The homeworker only rarely has a meaningful choice in how much work she takes on. The supplier sets the times for the collection of finished work. The homeworkers said that they often had to work to tight deadlines. When an urgent order was brought to the homeworker by her supplier, household chores had to be put off until late, or even until the following day so as to allow time for completion of the waged work. The real situation seems to be that homeworking, once provided, permits the worker to go on working until she drops, far from the claims of some suppliers that 'homework is done casually in front of the TV'.

According to S. Allen and C. Wolkowitz (1986: 243–4), the low piece-work rates and the need to have homework ready for collection form a mechanism to determine the homeworkers' pace, though control is not in the form of direct supervision.

Instability

Since one of the reasons for recruiting homeworkers is to cope with fluctuations in orders in an uncertain market, it is not surprising that almost 40 per cent of respondents listed the fluctuation in the volume of orders, rush jobs and pressure to meet deadlines as the worst aspect of industrial outworking. Homeworkers face uncertainty as to the amount of work, when it would be available, when it would have to be returned, and even the kind of work they would be given. The employment in home-based work is very unstable, and it does not guarantee an assured amount of income, given irregular and insufficient workloads.

More than a half of the homeworkers (56.1 per cent) said they either changed jobs or experienced unemployment at least once due to intermittent work orders during the year prior to the survey; their employment status alternated between on-site work and homework, or between one operation of the homeworking and the other operation. The homeworkers surveyed were unemployed for an average of five months during the year. The extracts from the interviews give a clear illustration of the lack of employment security.

Woman P was involved in the assembling of electronic parts for cassette tape recorders. She was employed for only seven months and unemployed for five months during the year prior to the survey, that is, August of 1988 to July of 1989. The work was given intermittently, and even when the work was provided, there were weekly or seasonal variations in the amount supplied. Nevertheless, she was expected to complete the work, filling rush and seasonal orders as necessary and going without her income when no work was supplied.

Woman Q was in a more unstable situation. She said she tried to take whatever jobs were available for her. The insufficient workload and low

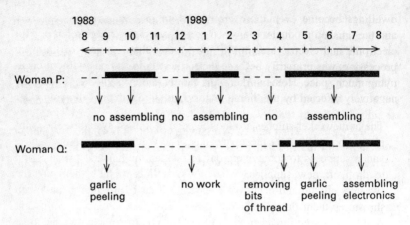

Figure 13.3   Two Examples of Lack of Employment Security

wages of homework were mentioned as the reasons for the frequent changes in her employment situation.

Health Hazards in Home Factories

The home becomes the work place, but a normal house is not suitable for such production in terms of space and safety installations. The labour process of homeworking is not only dull, but even harmful with potential nuisances such as noise, dust, odours and fumes. The use of domestic space causes, first of all, health hazards to the workers and their families. In fact, health and related problems were the major reason that homeworking was resented by family members, causing general upset in the family. In most cases, dissatisfaction was expressed in terms of 'the mess in the house from all the fluff' or inconvenience.

Some women in our survey worked with organic solvents, or with glue, in unventilated rooms. These women and their families were exposed to possible danger of developing toxic symptoms due to the detrimental work environments. Some interviews with the homeworkers of machine sewing or machine knitting were difficult to conduct not because of their refusal but because of the dust and noise from sewing or knitting machines. These homeworkers were co-operative to our survey but were unwilling to stop working for fear of failing to meet their deadline. These interviews were barely completed by revisits in late evening or early morning.

In addition, 'storage' aggravates the situation. Half the women in the survey reported that they lived in a house of one room. Already tiny dwellings become even more crowded with raw materials, accessories, and the finished products. Many women revealed that their preference for electronic and electric assembling jobs, rather than garment or knitwear processing, was primarily because the former could be done without occupying much space. Homeworkers, the family and even the neighbours are negatively affected by the 'home factory', as shown in the following case.

The homeworker stitches around the edge of knitted sweaters; she completes about 500–600 pieces per day. The volume is enormous, and a van is supposed to come every day to pick up the finished sweaters and to drop off new supplies. When the van fails to pick them up, the sweaters pile up and occupy the space for four family members. When she stores them outside her one-room house, the neighbors complain. And the dust and thread from sweaters become too much, and she must stop this work at times.

WHO ARE THE HOMEWORKERS?

A primary question is, why is it women who are so disproportionately represented in homeworking? Some crucial answers lie in the requirements laid on women in a family situation. What type of family context is most likely to provide female outworkers? First of all, class position and income level of homeworkers's family need to be analysed.

According to the household survey, the majority of homeworkers' husbands (93.2 per cent) worked in production and related sectors including construction workers, unskilled or semi-skilled mechanics, and taxi or truck drivers. Only 0.8 per cent were engaged in professional or managerial occupations. They earned on the average about 366 000 won during the previous month, which is somewhat less than two-thirds of the 560 000 won which constituted the average urban worker's income during a comparable period (Korean Economic Planning Board, *Monthly Statistics of Korea*, 1989, No. 9: 100).

Furthermore, there is no guarantee to earn even that low wage monthly income because the employment status of most husbands was casual rather than stable and permanent. The earning of women homeworkers which was on the average 100 000 won makes an indispensable contribution to the family living. On the basis of the data presented above, the level of the husband's earnings was an important factor in determining women's participation in income-earning activities such as homeworking.

Another significant factor is the importance attached to the women's

Table 13.5   Demographic Characteristics for On-site Married Women Workers and Homeworkers (urban area only)

Age	On-site* (%)	Homeworkers (%)
less than 30	20.4	26.2
30–34	18.8	31.2
35–39	15.8	18.2
40–49	27.8	16.7
over 50	17.2	7.7
Total	100.0	100.0
Pre-school children at home	30.7	34.2

*   Source: Korean Women's Development Institute, 1986, *A Study of Women's Employment*, pp. 51–62.

role in the house. Women homeworkers are further analysed in terms of their position within the family. Women in low-income families are in need of gainful employment, but face difficulties in entering the formal workforce. The typical woman outworker is in the ascendant phase of the family cycle, children are still young and dependent, therefore requiring longer periods of close attention.

As seen in Table 13.5, homeworkers were more likely to be younger than conventional workers; more than a half of the homeworkers were 35 years of age or younger, which would suggest that young children were over-represented among homeworkers. Though the rate of having at least one pre-school child was not much higher in homeworkers than in-workers, nearly half of the women (44.8 per cent) had at home either children under six years old or a sick or disabled family member. These women are expected to adjust their paid work around family responsibilities.

In response to questions concerning their reasons for homeworking, three-quarters of our sample cited the obligations of child-care and housework, while a quarter named 'poor health' and 'no other jobs available'. Two-thirds of the respondents expressed their willingness to remain as homeworkers even if jobs with better work conditions were provided, or even if children were grown up. The clearest example we found of it was the homeworker who stated:

Grown-up children still need a mother as much as or even more strongly than babies. I have a daughter of ten years old and a son of eight years old. Thus, I have no babies requiring close attention, but I cannot go out and earn. As you know, things are getting hostile for teenagers. There should be a person at home to protect my daughter from kidnapping and making prostitutes by force and to keep my son out of the growing rate of juvenile delinquency.

In fact, the decision to do homework seems frequently to be made by the husband. During the in-depth interviews the husband's opinion was proved to be crucial. The husbands expected their wives to fit with their definition of satisfactory family life or acceptable standards of housekeeping. More usually the husband's preferences for a wife at home was explained in terms of the wife's obligations to their children. They also made preferences to their own needs. They showed a high expectation that the wife should fit in with the husband's routine:

My husband is a taxi driver. He starts his work at 3.00 p.m. and he finishes the work at 3 or 4 o'clock the following morning under a shift system. He expects me to be in when he gets in from work. He doesn't like being in an empty house.

It is true that homeworking enables mothers to be at home with children young enough to require the presence of an adult, and wives to undertake the household chores. But it does not mean that these women look after all of their 'duties' properly. Homeworking is not as readily combined with the care of young children as is sometimes supposed.

Since they work as much on a full-time basis (when work is given) as women going out to work, they face most of the same problems, or they are more constrained than those who go out to work. Homeworkers experience the two sets of constraints simultaneously on a day-to-day basis. According to Allen and Wolkowitz (1986: 262–3), homeworking is very far from being a boon to women, for instead of liberating them from or reducing the burden of the 'double day' it intensifies the pressures of both waged work and unpaid domestic labour. Indeed in many respects homeworking is more onerous than going out to work, partly because there is no spatial separation between paid and unpaid work. The homeworker's family still expects the services of a full-time housewife. The domestic sphere incorporates other work obligations enforced by the explicit demands and implicit expectations of other family members. Autonomy will remain as a highly functional myth.

However, due to the taken-for granted ideological expectations of division of labour, a high priority is given to 'working at home'. By accepting the primacy of their family responsibilities and the supposedly subsidiary importance of their paid employment, women usually put up with unsuitable conditions such as low piece-rates, no fringe benefits, insecure or uncertain employment, irregular workloads, and harmful working environment, saying, 'it is better than nothing'.

Homework also becomes the wife's choice in the use of her free time rather than an extension of the working day. The homeworker is discouraged from seeing herself as a regular worker and earning a regular wage. The husband interprets her work as leisure-time activity, and prefers to ignore the reasons why women are forced to accept such low-paid work. However, many of the husbands are well aware of the competing demands for their wives' labour, and of the importance of meeting these demands for the functioning of the household. These husbands benefit materially from homeworkers' earnings, while they are still able to enjoy the status traditionally associated with being able to keep a wife at home.

CONCLUSION AND ORGANISATIONAL IMPLICATIONS

The empirical data collected in this survey showed the extent of the involvement in homeworking of married women in low-income strata, and that the decision to work at home was by-and-large made on the basis of a lack of viable alternatives, the limited care system, and/or the women's socially-defined responsibilities of running the family.

This chapter also characterised homework as a distinctive and highly exploitative form of work. Women are regarded as 'helping hands' at best, since they work in the home. Poor labour conditions prevail. Working at home probably precludes the development of a national policy of child-and-early-care support, and does not challenge the place of women within the home.

Women's entry into the labour market may be a source of social relationships outside the home, but industrial homeworking serves to isolate women further. Since all they see are the agent who collects and pays for the finished product, they are hardly conscious of the fact that the subcontractors of various levels make a profit on their labour. Their consciousness as workers is not developed, nor their working-class solidarity.

Furthermore, low wages, long hours, unhealthy sanitary conditions and inadequate safety standards for industrial homeworkers can threaten the labour and employment conditions of factory workers generally. They could be used as weapons against their sisters in the organised manufacturing sector when the latter make demands.

Optimally, the very existence of industrial homework in contemporary

Korean society should be ultimately abolished, and incorporated into formal external waged labour. This is in accord with the position and conclusions adopted by regional and international conferences. For example, a tripartite technical meeting concerning industrial homework sponsored by the International Labour Organisation (ILO, 1980: 112–13) asserted this strategy in its Resolution No. 2.

Recently, neighbourhood workshops have come into existence where women in communities come together to do what had been only home-based work previously in South Korea. These workshops provide a flexible work pattern, allowing women to go home two or three times a day for feeding, caring for children, etc. This arrangement has been established for the purpose of maintaining quality control and supervision of workers by manufacturing firms which have had difficulties in attracting in-workers. But women have a chance to stay together in this context, and to develop social relations with other women workers. In this sense, even workshops may serve as an intermediate stage between factory and homeworkers.

But it will take time before few women are engaged in homework. The Resolution also took the impossibility of this elimination into consideration and argues for strict application of government regulations in an attempt to ensure that labour conditions and social security standards of industrial homeworkers are to the maximum possible extent identical with those of factory workers.

The state should take part with a number of relevant policies and legislation. It is necessary to provide homeworkers with legal protection by an amendment in the labour law, whereby homeworkers' basic rights and minimum levels of piece-rate pay should be guaranteed. There should also be regulations to end unfair employment practices, and to extend legal liabilities along the sub-contracting chain. It is also necessary to point out the fact that the state has played a role in creating exploitative conditions of work by doing nothing to help women combine their domestic responsibilities with paid work. Through this, we could influence government officials to concentrate on developing conditions under which the decision to work at home is truly one of free choice.

However, there are inherent difficulties in effectively controlling industrial homework, and the state's efforts may be seriously limited. In Japan, the Homeworkers Protection Law – including legislation of minimum wage and registration of homeworkers, agents and employers, the duty to write a contract between homeworkers and agents about the wage, due date, etc. and provisions on safety and protection from health hazards – was established in 1971 when the number of homeworkers reached two million. The 20 years' experience of Japan demonstrates that these regulations are exceedingly difficult to enforce in terms of coverage, implementation and relevance in the context of homeworking. Thus, most of these regulations are more honoured in the breach than in compliance.

More practical strategy for action in relation to homeworking is for women to unite their own forces. This uniting could be created and sustained by organising. In South Korea, casual workers, including construction workers, have created unions. Though organising homeworkers is probably more difficult than organising construction workers, since at least the latter work together on site, organising homeworkers is not impossible.

During the workers' struggles of 1987–8 which brought about the social and political democratisation of the country, married women as wives of workers made an authentic contribution to the defence of workers' struggles, carrying their babies on their backs; this was known as 'family struggle'. What is needed is a long process of consciousness-raising about work conditions, women's location in the family, and their relation to the overall situation of Korean economy.

Fortunately, there are a number of devoted women activists and organisations, including the Korean Working Women's Association. Such organisations have established support structures in urban poor areas and have provided useful information related to improving wages and working conditions along with child-care services to women workers. They have also dealt with issues such as domestic violence and housing rent.

These women workers' associations should make efforts to build links among homeworkers and between homeworkers and women in-workers. They should help homeworkers to define their own experiences of oppression and develop their own framework for struggle against it. They should also continue to support homeworkers to enter into the organised production sector whenever possible.

Lastly, trade unions and women on-site must begin to think creatively about linking with women working in isolation in the home, as work moves increasingly into smaller, non-factory-based units and membership of traditional unions tends to dwindle during the industrial restructuring process.

NOTES

1. The data analysed in this article were originally collected for *A Study on Home-based Production in South Korea* published by the Korean Women's Development Institute (KWDI) in 1989. This research was directed by me in collaboration with colleagues of KWDI; a colleague and I also carried out the in-depth interviews. Our thanks to 20 women interviewers, and to the homeworkers who spared precious time to answer our questionnaire. Finally, I am indebted to the participants of the workshop and especially to Renée Pittin and Amrita Chhachhi for detailed criticisms and suggestions on an earlier draft.

2. For some important discussions, see, for example, V. Beechey, 1983, 'What's So Special about Women's Employment?: A View of Some Recent Studies of Women's Paid Work', *Feminist Review*. No. 15 (Winter); N. Folbre, 1982, 'Exploitation Comes Home: A Critique of the Marxian Theory of Family Labour', *Cambridge Journal of Economics*, Vol. 6, No. 4; and H. Hartmann, 1979, 'The Unhappy Marriage of Marxism and Feminism: Towards a More Progressive Union', *Capital & Class*, No. 8.

3. In the cases brought before industrial tribunals by homeworkers seeking to establish their right to benefits conferred on employees by the Employment Protection Act 1978 in the UK, tribunals judged in one case that insofar as the supplier of work determines 'the thing to be done, the manner of performance, and in reality the time and place of performance', the homeworkers should be considered as employees, with the same rights and benefits as other employees (Airfix Footwear vs. Cope (1978) quoted in Allen & Wolkowitz, 1986: 240–2).

4. According to the *Annual Report on the Labour Demand Survey* of the Ministry of Labour, the vacancy rate (the number of vacancies over the total number of employees) in production and related occupations increased from 3.20 per cent in 1986 to 6.85 per cent in 1990. Thus, the estimated number of workers needed nationwide reached 166 000 in the corresponding jobs.

5. For further information on PPS sampling, see P. H. Rossi, J. D. Wright and A. B. Anderson, *Handbook of Survey Research*, NY, Academic Press, 1983: 60–2.

6. The premium rate for overtime was 1.5 times the regular wage, and the wage for a regular working hour for Firm D was 600 won. Thus, the wage for an eight-hour working day and two hours' overtime was 6600 won.

7. The same strategy was also observed in a toy manufacturing firm (G) which had had difficulty in coping with the extreme fluctuation in orders, as seen in Figure 13.4.

8. A report of the US Bureau of National Affairs (BNA) provides comparative data demonstrating that the use of contracting was higher in highly unionised firms than in other firms in 1986 in the USA.

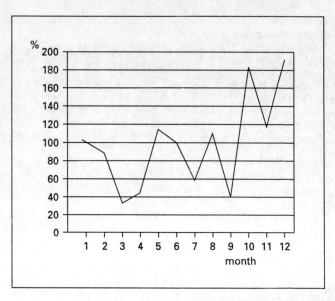

Figure 13.4 Fluctuation in Monthly Sales of Firm G, 1988 (sales in June = 100.0 per cent)

REFERENCES

Allen, S. and C. Wolkowitz. 1986. 'Homeworking and the Control of Women's Work', Feminist Review (ed.), *Waged Work: A Reader*, Virago, London.

Beechey, V. 1983. 'What's So Special about Women's Employment?: A View of Some Recent Studies of Women's Paid Work', *Feminist Review*, No. 15, Winter.

Beechey, V. and T. Perkins. 1987. *A Matter of Hours: Women, Part-time Work and the Labour Market*, Polity Press, London.

Cho, Hyung. 1985. 'Women's Labor in the Informal Sector', *Korean Women and Work*, Ewha Woman's University Press, Scoul.

Christensen, K. E. (ed.). 1988. *The New Era of Home-based Work*, Westview Press, New York.

Dakahuji, S. 1972. 'Legal Characteristics of Homeworkers', *Social Study of The Labour in Japan*, Vol. 18, No. 1.

Folbre, N. 1982. 'Exploitation Comes from Home: A Critique of the Marxian Theory of Family Labour', *Cambridge Journal of Economics*, Vol. 6, No. 4.

Hartmann, H. 1979. 'The Unhappy Marriage of Marxism and Feminism: Towards a More Progressive Union', *Capital & Class*, No. 8.

Hirota, Kazuko. 1969. 'Variation and Background of Work at Home', *Journal of the Japanese Labor Association*, No. 120, March.

International Labour Office. 1980. *Standards and Policy Statements of Special Interest to Women Workers*, ILO, Geneva.

Kim, Jae-won. 1983. *A Survey on Subcontracting in Korea*, Study Series No. 83–06, Korea Development Institute, Seoul.

Kim, Young-ock. 1986. 'The Position of Women Workers in the Manufacturing Industries in South Korea', Working Paper No. 6, Sub-series on Women, History and Development, Institute of Social Studies, The Hague.

Korean Economic Planning Board. 1987. *Report on Mining and Manufacturing Survey*, KEPB, Seoul.

Korean Economic Planning Board. 1989. *Report on the Second Nationwide Employment Structure Survey*, KEBP, Seoul.

Korean Economic Planning Board. 1989, 1990. *Monthly Statistics of Korea*, KEPB, Seoul.

Korean Federation of Small Business. 1988. *Report on the Present Conditions of Small Business*, KFSB, Seoul.

Korean Women's Development Institute. 1986. *A Study of Women's Employment*, KWDI, Seoul.

Korean Women's Development Institute. 1988. *Childcare and Environment in the Low-Income Areas*, KWDI, Seoul.

Korean Women's Development Institute. 1989. *A Study on Home-based Production in South Korea*, KWDI, Seoul.

Mitter, S. and A. van Luyken. 1983. 'A Woman's Home is Her Factory', in W. Chapkis and C. Enloe (eds), *Of Common Cloth: Women in the Global Textile Industry*, Transnational Institute, Amsterdam.

Ministry of Labour. 1987. *A Report on Occupational Wage Survey*, MOL, Seoul.

Ministry of Labour. 1988. *A Report on Labour Costs per Workers*, MOL, Seoul.

Ministry of Labour. 1986, 1987, 1988, 1989, 1990. *Annual Report on the Labour Demand Survey*, MOL, Seoul.

Pineda-Ofreneo, P. 1982. 'Philippine Domestic Outwork: Subcontracting for Export-Oriented Industries', *Journal of Contemporary Asia*, No. 12–13, pp. 281–93.

Roldan, M. 1985. 'Industrial Outworking, Struggles for the Reproduction of Working-class Families and Gender Subordination', N. Redclift and E. Mingione (eds), *Beyond Employment*, Basil Blackwell, Oxford.

Rossi, P. H., J. D. Wright and A. B. Anderson. 1983. *Handbook of Survey Research*, Academic Press, NY.

Ryu, Jang-soo. 1986. 'A Study on Home-based work in Korea – A Case study of Taegu Area'. Unpublished MA Thesis, Seoul National University.

Vocational Training Research Institute. 1989. *A Survey of Inactive Labour Force and Utilization Strategies*, VTRI, Seoul.

14 Purple and Red Banners: Joint Strategies for Women Workers in the Informal Sector
Nandita Gandhi

This chapter examines the emergence of new unions in India which have organised women workers in the unorganised sector in new and innovative ways. The possibilities and the limitations of these organisations and the women's movement to develop strategies to transform class and gender relations are discussed and suggestions for joint strategies for future struggle are explored.

An economic and political crisis shadowed India during the decade of the 1970s. It was hardly what had been visualised when Indian leaders and planners after Independence placed their bets on the development model of rapid industrialisation and land reforms through Five Year Plans as the way to build a strong and self-sufficient country. After an initial spurt in economic growth, there was a steady decline into stagnation with glaring polarisations in society, poverty, unemployment and social confusion. People were losing faith in the government, political parties and the democratic process. For the first time, the ruling party, the Congress, was being rejected and coalitions of opposition parties formed in different states. There were massive demonstrations and movements throughout the country, some of which, such as the student movements, Navnirman in Gujarat and the Bihar movement, had emerged from outside the party structures. Radical student groups initiated a series of struggles. Some split from the communists and led agrarian upsurges which came to be called the Naxalite Movement. Others worked with caste, tribal, landless and impoverished groups. By the beginning of the 1980s, women took to protest and initiated a new phase of their movement.

This period of upheaval inevitably raised conceptual, organisational and strategic questions, as it saw the emergence of new organisations. Some of the organisations emerged from older ones, or were newly formed, some were small, others mass movements; some had a developed ideology whilst others struggled to form one. What was common to most of them was a criticism of traditional Left ideology and structures, of the existing structure of unionism and the neglect of workers in the unorganised sector. Some of these organisations, influenced by the women's movement, gradually realised the necessity of involving women and broadening the agenda of trade unions. The Chhatisgarh Mines Shramik Sanghatana (Mine Workers' Organisation), the Tamilnadu Construction Workers' Union, Bandhua Mukti Morcha (Bonded Labour Liberation Front), Self Employed Women's Association, the Kerala Fisherworkers' Union and the Chhatra Yuva Sangharsh Vahini (Young Students' Movement), were born during this period of crisis. These organisations reflected a new generation of activists. Working outside the traditional Left parties and other structures, they could highlight the theoretical and strategic blindspots and dogmatism of the established parties and unions. Although the established parties and their unions have a long history of hard work, of organising, of successes, failures, of compromises and obduracy, many of them have unfortunately become set in an economistic groove which substitutes for the creative application of Marxism. In addition, in spite of sincere intentions, they have neglected women workers in the formal and informal sector, their participation in the trade union and their issues.

TRADE UNIONS AND WOMEN WORKERS

Trade unionism has existed in India for over a century and grown in numbers and strength, successfully striving for better wages and conditions, unfortunately failing to prevent splits and intra-union rivalry, but on the whole firmly establishing workers' rights and struggles in society. We will focus here on trade unions which have, whether individual unionists consider themselves Left or not, derived their ideological strength, terminology and militancy from Marxism. The communists and socialists in India have strictly adhered to the Leninist understanding of Marxism and perceived unions as schools of solidarity and socialism, which at the day-to-day level protect workers and struggle against capitalism. Trade unions should feed into the larger labour movement which in turn would aid the revolutionary struggle, conducted by the vanguard party, for a socialist society.

The vanguard party was to concentrate mainly on industrial workers who were strategically located to bring capitalism to a halt, support them, develop their consciousness as a class and lead them to overthrow the wage system and ultimately capitalism. Workers who were not directly at the point of production such as most women workers, workers in the informal sector and the peasantry were considered peripheral and not the agents of revolutionary change. These oppressed groups, it was hoped, would in the course of the struggle join in, as they too had a stake in the formation of a new economic order and society.

This Marxist understanding was translated by the Indian Left parties into a strategy so stringent and literal that most agricultural workers (except in plantations), white collar workers and casual and contract workers were ignored. A break-up of the TU membership of all organised workers according to industry shows that:

40% of workers belong to manufacturing units;
25% of workers belong to the transport industry;
10% of workers belong to agriculture, forestry and fishing works.

(Ramaswamy, 1987)

Trade unions in India based their understanding and relation to women workers also on a Leninist framework.[1] They usually make a conscious effort to have women members. However, they have found that women usually participate in demonstrations, but are hardly ever interested in involving themselves in union work. The experiences of the Centre of Indian Trade Unions (CITU), one of the oldest national unions in the country, affiliated to the Communist Party of India (Marxist), which still has a sizeable following and a spirit of struggle, is typical. Its women's wing, the All India Co-ordination Committee of Working Women (AICCWW) was formed in 1979 in Madras in a meeting prior to the CITU convention. It was established as a national body with a membership of all CITU women's wings. It has no formal constitution of its own, but has separate state level meetings, holds elections from a general council of 500 members, and has a working committee of 300 members who represent 42 industries and services. Its objective is to provide a national forum for the problems of working women and influence their trade unions to encourage the participation of women in union activities.

The CITU and the AICCWW have spared no pains in urging men and women at every meeting to take up women's issues and encourage their participation. In 1982, B. T. Ranadive, then the president of the CITU, asked leaders of the Railways and Post and Telegraph to appoint special women's committees to work among women, because unions are not men's, but common organisations. However, until now, the membership of women workers in trade unions in India is a minuscule percentage of the total number of women workers.

Table 14.1 shows the low participation of women in trade unions. In a sample survey of 336 of its unions in Maharashtra, Tamilnadu and Kerala, the CITU found that:

Table 14.1   Trade Union Membership in India

Year unions registered	No. of returns	Submitted	Membership men	women	% of women to total membership
1961/2	11 614	7 087	3 607 039	370 164	9.3
1976	29 757	9 102	5 751 000	400 000	6.5
1977	30 810	9 005	5 548 000	486 000	8.1
1980	36 507	4 432	3 509 000	218 000	5.9
1981	37 539	6 687	5 012 000	385 000	7.1

Source: S. Sood, 1986.

women members of the union made up just 8% of the total membership, women office bearers were only 34. . . . In the industries where women constitute the overwhelming majority of the workforce – plantations, coir, bidi, tobacco, the executive of the union consisted mainly of male members and at conferences, they made up hardly 1 or 2 per cent of the delegates.

(AICCWW, 1987)

Most unions like the AICCWW are pained by women workers' indifference, and frankly admit that there are miles to go.

In the 1st convention it was found that women, even in industries and occupations where they formed a sizeable section were hardly represented in the leading bodies of the unions. After 7 years we are not in a position to say that the situation above has changed considerably . . . [whereas] the membership of the women in the union under socialism is about 45 per cent to 50 per cent of the total . . . In GDR the TU membership is 51 per cent . . .

(Vimal Ranadive, 1987)

What comes through clearly is the Marxist concern for women workers and what they termed as 'the woman's question'. Communists are aware that women are an oppressed group dominated by men, burdened with the drudgery of housework on one side and subsisting on low-paid work on the other. Since they constitute a large section of society, their issues could not be ignored by the party. Special but not separate organisations such as the AICCWW or mass fronts are necessary for them. However, in the overall context of their ideological framework and strategy, women played only a small part – as factory, or other organised sector workers they were primarily in marginal or clerical or 'non-essential' jobs; in the informal sector or as housewives, they did not have the basis to develop a revolutionary consciousness. The Communists' strategy for women was therefore more complementary than independent or cohesive. Their main thrust was to encourage women to join the production process, and unionise and struggle alongside industrial men workers to overthrow the capitalist system. It was assumed that women's interests and problems would more easily be redressed with radical change and the establishment of a socialist society.

Women leaders of the Left with dual membership consider themselves primarily party members and are heads of women's wings as part of their duties and tasks. Their attention and creativity is thus concentrated within the party. The primacy of the party is reflected, indirectly and quite unconsciously, in the policies and functioning of all their bodies. A review of journals published by the three major unions: the All India Trade Union Council (AITUC), Indian Trade Union Council (INTUC) and Centre For Indian Trade Unions (CITU) shows that 'workers' to them meant the majority – the men. More attention was given to women as wives, mothers and sisters of workers who were glorified specially in encouraging their men and sustaining strikes and lockouts (Menon, 1986).

Most women's wings and unions agree with each other that women workers have a general apathy towards unions. They are more inclined towards solving their problems at the individual level or with the help of supervisors and managers. The other set of factors are domestic responsibility and lack of mobility. But instead of attempting to alleviate problems such as domestic responsibilities and restricted mobility, as well as attempting to go beyond them, the Left women's groups periodically renew their dedication without making any breakthroughs.

Besides the influence of the Leninist theoretical framework, these trade unions succumbed to the practical difficulties in organising workers outside the factory. Immediate political gains for the short term took the place of a long-term perspective. Large industry workers are easy to unionise through contact with local worker leaders who have large followings based on regional, language and caste lines. Workers owe their first loyalty to them, though they are also aware of their limitations and need for TU and party involvement (Gandhi, 1985). Secondly, it is more painstaking, long term, and difficult to build unions from bottom upwards by maintaining regular contacts and having dialogues. Take-overs of already established unions are much easier. Thirdly, unions can rally the entire body of workers effectively to shut down the production process. This contrasts sharply with the scattered handful of workers in small units, mobile contract workers

and seasonal or casual workers who are employed under numerous proprietors. Thus the possibility of protest and successful strikes is much greater
in big industry, which unlike small ones cannot shift out or employ other
workers. Fourthly, successful strikes and increase in wages enhance the
image of the union and its leader.

These ideological and practical drawbacks have cost communist trade
unionism dearly. White collar workers such as government employees and
teachers from primary to university level have formed powerful and large
unions under non-communist-party affiliated trade unions or independent
unions. The other significant development has been the emergence of
numerous independent unions organising informal workers such as the
Marxist-Leninist motivated Akhil Maharashtra Kamgar Union amongst
contract construction workers in Chandrapur, and the Bihar Collieries
Kamgar Union in Dhandbad, formed by individuals from a voluntary
organisation. Even some formal sector unions such as the Kamani Union
in Bombay are attempting the organisation of informal workers.

These new unions could perceive some of the ideological and organisational lapses on the part of the traditional Left unions, and chose to
concentrate on the non-prestigious informal sector and its scattered exploited
workers. Perhaps their political instincts and experiences with people made
them aware of what was gradually being 'discovered' by research and
government bodies: that the factory sector was not only static, but frag-
menting and decaying. In the course of organising, they publicised the
terrible plight of these workers, which raised visions of early capitalism
and its shocking cruelty and degradation.

The significance of the unorganised sector, particularly as the main site
for women's work and a sphere of extreme exploitation, has been highlighted due to:

1. Recent developments in research and international and national
   recognition;
2. Restructuring of industry and the decentralisation of production; and
3. The growth of the women's movement in India and its advocacy for
   women-specific issues,

The International Labour Organisation conducted a series of country and
city studies under its World Employment Programme which established
the concept of the 'informal sector' in the decade of the 1970s.[2] Recently
it reported that twice as many jobs have been generated in the unorganised
than organised sector (*Deccan Herald*, 12–1–90). The ICICI, one of the
influential finance institutions of the country, saw a shift within the formal
industrial set-up in favour of the unorganised sector worker. For example,

one third of all workers in power generation, chemicals and non-ferrous metals are contract or casual workers (Ramaswamy, 1987). The Indian government and planners too are turning their attention to the informal sector. The establishment of the Commission on Self Employed Women and Women in the Informal Sector in 1987 is one instance. Political parties see the possibility of a new constituency which they are willing to explore through employment schemes like the Congress (I)'s Jawahar Rozgar Yogna for farm labour.

Recent trends in industrial restructuring have led large established unions to see the complex and intricate connections between the formal and informal sectors. The impressive textile strike in 1981 in Bombay created no shortage of cloth mainly because of sub-contracting to smaller units or out-of-town mills. Decentralisation and encouragement of auxiliary units has reduced the striking and bargaining power of organised workers.

A large number of women, working class and middle class, had participated in the social movements of the 1970s. They had participated in developing a critique of the Left and its unionism and gradually extended it to include gender as well. They formed themselves into small groups within larger bodies, loosely affiliated, or were autonomous. Unlike the established women's wings and organisations they took up issues such as sexual violence, wife-battering, sexual harassment and dowry as political issues with street demonstrations and militancy. They were a loose coalition of women belonging to different political ideologies, coming from different classes and castes, united by the issue of women's oppression, its neglect by political forums and the urgency of developing a theory and practice for struggle.

Their protests and actions moved women's oppression from the margins to the centre of public consciousness and debate. They questioned not only the Left's perception of the women's question, but also that of their own mixed groups. They reclaimed and established the concept of patriarchy as the theoretical backbone of their argument for the cross-class and caste nature of women's oppression. Patriarchy, or the control of women's labour, fertility and sexuality by men, was located as oppressive a system for women as capitalism was for the working class and the caste system was for the *dalits*. It was the interplay of these systems that determined the conditions and status of women.

By the mid-1980s, these small women's groups, scattered in different parts of the country, had with militant actions, public debates, use of the news media and drama, generated both hostile reactions as well as solidarity. Today, violence and atrocities against women as issues have gained an accepted place on the agendas of most political groups. As a consequence of the women's movement, women workers have, to some extent, been able to gain a foothold in the general process of theoretical and organisational democratisation in mass organisations. Secondly, the very large number and militancy of women workers in the informal sector itself is another factor for unions to give serious attention to their needs and demands.

POSING CHALLENGES: NEW GROUPS AND NEW WORKERS

The Chhatisgarh Mines Shramik Sanghatana (CMSS) was launched in 1977 after a spontaneous protest by contract mine workers. One of the CMSS leaders was Shanker Guha Niyogi, who was earlier a member of the Communist Party of India and its trade union wing, the All India Trade Union Congress. He was also for a brief time with the Communist Party of India (Marxist).[3] Both these parties had recognised unions of the mechanised mine workers but had neglected the demands of the manual, contract workers. Women workers from amongst them formed the Mahila Mukti Morcha (Women's Liberation Front).

The Tamilnadu Construction Workers' Union found that as a single category, construction workers number two crores (20 000 000) in the country and work under terrible conditions. After an intense period of lobbying and public demonstrations, the union was able to introduce a Bill in the state legislature to regulate their wage terms, bring better working conditions and introduce welfare schemes. A large number of these workers who are the most unskilled, lowest paid and overworked, are women.

In Harayana, the Bandua Mukti Morcha has painstakingly brought together seasonal workers working in kilns or farms as bonded labour. Having accepted loans at usurious rates from contractors and unable to pay them back, they remain bound to work for the contractors, sometimes for life. Swami Agnivesh, an Arya Samajist and social activist has done remarkable organisational work with these invisible workers as well as forcefully protesting against anti-women practices such as sati. The People's War Group, a Marxist-Leninist party operating from the tribal belt of Andhra Pradesh and Maharashtra, has been able to pressure contractors and the government into raising the price of tendu leaves collected from dense forests by the tribals.

The Self Employed Women's Association in Ahmedabad, organised into a union a broad category of women working in jobs where there was no clearly identifiable employer. The established unions scoffed at the efforts of the Self Employed Women's Association (SEWA) to unionise these workers, as they had no employer nor were they employees. In a matter of years, it had a membership of 25 000 different self-employed women who were using SEWA banking facilities, working in its co-operatives and benefiting from its welfare programmes. Besides, SEWA has staged some militant protests, moved the courts and appealed to the state government to set up an Unorganised Labour Board and the central government to institute a commission.

Traditional artisans have been losing their livelihood to large capital-intensive, mechanised ventures. Fishermen along the western coast have been fighting a pitched, often bloody battle with mechanised trawler owners who are competing with them, destroying their nets in shallow waters and monopolising fish markets. Fisherwomen cannot compete with big auctioneers or race their trucks to the market. The Kerala Fisherworkers' Union joined a national forum which demanded a reservation of sea waters, a ban on night trawling and welfare benefits such as pension, education, and accident compensation.

Most of the landless are seasonal wage labourers who are underemployed and often not even given the statutory minimum wages. Most of them live and work under conditions of feudal oppression. The Chhatra Yuva Sangharsh Vahini was formed during the Bihar Movement by Jayprakash Narayan, a colleague of Gandhi and a sarvodaya leader. It was a student body of persons below 30 years who wished to support the movement. It established itself as a mass organisation with state-wide branches and today defines itself as an organisation with a class, caste and women-oriented perspective. The women activists of the Vahini were associated with the women's movement and were some of the first to take up the anti-obscenity campaign in their state. They had demanded and were granted space or a caucus called the Mahila Vahini, and representation at the national committee. The Vahini organised *dalit* landless labourers to struggle against the Math (Hindu temple) which owned the land. The *dalit* men and women refused to either plough the land or allow the Math to plough it. In one village called Pesre, women reaped the harvest and instead of taking it to the Math, kept it for themselves. When the government was finally prevailed upon to allocate the land to the landless the women raised crucial questions of ownership.

NEW QUESTIONS AND NEW STRATEGIES

Women within the new organisations and informal sector workers' union have to an extent been able to get some space in the form of a wing, caucus or even a separate identity. They have been encouraged to take their issues and make demands. Women have blossomed with confidence, learning new skills and taking responsibilities. However, even in these new organisations there are issues which remain unsolved. The following section will examine some of the questions which form part of the debate within these organisations. Why are women still excluded from leadership positions? The continued existence of these organisations demands a different pattern of union functioning and extension of its activities to cover women's non-waged lives. Should the union be engaged in development activities or only struggle for the rights of workers? Do unions consider it important to handle the class and gender contradictions without relegating either to a secondary status? This is particularly important since struggle and consciousness around issues of work invariably lead women to a search for an equal relationship with men in the home, at work and in politics.

THE QUESTION OF AUTONOMY AND LEADERSHIP

The Tamilnadu Construction Workers' Union, like the AICCWW, was also formed in 1979 in Madras. And like it, the union was aware that women were inactive in unions because of domestic responsibilities and organisational inexperience; that they were losing jobs because they were unskilled, and that they were being deprived of basic necessities like crèches and maternity benefits. Recognising that women also formed half of the union's constituency, the union formed a women's wing.

> Construction workers come from traditional earth workers communities which built the earliest dams and ponds. Women have always been a part of the construction team. We formed a women's wing because it is necessary for women to have organisational experience which does not come through only participating in morchas.
>
> (Unionist)[4]

The Tamilnadu Construction Workers' Union's women's wing has its own committees and elected officers at the village, district and state levels. It has made it compulsory for the main body of the union to have at least one woman on each of its committees. As women do not have the free time to attend meetings or, as men, may be working on different shifts, the union declares a holiday each month for all units and women's wings to meet as a general body. Each unit has a graded system of contribution towards union expenses. A unit can be formed with a minimum of 30 members who elect a committee with at least one woman member. Instead of level-based elections, the district, state and the council committees are directly voted in by all the units.

These parallel structures with women officers provide a special space for women, as well as keeping them linked within the overall structure of the union. Women who may be reluctant to come to union meetings because of time, diffidence or lack of procedural knowledge bring their problems to the more informal women's wings. Everything from wages to desertion to lack of water supply is discussed, analysed and decided upon. Some of the issues are again raised in the union meetings for action and consolidation.

For example, some women workers, very hesitantly, approached a woman unionist with a complaint about *mistries* (foremen) hiring local women to work for lower wages. The women were afraid to raise this in the general union meetings because the *mistries* had the power to recruit labourers and could take their revenge by not employing them.

> We did not want a men versus women or higher paid workers versus labourers fight. So we had a series of meetings with the women then with the men and finally decided that as the local women were also workers they should be made union members and be paid minimum wages. The mistries realised that they should employ union women.

Perhaps this might have been possible even without a women's wing, but its existence and the availability of a woman unionist had given the women workers the courage to raise issues of wage discrimination by their own co-workers. There are other incidents of women's demands being put forward in the general union such as skills training, night shift and even social issues of desertion, maintenance and domestic conflict. Geetha, one of the unionists, finds that the women's wing has encouraged women's participation: women are 30 per cent of the 20 000 paying members; they are active and articulate in union meetings; and in general militant and confident. Why then are women still reluctant to take up union leadership posts?

The women of the Chhatra Yuva Sangarsh Vahini went one step further when they asked how women's leadership could be encouraged in mass organisations. They recommended that women should be given representation not only at committee and lower levels, but also in the central decision-making bodies. However, they think that it is extremely difficult for women to reach the top via the tiered elective path or fulfil other requirements like rural or mass involvement, which are the necessary criteria for election. If their male comrades were serious enough to go beyond mere tokenism, then it was felt they should go all the way and give direct representation to women in the National Council. This would break the vicious circle of women's partial participation, which leads to the marginalisation of their issues and demoralises them into inaction.

A group of social workers involved in organising *dalit* labourers in Tamilnadu have attempted to address this issue in yet another way. They have set up two groups, the Landless Labourers' Movement (LLM) and the Rural Women's Liberation Movement (RWLM). The two are organisationally linked, but are separate, autonomous bodies. The RWLM has been organising women in over 55 villages of Arkkonam and Tiruttani area in Tamilnadu since 1981. The organisers describe the fundamental aim of the movement as establishing women's associations in town and village areas in order to create a socialistic pattern of society and economic upliftment. The RWLM works closely with the Landless Labourers' Movement (LLM) in taking up what are called 'general' issues such as wages, caste atrocities and meets for common discussions and planning of strategies.

Each organisation works independently with distinct internal hierarchies; however, at the apex they are both on a equal plane. Membership is also distinct: even when some LLM members wanted to join the RWLM, all the women were firm in refusing and insisting that they wanted their own organisation. By giving equal theoretical importance to class and patriarchy, the RWLM and the LLM have questioned the accepted sovereignty of the 'general' body or party as leader of all mass fronts. The RWLM's separate structures force women to confront their reluctance to take leadership positions. Not many women, and especially rural landless women, have the confidence or want the responsibilities of leadership. It is relatively easier for middle-class leaders to head and control mass organisations of landless peasants and workers. The RWLM's middle-class activists are called 'organisers', and their main activity is to catalyse people.

> There are different people: activists, villagers, non activists etc. at different levels of consciousness. We have been slowly motivating and involving them. If women don't call their own meetings, we try to find out the reasons, help organise them and show them the procedures. The tough part is decision-making. Women are not used to taking decisions without their husbands or fathers.
>
> (Unionist)

By deliberately withdrawing from formal posts, RWLM middle-class activists encourage and train local, landless women to develop the skills and confidence to manage and run their own organisations.

On the other hand, the RWLM is also conscious of the problems of entrenched leadership so common within parties and mass organisations. Leadership, whether it is middle or working class, has its own problems and tensions within a democratic framework. Leadership when concentrated in one person's hands gives him/her total control of information and decision-making. No effective opposition can be organised, and dissidents either have to toe the line or drop out of the group. Leadership also places a formidable burden on leaders, requiring total dedication and time. Women are rarely supported by their families to have such free time or commitment. There are numerous examples of women leaders having chosen to remain childless or having given their child-rearing responsibilities to their parents.

The RWLM tried to form a collective leadership of eight women to distribute the tasks and responsibilities of a leader. It is significant to note here that the men in the LLM refused to indulge in such an experiment. They were willing to bear the burden as well as the glory of leadership. After a few months, it was observed that it was not always possible for the women leaders to come from their villages, meet, share tasks and formulate plans. One of them took over the tasks and finally the leadership post. The experiment did not succeed, so the RWLM adopted the yearly rotation system. However, the present president has quite come to like her exalted position, the honour and the garlands. For the RWLM the opposing pulls between encouraging *dalit* women's leadership and preventing them from becoming too established still continue.

From these and other examples, there is no doubt that women need their own space to develop their organisational skills and confidence. This was recognised a long time ago for different reasons, either as a practical necessity in a sex-segregated society, or to take up their special issues or to be a launching pad to a revolutionary consciousness. The crux of this issue is what sort of space are mass organisations ready to provide? What sort of autonomy do women visualise for themselves? How can one create a genuine autonomous space?

Any autonomous space for women, within or outside a mass organisation, is suspiciously viewed as separatist and divisive of the common revolutionary struggle. The two have to be differentiated because separatism means the policy of keeping away from certain people or organisations, whereas autonomy is a complex political concept. Autonomy does mean a certain amount of separatism, i.e. distancing oneself in order to develop one's own theory and strategy. But it also means empowering oneself individually and organisationally to overcome all obstacles to an equal, happy and just existence in society. Usually autonomy is measured by factors such as decision-making powers, separate bodies and freedom of functioning. Autonomy goes beyond organisational forms since it is simultaneously an ideal – freedom and self-assertion – as well as a process – resisting marginalisation of women's issues and developing theory and strategy.

Perhaps women have to decide how they want to exert their autonomy, within mixed organisations or in unions (infinitely more difficult but effective in the long term), or split from them. The Tamilnadu Construction Workers' Union has separate wings, but from its functioning it is apparent that women's issues are taken up at the union level because of the strong support of its leaders. The lone (compulsory) woman member on the committees can easily be sidelined or ignored. The pressure to include women and their issues has ultimately to come from the women themselves. The Union is aware of this problem.

> It is important to remember that though women have come a long way since union activity began, they still have a considerable ground to cover ... women still suffer from wage discrimination and skill barriers ... One of the major problems the union faces today is the tension between men and women workers on these issues.
>
> (Geetha, in Gandhi and Shah, 1992)

It is necessary to reconsider widely prevalent assumptions which link the subordination of women to marginalisation from positions of power within organisations. We do not suggest that the struggle to develop women's leadership be abandoned. It is necessary to confront the sexual division of labour and the division between the public and the personal which places patriarchal restrictions and norms on women. But power itself is heady and addictive, as suggested by the RWLM example. We therefore have also to concentrate on building a democratic process within organisations which will not only allow women the freedom to participate more fully, but also control the excesses and domination of leaders.

Conflicting Strategies? Development Programmes and Unions

Informal sector women workers, as SEWA (Ahmedabad), a trade union of over 25 000 self-employed and home-based workers found, have many specific problems, such as inaccessibility to credit, police harassment, problems of securing stocks and low pay. They were harassed and exploited by different groups such as dealers, money-lenders and the police. Defined and recognised as workers through the struggle of SEWA, resolution of their problems continued to demand unconventional solutions. In 1977, a struggle for minimum wages for women *chindi* (rag) workers, hand-block printers and bamboo workers provoked merchants to harass women by refusing to give them work. SEWA felt that women on the brink of survival could not struggle endlessly. A year later it set up the SEWA Arthik Vikas Nigam (SEWA Economic Development Organisation) for the creation of worker-owned co-operatives.

> Pressure and development or union and cooperative – by linking the two, both the arms (of SEWA) have been able to uplift the worker from exploitation and unemployment.
>
> (Bhatt, 1979)

Though most of SEWA's programmes were developed jointly, its rapid growth and its policies strained its relationship with the main body, the Gandhian Textile Labour Association. It argued that such developmental activities meant getting into business which would invariably affect unionising and struggle. Sure enough, SEWA found that for its block printing co-operatives, it had to deal with traders, cloth merchants, and *dalals* (middlemen) for raw materials and marketing. These were the same people they have to oppose for better wages and conditions for the self-employed. Marketing the *chindi* workers' quilts meant setting up a shop and becoming shopkeepers. SEWA recognises this contradiction but sees no other viable solution.

In 1977, the Comprehensive Rural Operations Service Society (CROSS), Andhra Pradesh, organised poor peasant and agricultural women labourers to provide them with government funds for economic programmes. The organisation stated that 'even a struggle for higher wages or for land would be doomed for failure if they (women) did not have something of their own to fall back upon' (Mies *et al.*, 1983). Their strategy was to combine economic programmes with conscientisation and education. The leaders of the women's groups had to choose deserving women recipients for loans, animals and other facilities, which led to fierce competition and quarrels between women. This has been the experience of many other groups which have tried to use income generation as a means to an end, but have found that in effect it becomes counter-productive.

The most commonly proposed alternatives are co-operatives of workers or landless. In most cases, the intervening group takes the role of intermediaries, putting women in touch with a potential market and teaching them managerial and technical skills. Such endeavours have to face the stiff competition of a capitalist commodity market. There are very few success stories such as the Lijjat Papad Udhyog, which has flourished by their own advertising, attractive packing and changes in taste. The problem, however, is that in its rise to success, Lijjat has become alienated from its shareholders who, like all badly-paid workers, went on strike.

Organisations have usually found that in entering the market, they are compelled to operate like commercial ventures: i.e. they too have to take or give work on contract or piece-rate basis, give low wages etc. They are thus forced to go out of business or seek protected markets within the country or abroad through direct selling to consumers or through a Third World shops network. Both are uncertain and whimsical markets. The maximum these income-generating efforts have achieved is to eliminate middlemen, pay the producers a little better and make sections of the public aware of the producers' exploitation and problems.

Many women's organisations, such as Women's Voice, Bangalore, think that such attempts, which are anyhow short-lived, divorce the group from struggle and will not aid women's emancipation in the long run. RWLM activists too reject such programmes as being ultimately the same as capitalist exploitation.

What then is the alternative for unions or organisations which are involved with women in the informal sector, who barely manage to survive? One way of finding employment which most groups agree with is through propagating non-traditional vocational training. Many are developing training programmes for women in plumbing and electric wiring (Young Women's Christian Association, Bombay), masonry, carpentry and cycle repair. The Tamilnadu Construction Workers' Union is encouraging women to join state-sponsored skill training programmes. Such efforts simultaneously challenge sex-stereotyped work notions and develop women's skills.

The Construction Workers' Union believes that income-generating schemes can help only a few. If an entire group of workers like those in the construction industry or self-employed had to be addressed, then the state should be pressured to pass and implement laws recognising, regulating and giving protection to these workers. The TCWU has alternated between agitating for legislative reform and putting forward welfare and social programmes for workers. With the help of lawyers, the union introduced a bill in the provincial and later central legislature, and then through agitation pursued amendments and made its recommendations. During elections it put itself forward as a bloc which would give its vote to the candidate who supported its demands. On the other hand, the union solves domestic disputes, conducts weddings and funerals, pressures absconding men to pay maintenance to their deserted wives, etc.

Organising workers and their struggles are known and accepted methods of unions. But many have emphasised only their short-term economic interests and marginalised women's interests in favour of men's. Yet unions remain the best vehicles for workers' demands and struggles. On the other hand, development programmes have traditionally been associated with welfare and charitable activities. They can be training grounds for women to learn and develop themselves. We have yet to explore the potentiality of such organisational forms for raising consciousness. Co-operatives are an alternative to the wage system and therefore capitalism. They have the potential to question the organisation of the workplace, the hierarchy, division of labour, the care of infants, etc. Developing co-operatives, even if they are not economically viable, is an experiment for an alternative society. It is necessary for us to move out of the paradigms set by traditional Marxist thought and strategies of struggle which juxtapose reform against revolution. Organising as well as creating work opportunities are part of the struggle because both expose women to the workings of the capitalist patriarchal system.

We need to elaborate strategies on the basis of clearly identified forms of women's labour in the informal sector. Women's work in the informal sector, women's weak bargaining position with their employers or the state, their economic desperation, social restrictions and vulnerabilities and the changing economic scene have to be taken into consideration for the formulation of strategies. The production relations of each category of workers such as the self-employed, the contract workers and the home-based should be investigated.

Home-based workers are the most invisible and exploited by middlemen or contractors. They seldom know anything about the chain of production of which they are a part and, because of their isolation, limited skills and easy availability of such labour, cannot make demands. Their most immediate need is the formulation of minimum wages for different types of work, registration and identity cards, and a more long-term struggle against the 'housewife ideology' which perpetuates the myths around home-based work. An experimental co-operative might be able to combine a legal, economic and ideological struggle.

Contract workers are visible but mobile and do not have any single employer. They too function in a highly competitive and low-wage market. They need to be organised like the construction workers of Tamilnadu to give themselves a collective identity and bargaining power. Established trade unions have resisted organising them because they are often employed as strike breakers or casual labourers. Their interests conflict with those of the organised sector workers. But it is in the interests of both categories of workers for the unions to organise them together. They will then be challenging the management ploy of dividing workers on the basis of permanency and wages.

Self-employed are the only informal sector workers who can be supported materially, as they are in capitalist terms small entrepreneurs. Some
see the provision of facilities as a lesser evil than income-generation
schemes. The setting up of credit and other facilities basically helps women
to stay afloat. In fact, their size of operation invariably brings them in
conflict with the police, the state and financial institutions. They live with
the working class in worker colonies and *bastis* (slums) and can align with
them. Though it is difficult for them to see themselves as workers, they are
aware that they provide cheap services to society and can therefore make
demands from the state for education, pension and medical benefits.

Handling the Contradictions of Gender and Class: The Issue of Priorities

Struggles project the commonality of the exploited as a group in the fight
against their oppressor. In rural areas it is the caste and class contradiction
which is highlighted, whereas unions in urban areas focus on the class
conflict. It is assumed that men and women of the same class or caste
share and suffer from a similar oppression. In defence of this argument
cogently put forward by the communist and socialist parties and their mass
fronts, it is said that women do not form a special caste, class or community but are part of them and feel more close to their own men than
perhaps to women of another caste or class. And yet it is true that women
are subordinate to men no matter what caste or class they belong to, and
are oppressed and controlled by them.

Thus women form a category which crosses caste, class, and ethnic
boundaries, yet are divided by these structures, forming a differentiated as
well as a common group of people. They are linked not only by their
biological characteristics, but also by patriarchal norms, similar oppressions and subordination. Traditional socialist political theory has been
unable to explain or reconcile these opposing and converging links and
has, in the interest of the general revolution, chosen to be sex-blind and
subsumptionist. There is no doubt about women's militancy and anger
over their caste and class oppression. And with the space and support of
women activists, women have now begun to articulate their gender oppression too. There are many such examples. The question is, how do
mass movements or unions weave the two into their strategy?

One inspiring example is provided by the CYSV movement in Bodhgaya.
With the slogan 'Jo jameen ko boye jote, voh jameen ka malik hai' (Those
who sow and plough the land are the owners of the land), some hundreds
of *dalits* of Bodhgaya fought against the Math (Hindu temple), which

owned 12 000 acres of village land in 1978. They would neither plough the land, nor allow the Math to; if already ploughed they kept the harvest. People were determined to risk everything in this struggle. Some of them worked at a food for work programme and shared the grains with the whole village.

In the course of their struggle for land, women activists of the CYSV felt that:

> the Vahini men activists were mainly interested in women's participation in large numbers in action programs, but were less interested in their developing an independent identity.

> (Manimala, 1983)

They questioned such an attitude and pointed out the lack of women in the leadership of the movement. Why could the struggle for land rights not be combined with the struggle concerning violence against women? They constantly raised the issue of inequality and power at all levels. Their comrades' response was that such issues would only divide the landless and diffuse the issue of land rights.

When the government was finally prevailed upon to intervene and distribute the land amongst the landless labourers, the women asked why should they not get land in their names. A fierce debate ensued. Male activists and the landless agreed that single women should be given land in their names. However, for couples it was felt that the land should be in the men's names because it really did not make much of a difference. The women's reaction was not only to reject the notion of male ownership, but also joint ownership of land. Their logic was simple and irrefutable. If it really did not matter in whose name the land was, then why could it not it be in their names?

The debate within was extended to include government officials. So strong is the notion of male proprietorship over property that women had to put up a fight because the officials refused to register land in women's names. Finally only 150 acres of land was actually distributed to women. But the change in their confidence was obvious.

> If the men snatch away our wages . . . now we are at least able to feed our children from the produce of the field . . . (nor) can the men so easily throw us out of the house.

> (Alka and Chetna, 1987)

Small as the victory may be, the Bodhgaya Movement has set a precedent.

Unfortunately, such a victory for women has been an isolated incident. There are more examples such as the Chhatisgarh Mines Shramik Sangh in Madhya Pradesh and the Fisherworkers' Struggle in Kerala where there is an ongoing tension between the union and women's group, and men and women's interests. The CMSS has always considered women's involvement in the union to be extremely important and necessary. The Chhatisgarh region, especially Dalli Rajhara, has a large number of women mine workers who work along with their husbands on a piece-rate basis and have militantly participated in union struggles. The union has clearly supported women's work issues, encouraged their union participation as well as 'social' issues like the anti-alcohol campaign, and women's activities at the *basti* or worker colonies level. The CMSS's Mahila Mukti Morcha has thus been able to reach a wide number of women and men workers, benefit from the legitimacy offered by the union to women's issues, and widen the scope of their campaigns. Women, on the other hand, swear by the union and are more loyal to it than the men. They have become more vocal, confident and experienced.

But so strong is their identification with the union and so intricate their dependence on it that 'women themselves . . . often do not see any dichotomy in their organisational affiliation'. They may not 'see' that the MMM has no organisation of its own, or that their theory and practice is dominated by the union or that there was little generation of their own leadership, but they could 'feel' solidarity for other women-related issues like dowry or the unequal relations within their own families.

> But by and large such questions are suppressed, for the union leadership is not clear whether the women's question should be allowed to get into such 'divisive' channels.
>
> (Sen, 1990)

The small catamaran fishworkers of Kerala have in the last 15 years been involved in numerous violent clashes with the mechanised trawler-owning fishermen and companies and the government. Women have been enraged by the loss of their traditional net-making work to imported machines, the refusal of permission to ride in state transport buses and their vanishing retail markets to frozen fish. Perhaps it was seeing the fishermen's co-operative society (which excluded women) function at close range that led women to feel the need to meet, hold discussions and learn to function as a committee. Gradually, as the co-operatives spread to other areas, so did the women's committees.

As the unequal battle between the catamarans and mechanised trawlers grew more fierce, the small artisanal fishermen turned desperate, violent and began to attract public attention. The Church supported their struggle and slowly they began to organise themselves into a union.

Although there was some talk about a women's wing within the newly growing fishworkers' union in Trivandrum, it was eventually decided that there was no real need for a separate women's wing.

(Nayak, 1990)

Women continued to struggle, lead demonstrations and meet independently at the local level. When some of the union sympathisers and activists moved from issues related to women as fisherfolk to women as wives and mothers, they opened the questions of their subordination to men, of control and taboos. But it was difficult to transfer this new consciousness to men, make organisational changes or convince the union to take up their issues.

Inevitably, the women quite spontaneously formed their own informal Coastal Women's Front which highlighted the issue of rape and domestic violence and held joint solidarity demonstrations and 8 March celebrations. If the union leadership were worried that taking up women's issues might distress men and prove divisive, their not taking them up also proved divisive. They felt obliged then to accommodate an autonomous women's wing within the union structure. The women's struggle does not end here, they are aware that they still have a long way to go.

The class and gender dilemma does not exist only in mixed mass organisations. It was present in SEWA, an all women's union, but was perceived in a different manner and was closely related to the role of unions in the informal sector. SEWA saw unions as vehicles of economic and social change which had to oppose all anti-labour or community policies. In SEWA's perception, unions should involve themselves with not only the organised workforce, but also the unorganised and their family members. They stressed that though it was relatively harder to organise the self-employed, that their problems were different, and there was stiff competition between them, all these negative factors did not mean that they could never be organised.

Women perceive themselves, as most of society does, primarily as mothers and wives and not as workers. It is our objective as a union to impress on them that they are workers, contribute something to society and can be organised. And we have made some impact in this direction . . . in SEWA there is a written rule not to talk of family. Our members should rather talk of work. They seem to be dealing with beating and other social problems by themselves. We do not deny that there is conflict for example when women start earning and saving [and] the men step in. We speak of social change. When women get economic power, the balance changes and society changes. Women have suffered so much at the hands of those more powerful, been so oppressed and exploited that when women build a new society, exploitation should have no place in it.

(Bhatt in Gandhi and Shah, 1992)

However, in spite of such a strict policy of keeping gender issues at a distance, SEWA cannot escape from them completely. The organisation has been under constant pressure by other unions to organise and include men, as it was perceived as dividing the labour movement. Some of the leadership were not averse to reconsidering their policy.

We are always pushing the cause of the self employed in all areas and with all people. As a strategy it does not work to speak of only women . . . in order to become big (as an organisation) men's and women's groups will have to merge. At present, women refused to open SEWA to men in spite of pressure from the banks and other unions. But we must reach a stage when women will feel confident to handle matters.

(Bhatt in Gandhi and Shah, 1992)

Another SEWA activist said that the self-employed women who are on the Karobari (executive) were absolutely clear.

They just said no. There was no debate. Their fear was that we are too fragile an organisation to have men come in and take all the leadership positions. Then they felt their voices and issues will not be heard . . . Some spoke from the experience of working with men and their husbands in the Textile Labour Association.

(Chatterjee in Gandhi and Shah, 1992)

Most staff members of SEWA find that:

the members think that SEWA is a place where all their problems can be solved. We try to avoid their domestic problems but it is impossible, they bring them up. Everything is intermixed, the economic side of their lives and all other problems. Individual counselling takes a lot of time and at present SEWA is centred around struggle and organising. It is not that it is unimportant, but that we have to allocate our time and re- sources to what will have an effect on a mass of women rather than on an individual woman.

Yet SEWA cannot avoid attending to the problems of their long-standing members. The rest they refer to other organisations with legal funds, per- sonnel and shelters for distressed women. The organisation has yet to acknowledge that some of these 'individual' problems are common to all women and should be taken up at the union level. Perhaps in the future SEWA might attempt to take up a CMSS type of anti-alcoholism campaign or a campaign against sexual harassment. The disadvantage is that SEWA as a union has no influence with their members' male relatives, whereas CMSS and others are in a position to persuade and even pressure them. On the other hand, SEWA's position might be advantageous as it could act as mediator as well as support group for women in distress. SEWA has already highlighted the gap between the organisation of formal and informal sector workers, boldly united the controversial development and struggle approach and hopefully, with its growing stature, will be able to integrate their perception of women as workers and as women by some innovative strategies.

BRIDGING THE DICHOTOMY

The new unions or organisations, having emerged from the critique and hope of the 1970s, its political events, social chaos and economic crisis, broke new ground and posed as alternatives to the established political organisations. These organisations had already decided on a different political and ideological path which facilitated their growth as something more than a union. Geetha, an activist of the Tamilnadu Construction Workers' Union confirms this:

> We don't see ourselves as a trade union. So everything connected with construction workers and not only their wages is taken up. Ours is a construction workers' struggle which is more of a movement for basic rights in society.

> (Gandhi and Shah, 1992)

Ilina Sen (1990) sees a dialectic relationship between the nature of the organisations and the extent and intensity of women's participation in them. Given their reservations about democratic centralist organisations, these unions have a more open and non-bureaucratic way of functioning, and are willing to experiment and tackle different issues. They have been particularly amenable to include women's issues. Many like the CSYV have taken pains to give women space, encourage their leadership and in their own way take up their issues. These are some of the rays of hope on our political scene. However, we are conscious of the fact that this has happened more wherever there have been militant women activists or men who have been influenced by the women's movement.

In many ways the growing women's movement around the country stimulated a new thinking process even in the fish-workers' movement. For the first time the problems of women fish vendors also became the problems of women and mothers ... Questions from feminist friends such as 'why don't women go fishing?', 'why don't women cycle to market instead of walking for miles?' were earlier turned down as 'intellectual theorising and utopian ideas'. But they gradually became serious questions.

(Naik, 1990)

In spite of this, the labour movement (both the new and older groups) and the women's movement have not forged an alliance or a joint strategy. They are suspicious of each other and often harbour simplistic and stereotyped notions. Though there are shades of differences between the two, very broadly we can say that most of the established Left unions and the newer ones have been critical of what they call the women's groups' single-minded focus on family violence, highly individualist and campaign oriented style of functioning and lack of a larger political perspective and struggle. Many of the earlier attempts at working together collapsed.

Some of the women's movement groups perceive unions as mass organisations which are basically hierarchical, economistic, male-dominated bodies and indifferent to the travails of their women members and unwilling to take up a struggle against patriarchy. Even the 'progressive' amongst them refuse to grant autonomy, patronisingly encouraging women without making any fundamental changes in either their structure, theory or strategy. The unions and women's organisations are trapped by their specific emphasis, theoretical focus, organisational boundaries and functioning. One is inherently prone to economism and the day-to-day pressure of work and struggles in a deteriorating economic climate and new capitalist strategies. The other is determined to put women's issues, especially the unequal men–women relations, neglected for so long, on the political map for revolution.

Nowhere is it more clear that both movements need to involve each other in their struggles than in the case of unorganised sector women workers. Here the areas of work and home cannot be segregated, but rather depend on each other, and the struggle against capitalism cannot ignore the struggle against patriarchy. As we have seen, some unions have opened their doors, given space to women's caucuses and shown their intention to be more sensitive to women's issues. But as Naik (1990) says of the Kerala Fishworkers' Struggle:

Developing a feminist perspective is a long process which does not happen if mere structural changes within the union take place. These are the first steps but if they are to be effective a number of other changes have also to take place.

We believe that this process has already begun. But the onus for taking it forward does not lie only with the unions but equally with the women's movement and its groups. Women's groups have raised several important issues about women's work and lives, but have not followed them up and into the unions. There are not many examples of dialogues initiated by women with unions like the one organised by the Stree Mukti Yatra in Maharashtra in 1984. Sometimes unions are not only indifferent but hostile to women's groups. Efforts will have to be made to maintain contact with women unionists and support them. It is possible to involve them in their individual capacity or as union members in common campaigns which involve women as workers and as women.

CONTACT POINTS: COMMON ISSUES

At present there are several common issues raised by women workers, the women's movement and the labour movement. Although taken up independently, they could be brought together and supported by each other. For example, there is consensus that women are losing jobs in the formal sector. Some trade unions are fighting with their backs against the wall in trying to prevent job loss. The CMSS has opposed the voluntary retirement scheme which was first mooted in 1976. The scheme proposed that a woman worker below 57 years could voluntarily retire at any age and nominate her son, husband, brother-in-law, son-in-law or any other male relative to take her job and position. This resulted in a large-scale buying of women's jobs, especially in tribal areas, by middle-class non-tribal men having fake marriages for a couple of thousand rupees. CMSS and its women's wing, the Mahila Mukti Morcha, linked the issue of voluntary retirement with the larger issue of mechanisation and its effects on women. Both mobilised and conscientised women and men against this and other such schemes. A large seminar was organised on Mechanisation and Women, and women from different trade unions were invited for a dialogue and formulation of strategies.

In the urban centre of Bombay, another variation of the same type of scheme was being discussed for government women employees. A voluntary part-time work scheme for women workers was put forward as a boon to working mothers who have to perform the double burden of work at the office and housework. Many working women and women's groups were quick to point out its drawbacks. Firstly, a part-time job would mean reduction in wages and all other benefits such as holidays, casual and sick leave, provident fund, and a longer period of probation, while women would be spending the same time and money travelling to their workplace. Secondly, the scheme reinforces the notion that housework is women's responsibility. Thirdly, such schemes create a special category of jobs for women which are invariably of a lower status (N. Gandhi, 1989). After these strong reactions, the scheme was shelved.

The issue of 25 per cent job reservations for women with a special emphasis on scheduled tribe and caste women in all government, municipal and other local bodies was proposed by the National Federation of Indian Women (NFIW) in 1982. It provoked a heated debate within the women's movement. Some agreed that reservations might be instrumental in helping women to regain work, confidence and skills. Others such as the Mahila Utpidan Birodhi Sangharsh Manch (Forum against the Oppression of Women), Ranchi, Bija (Seed), Pune, and the AICCWW rejected it on the grounds that it sidetracked the main issue of unemployment and might create divisions between men and women instead of a struggle for 'work for all'. The CYSV feared that unless the sexual division of labour and the double burden was challenged, such a demand would make the position of women worse. Unfortunately this debate was not taken up with unions and other worker's organisations.

Wages have been the single most central issue for unions and their struggles. But equal wages for equal work has neither been supported by them or the courts. The air hostess case is a typical example. The work of an air hostess and a purser is basically the same, but their job classification, salaries and promotions are different because the former are 'a separate sex based category'. The cabin crew association consisting of pursers and pilots was uninterested, the larger union did not want to antagonise them, and the courts found technicalities to dismiss the case. For women's groups, the issue of equal wages also raises the broader question – how can women break the equation between women, inferior work, and low wages in order to reclassify work on the basis of skill and value, and not gender? This is an extremely difficult process and will undoubtedly need a multi-pronged strategy with all the support other organisations can give. It challenges deeply entrenched notions of 'family wage', 'sexual division of labour in society' and patriarchal control over women's labour.

There have been some instances of women's groups supporting women workers, especially the unorganised. Vimochana, Bangalore,[5] heard that 400 women from an ancillary unit linked to Hindustan Machine Tools had gone on strike. The unit had been formed by wives of HMT executives and some concerned individuals as a gesture of philanthropy towards poor, destitute and handicapped women. A demand for higher wages was rejected. Vimochana struggled along with them for a year (1983–4), asking for recognition of their union, focusing public opinion on their plight, performing street plays and helping them financially. In the absence of support from the larger HMT union, and given the vulnerability of women's position, the management broke the strike and threw out the leaders.

Unions, even an all-women's union such as SEWA, have not put much effort in building links with women's groups. An activist of SEWA frankly admitted:

> We have not made too much effort, we feel that we are strong enough to get things done . . . We fear that other groups may find us patronising. For example, if there is a rally we can in moments get 200 women together. Then the newspaper refers to it as SEWA's event. There have been instances when women's groups have not carried out their responsibilities. So we only go when we are called.
>
> (Gandhi and Shah, 1992)

It is often possible to work alongside unions on particular one-time issues. A young woman was referred to the Forum Against Oppression of Women (Bombay) by the local communist party unit. Her father had deserted the family, was living with another woman and was unwilling to pay maintenance. Her parents' relationship was too complicated to try to unravel, and there were no local Muslim community organisations which could be approached. Court procedures would have taken too long. The Forum decided to go to the man's workplace, an engineering unit with an all male workforce. The personnel manager refused to consider sending part of the man's wages directly to his family. The Forum then approached the leadership of the union, put forward the problem and with their help organised that part of his income reached his family every payday. The young woman, his daughter, kept the Forum informed about this arrangement.

One of the most difficult issues for women's groups to take up with unions has been the sexual harassment of women workers. There are several instances of women's organisations such as the Mahila Mukti Morcha of the CMSS taking up cudgels against criminals, contractors and the paramilitary for harassing or raping women. The union usually extends its full support when the class dimension can be played up. But if it is a case of harassment between workers, the union usually takes an indifferent or hostile attitude. Once again, the class divisive nature of women's or feminist issues is raised and the distance between the two groups widens.

There is no questioning the fact that some trade unions have taken several steps forward and changed their attitudes towards women and their issues. If women's groups find unions wanting in many areas, unions also find women's groups overly critical and unsympathetic to the problems of unionism and capitalist manipulation. Unions will have to take a closer look at their structures which reproduce sexism and bureaucratic power, and sensitively encourage women's participation. Women too are members of unions. Regardless of their numbers, their issues cannot be underplayed or traded off during negotiations. Unions cannot afford to be economistic without alienating women sector workers and their different needs. Just as they are experimenting with development projects or initiating welfare schemes, they will have to tackle gender issues.

Women's groups can align with individual women unionists or with the union itself in formulating joint campaigns. Women unionists are isolated within a predominantly male union, fight a hard battle to raise women's issues, and are caught in the double dilemma of focusing on mobilisation (as numbers are so important) or the longer drawn out conscientisation of women workers; and the conflict between class and feminist issues. They need the support of women's groups, who will also have to be sensitive to women worker's problems in the economic sphere and working within larger structures.

Joint strategises will have to be worked out carefully, with understanding on both sides. Women's groups' campaigns have shown that in the case of battering or dowry harassment, they have to tread carefully without alienating the distressed woman's familial and support base. Similarly, women workers often work with their men (for example in hawking or in workshops), and they may be fellow union members as well. Issues will have to be taken without affecting class solidarity, but without bypassing women's solidarity.

The Tamilnadu Construction Workers' Union and the Pennuramai Iyyakam in Madras have shown that it is possible to establish organisational links with dual membership in both bodies. Women workers have joined in the demonstrations organised by Pennuramai Iyyakam against obscene posters and dowry murders. Women's groups will have to understand more conscientiously the economic scene and capitalist anti-union strategies. Today, unions are desperately struggling and more often than not failing to bring in victories for the workers. At such times they might succumb to the tendency to relegate women's issues to the background and concentrate on economic issues. Women's groups will have to learn to ride these waves and continue to weave together gender and class issues.

Lastly, solidarity shown by women's groups at the time of strikes or demonstrations is extremely important, as this is a critical period for workers in general. Such solidarity not only legitimises the women's movement in the eyes of the union and its members, but also gives a different and wider class perspective to the general public. On the other hand, women's groups' involvement will give them a better understanding of class issues and problems of struggle. Women's groups are by virtue of their size and commitment creative, and self-directed. They reach out to all women, but they are also often short-lived. Trade unions are large, have an established membership and continuity but are bureaucratic and often dogmatic. In the interests of the labour movement and the women's movement, and the common dream of a society without class, caste and gender oppression, they will have to learn to unite.

NOTES

1.   Very clearly and explicitly, Lenin set the organisational principles for women's participation. He had said in his conversation with Clara Zetkin:

> real freedom for women is possible only through communism. The inseparable connection between the social and human position of the woman, and private property in the means of production, must be strongly brought out. We must win over to our side the millions of toiling women . . . there can be no real mass movement without women . . . Our ideological conceptions give rise to principles of organisation. No special organisations for women. A woman communist is a member of the party just as a man communist with equal rights and duties. Nevertheless we must not close our eyes to the fact that the party must have bodies whose particular duty it is to arouse the masses of women workers, to bring them into contact with the party and to keep them under its influence. . . . So few men, even among the proletariat, realise how much effort and trouble they could save women . . . if they were to lend a hand in 'woman's work'.
>
> (V. I. Lenin, 1978)

2.   The concept of the 'informal sector' is a contested one. The term is used here in a descriptive sense rather than in the ILO usage which has been criticised for its assumptions of dualism and homogeneity within the formal and the informal sectors.

3.   In September 1991, Shanker Guha Niyogi was murdered by local industrialists, in the midst of a long drawn-out struggle to get contract workers their legal rights. The struggle for regularisation of contract labour still continues in Chattisgarh.

4.   All quotes, unless otherwise stated, are from personal interviews with activists and members of organisations, based on material collected for Nandita Gandhi and Nandita Shah, 1992.

5.   A small group of women basically helping women in distress and managing a women's bookstore.

REFERENCES

AICCWW. 1987. 'Problems of Working Women and their Participation in Trade Unions', 6th Conference of CITU, 18–22 May, Bombay, Published by CITU.

Alka and Chetna. 1987. 'When Women Get Land: A Report from Bodhgaya', *Manushi*, No. 40, New Delhi.

Bhatt, Ela. 1979. 'Organising the Self Employed Workers (An Experiment)'. Paper presented at Regional Consultation on Strategies for Women's Development, 30 April–5 May, Colombo, Sri Lanka.

Gandhi, Nandita. 1985. 'When The Rolling Pins Hit The Streets: The Anti Price Rise Movement', Monograph, Bombay.

Gandhi, Nandita and Nandita Shah. 1992. *The Issues at Stake: Theory and Practice of the Indian Women's Movement*, Kali for Women, New Delhi.

Lenin, V. I. 1978. *Women and Communism*, New Book Centre, Calcutta.

Menon, Nivedita. 1986. 'Women in Trade Unions: A Study of AITUC, INTUC and CITU in the Seventies'. Paper presented at the 3rd National Conference on Women's Studies, Punjab.

Mies, Maria, *et al.* 1983. 'Landless Women Organise', *Manushi*, March–May, New Delhi.

Naik, Nalini. 1990. 'The Kerala Fisherworkers' Struggle', in Ilina Sen (ed.), *A Space Within the Struggle: Women's Participation in People's Movements*, Kali for Women, New Delhi.

Ranadive, Vimal. 1987. 'Problems of Working Women and their Participation in Trade Unions', 6th Conference of CITU, Bombay 18–22 May. Published by CITU.

Ramaswamy, E. A. 1987. Article in *Business India*, 7–20 Sept.

Sen, Ilina. 1990. 'Workers Struggle in Chhatisgarh', in Ilina Sen (ed.), *A Space Within the Struggle: Women's Participation in People's Movements*, Kali for Women, New Delhi.

Sood, Santosh. 1986. 'Women Workers and the Trade Unions'. Paper presented at the 3rd National Conference on Women's Studies, Punjab.

Index